MEASURING HIDDEN DIMENS
THE ART AND SCIENCE
OF FULLY ENGAGING ADULTS

(Volume 1)

Otto E. Laske
Interdevelopmental Institute

Interdevelopmental Institute Press 2006

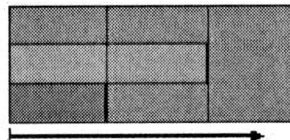

Library of Congress Cataloging-in-Publication Data

Otto E. Laske, Measuring Hidden Dimensions: The Art and Science of Fully Engaging Adults (volume 1).

Library of Congress Catalog Card Number: 2006900135

Includes biographical references and index.

ISBN, print ed. 0-9776800-0-2 [9780977680009]

Copyright © IDM Press 2005
First printing 2006

Published by:
Interdevelopmental Institute Press (IDM Press)
51 Mystic St.
Medford, MA 02155, USA
http://www.interdevelopmentals.org
orders@interdevelopmentals.org

Cover design by Will Tenney.

Copyright Acknowledgement
The author and publisher gratefully acknowledge permission for use of the following:
Lisa Lahey, Emily Souvaine, Robert Kegan, Robert Goodman, & Sally Felix (1988), *A guide to the subject-object interview: Its administration and interpretation.* Laboratory of Human Development. Harvard Graduate School of Education, Cambridge, MA, USA.

Contents

5

Illustrations

About the Author

Otto Laske is a writer, composer, poet, and developmental & organizational psychologist. Writing primarily in German and English, he has previously addressed diverse topics in cognitive science, artificial intelligence, cognitive musicology, organizational development (OD), expert systems, and adult-developmental assessment. Following his teacher, Th.W. Adorno, Frankfurt am Main, he has always combined in his thinking and writing an interest in the arts as well as the sciences.

If there is one term that sheds light on my motivation to write it is DEMYSTIFICATION. My feeling has always been that there is a lot of confusion in the world. I therefore initially studied philosophy, to cut down on the confusion. I did not see right away that philosophy contributes its own kind of confusion to the young mind. Only much later did I begin to see its real gifts: the ability to deepen an understanding of structure in contrast to content. What I felt was missing in philosophy was exact measurements.

A second term that sheds light on my writing in the social sciences is MEASUREMENT. I came to believe that measuring phenomena of the mind empirically was a help in knowing what one is dealing with and talking about. I was therefore delighted to meet Herbert A. Simon who invented the 'protocol analysis' of problem solving (1972) and Robert Kegan who invented the 'subject-object interview' for elucidating adult development (1988). Both scholars worked based on scrutiny of language, as did – more speculatively – my teacher Adorno.

These two preoccupations – demystification and measurement – are also primary concerns of this textbook. Especially beginners in developmental thinking need clarity, confused as they may be about how their life relates to the book's perspective. (Not that I don't remain confused about many things.)

So, this is my overriding 'credential': the urge to clarify! Clarity in the social sciences is important to me because these sciences directly feed into helping professionals' practice. I am concerned that the physical and technical sciences are far ahead of social science in this regard. That is a reason why I stepped back from the computer sciences and artificial intelligence in the 1980s: I found many of their conceptualizations to be too bereft of social content and action knowledge.

I have been prompted to write this book by the persisting absence of evidence-based procedures in the helping professions, especially in consulting and coaching (less so in psychology). It remains utterly astonishing to me that, despite the rich insights social science has unearthed during the last century, most people continue to use unclear, scientifically unsupported, short-cut (and cut-throat) methods and procedures in their work with others. To understand this is in itself a topic of studies in adult development.

This state of affairs is particularly harmful where *adults' developmental potential* is concerned. The reason for this harmfulness is simple: adults' cognitive capacity, when not strengthened through mentoring, loses its force to consolidate their social-emotional capability. In terms of this book, this is a major setback, especially in the helping professions.

You may take issue with my point of view, but it has a lot of scientific backing!

Preface

<u>Why this Book, and Why Now?</u>
Being an adult is a little bit like having spoken prose for many years without realizing it. It has become so natural, so second nature, that it is by now largely hidden from view. What <u>makes</u> you an adult is perhaps less hidden, but not many people think about how adults develop differently from children and adolescents. That's what this book is centrally about. It is an attempt to demystify adult development by teaching to use explicit developmental assessments.

Adult development, viewed scientifically, is complex. There are books, scientific handbooks, websites, research projects, all of which talk their own lingo. This book is different. While by necessity it also introduces a new vocabulary (and thus lingo), this book links issues of adult development directly to your professional and private life.

Demystifying adult development doesn't mean simplifying. As Einstein said, things should be kept as simple as possible, but made no simpler than they intrinsically require. For one thing, 'development' does not equal 'change,' nor is it 'learning.' Change and learning may have developmental effects, but they might not. Therefore, the book strictly distinguishes between these three aspects of how adults progress through time.

I speak in this book of development as MENTAL GROWTH, in distinction from mental health. To demystify mental growth, we first need to set it apart from what it is not. In this book, we do so by using assessments. We do so because of the fact the most convincing tools for researching and understanding adult development have been forged in the process of assessing how that development happens.

In my view, most people have a skewed view of assessments, seeing them either as something quick and easy to administer, or something almost like a 'test.' Neither view holds water in regard to the assessments introduced in this book. Developmental assessments are based on semi-structured interviews and constitute a type of *qualitative research* since the assessor uses him- or herself as an instrument of the research. The 'subject' of the research is an individual, team, or larger organizational or other group.

As said, the core of adult development is *mental growth*, or the growth of human consciousness over the life span. There is no shortcut for achieving it, as little as there is to achieving spiritual bliss. Mental growth is a multidimensional issue. Humans don't just develop in a single dimension, but in several, intertwined dimensions. In this book, we distinguish three such dimensions: *social-emotional, cognitive, and behavioral.* The first two are closely linked, but it is beneficial to differentiate them conceptually. This way, the interactions between them can be more easily grasped. The distinction between them does not quite match that of 'feeling' and 'thinking,' but as a first step of distinguishing them that conventional distinction is good enough.

As to 'behavioral' – not by definition developmental – dimensions, they are seen in this book as secondary, because they are determined by the first two. We say that social-emotional development together with cognitive development largely determine individuals' behavior, be it their conduct, their way of approaching tasks, making decisions, or their emotional intelligence and relationship with others. In shorthand, we refer to social-emotional development as ED, and to cognitive development as CD.

What about behavior? More than 95% of all assessments today are behavioral (MBTI, Enneagram, DISC, you name it), not developmental. In this book, we conceive of behavior as developmentally determined. This means that, considered outside of adult development, 'behavior' is a secondary phenomenon (epi-phenomenon) largely determined by where somebody presently is in terms of his or her adult development over the lifespan. **Behavior is a set of symptoms to be examined and explained developmentally.** More specifically, we conceive of behavior as based on two related factors called *Need* and *Press*[ure] (NP). By 'Need' we mean 'subjectively felt need,' while by 'Press' we mean the inner, as well as environmental, pressure that often makes subjective needs difficult or impossible to satisfy in an optimal way.

'Press' is another term for what is often called 'the real world.' However, from the vantage point of this book, the real world outside of us is considered strictly as a *mirage*, or an illusion. What matters in terms of this book is, rather, HOW THE REAL WORLD IS CONSTRUCTED BY YOU INTERNALLY, AND HOW THEREFORE IT SHOWS UP FOR YOU. In other words, the so-called real world is your internal construction. It is a projection that you make and then unknowingly (or knowingly) walk into. For this reason, nobody is responsible for the real world but you yourself!

When it comes to constructing the real world internally, humans don't just use a single perspective. In this book, we assume three fundamentally different perspectives, and these three perspectives actually determine the book's format. The book is laid out in four volumes, as follows:
1. Volume 1 (this book): the social-emotional perspective (ED).
2. Volume 2: the cognitive perspective (CD).
3. Volume 3: the behavioral perspective (NP).
4. Volume 4: a synthesis of the three perspectives in the form of case studies.

In general, ED has to do with the question **'what should I do and for whom?'** and is thus primarily about values (axiology). By contrast, CD has to do with the question **'what can I do and what are my options?,'** and is thus primarily about thinking (cognition). Finally, NP has to do with very concrete issues of self conduct, approach to tasks, and interpersonal perspective (emotional intelligence), especially as they shape behavior in the workplace.
The present, first volume exclusively deals with the social-emotional perspective on clients. Only in the Appendix some elements of NP (need/press) are introduced in an elementary way.

Purpose
Put briefly, the purpose of this book in four volumes is to present a theory of professional helping in the sense of *process consultation*. This term was coined by Edgar Schein (1999), and means 'consultation to the client's mental process.' The book in its entirety aims to assist professionals working with 'clients' (rather than 'patients'), whether these professionals are helping professionals, HR professionals, consultants (including

mediators and facilitators), or coaches. The book teaches helping professionals in general how to use methods of assessment that have emerged in developmental psychology over the last thirty years.

As will become clear, assessing and demystifying adult development is very nearly the same thing. The assessment is variously one of the client's developmental stage (ED), cognitive level (CD), and need-press profile (NP). Since consciousness is unitary and people are not operating differently in 'life' compared to how they function at 'work,' these three dimensions are equally essential for understanding what is going on for people in life and work. As is to be expected, the three dimensions – ED, CD, NP – are naturally and deeply interrelated, making up what is called *adult development over the lifespan*. When pulled together, the three dimensions provide comprehensive insight into how people think, feel, suffer, and blossom at different stages across the lifespan. I strongly believe that the assessments, once you master them, will count among your most valuable professional tools.

People tend to think of assessments as something concerning others, not themselves. While it is true that the book focuses on assessing others ('clients'), there is no way the tools taught in this book can be mastered other than by applying them to yourself. This is in fact a hallmark of the present book. **The book teaches assessments as a tool for engaging in, or bringing about, self transformation.** Once you have internalized assessment, it may initially be difficult to stand away from yourself enough to apply the assessment to others. For this reason, this book affords a substantial amount of mentoring, to prepare you for using adult-developmental assessments objectively, without interference by your own personality and current predilections. Studying the book and learning the assessments will substantially promote self insight, and boost your own social-emotional and cognitive resources. This in itself may well be the major benefit for you of engaging with the book!

<u>What Reading the Book Will Not Accomplish</u>
As much as you might benefit from reading a book, there are certain things that can only be learned in a classroom, together with others, and in interaction with an instructor. In the case of this book, this holds true especially for the arts of developmental listening, interviewing, and scoring. Although the book presents all the elements needed for listening, interviewing, and scoring – thus for gathering developmental evidence – actually carrying out qualitative research on clients is not easy to accomplish on your own simply by reading. This, however, is not a problem. At the Interdevelopmental Institute, there exist a large number of courses that help you acquire hands-on knowledge by making actual assessments, scoring them, and translating them into action with your clients!

Be daring, and take a first step!

Medford, MA 02155, USA
December 2005

Acknowledgements

This book is the synthesis of a life time of study, especially of studies undertaken by me at the Institute for Social Research and Institute of Philosophy, Frankfurt am Main, Germany, in my formative years, and the studies at Harvard Graduate School of Education in the 1990s. As a result, the reader will find in this book ideas stemming from the Frankfurt School ('Critical Theory') as well as the Kohlberg School at Harvard. For this first volume in particular, I owe thanks to R. Kegan, my Harvard mentor, and to E. Schein whose work has greatly influenced me since the late 1980s. I also owe thanks to C. Argyris and E. Jaques who personally challenged my thinking about organizations, and to M. Basseches who re-introduced me to the dialectical thinking whose discipline I first imbibed during my Frankfurt years.

Another influence on my work has been through Dr. John Blattner, owner of the Need-Press Analysis Questionnaire. Although in volume 1, the questionnaire is used only in the three case studies of Appendix B, I owe to my acquaintance with the Questionnaire most of my thinking about the relationship of developmental to behavioral data in process consultation. The Questionnaire figures prominently in volume C of this book.

More recently, Dr. Steve Stewart has influenced my presentation and interpretation of developmental research findings through his keen understanding of organizational functioning and corporate culture, both in the military and in industry. In particular, I owe to Steve elements of Table 1.1 (& I.1) that appears in many of the chapters of volume 1, as well as the final wording of the 'stage caricatures' I employ in chapters 1 to 3. Steve has also contributed to my thinking of how social-emotional development (ED) relates to cognitive development (CD). This is a topic he has investigated in his own research, as I did in my 1999 dissertation on transformative effects of coaching.

In addition, I owe a great many thanks to my clients, collaborators, and students. In my practice since 2000, my coaching as well consulting clients have greatly sharpened my insight into benefits and limitations of developmental methods, and have given me a more balanced view of the developmental framework here presented. I have also greatly learned from the reactions, questions, critiques, and suggestions of my students. Many of these students have been at the forefront of evidence-based coaching, not only in their course participation at IDM, but in their professional practice as well. I would like to name, in particular, Frank Ball, Antoinette Dawson, Jon Ebersole, Wendy Knowles, Krista Leirmoe, Nancy Moynihan, and Chris Wahl.

I also owe thanks to the IDM Ambassador Group directed by Antoinette Dawson. I have learned from members of this group why developmental thinking in consultation and coaching is experienced as such a novelty, in contrast to my own perception for whom this approach has been the most natural thing in the world for some time now. Antoinette Dawson and Jon Ebersole, in particular, have challenged my thinking in many ways, due to their intimate knowledge of the peculiar culture of North American coaching.

I also want to acknowledge important technical help I have received. My collaborator Nancy Moynihan, Co-Editor of the IDM Newsletter, took on the job of proofreading. In addition, Greg Welstead, Director of Administrative and Technical Services at IDM, stood by me throughout the process of preparing the book for print. I cannot thank both of them enough!

Finally, I owe thanks to Stephanie Taranto for her dedicated work on all matters regarding IDM during 2004-05. Stephanie never flagged in her belief in the benefit of my work for the larger consulting community, coaches included.

My thanks to all who directly or indirectly participated in producing this first volume!

Warning – Disclaimer

This is a textbook on developmental assessment for use in interventions with clients. I have made every effort to make this text as accurate as possible and as free of jargon as I could.

The purpose of this volume is to engage and educate. As to the former, the engagement occurs mainly in the realm of thought experiments, and who does not like those probably will not enjoy the book.

As to education, every book has limits beyond its control, such as the developmental level of the reader. It is a human condition that we 'understand' only as much as we are ready for developmentally. More specifically, there are also limits in what this book will, as they say in North America, DO for the reader. These limits have to do with the book's subject matter. The book focuses on two mental activities: *evaluating ('scoring') interviews* and the practice of *developmental interviewing*. This book has limits regarding both of these topics.

Nobody has grasped the challenge to make good use of this book better than Chris Wahl, Georgetown University, who has been an inspiring student in my Program One series of courses. In the October 2005 IDM Newsletter, Chris writes (quoted with her permission):

Word of caution. Reading this book alone is insufficient to setting coaches and others in the helping professions free to begin doing developmental assessments. And, it does not claim that any reader is ready to set up shop as a developmental coach after reading the book. In fact the opposite is true. Rather, readers are made aware of all they need to learn. No doubt, to learn to be a developmental coach, one needs the guidance and mentoring of a master developmental coach. Unfortunately, and Laske makes this point, few ICF MCCs fit this profile [i.e., being an MCC does not automatically qualify you as a developmental coach]. If his hypothesis that coaches are spread across developmental levels in the same statistical percentages as the general population is true, this book is a call to 55% of the coaches out there to get into purposeful education to stretch, broaden, and developmentally enhance the who that they are as coaches.

This captures the point better than I could. I would only add two things.

First, one can learn developmental interviewing in only two ways: (1) in courses led by an expert, and by working in such courses as a member of small groups, (2) in intensive one-on-one study with an expert in developmental coaching.
Second, to practice the developmental analysis of others is risky, and can be harmful if not properly done. This is so because an analysis must be 'fed back' to clients at their own present developmental level, and harm is caused if that is not achieved.
Another risk is losing your marriage or partnership, which could happen if you unwisely practice developmental stage analysis for the sake of employing labels meant to put loved ones or other people in their place.
In short, this volume – and the book as a whole – deals with mentally very powerful material and tools that must be expertly and wisely used.

Therefore, neither the author nor IDM Press shall have either liability or responsibility to any person or entity with regard to losses and damages inflicted as a result of reading and using this book!

Introduction

> One of the most important functions of process consultation
> is to make visible that which is invisible.
>
> E. Schein (1999, 84)

We have heard of hidden dimensions in many fields, most recently in physics. The universe seems to be full of them. When such dimensions are revealed, they typically raise people's awareness. Expanding awareness is a central purpose of this book.

Another, more specific purpose of this book is improving the professional standards of the *helping professions*. This is a broad term, referring to many kinds of consultations, – organizational development, mediation, facilitation, coaching, social work, and applied psychology. I refer to all of these by a single term, that of PROCESS CONSULTATION. As introduced by E. Schein (1999, 1987), this term has a very specific meaning. It refers to a particular way in which consultants formulate a model of the person who is seeking help, typically called a 'client.'

Three Models of 'Helping'
In an enlightening way, Schein distinguishes three models of consultation (1999, 1999):
  1. the expertise model
  2. the doctor-patient model
  3. the process consultation (PC) model.

This book centrally regards the third model, its depth and limits. More specifically, **it introduces an adult-developmental deepening of process consultation, thereby introducing *a related fourth model*.**

As Schein puts it "the (first,) telling and selling model of consultation assumes that the client purchases from the consultant some information or an expert service that she is unable to provide for herself" (1999, 7). What is being bought and sold according to the first model is *expertise*. A need is defined by the client, and a consultant is brought in to satisfy the need. End of story.

The second model is more complex. "The consultant is brought into the organization to find out what is wrong with what part of the organization and then, like the physician, is expected to recommend a program of therapy or prescribe a remedial measure" (1999, 11). In this model, the client "assumes that the consultant operates from professional standards; … that the consultant has the diagnostic expertise to apply the program only where it will help; and that the cure will take" (1999, 12). The 'doctor' (consultant) takes over responsibility for the diagnosis, only requiring that the client does her part in applying the remedy, just like a patient. This model makes the assumption "that the consultant can get accurate diagnostic information on her own" (1999, 13).

The third model, of Process Consultation (PC), is more complex since it is specifically geared to the client's mental process. Schein defines the model as follows (1999, 20):

Process Consultation is the creation of a relationship with the client that permits the client to perceive, understand, and act on the process events that occur in the client's internal and external environment, in order to improve the situation as defined by the problem.

As quoted, Schein's definition is emphatic about the following crucial aspects of process consultation:

- PC creates a relationship centered on the client's own mental process.
- The relationship must be such that the client comes to perceive, understand, and act on his or her own process.
- Process events relevant to the consultation are those occurring in the client's internal or external environment.
- The client's situation cannot be changed unless the client's internal and external processes are understood.

This definition implies that the more deeply the consultant understands the client's mental process, the more effective her intervention will be. However, the definition does not fully articulate that the client's external process events are INTERNALLY GENERATED. One could say it is not fully acknowledged in the definition above that the 'outside world' is a *mirage* that is internally constructed. This accounts for the limitation of the above definition, which is removed only when we adopt a *constructivist* point of view on the client as we do in this book.

In this third model of consultation, the assumption "that the consultant can get accurate diagnostic information on her own" is emphatically withdrawn. Both parties to the consultation are equally responsible for its outcome. In particular, it becomes the consultant's responsibility to understand the client's mental process, which is where the problem resides. However, the client remains responsible for, or "owns," her problem. Also, only the client really knows what will ultimately "work," or will take care of the problem. In this new constellation, what helping consists of itself becomes a topic of the conversation. Both the problem and the solution are initially unknown. It is only through the relationship between consultant and client, and by way of their shared diagnosis of the client's mental process that problems become defined and solutions, if any, emerge. These solutions are ultimately generated by the client herself, and only facilitated by the consultant. What is more, **the consultant's main task is to help the client help herself by understanding her own manner of generating problems, not to provide solutions to others' problems.**

As shown above, what the consultant provides according to the third model of helping starkly differs from the first two models. As Schein formulates the matter, "the ultimate function of PC is to pass on the skills of how to diagnose and constructively intervene so that clients are more able to continue on their own to improve the organization" (1999, 18-19). And, summarizing, he says:

> In a sense both the expert and doctor models are remedial models whereas the PC model is both a remedial and a preventive model. The saying "instead of giving people fish, teach them how to fish" fits this model well" (1999, 19).

<u>Deepening the Third Model of Helping Developmentally</u>
As said, once we adopt a constructivist perspective on people's 'real world,' we can take an additional step, that of demystifying the mirage of an 'outside world.' This is the step taken in this book. The step derives from the simple reflection that the client's process is developmentally determined, and cannot truly be understood in the 'flatland' of behavior (see below). Rather, the client's process can be viewed as being the function of a Center of Gravity shifting over the lifespan, and thus differing between different developmental stages from which the client may make meaning of the world.

Although this essentially holds true for both parties to the consultation, since it is the client's process that is central to the relationship, the developmental stage of the client is of primary concern. (See chapter 9 for consequences for the consultant.) The client's Center of Gravity (stage) determines how the consultant is 'seen' in and through the relationship. At the same time, it depends on the consultant's own developmental stage how the client is 'heard' and interpreted in the medium of natural language. Since the crucial medium of helping is *conversation occurring in language*, the way the two parties USE LANGUAGE is the crux of how they construe 'helping' and 'being helped.' Listening to how language is used is therefore a pivotal concern of this book. Differences between people in using language imply developmental differences. They also imply that there may be developmental levels at which PC cannot be carried out due to a lack of developmental capacity on the side of the consultant. As this book will show, **at different developmental levels helping looks different, feels different, is exercised differently, and is received differently by adults.**

An example will make this clearer. Say, a client seeks help in "communicating better with my reports as well as superiors." This is the client's '*presenting problem*,' that is, the problem as presented by the client. What exactly this problem consists of and comprises is initially not known, either to the client or the consultant, nor is the solution to the problem (if it turns out there is one). Understanding the problem is a matter of the consultant's insight into the client's mental process. (It is after all in this mental process that the problem is arising.) Therefore, what is needed is a consultation in which both parties exchange pieces of their knowledge and feeling about the problem *through language*. In such this 'give and take,' the problem gains contours and gradually becomes explicit.

When we consider that both consultant and client are human beings positioned somewhere in their journey over the lifespan, it becomes easy to see that "where the two parties are developmentally" is a major determinant of how they will engage in consultation. How the parties will work together is a matter of their respective developmental level (Center of Gravity). Since most of this book is concerned with helping clients, **the developmental underpinnings of the client's mental process are of uppermost concern**, not only in his or her interaction with the consultant, but the world at large. For this reason, the reader can best understand this book as going 'to the roots' (Latin 'radix') of the consultation process. In this sense, the book is 'radical.' As the reader will increasingly see, this radical conception of consultation is a natural one when coming from a 'constructivist' viewpoint. According to this viewpoint – followed throughout the book – 'the world' is *internally constructed* by individuals who, ceaselessly, walk into their own projection. **What is called the 'external world' is thus a**

secondary phenomenon, something not initially given but *made* (Latin 'factum') by way of both parties' mental process.

<u>The Multidimensionality of the Client's (and Consultant's) Process</u>
There are, of course, many ways of conceptualizing the client's mental process on developmental grounds. In this book, I have resolved to follow the *Constructivist Developmental Framework* (CDF) derived from research in adult development, especially E. Jaques, M. Basseches, R. Kegan. According to research, there are many dimensions of mental growth across the adult lifecycle. There is strong agreement among researchers (Wilber, 2000) that the two following dimensions have privileged status:

- Social-emotional development (ED)
- Cognitive development (CD).

As indicated earlier, when we look at adult development over the lifespan in terms of these two dimensions – how people make meaning and how they 'think' about themselves and the 'world' (constructed internally) – we are adopting a 'developmental,' not a 'behavioral' model of adult development. To make the difference between these two models more clear we can, following Wilber, distinguish between two diametrically opposed but nevertheless linked dimensions:

- The 'horizontal' dimension of behavior
- The 'vertical' dimension of human development over the life span.

Here, *horizontal* indicates that we are moving through a FLATLAND (Wilber 2000) in which adults incrementally "change" and acquire new competences and perspectives. The movement through flatland is linear throughout. There are no peaks and valleys at all.

By contrast, in the *vertical* dimension movement occurs discontinuously, by little jumps, and leads from one stage to another. As the term "stage" implies, you can't be at Stage 3 if you have never been at Stage 2. Also, whatever horizontal movement you have made has different meaning depending on where on the Vertical you presently are (your Center of Gravity).

Needless to say, in your life you always move both horizontally and vertically, but a specific horizontal movement (change or learning) may not get you any further vertically. This model is illustrated by the diagram below.

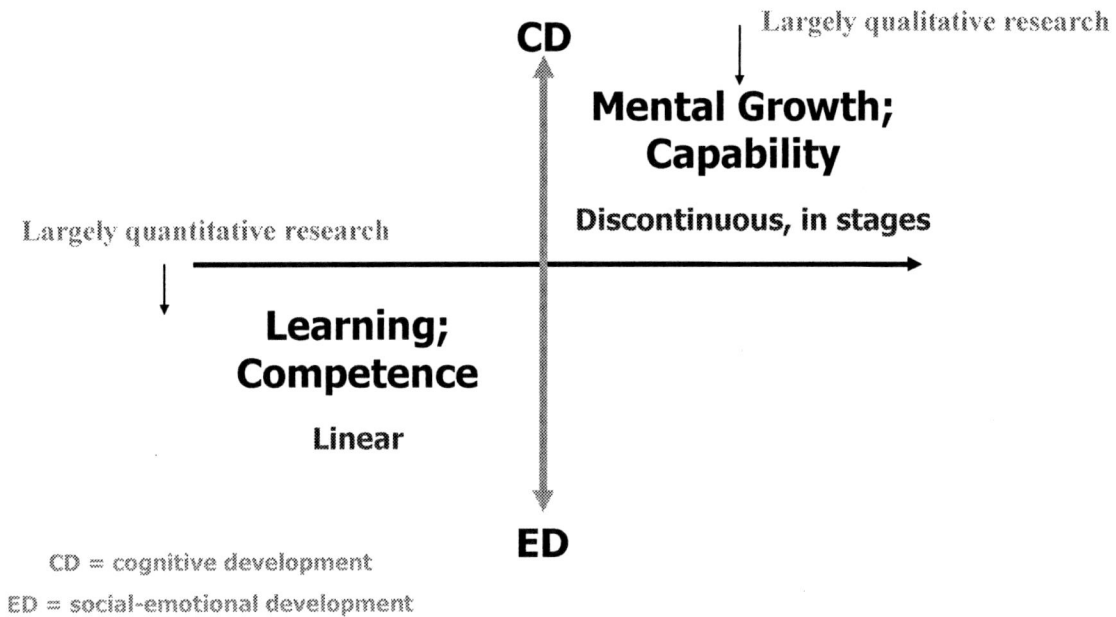

Fig. I.1 Two Dimensions of developmental assessment

Another way conceiving of this partition of life changes in terms of two dimensions is to distinguish 'learning' which is horizontal from 'development' which is vertical. As shown, most research into horizontal changes is *quantitative* research working statistically with large numbers of individuals, while most research in the vertical is *qualitative,* confined to small samples. This is so because the point in qualitative research is the richness of individual lives and small groups, not validity of results for statistic populations. However, throughout this book we are dealing with a *mix of quantitative and qualitative research* as will become clear to the reader as the book progresses.

What is Developmentally Deepened Process Consultation?
What, the reader will ask, is the difference between PC (process consultation) and its developmentally deepened version, DPC (developmental process consultation)? In particular, what is the responsibility of the consultant in the latter mode of helping? This question deserves a long answer, which is found by reading the book.

A short answer regarding **the fourth model of consultation introduced** in this volume should highlight the following aspects:
- As in PC, the client retains ownership of the problem.
- As in PC, problem diagnosis is mutual (albeit not reciprocal).
- As in PC, the consultant's main function is that of passing on "the skills of how to diagnose and constructively intervene so that clients are more able to continue on their own to improve the organization" (Schein 1999, 19).
- *In contrast to PC,* developmental process consultation (DPC) illuminates the client's problem on adult-developmental grounds (showing that the problem the client is 'having' derives from the client's present mind set, and cannot be solved within that mind set which created the problem in the first place).

- *In contrast to PC*, in DPC problem diagnosis is not restricted to the behavioral realm, but is extended to the developmental underpinnings of behavior, namely the Vertical which combines ED and CD, both of which explain behavior and behavioral problems.
- *In contrast to PC*, in DPC the consultant's function is to help the client make a *developmental shift* – in ED or CD or both –, not just a behavioral change, so that the problems that are focal in the consultation cannot only be 'solved' but 'transcended' in favor of a more systemic and self-aware way of conceptualizing them in the first place, and therefore, of 'solving' them in a more optimal way.

Gist of Volume 1

This is a book about adult-developmental assessment in the context of process consultation. The book focuses on how to provide developmental assessments, and how to use assessment results in feedback to clients and the structuring of conversations and interventions. While throughout this volume and its Appendices A and B the emphasis is on individuals, Appendix C and D are focused on how to apply developmental findings to teams and larger groups. The gist of the book is best explained in terms of the table below (which is revisited throughout the book):

Orientation [Frame of Reference]	Stage 2	Stage 3	Stage 4	Stage 5
View of Others				
Level of Self Insight				
Values				
Needs				
Need to Control				
Communication				
Organizational Orientation				

Table I.1. Changing orientations across adult stages

As indicated, the book centrally deals with the different Orientations people follow in constructing the 'world' at different developmental stages, whether in life or at work. Over the course of the book, **all the – now empty – entries of the table will get filled in**. People's orientation or frame of reference has to do with what is 'real' for them, and this has many facets. Some of the most important facets for process consultation purposes are named in the first column, under 'Orientation.' Others could be added through further hypothesis formulation and research.

In terms of the population addressed, the book focuses on *adults* between ages 25 and 100 regardless of education. Education is not a potent predictor of developmental level. Although age is not a potent predictor of developmental stage either, the age range indicated will orient the reader somewhat. Following the precedent of R. Kegan's work (1982), adult stages are identified by integers from 2 to 5, stages 0 and 1 having to do with children and young adolescents. As we will learn in the book, outside of the numerical shorthand stages also have non-integer names.

Structure of this Volume

Since adult development has many interwoven dimensions, a writer on the subject matter of this book needs to proceed in steps, like a weaver. What you presently have before you is the book's volume 1. It is a volume focused on social-emotional development (ED). This kind of development is calibrated in stages. Stages are like rungs on a ladder: you can't be Stage 3 if you never went through Stage 2.

In this volume, a distinction is made between "main" and "intermediate" stages (from 2 to 5). I introduce the main stages in chapters 1-3. In chapters 5-6, I follow up with the four intermediate stages (between each of the "main" stages). As a result, we will have at our disposal altogether 16 stages in terms of which to view and situate adult clients in their social-emotional development. By taking into account intermediate stages, we are able to address gradual developmental shifts that take place between the main stages across time. This will make for subtler methods of diagnosis, scoring, and design of interventions.

The book continues to chapters 7 and 8, to a point where the reader can expect to be reasonably expert at administering short developmental interviews and scoring them with some proficiency. Chapter 9 rounds off the subject matter of the book by focusing on the helping profession presently most in need of theoretical foundations, that of coaching.

This, then, is the journey undertaken in volume 1. At the end of the volume, you will have traveled *within* as well as *between* main stages, and will be ready for deepened practice of what the book has taught you. Having used the book in your practice for some time, you may then want to proceed to the other volumes the book comprises: volume 2 (cognitive consultation), volume 3 (behavioral consultation), and volume 4 (comprehensive developmental process consultation with individuals, teams, and larger groups.

In summary, the chapters of volume 1 have the following topics:

- Chapters 1-3: the theoretical background of adult developmental assessment.
- Chapter 4: introduction to developmental listening.
- Chapter 5: refinement of chapters 1-3 through intermediate steps between adult stages, together with a precise notation for these steps.
- Chapter 6: systematic overview of all 16 adult stages measured by the Constructivist Developmental Framework (CDF), the methodology adopted in the book.
- Chapter 7: (based on chapter 4) introduction to developmental interviewing.
- Chapter 8: in-depth study of a lengthy interview fragment, pulling together all that was learned so far.
- Chapter 9: broad overview of the consequences of adult developmental assessment for the young field of coaching and related fields.

Learning really new skills often implies learning a new conceptual framework. This holds true for this book. Volume 1 not only presents the *conceptual framework* of developmental process consultation. It also teaches the many skills needed to think in terms of that framework. By contrast, the Appendix to volume 1 is entirely focused on *applications*, including exercises. The Appendix shows the reader how to use what was learned throughout volume 1 and supports testing the acquired knowledge.

The Appendix of volume 1 is itself structured in four parts, A to D. In A, the reader finds exercises grouped by chapter, with or without answers, while Appendix B presents three case studies on which the reader can test his or her knowledge in working with individual clients. Appendix C introduces a developmental typology of teams, while Appendix D briefly introduces the reader to Capability Management, a novel form of Human Resources Management. Importantly, work with individuals, teams and larger groups is based on the same methods. For this reason, volume 1 is not eclectic as is so much present literature on consulting, but is consistent and comprehensive throughout. **It presents a consistent consulting methodology and constructivist philosophy of helping.**

Logistics of Using Volume 1 in the Classroom

When used as a workbook for a 32-hr class, such as the *Gateway* class of the Interdevelopmental Institute, or for any other introduction to developmentally based consultation, the chapters of volume 1 are best made use of in the way shown below. (I am assuming that the class comprises two physical workshops, one at the beginning and one at the end of the class, and intermediate virtual classes in between. Other arrangements are entirely possible.)

Module/ Chapters	Type of Instruction	Pedagogical Emphasis	Book Chapter
1	First workshop, AM	Basic notions of developmental thinking	Introduction & Chapter 1 (pre-class reading)
2	First workshop, PM	Interviewing demonstrations	Chapter 2
3	Teleclasses 1-4	Analysis of developmental stages	Chapter 3
4	Teleclasses 5-8	Interviewing for main stages	Chapter 4
5	Teleclasses 9-12	Analysis of intermediate stages	Chapter 5
6	Teleclasses 12-15	Interviewing for intermediate stages	Chapter 6
7	Second workshop, AM	Summary of stage theory; preparation of final case study	Chapter 7
8	Second workshop, PM	Students' interviewing and writing projects	Chapters 7 and 8

Table I.2 Proposed use of volume 1 in a 32-hr introductory class

Logistics of Using Volume 1 during IDM Courses

This book closely follows the course of post-graduate education provided by the *Interdevelopmental Institute* (IDM), in particular **Course One**. Below is the map for using the book chapters for the purpose of obtaining a Certificate in Developmental Assessment:

1. *Hidden Dimension Workshop*: volume 1, chapters 1 to 3 & Appendix A.

2. *Gateway*: volume 1, chapters 4 to 6 & Appendix A.
3. *Course One, Module A*: volume 1, chapters 7 to 9 & Appendix A.

The remaining volumes of the book provide class material for the remaining modules of Course One (as well as for <u>Course Two</u> that leads to Certification as a Developmental Coach or Consultant):

- *Course One, Module B*: volume 2.
- *Course One, Module C*: volume 3.
- *Course One, Module D*: volume 4.

Volume 2 is centered on process consultation from a cognitive perspective. It introduces to dialectical modes of thinking and provides answers to the question 'how systemic does my client think?' Volume 3 is focused on evidence based behavioral consultation, dealing with organizational behavior assessed through a questionnaire, and including an analysis of corporate culture from an individual's point of view. Volume 4 provides a number of comprehensive client assessments, including assessments of teams and larger groups. It introduces to some concrete examples of *Capability Management* (previewed in volume 1, Appendix D). Volume 4 comprises my own and my students' case studies in which all three developmental perspectives (volumes) are drawn together into a holistic and comprehensive demonstration of how to help organizational clients. I hope also to present some coaching outcome research.

In my own courses at IDM, I recommend to students to do exercises with at least one other person, or 'buddy.' A small group works even better. Through group work, students' critical thinking is schooled, and their learning is reinforced. In my experience over the years, work in small groups is the optimal way of learning about social-emotional development.

1
You Already Know What Adult Development Is

However you have lived your life, you have gathered a lot of unconscious and conscious knowledge about how human beings develop, from infancy to childhood to adolescence and into adulthood. The first two phases of life may be more or less vivid in your memory, but you most likely have a distinct notion of 'earlier times' in your life, your successes and struggles at that time, and your yearning to grow up. You may also be at a point where you see childhood and adolescence in a somewhat rosy light, now that you are being tested daily as an *adult*. Wherever you are is good enough to begin to learn more about what social science has found out about adult development.

The term *adult development* has an unconventional ring to it, since grown-ups don't typically think much about their own development, except when they get into a crisis, come to what feels like a turning point in life, or compare their life to that of others. That is, adult development is a kind of HIDDEN DIMENSION. This holds true not only in our own life, but also, unfortunately, in the helping professions where developmental knowledge would be a priceless tool.

This book invites you to make an excursion into the Hidden Dimension of adult development. **The book is written for anybody working with adults for the purpose of their mental growth:** consultants, line managers, social workers, psychologists, mediators, coaches, and HR professionals. As the term 'adult development' implies, the way adults develop – approximately from age 25 to 100 – is distinctly different from what we see happening with children and adolescents. The reasons for this are manifold, but the foremost reason is that adults live in a physically mature body focused on the development of CONSCIOUSNESS. At 25, the development of adult consciousness has barely begun.

Interestingly, adult consciousness has been found to develop in a discontinuous, not a linear fashion. We say therefore that it develops in "stages." A stage is a position along a growth curve to which you proceed in your life, given the potential to do so, with the result that the "world" you have so far known is suddenly and dramatically changed. It's a different world, and you are still trying it out, so to speak, – it is that new to you. Sometimes you need help to get to a new stage, sometimes you get there by yourself and then need support to stay there, not to speak of going beyond. Does this sound familiar?

What you don't know at this point is the vocabulary needed to talk about adult development knowledgeably, or in a precise way. This vocabulary is exactly what this book is about. The book introduces verbal distinctions and numerical notations that will be helpful to you in figuring out the meaning of what is said to you, the issues you are struggling with yourself, what is going on in relationship with others, and how you make decisions from an ethical point of view. These distinctions and notations will also help you improve your listening, not only to yourself, but to your clients. What has language to do with adult development, you will ask.

Here are some first answers. The way people use language, when listened to by a developmental expert, is revealing far more than the content of what is said. What people talk about is only surface structure, so to speak. There is a hidden *deep structure* that has to do with how they make meaning of the world they encounter inside and outside of themselves. This deep structure is 'deep' not only because it's hidden from view, but because it reflects a *Center of Gravity* from which people are thinking, feeling, relating to others, and making decisions about what they should do, why they should do it, and for whom. We say that the Center of Gravity – or developmental stage – colors everything people do. This center is their comfort zone, hidden from view that they are not really in control of. As we will see throughout the book, people are strictly SUBJECT TO their present Center of Gravity.

Why subject to? What you don't know controls you, more or less. It is not something you can lay your hand on or make an object of reflection of. In fact, you only get to "see" (understand) your Center of Gravity once you have grown out of it, have gone to another, 'higher' stage. This is simply the human condition of being – to speak with Heidegger – thrown into your existence (Dasein), with no choice on your part. You are developmentally where you are, and that's it.

Why is this important to know for you as a member of the helping professions? Clearly, what you don't see in, and know about, your clients you can't attend to in your services. You have a blind spot that your clients cannot remove because they themselves have it. But you have a greater chance to see it than they do! If you have a vocabulary and notation, as well as an understanding of the theoretical framework of adult development, that is! What you can describe and notate you can manage better.

This said, let's move on to some detail. At this point, we need some kind of an overview that will be more of a show and tell. First, let's look at a visual depiction of adults' journey across the life span, as seen below (Kegan, 1982, 134):

Focus on
SELF

Focus on
OTHERS

**Level is NOT strictly
bound to age!**

← Toward Stage 5

← Stage 4 (ca. 40 years)

← Stage 3 (ca. 25 years)

← Stage 2 (ca. 15 years)

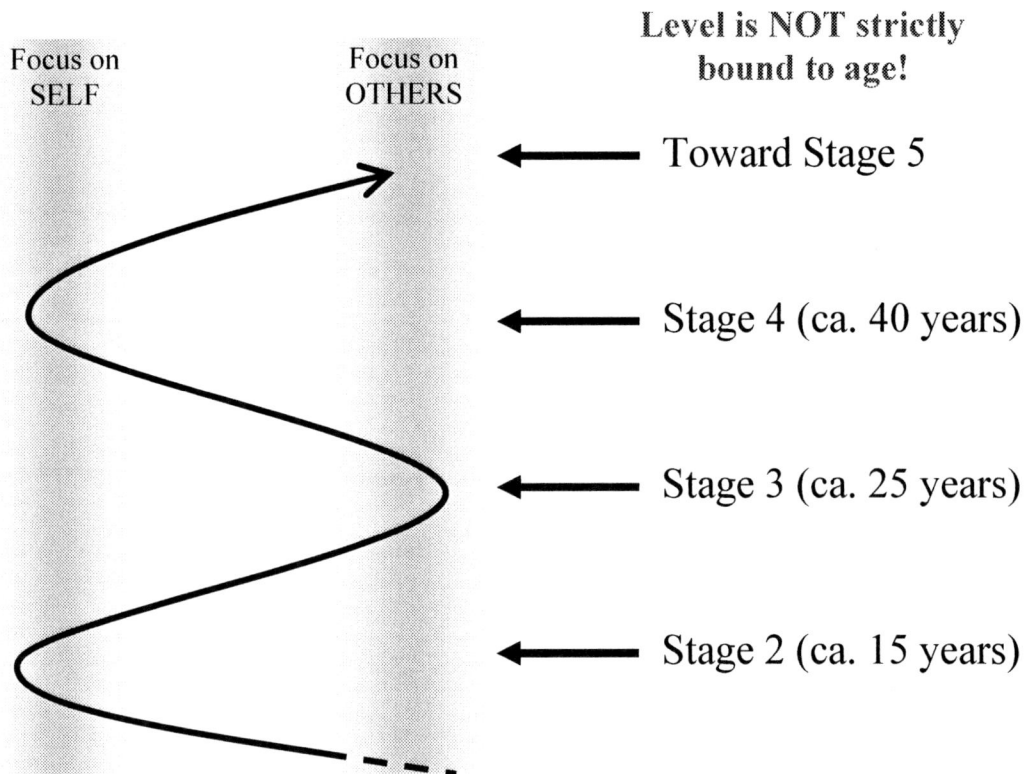

Fig. 1.1 The helix of adult development
(Courtesy John Spencer)

The depiction of the adult journey, above, is based on the assumption that humans struggle with two contradictory tendencies all of their life: the need to be autonomous or 'myself,' and the need to be included in a community or group, even if it is only a two-group (Kegan, 1982). As shown, adults oscillate between one focus and the other all the time, and this oscillation is what defines their social-emotional life. It's important to understand that the stages shown, and numbered from 2 to 5, are not aligned with age. Age is only a 'boundary variable,' in that most of the time you don't expect a twenty year old to be at stage 5. But everybody knows people in their thirties who are more mature than others in their fifties.

Let's investigate what seems to be the thrust of Fig. 1.1. (Stages 0 and 1 are not shown since they pertain to childhood and early adolescence.) The half-ellipsis, on the left, shows that there are certain similarities between Stages 2 and 4, and 3 and 5, respectively. Stage2 and Stage 4 are centered on the self, while Stage 3 and Stage 5 are centered on others. We will find out in due time in what sense this is so. Obviously, there are different, in fact starkly different, ways of being centered on oneself and on others.

You might ask: why do we stop at stage 5? The short answer is that stage 5 is the limit social science research has so far reached. Needless to say, there is ongoing research that leads beyond (e.g., Cook-Greuter, 1999). In this book, we will stay with Kegan's theory (1982, 1994), referred to above. (In what follows, I will abbreviate 'Stage' to S, and write S-2 for 'Stage 2,' etc.)

To understand the thrust of Fig. 1.1, it is important to realize that the movement from 'lower' to 'higher' stages never ceases (except if your developmental potential runs out, or at life's end), and that you can't be at S-3 if you have not previously been at S-2. It is also important to understand that nobody advances from S-2 to S-3 in one jump. In fact, we will introduce four intermediate levels that typify the journey from one stage to another and repeat between all of the stages (that is, they are 'recursive'). So, all in all we actually have about 16 levels to work with. As will you see later, nobody ever lives at a single level. Typically, people's developmental profile comprises, at any time, about 3 to 5 levels (most often 3).

Another, more esoteric, point is worth making. Research in the social sciences typically takes snapshots at a particular point in time to find out about how people act and experience the world. Fig. 1.1 above is based on a different perspective, replacing an 'in time' with an 'across time' perspective on life. The notion in the figure is that only if you can observe a very slow motion continuing over decades of adult life, can you really see what is going on in people's life. (Using scientific jargon, we speak of 'longitudinal' data.) Across time, you begin to see PATTERNS that elude you when you are only taking snapshots, as in typical assessments. The stages we are talking about in this book are such **long-term patterns invisible to the naked (developmentally unschooled) eye.**

Clearly, making such fine distinctions as we did above is both a skill and an art. It is something that can be learned. Let's begin this learning by looking at Table 1. The table points us to some of the major distinctions between stages:

Orientation	S- 2	S-3	S-4	S-5
View of Others	Instruments of own need gratification	Needed to contribute to own self image	Collaborator, delegate, peer	Contributors to own integrity and balance
Level of Self Insight	Low	Moderate	High	Very High
Values	Law of Jungle	Community	Self-determined	Humanity
Needs	Overriding all others' needs	Subordinate to community, work group	Flowing from striving for integrity	Viewed in connection with own obligations and limitations
Need to Control	Very High	Moderate	Low	Very low
Communication	Unilateral	Exchange 1:1	Dialogue	True Communication
Organizational Orientation	Careerist	Good Citizen	Manager	System's Leader

Table 1.1. Changing orientations across adult stages

The table above presents a brief summary of salient differences between successive stages. As you can see, views of others, level of self insight, values, needs, need to control, and communication all change from stage to stage, as does the way people live and work in organizations. Admittedly, the verbal distinctions made in the table are somewhat cryptic. They are meant only to facilitate getting an inkling of the broad patterns of adult development.

You will rightfully ask what is the process that holds together all of these different orientations? This is a very good question since it illuminates what the book is centrally about. The answer is: the process underlying the change of orientations is one of MEANING-MAKING, – the way people construct their life and work at different points of their adult journey. As R. Kegan formulates, being a person and being a meaning maker is really the same thing. This statement expresses a *constructivist* point of view where meaning making is seen as constructing meanings internally, and 'walking into them' like into a projection. Whether you know it or not, whatever you do is based on an underlying process of meaning making. It is virtually impossible to stop making meaning of yourself, others, and situations that you move through, except by falling dead. In short, meaning making is the life blood of social-emotional development.

To begin reading the table, let's look at the first two entries: views of others and self insight. They are salient indicators of social-emotional maturity.

Orientation	S-2	S-3	S-4	S-5
View of Others	Instruments of own need gratification	Needed to contribute to own self image	Collaborator, delegate, peer	Contributors to own integrity and balance
Level of Self Insight	Low	Moderate	High	Very High

As you see, the way people use each other largely depends on their level of self insight. So does the ethics of relationships. Level of self insight is not simply low or very high. It also has physiological limits depending on the development of the brain. Before age 25, the human brain is not in full possession of formal logical thinking, nor has it 'learned' (mostly the hard way) that if you use others as instruments of your desires you'll be punished for it, possibly publicly. However, acting from S-2 is not just a physiological but also an *epistemological* matter, where 'epistemology' translates to **ways of knowing**. People at S-2 can only hold a single perspective – their own – and this cognitive limitation necessarily leads them to act as they can be observed to do. Consult your resident teenager.

As indicated in Table 1.1, in late adolescence people start with a low level of self insight, and therefore tend to use others as instruments of their own need fulfillment. (Some people, and corporations guided by them, never get beyond this mental stage, see Enron). The only way to get out of this frame of mind is to become able – both in terms of consciousness and behavior – to hold other people's perspective, This motion simultaneously raises one's level of self insight and changes one's view of others. Others are now seen as having their own mind and feelings, and as requiring the respect of people living their own lives in their own way. Others also become 'hand holders,' models, examples. They are now needed to facilitate one's own decision making and way of living since they define conventions one feels it is important to follow. (Ask you resident advertiser or community buddy.) In this sense, people at S-3 are internally dependent on others. We call them, with Kegan, *other-dependent*. This is not cause for lamentations. As the remaining orientations under S-3 in Table 1.1 show, other-dependent people are the core of community. They are able to function as members of a team, with only moderate needs to control others. They are typically fair and "good citizens."

You will realize at this point that I am drawing up some caricatures. They are not meant to be funny as much as giving you a first, raw impression of the differences between adult stages. So, keep in mind that I am dealing with a typology here, nothing more. People 'are' not their stages, they just live there for the moment, without knowing it. There are millions of people living at the same stage, all of them are very different in behavior and culture. Still, knowing their stage tells a lot about what they strive for, what they need, and what their limitations in the social realm might be.

What kind of a person can be said to live at S-4? What is needed to go beyond defining yourself according to others' expectations? You guessed it: developing your own, very unique way of seeing and doing things, and being prepared to defend it if need be, marching to your own drummer. You might say: isn't that S-2? No. Because while at S-2 it is your needs and desires that are in focus, at S-4 it is your integrity and values that are. Although they are intimately linked to your needs and desires, you are holding yourself to a higher standard. Not only do you respect others who are different, you also acknowledge them as peers and colleagues. You are open to dialogue with them and, given that you can manage yourself reasonably well, you can also manage others, at least at work. You are also aware of your own uniqueness in relation to others (perhaps a little much so), and you are willing to pay the price of 'going it alone.' In this sense, your self insight is high, much higher than at S-2.

So what's missing in you, once at S-4, to act as thoroughly self-aware (S-5)? As I said before, people are subject to their present stage, and being at S-4 is no different. You literally don't see the cage of high integrity you are in from the outside. You are over-defined by yourself, your accomplishments, successes, merits, and what not. Thus you come to grief, either in life or at work, and have to learn the hard way that you have extensive limitations, often pointed out by others, and that you actually need others to safeguard your own integrity and balance.

As a self-authorer (S-4), you are just not humble enough and you often don't see the bigger picture (although this depends also on your cognitive resources). You are also not supportive enough of others, especially those who don't see things your way. You can manage them but cannot lead them, motivate them, foster their development even if that should be against your own best interest. (Erickson spoke of *generativity*).

As you see from this narration, life isn't getting any easier or 'better' as you rise through the stages. It's just that your joys and sorrows are different, and you have an increasingly clearer perception of being just a speck in the universe that will outlast you, including your successes and achievements. The world is becoming an ever larger object for you, with you deeply embedded in it until death comes. So, if you are lucky you are going to die knowing all this: the tragedy, comedy, struggles of life, and life's great beauty, including the beauty and frailty of your own life.

***

Now let's look at some statistics that the social sciences provide us with (Cook-Greuter, 1999, 35). For helping professionals, these make some sobering reading:

Organizational Perspective	% of Developmental Attainment	Short Characterization
S-2: Individualist	10	Instrumental
S-3: Group contributor	**55**	Other-dependent
S-4: Manager	25	Self-authoring
S-5 Leader	<10	Self-aware

Table 1.2 The sober reality of adult developmental attainment

We can summarize this table as follows:

- Most people never leave S-3 (other-dependent stage)
- No more than 25% make it to S-4 (self-authoring stage)
- Less than 10% become self-aware and can lead (self-aware stage).

If this sounds frightening, remember that society needs people at all stages. We can't really imagine a world filled with leaders – whom would they lead? It's true that we are dealing with a stratified universe (which is hidden), not a flat one. But just because of that, there are some good sides to this statistic, too, especially for process consultants.

For one thing, there does not seem to be a social *forcing function* for getting people beyond S-3, to S-4. Nothing but you yourself prompts you to go there, and you do so at a price. Society is already satisfied if you get to S-3, where you constitute a member of the civil community. To go beyond the conventional realm of S-3 is left to everybody him- or herself. This is another facet of the human condition we spoke of. Importantly, it's not a matter of education or age either. These two variables are weak predictors of developmental stage. The best, if not only, predictor of stage is a person's level of consciousness (or meaning making) as revealed through natural language.

As Robert Kegan (1994) has shown in detail, this epistemological situation – regarding ways of knowing – poses many problems for present society and its members. Since most professional jobs require at least S-4, which is not where most people lead their life, working people rightfully feel as if they were 'in over their heads.' In this context, it is interesting that a movement like that of coaching should have come about. As an outgrowth of the North American self-help movement, coaching could be seen as society's attempt to create, if not a social 'forcing function,' at least a social *helping function* for people to move to a self-authoring stage. I leave it as an exercise to the reader to decide whether the coaching movement has attained, or is likely to attain, this lofty goal. Clearly, coaches who are not themselves self-authoring cannot hope to assist others in the journey to, or beyond, S-4. Most likely, many coaches use their professional work to move out of S-3 themselves. This is a little like 'the blind leading the blind.' (See Chapter 9 for further thoughts on issues peculiar to coaching.)

A related issue that is the focus of volume 2 is people's *cognitive profile*. Adults' social-emotional development is strongly correlated with how complexly and systemically people can think. The correlation is about 0.6, which is high for social science findings. Since correlations are by definition not causal, they don't reveal which one of these main strands of adult development functions as the motor of the other: does a highly developed cognitive profile (not identical with high 'intelligence') promote social-emotional awareness, or is it the other way around? All we can say is that these two developmental strands – the cognitive and the social-emotional one, referred to in this book as CD (cognitive development) and ED (social-emotional development) – are *inseparable*. This is important in the helping professions, because 'cognitive coaching' might just be what a client needs to make it to the subsequent stage (see volume 2 of this book).

Intermediate Summary

In this chapter, I have introduced the reader to some fundamental notions of adult development over the life span. Many of these notions are either unknown or contradict conventional assumptions. They are therefore often 'hidden' from view. Nevertheless, the findings of more than 50 years of research cannot be disputed. They are findings which 'coaching research,' as it is called, is only gradually waking up to.

Here is a short summary of what we have – potentially – learned:
1. The social world is built on a hidden stratification of developmental stages.
2. People's joys, problems, struggles at different stages are different (not better).
3. There are altogether about 16 stages (see Chapter 6).
4. Most people do not live at a single stage, but at a Center of Gravity associated with a "lower" and "higher" stage (Chapter 5).
5. People's potential to attain higher stages of development starkly differs.
6. Some people reach their capability ceiling in their fifties, sixties, seventies, eighties, – and some die before having reached it.
7. The proportion in which people make meaning of their life and work is skewed toward S-3, of other-dependence (55%); this presents a problem for modern society whose professions require S-4.
8. Age and education are poor predictors of developmental stage.
9. The helping professions can be seen as an attempt of society, to introduce tools supportive of adult development over the life span.
10. Whether the helping professions can become an effective force in society depends on the self development – adult maturity – of its members.

The Full Scope of Developmental Assessments

Let me put what I have said about developmental stages so far into a more comprehensive perspective. From my experience as a developmental consultant, I would emphasize that working based on knowledge of developmental stages alone does not do justice to the full complexity clients bring to an intervention. Although these other, additional, assessments are the topic of volumes 2 and 3 of this book, I briefly introduce them here, to give the reader a fuller account of the design of the book as a whole. This will also help the reader to anticipate more succinctly what the rest of the book will be about.

As said, this is a how-to book on making client assessments in the context of developmentally based process consultation. Since the methods remain identical throughout, it is of no concern whether the client is an individual, team, group, or entire organization. What matters is that we work in an assessment based way, eschewing all 'hand-waving.'

The best way to understand the layout of the entire book – its four volumes – is to distinguish between an assessment KERNEL and a set of assessment TOOLS, as shown below:

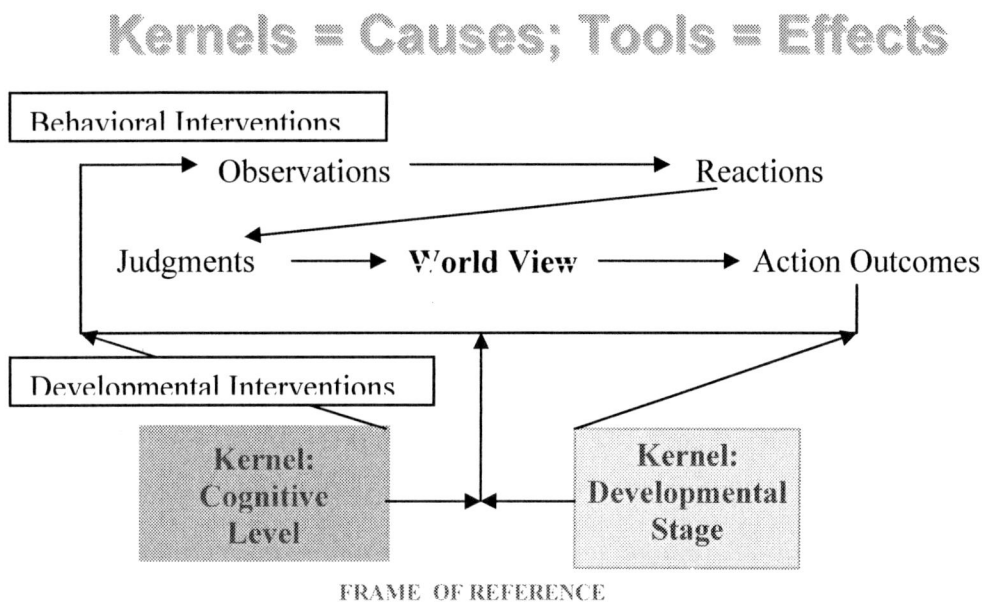

Kernels = Causes; Tools = Effects

Behavioral Interventions

Observations → Reactions

Judgments → World View → Action Outcomes

Developmental Interventions

| Kernel: Cognitive Level | | Kernel: Developmental Stage |

FRAME OF REFERENCE

How people <u>use</u> competences depends on their World View, that is, on how they observe, react emotionally, judge things, set goals, and act, and this is a function of their cognitive level and developmental stage (Frame of Reference)

Figure 1.2 CDF Kernel and Tools (adapted from Schein 1999)

In Fig. 1.2, I have brought together Schein's ORJA cycle with its developmental base. As shown, two kinds of interventions are distinguished: *behavioral* and *developmental* interventions. Behavioral interventions (such as coaching) attempt to influence how people set goals and use competences, in short, individuals' performance. As shown in this book, performance can't be understood apart from developmental level. Accordingly, developmentally based consultation must comprise both behavioral and developmental assessments, or as I say in Fig. 1.2, *Kernel and Tools*. Kernel assessments regard causes of behavior. In the *Constructivist Developmental Framework* here detailed, the Kernel comprises two developmental assessments. Tool assessments provide additional information about clients' behavior and performance as a function of their needs and the environmental (organizational) pressure they are under (volume 3).

As Schein rightfully emphasizes, process consultants work from the assumption that in the beginning of a consultation, neither client nor consultant know precisely what is going on. Neither the problem nor the solution is known to them. What is known is only that some assistance is needed. Most likely, the client's presenting problem is only a first stab at what might be going on for the client. Developmentally considered, 'what is going on' for the client can largely be predicted from the knowledge of his or her developmental stage. In fact, the client's initial problem formulation succinctly encapsulates his or her developmental stage. Stage is the cause, behavior the effect. This fact precisely explains the relevance of stage in developmental consultation.

From the vantage point of Kernel and Tools assessments, above, I can now speak very succinctly about the four volumes of this book. Volumes 1 and 2 regard the Kernel, while volume 3 concerns Tools. Volume 4 pulls Kernel and Tools together into a comprehensive synthesis where all three perspectives on a client are fully realized.

The best way to reinforce the distinction between Kernel and Tools is to distinguish between *vertical* and *horizontal* assessments (Wilber, 2000, 53-54). Most existing assessments are horizontal, and thus are *Tools*. They produce snapshots of the past more than the present, and presuppose a linear development occurring *in time*. The predictive value of such snapshots is very small (although this is often denied). By contrast, vertical assessments – of which only a few exist at this time – capture developmental patterns that occur *across time*.

When looking at human change 'in time,' much remains hidden that becomes visible only when focusing on change 'across time.' Patterns, such as stages, are across-time patterns, and they derive from Kernel assessments. To make such patterns visible requires a vertical approach, both in eliciting data and in using it in interventions.

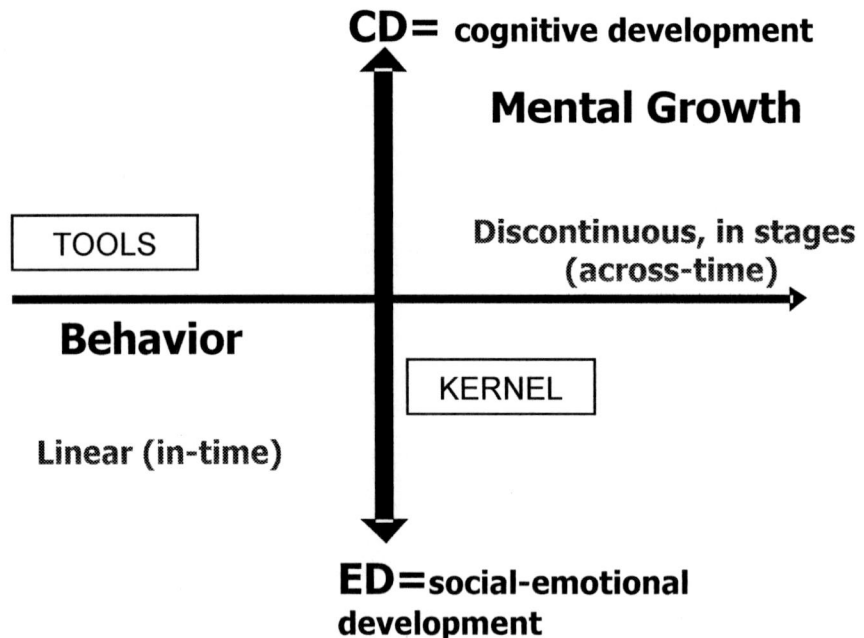

CD = cognitive development

Mental Growth

TOOLS

Discontinuous, in stages (across-time)

Behavior

KERNEL

Linear (in-time)

ED = social-emotional development

Figure 1.3 Kernel = Vertical, Tools = Horizontal

As shown, client behaviors are typically assessed from an in-time, linear perspective, the notion being that behavior changes through learning. Learning is a linear process that can be captured 'in-time.' By contrast, clients' mental growth, since it follows stages, is discontinuous in nature, and is different from mere learning. Rather it enables learning to occur or obstructs learning. Progression through stages occurs across, rather than in, time, according to patterns of movement between stages that in-time snapshots cannot capture. The reason for this is simple: an across-time approach to intervention is 'longitudinal,' meaning data is being elicited across time, possibly entire decades or even the entire human lifespan.

The distinction between 'horizontal' and 'vertical' assessments, above, means also that one and the same horizontal (behavioral) fact or data set can have many vertical (developmental) *interpretations*. For example, a client presenting with insufficient time management will 'have' that issue for very different reasons, depending on his or her cognitive capacity and developmental stage. To know the client's developmental profile is therefore highly important, since intervention focus and approach to improving client issues will have to differ from stage to stage. (This is not taken into account by 'best practices', of course, so the question arises: 'best for whom?') Or take some horizontal assessment like the Enneagram or the MBTI. What it means to be 'Type 8' of the Enneagram, for instance, depends on the vertical, developmental stage of the client. In itself the finding is too generic to be very meaningful, at least for process consultants.

We can now summarize. The important fact about the distinction between Kernel and Tools assessments – or, equivalently, Vertical and Horizontal assessments – is that the former assess the **Causes of behavior**, and the latter assess behavioral **Effects (of the Kernel).** To give an example of this distinction, let's say, you have made a 360-degree assessment of a client, and you now want to add a developmental one. To be comprehensive, you will want to add two developmental assessments: one for social-emotional development (ED), and one for cognitive development (CD). The relationship between Kernel and Tools assessments in the framework of this book is visualized below:

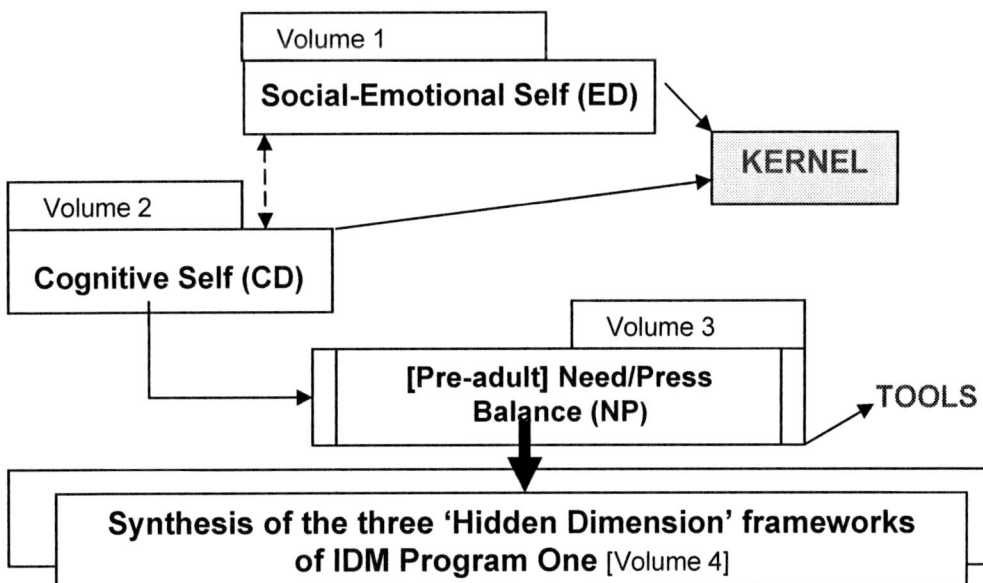

Fig. 1.4 Relationship of the three client perspectives

As can be seen, volume 1 of the book exclusively deals with the social-emotional self and its levels, while volume 2 focuses on the cognitive self. Together assessments of these two selves constitute the Kernel. Then, in volume 3 of the book, we learn an assessment that provides us with very broad insight into the nature of clients' *behavior* and strongly suggests how to proceed with clients in feedback and coaching sessions. The purpose of this tri-partition into volumes 1 to 3 of the book is outlined below:

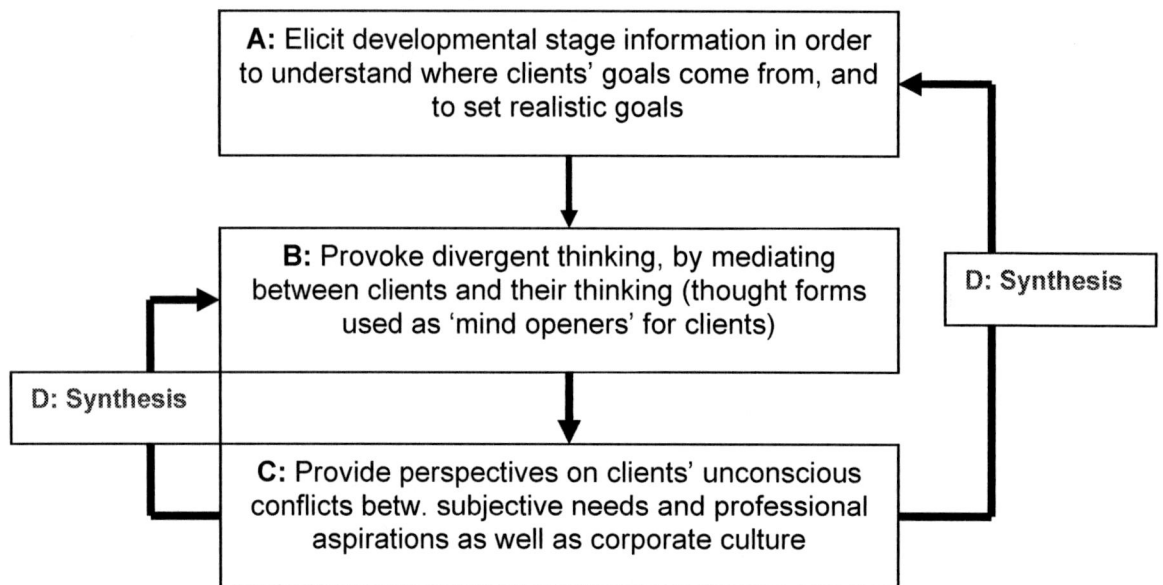

Fig. 1.5 Three steps in working with clients

As shown, in volume 1 of the book we focus on understanding the client's goals, their nature and where they come from. For this purpose, determining developmental stages is a priority. As you will increasingly understand, people at different stages have very different basic goals that inform their entire way of approaching life and work, including their 'desires' and 'needs.'

The second issue in the Kernel assessments is the way clients *think*. We refer to thinking as *cognition*, focusing on the cognitive self. By cognition we mean how deep and systemic clients are able to think, as indicated by the *thought forms* they have mastered to various degrees. Findings about cognition tell us what clients CAN do, while findings about stage tell us what clients think they SHOULD DO and FOR WHOM they should do it.

Once we understand clients' KERNEL, we can then use various tools to learn in more detail about what clients' actual behaviors are. We thus arrive at the following equations:

Kernel = Causes of behaviors (ED & CD): long-term development.
Tools = Behavioral effects of causes: short-term change perspective.

PRACTICE REFLECTION

At the end of each chapter of this volume, the reader will find some pertinent topics of reflection through which to deepen his or her understanding of the content of the chapter. These reflections are separate from the Exercises in the Appendix, all of which are voluntary, and some of which have stated answers.

- Think back 10 years in your life and think about what, since then, you have acquired in terms of:
    a. knowledge about yourself
    b. knowledge about others
    c. intellectual clarity about how the world works
    d. self awareness
    e. sensitivity to others
    f. etc.
- How, up to now, have you discerned the level of your clients' developmental maturity?
- What do you do if, in your estimation, your client is more highly developed as an adult than you are?
- What are your thoughts about there being stark developmental differences between people, even of the same age? How do you approach such differences in your practice?
- Since you presumably have worked exclusively from a Tools perspective, how might integrating Kernel assessments, as taught in this volume, change your work?

2
What is Your Hypothesis as You Listen?

The high-level overview of Chapter 1 will enable us in what follows to begin thinking about the abilities that are central to leading powerful conversations. The most important of these capabilities is *listening*. This chapter presents a first example of developmental listening, using utterances taken from an S-2 individual. We will get a 'feel' for how such a person sees the world, and what, as process consultants, we need to pay attention to in order to be of help. The chapter also presents two 'counter-hypotheses,' meaning guesses as to what is the speaker's Center of Gravity. In this way, readers will learn to make distinctions between different main stages that they might initially have in mind when attending to the speaker.

The reader would do best to proceed as if in the utterances presented *every word* counted. Since developmental listening is all about clients' spontaneous use of verbal language, readers are encouraged to use their own abilities as native speakers of English, to puzzle out what is IMPLIED by what is said (and thus not said directly.) The ability to infer from – rather than interpret – verbal utterances is a major tool that needs to be mastered in order to become expert in developmental listening.

***

Listening is an internal process that is not easily mapped and understood, whether we deal with listening to language or to music. It is different from *hearing* (an acoustic term) in that it is entirely based on meaning making. This fact ties it to our own development, thus our own life, since the meaning we make of things we hear is specific to our own adult history and profile. For this reason, this chapter is not so much an analysis of listening to clients (or other stake holders) as it is an outline of what can be accomplished by a developmentally schooled professional.

The first thing that is striking about listening is that it is an effort to *understand* somebody else. The underlying notion is that what is said to you makes the claim to be true, and that your task is to understand that truth. In the helping professions, the verbal material brought forward is also meant to be understood in the sense of being analyzed, in some way. There are many ways to analyze interviews, for example, most of them concerned with literal content (themes, etc.). It is here that developmental listening is in a category by itself since it strives to understand the STRUCTURE, not the CONTENT, of verbal utterances. After reading chapter 1, it will not astonish you to hear that what is meant by structure is really STAGE.

So how, during an intervention, do you listen to discern the stage from which a client is speaking to you? While listening happens throughout the helping process, in evidence-based developmental coaching it happens very emphatically at the very beginning of the helping process. Provoking people to reveal their Center of Gravity is the core of what is called **developmental interviewing**. Such interviewing is carried out with a hypothetical developmental stage "in mind." Such hypothesis based interviewing is what we are exercising from the beginning to the end of this book.

Where do you begin to learn developmental listening and interviewing? The first thing, clearly, is "to know your stages." This means to know their characteristics, "know them when you hear them," and, to help that along, *probe* for them. This is not easy, but it can be learned from examples and illustrations and, of course, from observing an expert. Probing is the real core of this enterprise. Probing presupposes that you know what information you are missing, and how and what, therefore, you have to ask a client. **In fact, if you don't know what information is missing for you in what you hear, you cannot probe.** And to know what is missing, you have to know what to listen FOR. This means you need an hypothesis as to what you are listening TO. Are you sufficiently confused?

Let's start over. Developmental listening by way of probing is not so different from any other *discovery procedure*. When you studied biology as a child, you were given certain properties of bugs to look for so that, when you saw them under a microscope, you could formulate a HYPOTHESIS (a guess) as to what bug it might be you were seeing. It's not so different in developmental listening except that there are no visual cues, because the hypotheses you are following are all 'just in your mind.' And the better you become at developmental listening, the better your hypotheses and your probing for the purpose of engaging fully with them will become.

Look at the developmental enterprise this way: You are using yourself as the instrument of your research: your feelings, your mind, your own developmental stage. In academic jargon, this is called *qualitative research*, since what you are trying to do is to come up with qualities of a person, situation, or environment that one can classify and give a name to. It's no different here. Developmental interviewing is 'research' (coaching research or other). You are doing qualitative research on a single person, for the purpose of finding out how that person makes meaning in her life and work right now, in order to know how, based on forthcoming information, you might effectively help that person. To do so, you are wearing developmental glasses, that is, you are adopting a perspective linked to knowing developmental stages and their differences. On account of this knowledge, you can formulate hypotheses (make guesses) as to what it is you are listening to. In short, developmental listening is a (stage) *discovery procedure*.

Now, the important thing about this discovery procedure is that you need to be able to **probe** for what is missing to test your hypothesis, or confirm its accuracy. This is the tricky part which entirely depends on your own understanding and expertise. As if this wasn't difficult enough, in addition you have to cope with the distinction between CONTENT and STRUCTURE, introduced above. What is that all about?

If we equate STRUCTURE with STAGE, then clearly, the distinction of Stage from Content is a matter of discerning what Stage the Content expresses or manifests. That means to accept the notion that ANY content can express a particular stage, and that there is no one-to-one relationship between content and structure (stage). Put differently, when somebody speaks of being, and loving to be, a member of a community, it is easy to hypothesize that the person speaking is an 'other-dependent' person living at S-3. However, this can be highly misleading, since somebody at other stages, certainly S-5, could say the same or similar thing. So, what matters, obviously, is the CONTEXT in which something is said, and the EMPHASIS that is falling on what is highlighted by the speaker. All of this can be mastered in due time with extended practice.

Let's start with some *illustrations*. In fact, that's what we are going to use in this book most of the time, except at the end, where we use actual interview texts. Let me explain why illustrations are different from real interviews.

Developmental Illustrations are texts composed for the purpose of highlighting a particular adult stage. They are contrived to make a point. Typically, they fall into a particular *range* of levels. (Henceforth, I am going to use the term "levels" to indicate that there are 'intermediate' stages between 'main' stages). By contrast, in a real-life developmental interview, you are initially without any sign posts. You don't know 'where the speaker is coming from.' The origin of what has been composed by the speaker is unknown to you (and the speaker as well). Although what you hear or read is composed in some way, you initially don't know what is the range of levels that are being expressed. As a consequence, you don't immediately know what stage to listen FOR. There are no visible or audible markers, only inferred ones. You yourself have to determine a possible range *by hypothesis formulation*, and within some postulated range have to find out exactly what levels are part of the client's present meaning making range. In a real interview, then, **context** becomes all-important, and nothing is highlighted for you in advance. You are the sole arbiter in defining a range of levels based on which to 'score' (evaluate) an interview. How does this become possible?

The main reason why this is entirely possible to do is that people live, as I've said, at a particular Center of Gravity. And although they live at more than a single level, such as a lower and a higher one, they are typically not spread out over 10 levels or so. If they were, they might be considered as mentally ill. For this reason, anybody able to postulate a Center of Gravity below and above which a person may be making meaning of the world typically succeeds in delimiting the range of levels within which the speaker can be said presently to function developmentally.

This brings me to an additional requirement of developmental listening, and that is PLAYING DEVIL'S ADVOCATE. We reasoning beings are all hell-bent on *satisficing*, to speak with H. Simon. This entails that we don't really search for all possible alternatives but make an assumption that comes easy to us, and then go with that assumption. Under these circumstances, we lose track of the critical voice in us that says "but couldn't it rather be stage X?" And that is exactly what we have to learn to ask ourselves. In a small group, this happens naturally (and groups are therefore the preferred context in which to learn developmental scoring). Somebody other than you will question your hypothesis and say: "but I think it's rather Y, and here is why!" This then leads to a process of justifying one's hypothesis. And justifying one's hypothesis is best provoked by becoming critical of oneself. By internalizing the critical voices of the group one starts to learn to make better assumptions and formulate better hypotheses.

***

Let's now look at some illustrations of levels, to get a better grasp of the matter, keeping in mind that these are contrived examples (illustrations) meant to make a point.

EXAMPLE 1 (adapted from Lahey et al. 1988, 94)
The client has been speaking about being new in the company, and trying to find her way in the new, unknown environment. She has been speaking of a number of colleagues, particularly of S. with whom she seems to have closely associated herself:

Client: I'm really sad that my colleague lied to me regarding his salary raise. Now I can never be sure whether he's telling me the truth. Like if you know a person has lied to someone else or to you before, then you know you just can't count on them.
Interviewer: What do you mean by "count on them?"
Client: You need to know who the people are that you can turn to when you need truthful information or help.
Interviewer: Like what kind of help are you thinking of?
Client: Like if you're new to a workplace and working very hard to get to know the cultural climate, and you don't know whether it would make any difference whether you work hard or not, you need to know who you can ask to give you the right answer. You need to know whether the person you are asking will tell you the truth.

Disregarding, for the moment, the procedure of the interviewer: what is this client saying that could be of interest in determining the range of adult levels within which she makes meaning of her social environment, – not to mention ethical issues like standards of work excellence, and notions of truth she is holding?

Apparently, the client is not on too sure footing in her new environment. She is dependent on other people for knowing how to behave properly, how much effort to invest, etc. She is concerned about something she calls 'truth,' which seems to be either black or white ('the truth'). Moreover, this 'truth' is identical with what is perceived by her as being helpful to herself, and is thus of very limited generality. Her notion seems to be that you either lie or you don't, and that 'truth' is an absolute. In this context, 'counting on' is still another absolute indicating absolute dependency on somebody for survival. And who has lied to you or somebody else before is therefore by definition a 'liar,' period.

So far, our comments have been strictly content oriented. So, how can we shed some light on the stage the client above is presently speaking from? To illuminate the underlying **Structure**, we could rewrite this illustration with totally different content, nevertheless retaining the Structure. This would show that content is not really what matters, and would be a good exercise to show ourselves that we should begin to see content for just what it is: content. For instance, we could substitute the following content for the one above without moving away from the focus of the illustration.

EXAMPLE1b.

Client: I'm truly sad that my friend lied to me about why he has avoided me in recent days. Now I can never be sure whether he's telling me the truth. Because if you know a person has lied to someone else or to you before, then you know you just can't count on them.
Interviewer: What do you mean by "count on them?"
Client: You need to know who the people are that you can turn to when you need truthful information or help.

Interviewer: Like what kind of help are you thinking of?
Client: Like if you're doing your best to be liked by others by being on your best behavior, and you don't know whether your efforts make any difference at all in how they view you, then it is helpful to be able to ask them about the truth, so you henceforth know what not to do or to avoid. You need to know whether that person will tell you the truth about yourself.

While the content details above are somewhat different, as previously they concern human relationships, and the perceived requirement to be able to count on somebody to tell the truth, so as to arrange one's behavior accordingly. Clearly, the need to be able to count on somebody is a fundamental issue in both illustrations. In both examples we perceive:

- The same focus on one's own needs and desires and their instantaneous gratification.
- The same fixation on one's own perspective, with the inability to take another person's perspective, especially on oneself
- The same indifference to what others think, feel, and experience.
- The same inability to be influenced, in one's own thinking and feeling, by others thinking and behavior.
- The same rigid understanding of 'truth' (restricted to 'my needs').
- The same ignorance about the self's position in the social world, and therefore the same cloying behavior.
- The same need to be able to use others as a resource in the case of a crisis.

Somewhere in this sameness lies the STRUCTURE of the speaker's present meaning making process. Let's spell out this Structure in positive terms:
1. I am defined by my needs and desires (as far as I know them).
2. I am ignorant of what others think and feel; as far as I am concerned, they are living in a different world ('two-world hypothesis').
3. I have no intention or capacity to penetrate others' world.
4. I therefore am dependent on others' absolute truthfulness which alone can save me in moments of crisis.
5. I need to be able to use others as instruments of my need gratification, either by exerting absolute control, or by adapting myself to what I perceive to be their motivation to help me out (preferably the former).

How does that fit with the entries for S-2 in Table 2-1?

Orientation	S-2
View of Others	Instruments of own need gratification
Level of Self Insight	Low
Values	Law of Jungle
Needs	Overriding all others' needs
Need to Control	Very High
Communication	Unilateral
Organizational Orientation	Careerist

Table 2.1 Parameters of acting from S-2

Many, if not all, orientations listed above appear in the two illustrations. Here is how and why.

Extrapolating from the two examples, it seems that the values manifested therein signal a view of society where everyone is on his or her own, and the stronger will eat the weaker. In this kind of society, the Law of the Jungle reigns supreme. In this terrifying situation, people's only recourse is to strive for absolute control. There is no other safety, since nobody tells the truth, and nobody can be counted on. In this case, people's communications will be unilateral, in the sense of 'you are either for me or against me.' There will be crusades, designated enemies, fear-based campaigns and wars, since the only thing that unites people is their common fear, risk, or crisis. In an organizational context, once somebody has enough power to dispense with the craving for others' truthfulness, s(he) can dictate the truth, and decide the Law of the Jungle in his or her favor.

We are talking here about a developmental stage that society is rightfully apprehensive of, for the reason that there exists no notion of a civilized society in which conventions are in force. A community of interests, solidified by commonalities and implicit agreements between people does not seem to be in place. Communication is dictatorial (unilateral) and replaces consensus. THESE ARE THE CHARACTERISTICS OF S-2!

Looking now at the principal features of this stage, we find that people at S-2:
1. can separate themselves from their perception, making a distinction between what something seems and what it is (this is the advance over S-1)
2. have the ultimate concern of whether they will lose in others a source of help for themselves in a situation of danger or crisis
3. take their own self interest as a guide in the complex and dangerous social world regulated by laws of the jungle
4. have no clue, either of their own self or that of others, and lack a theory of mind
5. live in a *split universe* where everybody is separate from the other's knowing
6. cannot see in others anything beyond the importance of their actions and their actions' consequences for their own life's security and well-being
7. use others as instruments of their own survival.

If you think as Thomas Hobbes did in the 17th century, that this scenario describes the origins of human society, you may be on the right track. We can think of society as a set of conventions made to escape from the laws of the jungle that, at S-2, reign supreme. Clearly, the speaker in the last two illustrations is not entirely part of civil society, or at least not yet.

Let's briefly summarize S-2:
- **Distribution:** about 10% of adults.
- **Advance over Stage 1:** a distinction can be made between what something seems and what it is. This requires the ability to separate oneself from one's perception (stage 1), of taking one's perceptions as object (S-2).
- **Essence of this stage:** As a self subject to my needs, wishes, and interests, I relate to another person in terms of possible consequences for my world view. I "know" you in

terms of how helpful you can be to me, and am thus unable to consider your independent view as I am taking into account my own.

- **Instrumentalism:** The ultimate concern is with whether I will lose you a source of support or help for myself. My own interest constitutes the ground from which I attend to your perspective.
- **Pervasive limitation:** a 'split universe,' where each individual's knowing is separate from that of others.

Movement toward Stage 3

Except for the 10% of the population which typically remain at Stage 2, most people move beyond, thereby becoming more socialized and at ease with convention, at least on the surface. We can infer from the characteristics of S-2 what this move requires. Here are some highlights:

- A person must be able to distance herself from being embedded in her own needs and interests.
- A person must begin to take a second perspective on things, that of others who are different from herself.
- Increasingly, the person must *internalize* other people's perspective, by "bringing them inside" (Lahey et al, 1988)
- A person must begin to be influenced by that second perspective in his/her thoughts and feelings.
- A person must begin to act in recognition of others' needs and desires, acknowledging that others are taking their own peculiar perspective on other people, including the person herself. (We can call that a *theory of other minds.*)

***

Let us pause and look back. In this chapter, we introduced the notion of listening based on the formulation of a hypothesis about a speakers developmental stage. We referred to stage as *Structure*, and explained in some detail the mental processes of probing for Structure. Below, let's return to this topic, by having another look at Example 1.

EXAMPLE 1 (adapted from Lahey et al. 1988, 94)
The client has been speaking of being new in the company, and trying to find the way in the new, unknown environment. She has been speaking of a number of colleagues, particularly of S. with whom she seems to have closely associated herself:

Client: I'm really sad that my colleague lied to me regarding his salary raise. Now I can never be sure whether he's telling me the truth. Like if you know a person has lied to someone else or to you before, then you know you just can't count on them.
Interviewer: What do you mean by "count on them?"
Client: You need to know who the people are that you can turn to when you need truthful information or help.
Interviewer: Like what kind of help are you thinking of?
Client: Like if you're new to a workplace and working very hard to get to know the cultural climate, and you don't know whether it would make any difference in the company whether you work hard or not, you need to know who you can ask to give you the right answer. You need to know whether the person you are asking will tell you the truth.

Rereading Example 1, a listener might be tempted to formulate two different hypotheses:

1. The client speaking seems to be very dependent on her colleague for orienting herself in the new company environment. This dependency sounds to me as if the client is defining herself by the colleagues' expectations as to how effort is rewarded in the company. The client seems to identify with her colleague, and indirectly with the work community as a whole. It is for this reason that the client is so dependent on being told the truth. Therefore, I would hypothesize that the client's stage is presently at or close to **S-3,** where people define themselves by others' expectations.

2. The client is speaking as if truth was highly important to her, defining her own integrity. Not being told the truth is so upsetting to the client because she thinks she cannot live and thrive in a climate in which truth lacking. Therefore, I would hypothesize that the client's Center of Gravity is presently located around **S-4** where people are defined by their strongly held values defining their moral integrity.

Playing Devil's Advocate Regarding Counter-Hypothesis #1 (S-3)

Let's take these *counter-hypotheses* as material for playing devil's advocate regarding our initial notion that the client speaking is presently at S-2. Here is what we would have to respond to the first counter-hypothesis. (You can imagine this being done in a group discussion where members of the group collaboratively evaluate, or 'score,' a developmental interview).

While it is true that the speaker (client) seems to be very dependent on her colleague, and to a great extent identifies with him, we have to consider the *kind* of dependency that is being articulated by the speaker. We also have to take into account the kind of relationship the client entertains with her colleague.

As to the dependency expressed, it really centers on the client's need and desire to be safe, and to be helped out in situations of crisis. This dependency is not based on any kind of identification with the colleague, neither with the colleague as a person, nor with the colleague as a representative of a larger group. There is no evidence that the client has a way of even establishing dependency in the sense of S-3. She presently cannot take a perspective other than her own, and thus cannot be influenced in her thoughts and feelings either by her colleague as a person, or as a representative of the larger community.

Playing Devil's Advocate Regarding Hypothesis #2 (S-4)

What about the second hypothesis that the client is speaking as a self-authorer, entirely acting from her own principles and values?

While it is correct that the client conveys an ardent desire for hearing the truth, what she calls *truth* is the expression of a personal (and possibly erroneous) view of how to operate within a workforce community. 'Truth,' as the term is here used, is also external to – or excludes – the colleague that is being addressed, since it is one-sidedly a matter of the speaker's own interest (for whom the colleague is an instrument). There are no indications that the client has enough self insight to know whether speaking the truth is at the center of her own integrity, nor does the client seem to be able to formulate even an elementary theory of her own self (of what she stands for), except for her need to be helped in situations of risk or uncertainty. Therefore, the hypothesis that the client is speaking from S-4 is not persuasive. It is, in fact, contradicted by most of what is expressed by the speaker's discourse.

The above discussion of two counter-hypotheses is a good example of the internal process that occurs in a developmentally schooled listener. The listener is making inferences from what is heard, and is matching these inferences to his or her knowledge of what individual stages imply. The listener clearly separates content from structure, and is thinking exclusively in terms of structure (in this case main stages). As far as the listener is concerned, the client could be talking just about anything. By putting the content of what is said *into brackets*, the listener focuses on how meaning is made by the speaker. This, in a nutshell, is what developmental listening is all about.

Having settled the counter-claims regarding our S-2 hypothesis, let's now return to the question of how to probe for the sake of formulating a correct hypothesis. We have said that a lot of information is often missing when we listen for structure in clients' verbal material. As a consequence, we have to ascertain what exactly it is we do not understand about a client's meaning making relative to our stage hypothesis regarding the client. Focusing the client's attention on what s(he) is saying, we'll want to compare what we hear with our initially formulated stage hypothesis.

For instance, if our hypothesis is that the client is speaking from an S-2 vantage point – and we are thus discounting that there may be true S-3 dependency or S-4 integrity at play – we could formulate the following **additional probes,** to be sure we follow a correct hypothesis in our listening:

Client: I'm really sad that my colleague lied to me regarding his salary raise. Now I can never be sure whether he's telling me the truth. Like if you know a person has lied to someone else or to you before, then you know you just can't count on them.
Interviewer: What do you mean by "count on them?"
Client: You need to know who the people are that you can turn to when you need truthful information or help.
Interviewer: What is so vital for you in being able to turn to others for help when you are uncertain of how to proceed?
Client: Well, since I don't really know the culture of the company as of yet, and I want to invest just enough effort in my work but no more than I need to have as much free time as possible for my own pursuits, I really have to know how to proceed in this situation. So I need his help.
Interviewer: Why do you think that your colleague knows more about that than you do?
Client: Well, he has been with the company much longer than I!
Interviewer: Have you asked your colleague how he feels about the degree of effort needed to succeed in this company?
Client: No. I didn't see a need for that.
Interviewer: Tell me a little more about why not working more than you absolutely have to is so important to you.
Client: Well, I am in this job really for my own sake, I don't really care what the company gets out of it as long as my own needs are satisfied. I have long been seeking a place to work where I

could develop my own interests and buy things that I need for my recreational goals. I have chosen the company for exactly that reason, and that is why I have to rely on being told the truth about the company.

You will have observed that the interviewer's questions are always staying very close to the client's stream of consciousness. For instance, the interviewer is not asking questions out of the blue, questions that have nothing to do with what the client is presently focusing on. That is, **the interviewer supports the client's focus of attention**. The interviewer is also not asking extraneous 'Why' questions (just out of curiosity), because doing so would most likely derail the client's present train of thought. (Clearly, the client could make up any number of reasons to answer 'Why' questions that have nothing whatsoever to do with his or her own present mental process.) This procedure, of staying where the client is, is one of the **central tenets** of developmental interviewing. In this way, developmental interviewing is very different from conventional (content-based) interviewing. As we have said, it is focused on structure, not on content.

Let's conclude this chapter by highlighting some salient features of developmental interviewing:
- Developmental interviewing is *qualitative research* for the sake of determining the client's present mode of meaning making.
- Developmental interviewing is based on formulating stage hypotheses, and on probing for their verity in order to locate missing information about the stage structure of the client's discourse.
- Developmental interviewing is based on a conceptual framework that requires of the interviewer/listener to refrain from any haphazard and gratuitous questioning of clients. Consequently, this kind of interviewing introduces a highly focused and structured consultant-client discourse where every question asked by the interviewer/consultant is rooted in probing for the sake of confirming or rejecting a developmental hypothesis.
- Developmental interviewing is about focusing the client's attention on his or her own internal mental process, in order to go beyond mere content to the roots of how this content is constructed by the client through language.
- Logistically, developmental interviewing precedes the intervention proper, whether it be coaching or some other intervention.
- Even beyond the purposes of the initial developmental interview, developmental thinking and listening pervade the process of giving feedback to clients, of formulating coaching plans, and of leading coaching conversations (as is shown throughout the book).

SUMMARY OF STAGE 2 (final wording by S. Stewart)

S-2 is an 'I' stage, characteristic of late teenage and early adulthood, although in our own culture, private sector profit concerns often drive many adults to revert to this stage, at least in their 'world of work.' Persons on this stage are highly, if not totally, steeped in their own wants or needs. They are impulsive, seek immediate gratification for those needs and wants, pay little attention to what others say about them, but will vehemently deny feedback that is not concordant with their own rigid self-perception. Above all else, they are interested in preserving the image they have established for themselves, regardless of how accurate it might be. When challenged, they can be very emotionally explosive and abusive to the feedback's source(s). S(he) readily understands others' perspectives, not out of empathy, but for the sake of knowing how to manipulate them to satisfy their own needs and ends. They will follow socially established (Stage 3) community rules and conventions when beneficial to them, or as long as they believe they will not be caught or punished. Thus, cheating, lying, deception, and falsification will be used, as necessary, to achieve self-set goals. They can work effectively and productively, if working alone and if their objectives happen to be aligned with those of the organization. In a Leader role, they will tend to micro-manage, exploit others, create ill will and mistrust, and misunderstandings will abound within the team or work group. Unbridled 'careerism' typifies this stage, for those individuals who manage to work their way into positions where they are given any degree of social authority.

CHAPTER SUMMARY

In Chapter 2, I have introduced the reader to developmental listening and interviewing as discovery procedures for the sake of conducting an intervention. It is probably clear to the reader that these procedures are the basis of process consultation. I have shown why, and to some slight extent how, these procedures are used. I have also introduced two examples of meaning making at S-2, and have justified that and why they are indicative of S-2, rather than of S-3 or S-4.

Here is a short summary of what the reader has – potentially – learned in this chapter:
1. Developmental stages are expressed by people through their use of natural language
2. Since people are subject to their present *Center of Gravity* (stage), and are moreover, centrally focused on contents of one kind or another, they are not aware of the fact that they are expressing their level of meaning making along with the content they focus on.
3. In order to substantiate a developmental hypothesis, the interviewer has to stay close to clients' train of thought as the medium in which structurally relevant information (stage) is being revealed
4. Developmental interviewing is a *discovery procedure* that requires the ability to play devil's advocate regarding one's own hypotheses (an ability that is best learned as member of a group).
5. Developmental interviewing is a learnable art that is based on, first, formulating developmental hypotheses, and second, probing for missing information needed to confirm or reject them.
6. Developmental listening is the crux of developmental interviewing; it is the art of testing hypotheses regarding the other party's present developmental level
7. Developmental listening is based on a strict distinction between content and structure, where 'content' is anything that can be substituted for by another, similar content.
8. Developmental listening is qualitative research in which the interviewer uses him- or herself as an instrument for understanding how the other party makes meaning of self and world.
9. Developmental listening, probing, and interviewing introduce into process consultation with adults a highly focused mode of conversation that eschews all haphazard questioning and commenting.
10. When developmental listening and probing is continued into interventions such as mediation, performance review, giving feedback, formulating coaching plans,

designing powerful conversations, clients are given the opportunity to reflect deeply on their own, hidden assumptions.

PRACTICE REFLECTION

1. Considering the content of this chapter, what have you learned – directly or by extension
– about one or more of the following topics:

- Coaching
- Mentoring
- Mediation
- Facilitation
- Social work interviewing
- Psychological interviewing
- Hiring
- Performance review
- Performance management
- Succession planning
- Formulating 'development' programs
- Career counseling
- HR resources management?

2. How will you have to revise your theory of *helping* given what you now know about adult levels of development?
3. How do you think you can refine your *active listening* to clients given what you begun to learn about developmental listening?
4. What do you think are the difficulties in learning developmental interviewing?
5. In what way is developmental hypothesis testing different from the kind of questions you are used to asking yourself about your clients?
6. How do you think you presently formulate hypotheses as to *who your client is developmentally*?
7. What does it tell you about yourself as a helper, to realize that the client him- or herself can never be known directly, but only with the aid of a model that you – unconsciously or consciously – formulate in your mind?

3
Where is Your Client's Center of Gravity?

In this Chapter, I lead the reader further into the universe of adult development as circumscribed by way of four 'main stages' (S-2 to S-5) introduced in Chapter 1. Based on illustrations of S-3 to S-5, the reader will acquire a first, rough overview of the developmental trajectory typically encountered in developmental process consultation. The chapter will also indicate what is required of individuals, in a general way, to proceed from one stage to another.

As will become increasingly clear, over life's journey an individual encounters a periodic *loss of self* which is the price to pay for moving on in terms of maturity. No gains without losses, and nothing is gained by resisting loss of self. This loss is like the shedding of a fur in an animal. What is lost depends on the Center of Gravity left behind. This chapter demonstrates what particular 'main' Centers of Gravity beyond S-2 entail for individuals' Frame of Reference (outlook on self and world). Understanding individuals' Frame of Reference in leading their life and pursuing work is a major factor in being of help to them.

The reader will by now have at least an inkling of what developmental interventions are all about as far as the client is concerned. The related issue of what such interventions demand of, and accomplish for, the process consultant him- or herself will emerge more clearly in subsequent chapters. However, before going forward, it is appropriate to say something about the *interdevelopmental* nature of developmental interventions (as in 'Interdevelopmental Institute)..

The mental demands that adult development makes upon individuals are, of course, shared by client and consultant. Everything said in this book about clients equally holds for consultants. Helper and 'helpee' are subject to the same developmental dynamic without exception. But more is involved than equality of the human condition. The helping relationship itself provides extra stimuli for adult development to take place in both parties, and can therefore be called *interdevelopmental*.

If you recall what I have said about the developmental interviewing process, – that it requires formulating hypotheses, testing them, and using yourself as an instrument of research in a disciplined manner – it may dawn on you that a shift may be required in how you work as a consultant. The essential shift in evidence-based interventions is that from relying solely on your "own little personality" to mastering and using a *conceptual framework* that sets you free to explore your own mind at least as much as that of the client. This shift is likely to happen simply because when you respect the developmental structure of the client's mind, you cannot but also begin to respect and begin to investigate your own. You are thus led to reflect on long-standing assumptions you have typically made, thereby engaging in what C. Argyris calls *double loop learning*. In this kind of learning, you not only change your action plans, but also the assumptions they are based on. Changing actions and action plans is just *learning*, while changing assumptions may actually signal an *adult-developmental shift*.

Another way of speaking about shifts that need to be made by practitioners of process consultation is to say that the key to their effectiveness with clients lies in their own self development. This is in contrast to the assumption shared by most coaching and other training schools, that assisting others is mainly a matter of acquiring and having "skills," knowing "best practices," and having a "strong" or "empathic" personality. Nothing could be further from the truth. I am not debating that a process consultant needs skills and expertises, as well as empathy. I am only saying that they are secondary to WHO THE PRACTITIONER IS DEVELOMENTALLY, an assumption that has been proven many times over in research on psychotherapy (Luborsky, 1988). In other words, it is not what the consultant HAS – skills, etc. – but what the s(he) IS that ultimately matters in developmentally based consultations.

In terms of methodology, the shift that occurs in evidence based interventions is mainly the result of using a validated conceptual framework rather just personal 'intuition.' In all helping professions, conceptual frameworks enable practitioners to make a distinction between their own personality and the *professional Persona* they need in order to be successful in their work. Professionals (in the emphatic sense of the term) share a knowledge base anchored in research that is quite independent of their own personality. Through their particular take on things, practitioners develop an idiosyncratic understanding of the framework they absorb through study. While intuition is always a fine thing to have, the more knowledge informs intuition, the more potent that intuition can be.

Moving away from one's own elementary intuitions and personality and standing outside of it – making it an object of reflection – is a developmental journey of great significance. This movement assumes central importance in the developmental range from S-4 to S-5. To start such movement as early as possible, within the range from S-3 to S-4, is a major goal of this book. To illustrate what the journey entails, I speak of acquiring a professional Persona. Like in acting, a persona carries the practitioner across the currents of own moods, dispositions, inclinations, achievements, and likes. **Persona is focused on the task at hand, and its mental demands.** In the work world, a practitioner's Persona is based on making meaning from S-4 and on knowing alternative ways of proceeding that are based on empirical research in one's domain of practice (not just *experience*).

What, you will ask, does acting from a professional persona have to do with self development? Very simply and bluntly put: **it is very difficult for a practitioner at S-3 to come across to a client who is a professional as a *professional*, rather than just a particular personality.** Why should that be so?

Orientation	S-3	S-4
View of Others	Needed to contribute to own self image	Collaborator, delegate, peer
Level of Self Insight	Moderate	High
Values	Community	Self-determined
Needs	Subordinate to community, work group	Flowing from striving for integrity
Need to Control	Moderate	High
Communication	Exchange 1:1	Dialogue
Organizational Orientation	Good Citizen	Manager

Table I.1. Changing orientations across adult stages

If you recall Table I-1, excerpted above, you will see what I mean. A consultant at developmental level S-3 is certainly a 'good citizen' and able to have fair one-to-one exchanges. S(he) has moderate self insight, knows how to subordinate her own needs to a community or work group, and thus has most likely only a moderate need to control others. Her values are focused on being part of a community and of benefiting that community, – all very honorable things, but not quite enough for a professional!

Can one, the reader will ask, develop such a Persona through training or education? Yes and no. As I said, education is a poor predictor of developmental stage, just as age is. Therefore, education alone will not make you a professional, only the degree to which that education has led to developmental transformation will. Whether it does or not largely depends on your own developmental potential, and on **where you are in your journey from S-3 to S-4.**

Speaking with R. Kegan (1994), being a *professional* means accepting – and ultimately fulfilling – certain MENTAL DEMANDS of the surrounding culture that lie far beyond any kind of consensus and group mind (*best practices*). We can say that these mental demands are partly embodied in conceptual frameworks for hypothesis testing and qualitative research. I would surmise that hypothesis testing and using yourself as an instrument of research – thus exploring your own mind – strengthens self-authoring (S-4), if it does not already presuppose it.

The best way to understand the distinction between personality and professional Persona is to explore what an S-3 individual sounds like, and what such an individual lacks in terms of self-authoring. As in chapter 2, I proceed by illustration.

EXAMPLE 2a (adapted from Lahey et al. 1988, 47)
The client is a line manager with responsibility over 5 sales people. She has been speaking of her relationship to her boss, the fact that she is eager to make decisions on her own, but also feels the need to consult and engage him in her decision making.

I have just been gathering data for the decision I and my boss have to make, rather than going ahead with the decision on my own, or waiting for the boss to come in. He really prefers to delegate, and I just didn't take up the challenge to make a decision on my own. But now I realize that he really doesn't mind if I make a decision that has to be made. More than that, he really likes me to make my own decisions because then he doesn't feel as if he's depriving me of authority, or as if he really should be making the decision himself. Before, it really was a strain between us, because we didn't get to make decisions as much as I really found necessary and wanted to, or else I harassed him about making the decision, and then felt guilty about it. Making the decision by myself occasionally makes both of us happier, and even makes things between us a lot smoother.

The focus of this self report is clearly on "I and my boss." These two individuals are almost indistinguishable, although we know next to nothing of who the boss really is. (We know the boss only through the client's self report.) What are we to make of this intermingling of the speaker with her boss? The boss she is speaking of is both a *physical* and an *internalized* other. (The boss is at times physically present, and is also present as an internal voice.) Apparently, the speaker is unable to distinguish these two aspects of the boss from each other. What is more, she can also not distinguish the two aspects of the boss from herself, her own meaning making. What she calls "my boss" is her own voice, merged with that of the other she projects herself into. The physical boss she works with and his internal echo in her are one, and she is merged with both. As a further result, she does not realize that she is presently defining herself by her boss's expectations, and is sustained by him in her role as a decision maker. In short, she is making meaning from S-3.

Specifically, this is what seems to be going on in the line manager's meaning making:

- She is able to distinguish her point of view from that of her boss (which moves her beyond S-2).
- She is also able to make both her own and her boss's points of view part of her own self, thus internalizing her boss's perspective, – she can hold multiple perspectives focused on her other, which puts her at S-3.
- What she calls "my boss" is the self authoring side she is presently lacking, which is delivered to her externally through her boss as 'physical other' and internally generated by her through the internalization of her boss (her 'internalized other').
- In her pseudo-independent state, she holds herself responsible for her boss's point of view (feeling guilty when and if the boss does not go along with her decision making) – *I harassed him and then felt guilty.*
- In this developmental state, she needs 'hand holding' by her boss to make decisions independent of him (*he really prefers to delegate …*).
- She ascribes to her (internalized) boss the desire not to deprive her of the authority to make decisions by herself, – this is her way of acknowledging his ascendance over her.
- She furthermore ascribes to the boss the feeling of contentment not to have to make (subordinate) decisions himself, or be relieved of them, thereby showing how she constructs her internalized other.
- As a result of the foregoing, the coherence of her self is dependent on the continued existence of her boss as an internalized other, rather than being generated by herself (as in a self authorer, or S-4 individual).
- In short, she is presently not ready to release her boss from his function as an internalized other who guarantees her wholeness as a professional and decision maker.

To drive home the lesson deriving from the above excerpt, it is of interest to ask how a process consultant who is a coach functioning at S-3 would come across in speaking about her client. Here is how it would sound.

EXAMPLE 2b
The coach works with executive clients of the Fortune 500 class. She has been speaking of her relationship with her clients, the fact that she is a model to most of them given her ability to move them toward action.

I have a wonderful relationship with most of my clients. They tell me that I am a great inspiration to them simply on account of my personality which leads me to tackle issues head-on, even difficult ones, with little hesitation. I can do that because I am able to intuit what it is they want and need to do. They really expect me to show them the way which, on account of my wide organizational knowledge, I seem to be able to do very well. So, we are really highly bonded, in a wonderful give and take. What most stands out for me about my clients is how careful they are not to deprive me of my authority, say, by correcting or challenging me. I have the feeling that they want us to succeed together, which is exactly my own wish. It even occurs that I feel guilty about my boldness at times, especially when having suggested an option they have not thought of. I then think "oh my God, can I really know this better than they do?" But on the whole, I feel quite at ease with them, relying entirely on my intuition of what they are groping for. And with my vivid imagination and active listening skills, I generally come across as an inspiration to them. In short, our conversations are really powerful.

Comparable to the line manager of the previous example, the executive coach speaking above has the following characteristics:

- She is highly bonded with her clients who give her permission to be herself and do her best.
- Her clients function both as physical and internalized others, and she cannot separate these two aspects either from each other or from herself.
- She is defined by her clients' expectations to take the lead and guide them to where they might not have thought to go.
- The give and take of which she speaks is largely one between her physical (external) and internalized Others, and may just signal her inability to perceive real differences between herself and her clients, or internal conflicts her clients struggle with (this is difficult to do when not relying on developmental assessments).
- Consequently, her professional Persona is weak since she mostly relies on her own little personality and an intuition largely uninformed about the nature of her clients (which she construes based on her own developmental level).
- Her authority is not so much self authored as it is condoned by her clients who do not dare to challenge or correct her (either in order not to derail her if they act from S-4, or because they don't know better since they are themselves acting from S-3).
- She ascribes to them her own wishes, and shies away from probing for real differences between herself and her clients.
- One might say she is colluding with being her clients' expectations, that is, the image she fashions of her clients, rather than being with who her clients really are.
- She is largely defined by the expectations of her clients which, in a conventional consulting relationship, remain more implicit than they are explicit.

In short, she has not yet begun the journey toward self authoring (S-4), remaining embedded in other-dependence, her skills and knowledge of techniques notwithstanding.

If we consider that between 50 to 60% of individuals developmentally stay at S-3, we can begin to understand the immensity of the problem of modern society and its organizations. In their professional work, these individuals are "in over their heads" because they have not mastered society's 'curriculum' (Kegan, 1994) that requires them to act in a self-authoring way (S-4). If most process consultants and coaches were found to make meaning from S-3, the outlook on professional life would be that much gloomier, not to mention effects on society as a whole. And since age and education are poor predictors of developmental level, the question may be asked: what can be done about it?

The reader may ask herself now: what is required of the line-manager and the executive coach living at S-3 to advance toward a true self-authoring position, and what would that position look like? The short answer is that both individuals, to speak with Lahey et al. (1988), will have to "gradually separate (their) internalized points of view from their original sources in (physical or internalized) others and make the self itself a *coherent system* for their generation and correlation" (p. 51). By "gradual" is meant that nobody makes a single leap from S-3 to S-4, but rather advances in successive steps to levels *intermediate between* the two stages. What that entails in detail is the topic of chapters 5 and 6.

SUMMARY OF STAGE 3 (final wording by Steve Stewart)
S-3 is a 'We,' or a sense of community stage. Self-image is determined entirely by what others think, whether these others are internalized or external others. Thus, people at this stage are highly, if not completely, identified with an external socially established norm or standard that has been internalized. If rank, position, power, etc., are viewed as being important by the system that defines them, then they are important to this individual, as are appearances – social correctness. Obtaining status, in whatever terms the external reference is based upon, makes them highly competitive, but they will not stoop to the stratagems Stage 2 persons will to achieve their ends. They 'follow the rules,' and are 'above board' about winning and losing. It is very unlikely that they will 'see' or think beyond the established operational principles and values of 'their' organization. Because their image is so caught up in the status quo, they will be unwilling to take the risks necessary to change it, even if they can stand apart from their unit, group, or organization far enough to objectively assess what could make it operate more effectively. Hence, they do not make good change agents, either in the sense of seeing what needs to be done or in actually doing it. Any change they believe might be beneficial will be whatever is being echoed by the majority. In a leader position, this person will follow what they believe the norms are and will try to establish a climate accordingly. Yet, they may have a very tough time doing so, unless those norms lead them to simultaneously gain recognition, or credits, within the broader social structure. What contributes to the climate first is how it will affect their stature. Hence, the climate will be focused as much on individual achievement as it is on the group's collective effectiveness.

Let's briefly summarize S-3:
- **Distribution:** between 50 and 60% of adults live (and remain) at this stage.
- **Advance over S-2:** theory of self now includes others' perspective.
- **Essence of this stage:** my self is made up by the expectations of physical or internalized others (family, religious or peer group), and I lose myself when losing membership in, and the support of, the group.
- **Conventionalism:** the ultimate concern is with whether I am adhering to what is expected of me. Being 'good' means following the rules of an institution larger than myself that I have completely internalized, and without which I will be 'at a loss'.

- **Pervasive limitation**: I cannot distinguish my points of view from those of physical, and especially internalized others; consequently, I have no 'theory of self' independent of what I have absorbed from the social surround, whether by adherence to, or strict negation of, existing conventions. My guilt is about not being sanctioned by others, not about failing my own standards.

An extension of this characterization to an S-3 professional, whether process consultant or coach, is straightforward:

- Lacking an idiosyncratic sense of self based on authentic values and principles, the practitioner follows community-generated rules and practices.
- The practitioner is in need of endorsement from the client as a physical and internalized other, and from the community that defines her/his identity.
- To fill in for the lack of a self-authoring stance, the practitioner relies on community based certificates, licenses, etc., or on sanctioned expertises and theories.
- Proceeding without a self-generated Frame of Reference (professional Persona), the practitioner is at constant risk of collusion with the goals and ideology of the client, under the guise of being *helpful*.
- Without an explicit model or theory of the client, the practitioner assumes shared values that (essentially) disregard the developmental uniqueness of the client.
- Focused on being in synch with the client, the practitioner is unable to challenge the client's values other than by referring to internalized community values she shares with him or her.

Having now acquired a better notion of an S-3 professional, we may ask: what does the journey from S-3 to S-4 consist of? **What needs to occur in individuals' consciousness in order to move from relying on others as a source of feelings and thoughts to a higher level of self insight (and thereby diminish the need to feel responsible for others' feelings and thoughts)?**
The following seems to have to happen for individuals:

1. First, individuals must internally distance themselves from their need of being acknowledged and accepted by the community; they must be able to 'go it alone' if their own inner voice tells them to do so
2. Second, individuals must develop a better and better notion of their uniqueness, of what makes them different from others, and find the courage to make that difference known to others while respecting others' otherness
3. Third, individuals must develop an ethical theory of integrity of self that is based on their own authentic values and principles.

The major difficulty in taking these three steps is that individuals at S-3 are NOT AWARE that they define themselves by physical and internalized Others. Therefore, espousing S-4 values is easy and natural for them (see the ICF core competencies). Not only are they not aware of acting from S-3, they also don't get any help from their own community to go beyond S-3. By this I mean that there is no 'social forcing function' for people to become aware of their dependency on others. Outside of educational curricula, there is no socially enforced curriculum to bring people 'up a level.' **In fact, if it existed,**

such a curriculum would run counter to what it means to become the author of one's own values and sense of self!

Although there are some demanding educational curricula that promote the move from S-3 to S-4, knowing that education, just like age, is a weak predictor of developmental level, one cannot trust that education will suffice to induce a developmental shift. Most likely, personal hardship – breakdown of a relationship, personal betrayal, illness, financial crisis, a painfully challenging task, etc. – will be more effective than mere education. Nevertheless, education might do some good, – as long as it meets with developmental potential in the learner and is evidence-based.

With regard to 'helping' through process consultation, it is here that the value of knowing a client's developmental potential to move from S-3 to S-4, for instance, is a highly valuable resource. If there is a way to determine such a potential, and feed knowledge of it back to the client, the benefits would be evident:

- The client would become aware of his/her other-dependency.
- The client would come to believe that s(he) can internally move from the present place in consciousness to a place of greater independence and risk taking (even if resisted or not understood by others).
- The client can be given tasks that just might challenge him or her in the upward developmental direction.

However, there are also developmental risks that have to be taken into account.

- Going from S-3 to S-4 involves taking the risk of *loss of self* since self is presently defined by others, and this self will be lost if an individual moves to S-4.
- Separating out internalized others that mimic being one's own voice – but are not authentically one's own – potentially requires painful and hurtful separations from previous guarantors of self.
- *Going it alone* in order to manifest one's uniqueness may come at some cost to one's own safety and security, if not to one's life..

All of these risks have to be taken, however, if the journey is to result in a successful shift to S-4!

In summary, the move to S-4 entails the task of "construct[ing] a … psychological organization which generates its own values in accordance with its own standards" without relying on others (Lahey et al., 1988, 79). If this challenge is taken up successfully, the individual will be able to:

- Act consistently from own, authentic values.
- Withstand outside pressures to 'back down' for the sake of some community's 'best practices or other interests and conventions.
- Take risks that may cost one others' trust.
- Work in community without being determined by community.

All of this is hard to do. No wonder, then, that individuals at S-4 quite naturally become wholly identified with their own cherished set of values and principles that have sustained them through the difficult and lonely journey that lies behind them. In fact, they become themselves the 'system' of values from which they act, rather than 'having' those values. They are dependent on their values for the integrity of their self, and essentially unable to stand away from that integrity (in particular, their theory of helping). As a result, S-4 individuals have a hard time viewing themselves critically, from others' point of view. As this shows, self-authoring comes at a price.

Let's briefly summarize the S-4 developmental position here:

- **Distribution:** between 20 and 25% of adults live (and remain) at this stage.
- **Advance over Stage 3:** I can articulate a coherent theory of self in terms of my values & principles potentially different from consensus.
- **Essence of this stage:** I am identified with my own value system as the root of my integrity (my highest value, and the grounding of my 'being in control').
- **Self Authoring:** the ultimate concern is whether I safeguard my integrity by following my own values and principles.
- **Pervasive limitation**: I do not have an objective, outside view of my own ways of acting on my principles. Therefore, I can only do *single loop learning*, examining outcomes but not assumptions lying beyond my own value perspective. While I can respect others for their differences, I cannot truly enter into their universe of discourse beyond what is understandable to me on the grounds of my own values and principles. Therefore, as a change agent I act according to norms excluding multiple perspectives, intent on shaping my group and organization in harmony with my own principles.

We have described the journey to be made from S-3 to S-4, and have summarized the S-4 world view. Let us now listen to a person who has successfully made that journey.

EXAMPLE 3a (Lahey et al, 1988, 131)

Last week a colleague and close friend of mine was telling me about an important feeling about his superior he had that was evidently very painful to him. I was mainly trying to listen and understand what was important to him in this. I believe that's the way I can be most helpful to him, by being an understanding, sympathetic listener, rather than, you know, trying to fix things up, or lay my own stuff on him regarding what I am thinking or feeling. So, I encouraged him to talk, and I asked him some questions to try to understand better. And basically, he did describe his experience, but I didn't really get a chance to respond at all, since he immediately asked me whether I would have felt hurt if I had been in that situation myself. From what I understood of the situation, I was pretty certain actually that I wouldn't have. But I couldn't tell him that, because that would have been like my ignoring how he actually was hurt. I would have felt like I was no longer staying with his take on things, kind of abandoning him. And that was exactly what I didn't want to do! What I really wanted to do was just to let him know that I understood how he must have felt.

Although the content of this excerpt is about a relationship, true to our goal of separating CONTENT from STRUCTURE (= stage), we cannot assume that it is therefore a manifestation of S-3. Utterances whose content is focused on relationships can equally be spoken from beyond and below S-3. We therefore need to understand from what Center of Gravity the above individual is speaking.

Here are some clues as to how to interpret what the speaker in Example 3a illustrates:

- The speaker fully understands (and respects) that the other's thoughts and feelings belong to a meaning making system different from her own.
- The task the speaker sees is to listen deeply to understand what the other's values (and related feelings) might be in contrast to her own.
- This 'objective' stance acknowledges the difference between two systems of identity or frames of reference, and does not imply any loss of relatedness (in fact, it is the proper way of being related to the other party at S-4).
- The objective stance adopted by the speaker expresses the ethical principles of S-4, not to impose her own perspectives and related feelings on the other party; it keeps the speaker focused on her own value system without proselytizing, and makes her curious to understand how the other party might generate feelings.
- The speaker is totally identified with – and thus subject to – her own 'feeling generator' (Lahey et al. p. 136), and is thus unable to take a perspective on it.
- The speaker in no way invites others to become critical of her own self-authoring.
- From this flows a THEORY OF HELPING that is peculiar to S-4. This theory requires:
    1. A move beyond community *best practices* as to what is entailed by assisting individuals different from each other and from oneself.
    2. The ability to do a kind of 'active listening' that fully acknowledges the uniqueness of the other party's way of making meaning, by assessing the other party's developmental potential.
    3. The insight that others have their own unique history and integrity that cannot be surmised but needs to be researched in open dialogue (rather than only a one on one exchange, see Table 1.1).
    4. The ability to form theories and hypotheses based on one's own values and principles, especially where they deviate from community practice.

With these clarifications in mind, let us now listen to a coach who has made the journey to S-4, as a counter-example to the S-3 coach who spoke above:

EXAMPLE 3b
You wouldn't believe how different my clients are from myself! I have finally understood that I should stop assuming they are acting from the same values as I do. I am often puzzled by what, to them, seems to be a problem. Some of them are in a never-ending loop that involves them with others from which they cannot extricate themselves. Others are so pinned on their way of seeing things, it's hard to move them to a point of reflection about themselves. They just don't see how ensconced they are in what they have become, their successes, ideologies, and so forth. For this reason, I have now adopted a way of listening where I consciously 'draw the line' between them and me, and I never suggest that I know what they are talking about. The difficulty for me is that I am often tempted to let them know my own take on the situation they are bringing to attention, especially if they ask me for feedback or advice. I will typically reply that resolving the situation at issue might best be done by our shared exploration of how it has been framed by the client in the first place. Might there be other perspectives or roles we could adopt to take multiple perspectives on it? In short, I invite them to join my diagnostic process. Most of my clients are not very good at stepping outside of the box they are in, and adopting multiple views on one and the same situation. Their emotional ties to the situation in question just paralyze them. Others, who are a little more advanced developmentally, at least have some

resources to question their own views, but often they are seeking recourse in some outside community or agency to proceed beyond the issue. The values they sponsor are thus not truly their own.

Given this scenario, I am really glad that I have a solid coach education that makes me quite independent of my specific personality and community-inspired best practices. I am working from within a conceptual framework that allows me to adopt a professional Persona different from my own little personality. And that is what keeps me out of my clients' loop. I will say, however, that the detachment from which I work often makes me feel somewhat guilty. But my compassion with myself as a professional coach usually takes care of that.

The reader might detect in this excerpt a slight capability of moving beyond S-4, indicated by the ability to reflect on where the speaker's professional identity comes from. However, there is no indication here that the speaker is inviting others to keep her on her toes as to the values on which her consultation is based. Such a coach is good material for developmental mentoring by a practitioner making meaning beyond S-4.

SUMMARY OF STAGE 4 (final wording by Steve Stewart)

S-4 is an 'I" stage, but one much different from S-2. These individuals, rather than trying to become someone, have found themselves or 'come of age.' They have been successful while pursuing S-3 goals and have, in their eyes, earned the 'right' to stand above the crowd and be noticed. Consequently, they are highly, if not completely, identified with the value system that they have authored for themselves, yet they are very respectful of others for their competence and different values and beliefs. They find great difficulty in standing away from themselves to discover their own voids, but they will accept them when they are discovered. In this sense, they can be more self-accepting, relative to those less well developed. They can stand back, however, from the institution that previously defined them far enough to be objective about what they 'see.' Since they are far more objective, they can be good at apprehending what could be done to change the system of which they are a part and, once doing so, will have enough strength in their own center-of-gravity to weather the storms that may come about in actually instigating a change or transformation process. The changes they author, however, will, more likely than not, be directed towards making the organization more responsive to themselves, authoring and moving it in directions approximating their own personal 'institution,' rather than one more universally self-sustaining. The climate they create will be one that follows the status quo, but taking on their own idiosyncratic values and operational principles as time passes. Since they are caught in their own frame of reference, they fail to appreciate the value of other frames of reference (that are) just as much, if not more, developed. This, by definition, limits the extent to which 'their' organization can learn-to-learn, grow, and further develop.

What, in light of this summary, can we say about the limitations of an S-4 practitioner? Here are some suggestions:

- The practitioner is fully, and without reflection, identified with a self-generated value system.
- Because that value system transcends community, it is also potentially detached from, and different from, the client's own meaning making process – except if evidence about the client is gathered on evidence based grounds.
- A professionally detached approach (based on a Persona) works well with less developed clients (S-3), where it leads to being critical of the client's embeddedness in others' expectations.

- However, the S-4 approach makes for difficulties in work with clients beyond S-4, and potentially even those at S-4 (since detachment on both sides hinders deep inquiry into idiosyncratic, or even mutually shared, assumptions).
- Being grounded in her own Persona, the practitioner has little or no grasp of the client's developmental potential beyond S-4; this is further reinforced by her *theory of helping* that is based on detachment from the client as a different and *untouchable* meaning making system (often covered up as 'respecting boundaries').
- With clients at S-4, the practitioner's best recourse – outside of insinuating her own values – is to regress to adopting the values of the community that as a person the consultant has already overcome. (This makes for sub-optimal interventions.)
- Alternatively, to avoid such regression, the consultant must be capable of challenging the client to reflection about his/her own value system (which is either impossible or not easy for an S-4 consultant because of having adopted the principle of non-interference and the need of saving face).
- With clients beyond S-4, the practitioner lacks insight into a state of mind in which individuals constantly invite others' feedback, – not to be swayed by it, but in order to achieve clarity regarding the limits of their own institutionalized self.

As can be inferred from these elaborations of what an S-4 Center of Gravity entails, *acting from a professional Persona* does not equate with S-4. It actually requires a step beyond S-4 that enables the practitioner to reflect upon his or her own Persona. Nevertheless, S-4 defines a minimal developmental position for professional – in contrast to 'personality based' – interventions. The former are evidence based, while the latter are based on a type of intuition that is in dire need of being boosted by way of developmental evidence (gathering).

We have now completed an overview of S-3 and S-4, and the journey from one to the other. To complete our overview of *main stages,* it remains for us to proceed to S-5. We do so by reflecting on what the journey to S-5 may look like, and by briefly illustrating the journey as best we can by way of examples. (We will be discussing the subtleties of moves beyond S-4 in Chapter 6, including the question of whether 'coaching' from a developmental position close to S-5 is a notion that makes any sense.)

How, then, is the journey from S-4 to S-5 made?

Orientation	S-4	S-5
View of Others	Collaborator, delegate, peer	Contributors to own integrity and balance
Level of Self Insight	High	Very High
Values	Self-determined	Humanity
Needs	Flowing from striving for integrity	Viewed in connection with own obligations and limitations
Need to Control	Low	Very low
Communication	Dialogue	True Communication
Organizational Orientation	Manager	System's Leader

Table I.1. Changing orientations across adult stages

As we already know, there is no *social forcing function* that will move individuals beyond an S-4 outlook on life and work. (If such a forcing function existed, the description of S-5 as *self-aware* would be pointless.) We also know that less than 10% of individuals ever reach S-5, the position of true leaders. While we can only speculate about the reasons for moving to S-5, we can succinctly describe what that move looks like in our culture and, correspondingly, in other cultures.

For one thing, it is evident that to be captive to one's own limited value system and sense of integrity, although it is the basis of ethical behavior 'above the fray,' is a rather difficult situation to be in, at least for an inquiring mind bent on examining underlying assumptions. To live under S-4 conditions is also fraught with risk of failure, especially failure in one's own terms (before one's own court). But as we know by now, intellectual rigor and curiosity as spawned by cognitive development (CD) alone will not guarantee a move to S-5. Certainly 'intelligence' can be helpful in bolstering an S-4 position, by using it defensively. The "higher" one's Center of Gravity and the stronger one's intellectual resources, the more defensive one can be.

Recalling the journey we have made to S-4, clearly the journey to S-5 has to begin with recognizing that the distinction between my own identity and that of others, while professionally fruitful, does not give me many resources for looking critically at my own splendid isolation. Also, the more I advance in my own development, the more I begin to see the idiosyncrasy of my own history, my character (which is a system of defense) and all my self-constructed certainties, assumptions, successes, and attitudes that so far have served me well. (They may indeed have led me to do pioneering work far transcending conventional assumptions and policies, and if this work of mine has been publicly acknowledged I may not care to move beyond S-4).

The issue at stake really is how far I am prepared to experience a loss of self that will occur if I give up my splendor and splendid isolation. This entails exposure of my limitations to others, especially intimates, who would potentially become midwives of my own development. However, this loss of self – which occurs in any developmental shift whatsoever – would in this case have to be preceded by the realization that I cannot impose my own 'institutional' self (Kegan, 1982) on others, nor can I make my own successes and triumphs the criteria of evaluating others. What to do?

Here are some suggestions:
- I must be shaken out of my unconscious identification with my life and career history, to grasp the limitedness of my own universe (even in terms of my own aspirations).
- I must embrace other, equally or higher developed, people as midwives of my self-reflection.
- I must embrace knowledge sources other than 'intellect,' such as 'heart' and 'spirit,' thereby bringing a sacrifice of my own rationality (many people espouse this, but only few are capable of it).

- I must extend what is REAL for me to a multi-perspectival view in which many different certainties can be balanced in search of the authentic action required of me at a particular moment.

All of this is easier said than done. Therefore, it is important to separate *espousal* (make belief) from real humility. **Entire S-5 ideologies have been, and constantly are being, formulated that one can learn to speak in terms of**, to give the false impression (even unconsciously) that one has really left behind S-4. The spiritually based helping professions are full of such templates for espousal, to judge from the literature and its use by practitioners.

To move beyond our discussion of S-4, it might be best to start with a caricature of S-5. Here is a pertinent description (wording by Steve Stewart):

> At this stage, people are no longer strongly identified with any particular aspect or asset of their own frame of reference. They know that no matter what they do it will be limited. Consequently, they have come to realize that learning-to-learn, life long learning, is not just a platitude, but becomes their life. Collaboration and collegiality become the means for exchanging different frames of reference openly, where exposure of self-limitations is routinely accepted as the only means to learn increasingly more about the self and others. This makes them potential unifiers – consensus builders at their level – and an invaluable resource for rethinking corporate goals, operational principles, and values that combine to create culture. Such a person is best positioned where visionary risk taking and development of others, their organization, and the broader social context are called for. Such a person is often highly self-critical, even humble, seeing clearly the limits to which s(he) can impose their perceptions and convictions on others. The climate they will create will be one that is open to exploration, risk taking within reasonable limits, and the emphasis, above all else, will be on promoting and sustaining growth and continued development of others and the organization as a whole.

While this is a caricature, it is the next best thing to understanding what the journey to S-5 leads to. Let's highlight some of the points made above:

- Persons at S-5 are aware of the limitations of their own identity, history, character, developmental level, and frame of reference.
- They realize that recourse to others as midwives of their further development is crucial, and that these others have to be at least as developed as they themselves, if not more highly developed.
- Exchanging different Frames of Reference which define 'who I am' must become the thoroughfare of personal development.
- Humility sets in when it comes to realizing one's own limitations as to who one is and what one can accomplish by oneself.
- Given resources of systemic (multi-perspectival) thinking, it becomes obvious that opposites should be unified, and consensus should be built – not as in S-3 based on 'community values,' but based on individuals all of whom are developed enough to see and articulate their own limitations.
- Emphasis must come to lie on the continued development of others, even where that is in conflict with one's own best interests.

- In organizational terms, this means that a CULTURE OF LEARNING has to be created in which 'learning organizations' can arise – but remember that 'learning' is not by definition 'development' (Chapter 1).
- In private terms, this means that one is able to create for oneself a CULTURE OF BEING IN THE FLOW, no longer fixated on this or that aspect of oneself.

We can summarize the above caricature as follows:
- **Essence of this stage**: I am transparently linked to others that I trust enough to ask for help in questioning my perspective, thus being open to uncharted pathways and unforeseen discoveries about myself.
- **(My Own) Learning Organization**: The ultimate concern is with expanding my view of potentials in me that I have so far not grasped, or have defended against.
- **Pervasive limitation**: I am not fully aware of the extent to which my 'languaging' of reality gives me the illusion of 'knowing what is going on' inside and outside of me; while I can represent 'objective reality' with increasing accuracy, I remain blind to much that escapes categorization and formulation, – the constant flux of life.

You will agree that the caricature and summary, above, lead us far beyond even the most consummate exemplar of S-4. We are here traversing the grounds that lead from managing things and people to visionary leadership. Since less than 10% of people become capable of fulfilling the above criteria, we must keep our eyes open for the many espousals that will occur, and the many disappointed expectations that are upon us, including those regarding ourselves!

The closest we can come to characterizing functioning at S-5 is to reflect upon the illustration of a person who has essentially made the journey, but remains in need of espousing S-5. 'Espousal' here means that the speaker feels compelled to emphasize his being at S-5, while actually still holding on to some elements of self-authoring. (If the speaker were fully at S-5, such espousals would be pointless. Thus when somebody lets you know about what a great leader s(he) is, you know you are listening to an espousal of S-5, not the real thing!).

The excerpt quoted below continues the story we previously heard from our S-4 speaker. Let's therefore pay close attention to what has happened to the speaker in the meantime (5-7 years or more), in terms of his/her level of self awareness. It is a long excerpt, and we will therefore summarize it below.

EXAMPLE 4a (Lahey et al., 1988, 140-143):
Last week a close colleague of mine was telling me about an important feeling he had experienced that was very painful to him. I was trying to understand what was important to him, because I felt my being an understanding, sympathetic listener would be the way I could be most helpful. But then he asked me how I would have felt in his situation. So I said, 'you know, I was feeling like really listening to you, creating a space for you talk this out, out loud, thinking that would be the most help I could be.'
And he said back to me, 'but that's not what I really want from you. I know how I feel, and I'm really wanting to understand whether there's another way I could be putting this experience

together.' Well, it really surprised me that my first instinct at helping was one that he wouldn't feel helped by, since I feel like we're so tuned into each other's needs. But what was really amazing was that when I actually jumped in to exploring right along with him, not just how he felt, but how I would have felt, I discovered another "good" reason why I might not have thought to respond to him differently when he asked me whether I would have been hurt.
I had thought, as I listened to his story, that I wouldn't be. In a way I hadn't wanted to answer his question, because I thought I wouldn't be upset, and I didn't want to restrict him into paying attention to why I wouldn't, rather than how he felt. But I ended up discovering how by looking at the situation the way he does, by paying attention to pieces I would have ignored but he looked at, I actually would be quite hurt. He helped me see that what was hard for me was that his situation parallels one that I'm in quite a lot with a colleague of mine, where I haven't paid attention to all the ways I really am hurt.
So, I guess I had a lot invested in not paying attention to that hurt (and that's a whole other topic …) – so much invested that I picked, and even rationalized, a way to attend to my close colleague that could keep me distant. You know, I really try not to do that, to get wrapped up in my own ideas of how to respond without giving him some choice. But I'm a sneaky one, I'll tell you! I've got to be on my toes all the time to keep from controlling everything, him, myself, what's him, what's me, every thing!
I almost have to keep from letting myself get too involved with my first take on things because, whatever actual merit it may have, I'm in danger of making it into the truth. And I also have a tendency not to want to see some other whole way I'm actually operating or feeling, because I might get pulled into making that the truth. That's kind of funny; like it's not that I've got a whole different take in there, too, because it'll make me leave the take I've been going with, but because I'm afraid I'll go too much with the new take. I'm lucky he's someone I can explore those kinds of things with. We really do help each other not to just take some stand that keeps us from exploring even the hard stuff.

This excerpt offers an example of two equally developed individuals, at work to clarify and critique their own idiosyncratic Frames of Reference. The interlocutors strive to be (– think espousal! –) fully transparent for each other, and they put themselves fully on the line to achieve this, almost regardless of where this procedure might lead them. This is a powerful conversation since it abandons any reservations and defenses meant to boost one's own safety and self-esteem.

We can highlight the changes that have occurred in the speaker since reaching S-4 as follows:

- Prompted by his self-searching colleague, the speaker is persuaded to reconsider his previous stance, of maintaining detachment vis a vis his colleagues' innermost feelings.
- The speaker has become open to being deeply influenced by his colleagues' analysis of what was hurtful to him.
- He is no longer willing to delude himself into thinking that he is 'helping' the other by remaining aloof, instead of seeing that he is engaging in a kind of self defense.
- The speaker has developed great sensitivity toward his own inclination to control, not only himself but others, and is now near relinquishing that inclination.

- The speaker is also highly aware that he is likely to identify with first (or second) impressions and 'make them into the truth' if that supports his present take on what is going on.
- The speaker is cognizant of the fact that he needs his colleague, and vice versa, since until the level of self awareness required at S-5 has become fully second nature, a single person will tend to be deceived by him- or herself.

Here, the mentioned espousals can be heard in the emphatic self critique the speaker is administering upon himself. For a person fully at S-5, such espousals would have shrunk in size or disappeared, since to be in the flow and to be aware of one's own tendency to deceive oneself ("I am a sneaky one!") would reliably have become second nature.

Let's now listen to a coach who may be said to be at a similarly high level of self awareness, functioning close to S-5:

EXAMPLE 4b

The most valuable aspect of the coaching I do, whether with executives or others, is the kind of ruthless truthfulness toward my own person that it enables me to acquire. I mean that all the subterfuges of professionalism, best practices, 'coaching ethics,' credentials, all that ideological crap just has fallen away as I confront internally what my clients reveal to me about myself. It has taken me many years, believe me, to see all of my own subterfuges for what they are!

In particular, I had to let go of the presumption that I can help people I do not fully understand, just by applying some learned templates, or even procedures based on my own values (or so I thought). I am now aware that unless I risk myself completely, including my professional identity and reputation, I cannot maintain even the trace of the Persona of a helper. It's not that I need to spill all these self-insights in front of my client, or even my internalized client. Rather, by risking failure with clients, I open up issues with them in a way that forces both of us to become completely transparent to each other. This is hard to do because I am supposed to help, and to know everything better than my client, right?

Well, I don't have to confess ignorance toward them all the time at all. I only need to follow the developmental data I have acquired with my clients' help, and begin a ruthlessly honest appraisal not only of this jointly generated data, but of my own way of interpreting the data to my client, and of the client's way of responding to my feedback.

So, typically, at the beginning of the coaching following the assessments, both I and my client embark on a discovery journey into the heart of my client's present meaning making issues. I am not simply 'buying' the findings my interviews have yielded; I am only 'renting' them, so to speak (Kegan), in order to provoke self analysis. And in doing so, we unmask whatever may stand in the way – either on my or the client's side – of observing ourselves being in a helping relationship.

Most of the time, I am simply focusing my client's attention on his or her own process. I am doing little or no interpretation, and no modeling of new behaviors either, except when I am certain my modeling (of the client) is selfless. I am simply being aware of the process that is occurring, and I convey this awareness to my client to check it out in his or her terms. So, we are both totally in the flow, and taking risks all the time to come upon sneaky moves of ourselves, where we hide behind some kind of expertise and 'knowing better' or whatever other excuse you may want to think of. We have completely debunked the 'let me show you' attitude. As a matter of fact, we have both been very humbled by this process, and leave it to others to speak of *successful outcome. Because we ourselves are really the successful outcomes!*

As can be heard above, there are still a considerable number of espousals of S-5 in this excerpt, – statements the process consultant wouldn't have to make if being in the flow would be truly second nature for her. However, the distance traveled since functioning at S-4 is evident. The consultant is no longer defining him- or herself by credentials, nor by any particular kind of 'intuition' or 'personality,' not even in terms of being an objective observer who practices in an 'evidence based' way (grounded in data and based on authentic own principles). The consultant does not even believe in 'successful outcomes' any longer, knowing very well that such outcomes are only the outer appearance of internal shifts and advances that no performance appraisal can truly measure. The consultant realizes that outcomes are for others, the community of on-lookers external to the helping relationship (S-3), or for boosting one's feeling of being an expert in the sense of S-4.

While letting go of fixed notions of 'who one is' is difficult enough in private settings, where there exists a holding environment of intimates, it is even more difficult in a competitive world where proving that one is worth one's pay or honorarium is a standard requirement. As a result, there are in our society many pressures that reduce those striving to reach S-5 to mere beginnings of the journey, especially since learning organizations have largely remained an ideology. (Knowing the percentage of people attaining S-5, we know why.)

In most contemporary organizations, any kind of authentic conversation itself is viewed with suspicion, as one prefers to stay hurried and busy, and content with descriptions rather than explanations. In this climate, self development toward S-5 cannot easily be attained, and many who have the potential to reach S-5 have to wait until their tenure in the commercial world has lapsed, or they have the courage (and the developmental potential) to leave it's world view behind.

CHAPTER SUMMARY

We have now completed the tremendous journey adults undertake in their consciousness from about 25 to 100 years of age. While we have not delved into details regarding the intermediate steps needed to reach successive stages, we have become aware of the overall outline of the ellipsis that leads from S-2 to S-5. We have also learned what this journey in consciousness means and entails for process consultants, whether it be practiced as coaching, mediation, social work, and even clinical treatment. With regard to professional helping, we have seen how many well-established personal and organizational subterfuges have to be left behind before authentically powerful conversations become even remotely possible. In sum, we have seen **that the level of self development of the helper is the singularly most important key to success in assisting others.**

The reader may now ask the following two questions:
1. Why are we stopping at S-5? Are there no higher stages?
2. Can we speak of 'typical helping issues' occurring for clients at S-2 to S-5?
Below, I turn to reflecting upon these two questions.

Development Beyond S-5

As far as we know today, developmental stages extend further to 'post-autonomous' stages (S. Cook-Greuter, 1999). Therefore, the answer to the question is Yes. (For a broader perspective on the development beyond S-5, see Wilber, 2000). While throughout stages S-2 to S-5, the major focus of development is the ever increasing distance between what a person is *subject* to (and thus cannot reflect upon) what s(he) can make into an *object* of reflection (subject/object relationship for short), – once we arrive at S-5, subject-object balance is replaced by *universal embeddedness*. In that mental state, a separation of subject and object – Me and Not-Me – moves to the background of consciousness. This means, essentially, that the scope of reflection – and thus of consciousness becomes very broad, based on the suspension of what is Me and what is Not Me. Consequently, qualitatively very different issues come into view, both cognitively and social-emotionally.

On the positive side, there is heightened *construct awareness* (Cook-Greuter, 1999), meaning that a person is increasingly aware of language as a straightjacket that reality is being forced into. For people beyond S-5, natural language can no longer render the ceaseless flow that, for them, is *Reality*. Due to this, what is experienced as real is of a very different nature than what people are believing reality to be up to S-5.

Let's listen to one of the experts of "transpersonal" research on adult development, Susan Cook-Greuter (1999, 128-129):

I am suggesting here that describing post-conventional development [that is, developmental beyond S-5, O.L.] in terms of a stepwise deconstruction of the constructed aspects of our symbolically mediated views of reality leads to a more comprehensive understanding of mature development than looking at increasing structural complexity only. In this view, post-conventional development outlines the dis-identification from the culturally supported fiction of the separation between the knower and the known. I have argued elsewhere (Cook-Greuter, 1990, 1994) that seeing through one's cultural and linguistic conditioning is a logical outcome of paying attention to the processes of meaning making that can lead one closer and closer to the metaphysical realm of intuitive, non-representational ways of knowing. … This different way of apperception has been explored in the field of transpersonal psychology … A common theme among transpersonalists who try to describe the meta-rational realm of higher stages of consciousness is the paradox of having to communicate the 'ineffable' of the subtlest inner experiences through the filter of [natural, OL] language.

What is here formulated in academic language – deconstruction, symbolically mediated views of reality, post-conventional development, dis-identification, non-representational ways of knowing, etc. – is really quite simple. Two personal experiences that are made beyond S-5 stand out:
  1. Loss of the 'Me' – 'Not Me', or subject – object distinction.
  2. Loss of faith in natural language as an adequate vehicle for understanding 'reality.'

While, as Wilber shows, these ingredients of *spirituality* can occur prior to S-5, it is evident that spirituality is always experienced by a human being ACCORDING TO HIS or HER PRESENT DEVELOPMENTAL LEVEL. In other words, spirituality at S-2 differs dramatically from spirituality at higher levels.

In summary, beyond S-5 there is a loss of the customary object world that our language and science seem to describe, along with a sense that the use of natural language <u>limits</u> awareness rather than promoting it. (For this reason, exploring development beyond S-5 through the medium of natural language, such as through interviews, is a self-contradictory undertaking.) In addition, linear experience is typically replaced by a *cyclical* experience of causality. We can say that a much more sophisticated *Weltbild* (picture of the world) is created, because the person beyond S-5 gains access to numerous layers of symbolic abstraction not available below S-5. Also, the person is immersed in the phenomenal flow in a way that cannot be mastered (or even imagined) below that stage, despite all espousal to the contrary.

In my own view as a composer of music, universally valued works of art are probably the most convincing embodiment of levels of functioning beyond S-5. Such works are typically the product of a highly mature individual who is (or has been) 'gifted' to articulate his or her own developmental level through artistic material. (This is a point of view on which H. Gardener's notion of 'capital C creativity' in contrast to 'small c creativity' is based).

<u>Typical Helping Issues between S-2 to S-5</u>
Looking back to Table 1.1, you'll see right away that there clearly are 'typical' helping and coaching problems at each of the stages. However, as we learned at the end of Chapter 1, stages are not the only determinant of what problems come up for a client at a specific time. We also have to take into consideration Kernel assessment #2, which is cognitive, and Tool assessments which are behavioral. Moreover, no person ever IS their stage, and there are millions of people living at the same stage, – all of whom have very different cognitive and behavioral profiles. For this reason, a simple one-to-one relationship of helping or coaching problems with social-emotional stages is too amateurish to stand the test of coaching research and practice.

This said, we nevertheless can single out some very generic helping issues that flow from the difference between stages outlined in Table 1.1, and will continue to outline such problems in subsequent chapters. The listing below gives us an inkling of what may be involved.

Stage 2: Clients can only hold a single perspective, their own, and therefore:
- Others are only known as instruments of satisfying clients' own needs and desires.
- Imagining others' thinking and feeling about others is not possible.
- Others' thinking and feeling do not influence or determine clients' goals, decisions, and actions.
- Competitive careerism is in the foreground.
- Individuals at this stage cannot function as change agents since their grasp of their environment and others' needs is woefully inadequate.

Stage 3: Clients define themselves by the expectations of physical and/or internalized others, and therefore:

- They cannot distinguish internalized others (conventions) from their own authentic and unique self (which they have not yet developed).
- They do not have a self-authored system of values and principles in place, and therefore act according to consensus.
- They experience loss of self (abandonment) when not approved by the group or community, and thus cannot 'go it alone' and stand up for their own decisions.
- They are not aware of how embedded they are in the social fabric, and are therefore confused as to where failures come from.
- They cannot 'manage,' and even less, 'lead,' others, even if their social position requires it and they espouse doing that.
- They are not good change agents since they cannot oppose and act beyond consensus.

Stage 4: Clients define themselves by their unique, history-derived individuality that determines their *integrity*, and therefore:

- They find it hard or impossible to stand back from their own peculiar individualistic values and principles (ethics).
- They can respect others but not really stand in others' shoes or motivate others.
- They are able to go beyond consensus and act on principles, but may be relentless in applying principles (their own unreflected principles).
- They are potentially good change agents but may NOT think systemically enough to take their environment, and their own limitations, sufficiently into account.
- They may be out of touch with their team(s), following the voice of a *lonely rider* or hero.

Stage 5: Clients have transcended their idiosyncratic life history, career successes and failures and, no longer identified with a particular part of themselves, can 'lead' others. This entails:

- While they are good change agents, able to embrace divergent opinions and motivate others, they may lack true peers operating at their own level.
- They may be 'lonely' and feel misunderstood, undervalued, and unseen.
- They may be seen as 'weak' because they are not interested in control.
- They may be unable to elicit others' truthful feedback, especially when in a position of power that hinders others' truthfulness from emerging.
- They may be acting on behalf of a vision they cannot fully convey, and may thus fail to get the support they need to benefit the whole.

From these client attributes, one may be able to infer some of the problem commonalities at individual stages, but at the risk of over-generalizing. One thing, however, is clear: process consultants who do not understand the range of developmental levels that underlie a client's perspectives, issues, and problems do not have much of a chance to bring about effective change, and certainly not developmentally relevant change!

PRACTICE REFLECTIONS

- Since, most likely, what you have learned about coaching outside of this book has been framed as a world best described as FLATLAND (Wilber) – a world that acknowledges no developmental differences between people – how are you beginning to re-think some of your coaching or consulting experiences in terms of what you have learned in this book so far?

- If you had to guess within what developmental range of levels you presently make meaning of your life and work yourself, what would it be?

- If you have been in conflict sometimes in the past, would you say that the developmental model helps you make sense of conflicts in a way that sheds light on your life?

- What other models of developmental conflict are you aware of?

- What do you suggest doing to clarify your professional agenda as a consultant or coach, given your newly gained insight into developmental levels?

- What new ideas do you have regarding clients you would like to work with given your newly acquired developmental knowledge?

- Are you still satisfied with your coaching work as far as it is presently out of context with developmental models, and if so, why?

4
From 'Active' to Hypothesis-Based Listening

A First Definition of Active Listening

This chapter has two parts. In the first, I review ICF's definition of the core competency of *active listening*, while in the second, I introduce the techniques developmental listening is based on. Since developmental listening can be called active in an emphatic sense – as we will see – it will be important to understand what the activity of developmental listening consists of in contrast to what we might call its conventional (S-3) definition.

We have learned in previous chapters that *espousal* – the enunciation of values that are at odds with one's actual practice – happens when there is a need to reassure oneself and others of doing things the way one thinks one should. As C. Argyris teaches us (1999), our 'espoused theories' of action are often at odds with the 'theories in use' we actually follow. We are all aware that espousal has a psychological, and potentially also a cultural, value, since it boosts reassurance, and may even stipulate 'higher values' than those presently acted upon.

Of course, espousal may also hide or mislead. As we now know, espousal happens especially in circumstances where a lack of inner certainty leads one – unconsciously – to project oneself into a state of mind and development that is presently 'above one's head.' **Whether a definition or value is espoused or not depends on the discrepancy between two human actions: doing and speaking.** Since 'doing' is determined by the Center of Gravity, the discrepancy can be determined by investigating the speaker's developmental level as expressed in language.

In this context, it is of interest to review a well known definition of LISTENING, and to contrast that definition with the developmentally grounded meaning of the term. In this chapter, therefore, I will inquire more deeply into the process of listening, and will reflect upon the mental demands on listening in process consultation. I will also introduce some crucial tools available for developmental listening.

I propose to investigate listening from the point of view of 'everyday conversations.' Wide-ranging in content as these conversations are, it is not immediately clear how one would go about discerning the STRUCTURE of such contents. One thing is clear, however. Special constraints have to be put in place to make it possible to elicit pertinent developmental information from clients. These constraints have mainly to do with demands placed on the developmental interviewer.

Let's start, then, with ICF's definition of *active listening* (www.coachfederation.org):

Active Listening – Ability to focus completely on what the client is saying and is not saying, to understand the meaning of what is said *in the context of the client's desires* [highlighted by OL], and to support client self-expression.

(The coach):

a. Attends to the client and the client's agenda, and not to the coach's agenda for the client,
b. Hears the client's concerns, goals, values and beliefs about what is and is not possible,
c. Distinguishes between the words, the tone of voice, and the body language
d. Summarizes, paraphrases, reiterates, mirrors back what client has said to ensure clarity and understanding
e. Encourages, accepts, explores and reinforces the client's expression of feelings, perceptions, concerns, beliefs, suggestions,
f. Integrates and builds on client's ideas and suggestion,
g. 'Bottom-lines' or understands the essence of the client's communication and helps the client get there rather than engaging in long descriptive stories,
h. Allows the client to vent or 'clear' the situation without judgment or attachment in order to move on to next steps.

From the above definition we can distill the following six highlights.
Listening:

1. is (based on) focusing of attention (including on what is 'not said'),
2. attends to the client's, not the coach's agenda, goals, values, beliefs,
3. aims to understand 'what is said in the context of the client's desires,'
4. summarizes, paraphrases, reiterates, mirrors back what is said by the client (to ensure understanding),
5. supports clients' feelings, perceptions, concerns, beliefs,
6. helps clients 'clear' emotionally laden situations.

As I will show, there is nothing 'wrong' with this definition. In fact, as a first attempt to define listening in process consultation more clearly, it is a good first step. However, from a developmental vantage point, the definition is *incomplete*. This is so since listening is a form of meaning making comprising different layers, and these layers stand in a close correspondence to developmental levels. Concretely, if you are presently making meaning from S-3, what you hear others say is decoded from S-3, and this may not suffice to make an optimal intervention. This chapter is about what's needed to broaden the listener's purview.

Three Important Issues in Active Listening
From what you already know about developmental stages and their influence on how people think, you will probably ask yourself what developmental range of stages this definition articulates. This is one of the questions to be discussed. Below, I am listing two additional questions that need addressing:

A. Coaching level: What developmental stage of the process consultant – *coaching level* – is assumed by the definition?
B. Epistemology (Way of Knowing): In the above definition, what assumptions are made about how the listener can 'understand' clients' concerns, goals?
C. Developmental balance: In the above definition, what is the developmental balance envisioned between coach and client (listener and speaker)?

A. Coaching Level

In the ICF definition, the separation of the coach's (consultant's) agenda from that of the client clearly, though superficially, articulates an 'S-4-ish' developmental stance. The definition says that only a listener who knows his or her own boundaries can focus on another party as 'other' or 'Not-Me,' and make the other party's mental process an object of discernment, reflection, and intervention. Equally, only a person making meaning from S-4 with an 'appropriate' cognitive grasp, can objectively summarize, paraphrase, etc. Not only has such a person learned to hold another's perspective (S-3), given a sufficiently advanced cognitive grasp, such a listener can also 'bottom-line' what is said and infer what is not said.

Holding both her own and the client's perspective in balance, an S-4 listener is able to let the client 'clear' a situation without judgment or attachment. The S-4 listener realizes that the client has a different generator of thoughts and feelings, together with a different life history, etc.

It seems legitimate at this point to draw two inferences:
1. An S-2 individual cannot meet the mental demands of the ICF definition
2. Minimally, an individual with an S-3 Center of Gravity is required for active listening to occur.

HOWEVER, the overall 'espousal' of the ICF definition is focused on S-4, rather than S-3. This issue deserves further attention. To begin, there are several ambiguous sub-clauses in the definition stipulated by ICF:
- "Ability to focus completely' (on what the client is saying and not saying)"
- "What is said and not said"
- "In the context of the client's desires"
- "Support client self expression.

All of these sub-clauses have to do with what, developmentally, is best called the practitioner's MODEL OF THE CLIENT. By *model* is meant that, from a constructivist point of view, there is no way in which a client could be *directly* understood other than by first formulating a model of WHO THE CLIENT IS. This model can be either implicit (unconsciously held), or explicit. Whether the client model is implicit or explicit is a direct consequence of the methodology of coaching that is applied. Simply put, in contrast to conventional coaching, which is based on *belief*, evidence based coaching follows an EXPLICIT, not an implicit – unconsciously held – client model. The belief is a set of implicit assumptions, varying from coach to coach, as to who the client IS.

Keeping this in mind, let's ask now: how do we have to approach the above four sub-clauses of the ICF definition when interpreting them from an evidence-based, developmental point of view? I think it is fair to say the following:
- The ability to focus completely is a matter of interview technique, especially of separating between 'content' and 'structure' (stage).
- What is said and not said sounds different to coaches at different developmental levels (coaching levels).
- Clients' desires are constructed differently by them depending on their present developmental level.

- Client self expression also differs according to developmental level as well as cognitive and behavioral profile.

What do these clarifications contribute to our discussion of developmental coaching?

First and foremost, they make us aware that the ICF definition will be understood, as well as applied, differently **depending on coaching level.** *Differently* means, in particular, that for some practitioners – all of those with a Center of Gravity S-3 – the ICF definition will remain a merely ESPOUSED, unrealized one! In other words, the *theory in use* of coaches at levels S-2 and S-3 will be inadequate to the task.

Let's review. We have focused on the ICF definition of 'active listening' to ascertain what Center of Gravity it espouses. We have distinguished this definition – really a stipulation – from practitioners' theory-in-use (or actual procedure) which depends on their Center of Gravity. In what follows, therefore, we will study in greater depth what it entails to UNDERSTAND THE MEANING OF WHAT IS SAID AND NOT SAID IN THE CONTEXT OF THE CLIENT'S DESIRES.

B. Epistemology

I mean by *epistemology* the coach's way of knowing (Greek episteme = knowledge), or as I put it above, the way the coach is constructing a *model of the client* for the sake of 'understanding' the client. Clearly, all a process consultant can ever understand of and about the client is a MODEL, not the actual person. The typical person, subject to their own Center of Gravity, does not even understand him- or herself, so there is no chance the coach could do much better. However, – and this is the true innovation in coaching,– the process consultant can develop a more or less evidence based model of the client which serves as a frame of reference for assisting him or her. Even when a model of the client exists, such as a developmental model, there is no guarantee that it will be adequately followed by practitioners. Rather, practitioners at an **S-3, S-4, or S-5 coaching level will follow one and the same client model differently.** This is what I mean when I say that – once we distinguish between CONTENT and STRUCTURE in listening – the ICF definition of active listening REMAINS ESPOUSED for a large number (up to 55-60%) of practitioners. And that indeed brings to light some essential pedagogical concerns!

C. Developmental Balance

I mean by *developmental balance* the balance between the practitioner's and the client's developmental level. As I show in Chapter 9, this balance is crucial for many reasons, above all for reasons of effectiveness, but also of ethics. (Coaching a client residing at a higher developmental level (than the consultant) may be unethical, since it may developmentally constrain and retard the client. At present, no coaching ethics provides for this case.)

More particularly, in the present context of 'understanding the client', let us review Table 1.

Orientation	S-2	S-3	S-4	S-5
View of Others	Instruments of own need	Needed to contribute to own	Collaborator, delegate, peer	Contributors to own integrity and balance

	gratification	self image		
Level of Self Insight	Low	Moderate	High	Very High
Need to Control	Very High	Moderate	Low	Very Low
Communication	Unilateral	Exchange 1:1	Dialogue	True Communication

Table I.1. Changing orientations across adult stages

It is clear from the Table, above, that "understanding the client's agenda, concerns, goals, values, beliefs" is very different at different developmental stages, thus *coaching levels*. Understanding what is said and not said therefore has <u>no unitary definition</u>, but only a stratified one, vaguely suggested by the Table.

As the reader will agree, "understanding what is said (and not said)" by clients crucially depends on all of the four orientations listed in the Table, not just one. Let us see in detail why this is the case:
1. View of others
2. Level of self insight
3. Need to control
4. Communication.

[1] When speaking of 'understanding others,' our view of who they are, in terms of the model we formulate of them, is of great importance. Consequently, at S-3, a coach's understanding of a client is very different from that of an S-4 coach. Only the latter can have an 'objective' view of the client, rather than using the client for purposes of professional – or even private – self cohesion (self-boosting).
[2] The same holds for level of self insight as a determinant of 'understanding the client.' As we have superficially understood, and will grasp in greater depth in the following chapters, 'level of self insight' centrally has to do with where I, as the practitioner, place myself in regard to my client. Here again, an S-5 (or near S-5) stance is the most powerful one, while both S-3 and S-4 'understandings' of the client are hampered by lack of self insight, although of a different kind. At S-3 the process consultant is hampered by the interference of internalized others, while at S-4 she is constrained by her inability to take an objective, 'outside' view of herself.
[3] Control can be handled in very subtle ways. Far from coercion, it can be exerted simply by some kind of other-dependency, as would be the case at S-3. Although it would seem that an S-3 process consultant is under the control of the client, the resulting collusion, reinforced by playing to the social surround, gives the consultant an effective, although unconscious, control tool. Unconscious control is still control!
At S-4, control is under the reign of the practitioner's own integrity, and therefore is typically low on account of his or her self insight and respect for others. Put differently, coaching conversations are more or less controlling, depending on coaching level.
[4] The way a practitioner communicates with clients – whether through 1:1 exchanges, dialogue, or 'true communication' (see Chapter 6), is equally central for the degree of understanding that can emerge between process consultant and client. The degree of understanding has centrally to do with the model of the client that underlies the communication. For instance, in the framework of an S-3 model of the client, a dialog of equals is only possible as long as the practitioner is at least as highly developed as the

client, and is more potent when the practitioner is at least one step ahead of the client developmentally.

As this demonstrates, there is no unitary definition for "understanding what is said in the context of the client's desires," nor is there a unitary definition for what "the client's desires" are! For this reason, the ICF definition is too generic to hold up for purposes of evidence based process consultation.

We surmised above that the ICF definition discussed implicitly requires coaches to be minimally at S-3, and ideally at least at S-4. Otherwise, no true dialogue, not to speak of true communication, is possible, thus no 'understanding of the client' *as a person outside of the practitioner's dependency on him or her*. As we have seen, as long as the coach makes meaning at S-3, what is understood of the client remains highly mixed up with the coach's self definition that is based on others' actual or inferred expectations. This kind of understanding is a mélange of the coach's internalized others and some emerging elements of self definition which have not fully matured.

Under these circumstances, the ICF definition is mere *window dressing*. The definition is being espoused for some assumed common good and/or for pedagogical purposes. This is honorable, but not good enough for a **profession**.

Summary of Comments on the ICF Definition
- The ICF definition of Active Listening requires a developmental range of minimally S-3 to S-4. Anything below this range cannot be called 'active listening.'
- Coaches' way of understanding clients, or their model of the client, is determined by their coaching level (developmental level from which they 'coach'). Understandings beyond the coaching level are espoused.
- There is no way in which an S-3 practitioner can strictly focus on clients' agenda, goal, values, etc. [as required by the ICF definition] since the practitioner cannot clearly separate his/her own agenda, goals, values, from that of the client.
- The royal road to becoming a professional in the evidence based sense of the word is the journey to S-4. Otherwise the practitioner is, to speak with Kegan, 'in over his/her head.'

The question now arises: how do we have to modify, or perhaps reformulate, the ICF definition of Active Listening, in order to arrive at a definition without elements of espousal, put into action at and beyond S-4?

Listening as Hypothesis Formulation and Testing
We have seen that to do justice to the ICF definition of Active Listening requires a practitioner to engage with coaching clients minimally at S-4 (as long as they are not developed more highly than S-4). As we know, typically 25% of adults make it to that stage. What of those who don't? This is a serious pedagogical question regarding coach education and certification standards focused on coaches' self development. Since we cannot legislate acting from S-4, what can be done to move the subpopulation of coaches to that Center of Gravity? I address this question in Chapter 9. For now, let's stay with the issue of defining Active Listening. **Essentially, we are striving for a**

developmental re-definition of what the ICF stipulation of Active Listening seems to 'have in mind.'

The best way to transition from a *behavioral* definition of active listening to the *evidence based, developmental* one presented in this book is to reflect upon, first, *who formulates hypotheses* and second, *what kinds of hypotheses are there*. The brief answer to the first question is that EVERYBODY FORMULATES HYPOTHESES ALL THE TIME, whether knowing it or not. The answer to the second question is that there are two ways of formulating hypotheses, of whatever kind: *unconsciously and consciously*. Unconscious hypotheses are characteristic of implicit, popular theories we can call *pop-theories*, while consciously formulated hypotheses have the purposes of testing actual, 'real' theories, namely those that can generate and frame empirical evidence.

The Inevitability and Ubiquity of Hypothesis Formulation
An example for the first, unconscious, kind of hypothesis would be: 'Going north and then slightly south will get me to the place I want to get to.' An example for the second, conscious kind of hypothesis would be: 'I think my client makes meaning of his work very close to S-4.' In defining Active Listening, therefore, the issue is not whether listening is based on hypotheses or not – it surely is – the issue is rather *what kind of an hypothesis* listening is based on, and how explicit that hypothesis is. Regarding work with people: **Since process consultants have no choice as to whether to formulate hypotheses or not – they do it unconsciously all the time – why not do it consciously, as in evidence based coaching?** All this chapter asks you to do is to consider transitioning from holding unconscious hypotheses about your clients to making such hypotheses EXPLICIT. Let's therefore reflect a little further about what is involved in formulating conscious, explicit hypotheses, – those that, when confirmed, yield empirical EVIDENCE.

Hypotheses, if they are not to be random, must derive from some conceptual framework defined beforehand, such as the *Constructivist Developmental Framework* (CDF) used in this book or another framework. Such hypotheses are **reasonable assumptions and guesses, meant to generate empirical evidence, and are empirically testable**. 'Testable' refers to some kind of experimentation, including scored interviews (see Chapter 8), as holds for CDF. A simple hypothesis could regard a developmental stage – e.g., "this client is operating from stage 4," as is needed for developmental intakes. A more complex hypothesis could involve, for instance:
- The relationship of a person's developmental stage to her cognitive grasp (see volume 2).
- The interrelationship of the Centers of Gravity of members of a team for predicting team dynamics (see this volume, Appendix C).
- The prediction of behaviors – say, of self conduct, or approach to tasks – on the basis of developmental stage(s) (see volume 3 of this book).

And so forth.

The Need for A Conceptual Framework
The reader will now ask: what are 'conceptual frameworks'? Such frameworks are also called *theories*. There are pop-theories (hunches) and scientific theories. In coaching, a

whole slew of theories (mostly pop-theories) is presently used, although by definition mostly unconsciously. The most important theory in coaching is BEHAVIORAL THEORY, which says that *behavior* can be learned, observed, investigated, changed, etc. In addition to behavioral theory, there is DEVELOPMENTAL THEORY. This theory says that behavior is a secondary phenomenon (epi-phenomenon), since it derives from developmental stage and cognitive profile. In this book, we follow Developmental Theory as made explicit through CDF in which both theories coalesce.

Intermediate Summary

At this point, the reader not used to theoretical argumentation may need a succinct summary that briefly highlights what we have worked out in this chapter so far in practical terms.

Up to this point, we have reviewed the behavioral definition of Active Listening, formulated by ICF, and have found that conceiving of listening as *understanding what is said and not said in the context of the client's desires* one-sidedly and unrightfully assumes that:

- clients fully understand their own desires;
- desires are something absolute, immutable rather than being a function of the individual's developmental stage.

By pondering what listening is further, we have also discovered that **all listening is hypothesis based**, and that hypothesis formulation is meaning making that goes all the time, 24 hours a day (even in dreams). We have distinguished between two ways of formulating hypotheses, conscious and unconscious. We said that unconsciously formulated hypotheses are good enough for verifying *pop-theories*, and that consciously formulated hypotheses are needed to actually gather empirical evidence. As a result of these deliberations, we have questioned the validity of the ICF definition of active listening to coaching levels lower than S-4.

Clearly, then, we can now define evidence-based LISTENING as **conscious hypothesis formulation and testing in search of empirical evidence**. This said, it's important to be aware that thereby we enter the realm of ***qualitative research***. What does this entail for working with individual clients in some kind of intervention?

Subject of the research – often referred to as *coaching research* – is the client. The research we do with individual clients is based on listening, through which the practitioner uses him- or herself as the instrument of research. The practitioner's listening is ACTIVE to the extent that the s(he) follows an explicit hypothesis that can be empirically confirmed or rejected, in our case a developmental hypothesis such as "this client acts from S-4."

As we will see in the next chapter, the research taught in this book is not only qualitative research – where we look for "qualities" of the subject we study – but is rather a mix of quantitative and qualitative research. This is so since we are using *measurements* that can be expressed in numerical form, and can be aggregated to higher than individual levels. (E.g., we can test an hypothesis such as "the majority of members of this team have not reached S-4," see Appendices C and D of this book.)

Active Listening as the Testing of Developmental Hypotheses

As everybody knows, *research* has to do with making experiments. In interventions with individuals, such experiments are conversational ones: we experiment by way of conversations. I have shown that such conversations can be 'powerful' to the extent that they are based on testing hypotheses about clients' developmental levels. In order to amplify the meaning of Active Listening in the developmental sense, I am now going to show how powerful conversations called INTERVIEWS can be used to:

- Formulate hypotheses,
- Test hypotheses,
- Confirm or reject hypotheses.

Since in the present framework hypotheses are *developmental*, I need to explain how such hypotheses are arrived at by the process consultant, how they are tested, and how they are confirmed or rejected. I also need to indicate how evidence deriving from confirmed hypotheses is given feedback about to clients, and is used by the consultant or coach to formulate coaching plans and structure coaching conversations (for examples, see Appendix B of this volume). This I cannot do in a single chapter, but only volume 1 in its entirety. In the present chapter, I am going to focus on the three main issues just stated above.

Developmental Prompts

The reader will remember from 'Research 101' or an equivalent class on science that the researcher follows a 'methodology,' and that there are 'research questions' and 'research methods.' In this book so far, I have already introduced some research questions, such as "what is the developmental level from which my client is presently making meaning?" I have also introduced the outlines of a methodology, framed within the conceptual framework called CDF. A methodology typically comprises a set of methods. Methods have an operational side that deals with "how to proceed." This is the question I will now take up. I will ask:

- What is required of the process consultant to formulate a developmental hypothesis about a client?
- How can such a hypothesis be tested for its truth value?
- What does it mean to confirm or reject such a hypothesis?

Here is the rub: **in everyday, 'open' conversation it is very difficult, if not impossible, to carry out developmental hypothesis testing.** Especially when undertaken with intimates, it can also be downright risky or harmful. Clearly, we need special tools for adequately *structuring* conversations so that they elicit correct developmental information. How can we achieve that?

What we need to establish is a firm structure for the conversation that is meant to tell us with certainty from what developmental stage a client is speaking. By 'firm,' I mean a structure that can be reproduced in each interview, regardless of who is administering it, with enough flexibility to adapt the interviewing to the specific client and his or her surroundings at the time. Such conversations are called *semi-structured* (partially structured) interviews, and they have the following characteristics:

- The interview is entirely focused on the client's agenda.

- The client's agenda is defined based, not on content, but on stage (structure).
- To have the client follow the agenda in a constrained way, s(he) is asked to choose from ten *verbal prompts*, or words and short phrases that lead him or her back to a memory of important experiences

In this way, the client is led to construct meanings of experiences from which a knowledgeable interviewer can infer the client's stage.

If the agenda is the client's, what's left for the interviewer to do?

- The interviewer's task is focusing attention – and nothing but focusing attention – on what the client is "saying and not saying," – this is Active Listening.
- To focus attention, as well as to know how to probe for missing information, the interviewer needs to *formulate and test (conscious) hypotheses* as to the stage the client is speaking from as a Center of Gravity.

Does that sound simple? It is not, but it can be learned. (Students of IDM learn to do this in Gateway and Part A of Program One.) It is difficult for beginners because *focusing completely on what the client is saying and not saying* (ICF) has a very different, <u>deepened</u> meaning in developmental coaching. It means to provoke the client to generate utterances that will reveal his or her developmental stage. This is an art as well as a science, as indicated by the title of the book. It is an art because of the skills involved in this kind of interviewing, and it is a science because, as we've said, it's qualitative research. This needs further explanation.

<u>The Nature of Probing in Developmental Interviews</u>

As we have seen, people are not only unaware of their developmental stage (needing a third party to give them feedback on it), they are also subject to it. *Subject to* means they can't know, control or manipulate it, except perhaps through very determined espousal, which a developmentally skilled interviewer will surely find out. Developmental interviewing is initially not easy because what clients say is highly contextual. Clients produce similar content at different stages, for which reason developmental experts can't rely on content. Rather, an expert interviewer is required *to probe* for what is the client's Center of Gravity by 'bracketing' content (putting content 'in brackets' as secondary to stage). Whether the client tells me about her pet animal, her grandmother, or her boss is irrelevant to me as a developmental interviewer in search of what the client's present developmental stage may be.

How is such interviewing done? It is done by asking two questions:

1. What assumptions about what is ME and what is NOT-ME are underlying the content I am hearing?
2. Given what I just heard, what additional information do I need to probe for, to tell what stage the client's content is based on?

The first question requires making inferences in the context of stage theory. The second question requires further probing, meant to test the limits of the client's ability to take responsibility for what s(he) assumes to be ME.

Let's consider an example here. A client says to you: 'I would like to work with you to become a better communicator. I have been frequently told that I don't communicate clearly, either with my reports or my boss, and I think this is a big issue in my work. So that's what I would like to work on with you.' This is the client's *presenting problem*, that is, the part that the client knows about. What the problem really is remains initially unclear. There is also no clear and immediate solution to the problem. (Accordingly, what is needed is process consultation.) Only you, the process consultant, know about the fact that 'becoming a better communicator' means very different things when coming up as a problem at S-3 compared to S-4 or S-5.

Imagine an S-3 individual communicating. What might that be about? Surely, whatever it may be about – that's just content – a primary assumption the individual will be making is that it's a first priority to remain acknowledged, supported, and valued by the group she is presently part of (peer group, company, or other). This unconscious assumption is going to define the ceiling of what the individual is going to be able to risk, and also defines the core of what the individual is going to want to *communicate*.

Now contrast that with an S-4 individual who wants to *communicate better*. What might that be focused on? Since the individual defines her own integrity by way of values and principles of an idiosyncratic kind, backed up by her life history, she will most likely be intending to make those values and principles better known to her interlocutors, certainly her reports. As to communications upward, she might want to become more forceful in holding and supporting her own point of view in a circle of peers. Or else, she might, moving beyond S-4, want to be able to become more risk-taking in standing away from her own meaning making and turning it into an object of reflection pointing up her limitations. Whatever it is, clearly these two meanings of learning to communicate better are worlds apart. And the same ought to hold for the 'coaching'!

This said, the question still remains: how does the interviewer know WHAT TO PROBE FOR? The answer is: **what is to be probed FOR is determined by the interviewer's hypothesis.** The process of formulating such a hypothesis is a kind of *Gedankenexperiment* – thought experiment – where the interviewer says to him- or herself: "Let me assume that what I just heard from the client is expressing an S-3 viewpoint." That's a developmental hypothesis. Clearly, to state a hypothesis, the interviewer has to know stage theory, just like in any other scientific undertaking where the researcher has to know the theory whose assumptions are being tested. Having formulated such an hypothesis, and knowing its implications for the client's meaning making, the next step for the interviewer is, of course, to ask: "If it's S-3, what information is missing that would tell me about how much below and beyond S-3 the client is actually functioning?" (see Chapters 5 and 6).

By the way, you already know how to formulate hypotheses. In a way, you don't ever do anything else, except that you do so unconsciously, like you speak 'prose.' When you enter an unknown building, for instance, you hypothesize that it is safe to enter, and if it is not, you enter with great care. Entering a room in the building and sitting down, say in a cafeteria, you INFER from the presence of others around you that they apparently feel safe, and you should do likewise. You hypothesize that in all likelihood the ceiling will not come down and the earth will not shake. As long as a hurricane has not been declared to be imminent, you can rest assured that the others around you are not kidding themselves regarding their physical safety. **Without these unconsciously held**

hypotheses you would be completely paralyzed in doing anything at all, including eating your meal.

Making Hypothesis Formulation Conscious

Making hypothesis formulation conscious, and making hypotheses thus explicit, is the hallmark of a professional. All you are asked to do in developmental listening (interviewing) is to make your hypothesis formulation and testing CONSCIOUS, and to do so in the context of a particular theory that concerns people's differences in meaning making. After all, you bought this book to learn how to do so. Let's summarize in general terms what is the task of the process consultant as a developmental interviewer:

- To distinguish 'structure' (stage) and 'content' in client speech.
- To stand in the client's shoes, *adopting his or her agenda.*
- To formulate and test (confirm or reject) hypotheses regarding the client's developmental level.
- To be sensitive to issues the client chooses not to discuss, is unable to 'see,' or cannot 'say' (and there is much the client *cannot say*; otherwise, the interview techniques the book is teaching you would be wholly unnecessary).

You'll have noticed in the second point, above, that *adopting the client's agenda* has changed meaning from what it is understood to mean in conventional (behavioral) interviewing. Conventionally, it means to make the content of the client's agenda an object of reflection. By contrast, here it seems to mean *standing in the client's* shoes as s(he) <u>constructs</u> the content from her Center of Gravity. These minute differences are really immense, methodologically speaking; they begin to point to the differences between behavioral (conventional) coaching and developmental coaching, as well as between conventional process consultation and its developmentally deepened version.

Constraining Clients' Agenda by Way of *Prompts*

I said initially that we can elicit developmentally relevant information only if we can find ways to CONSTRAIN the discourse with clients in some way. The reason for this is that we need a 'pure' medium in which, like under a microscope, the client's words can be screened (scrutinized) for their implications in terms of what is ME and what is NOT-ME for them at this time. What we really need is a kind of *projective test* with the aid of which clients **project themselves** into a notion or phrase in order to make their unconscious meaning making EXPLICIT for another party. This is exactly what we do through the use of so-called Prompts.

Prompts are single words or short expressions written on index cards that we can give to clients, asking them to think about 'what comes to mind.' In this way, we are tapping clients' stream of consciousness, or train of thought, based on their memory, which is exactly what we want to do, since it is in that stream of consciousness that meaning making actually happens. But the prompts do more than channeling the reporting of client memories through which meanings are formulated. Prompts also enable the interviewer to be an IMPARTIAL LISTENER IN SEARCH OF A DEVELOPMENTAL STAGE. This is so since prompts provide 'hooks' based on which the interviewer can guide interview conversations and construct hypotheses that can be tested in the course of the interview.

You will now wonder what exactly these prompts are. They are listed below (adapted and modified from Lahey et al., 1988):

- **Success:** Can you think of a time in your recent work where you felt somewhat jubilant, feeling you had achieved something that was difficult for you, or that you had overcome something?
- **Changed:** If you think of how you have changed over the last year or two, or even months, regarding how you conduct your life, what comes to mind?
- **Control:** can you think of a moment where you became highly aware that you were losing control, or felt the opportunity of seizing control, what occurs to you?
- **Limits:** If you think of where you are aware of limits, either in your life and/or work, something you wish you could do but feel excluded from, what comes up for you?
- **Outside of:** As you look around in the workplace or the family, where do you see yourself as not fitting in, being an outsider, and how does that make you feel?
- **Frustration:** If you think of a time where you were in a situation not of your choosing, where you felt totally frustrated, but unable to do something about it, what emerges?
- **Important to me:** If I were to ask you 'what do you care about most deeply,' 'what matters most,' are there one or two things that come to mind?
- **Sharing:** If you think about your need of sharing your thoughts and feelings with others, either at work or at home, how, would you say, that plays out?
- **Strong stand/conviction:** If you were to think of times where you had to take a stand, and be true to your convictions, what comes to mind?
- **Taking risks:** When thinking of recent situations where you felt you were taking, or had to take, risks, either to accomplish or fend off something, what comes to mind?

How to Use Prompts

As seen above, prompts consist of selected single words (noun, verb, adjective) or short expressions, followed by an appellation to the client, to search one's present or recent mind state. This explanation follows the general introduction by the interviewer who might have said at the outset:

I am meeting with you today in order to acquire a better understanding of how you presently function in your work and/or life. I am particularly interested in how you relate to yourself and others. To understand that better, I am going to give you ten index cards on which single words or short phrases are written. These words or phrases have the purpose of reminding you of certain recent experiences in your life or work that right now have significant saliency for you. I will essentially be just a listener, my task being to stand in your shoes and understand deeply how you feel. You will be in complete control of the agenda of this interview.

I will initially ask you to look through these prompts and then to choose whichever prompt seems to be most salient for you. **You'll call the shots.** Once you have selected a prompt, I will ask you to go into your memory to a specific event, situation, or person where the prompt chosen by you is in sharp focus. We will then have a conversation about this event or situation that you remember. For the sake of this interview, we will not have to use all the prompts, but only about 3 to 5 of them, all chosen by you. My main task in this interview is to stay close to your train of thought, and support your recollections. I will ask for your permission and forgiveness when I insist on more explanation from you in the case that I just don't "get it."

You should know that you can discontinue the interview at any point, for whatever reason (for instance, if it is uncomfortable). Since I will be tape recording you, you can also ask me to go temporarily off line and stop recording. Most importantly, remember that this interview is entirely confidential. Nobody will get a copy or transcript of this interview except you, and no information you share in this interview will be divulged to any third party. In short, **the results of this interview will not be shared with anybody, except with your consent and in a form you agree to.**

Something like that. In addition to having the interviewee sign an agreement that spells out the interview's purpose and its confidentiality, this introduction to the interview will put the interviewee at ease and build trust, as needed in any interview.

The reader now understands that the developmental interview is a *structured* conversation about some client-selected topics of importance to him or her in work or life. In contrast to conventional interviews, this interview is, first, *structured by prompts*, and second, *not about content but about stage (structure)*. In reading and evaluating the interview, the interviewer will not be looking for any specific "themes," "attitudes," "opinions," that is, for any CONTENT that might be of interest. Instead, the interviewer will strictly attend to the client's agenda as it derives from the individual prompts, and from the meaning making that is being projected by the client into the prompts.

During the interview, the interviewer will also abstain from any arbitrary remarks, comments, opinions, interpretations, etc. that stray beyond the client's "train of thought" (see also Chapter 7). Rather, the interviewer will single-mindedly be interested in decoding the client's utterances by relating them to the stage hypothesis s(he) has formulated at or near the beginning of the interview (for an example, see Chapter 7). Also, as we will see in later parts of this book, the interviewer will evaluate the interview by "scoring" it, that is, by assigning to different parts of the interview a notation specifying the particular stage that is clearly expressed by the interviewee. To do so is best learned in small groups. In Appendix A, this book offers many exercises for practice.

<u>Requirements of Developmental Interviewing Summarized</u>
Let's briefly summarize the main requirements of a **developmental interview,** following chronological time:
- Make sure the client has signed an interview agreement (see Appendix A).
- Make sure you have conveyed that the interview is an 'intake,' not a test, meant to enable you to build trust and work effectively.

- As soon as possible in the interview, START WITH A REASONABLE HYPOTHESIS AS TO RANGE OF STAGES OR MINIMAL (LOWEST POSSIBLE) STAGE (see more about that in Chapters 5 and 6).
- Leave behind any pre-defined agenda of your own – all good intentions to 'help' in particular, and adopt the *principle of non-interference with clients' discourse* (this is one of the most difficult mental demands for seasoned, conventionally trained 'coaches').
- Become a receptacle for what the client shares with you.
- Avoid deviating from the client's present 'train of thought,' e.g., by way of comments, why questions, interpretations that come to mind, advice – anything extraneous to their thought process.
- In particular, do not ask any "Why?" questions – they will only derail the client's associative thinking and destroy her train of thought right on the spot.
- Once recording the interview has begun, probe based on what you just heard, starting with what you think is a minimal lower stage ("I credit this client with being at least at S-x …").
- Stop probing only when sure that you are standing firmly in the client's shoes, seeing the world as s(he) does, measuring what YOU feel against what different stages 'feel like' FOR YOU.
- When probing yields a result discordant with your initial hypothesis, revise your hypothesis and start over (this requires knowing intermediate stages, see Chapter 6)
- When 12-15 minutes have elapsed, check with the client as to whether s(he) feels s(he) has exhausted the prompt and is ready to move to another one.
- If all the prompts the client chooses tend to support self boosting ('look how great I am!'), suggest choosing a prompt that deals with what the client is experiencing as difficult or as generating discomfort and frustration; explain that you want to get a balanced picture of the client's strengths and challenges, not a self-eulogy of the client.
- At any point, feel free to paraphrase and/or summarize recent client statements, choosing the client's vocabulary and abstaining from any grandiose interpretations of your own; avoid abstracting from what was said by the client.
- By formulating short summaries, locate through interaction what remains unclear to you and what therefore needs further probing. (In fact, if you don't know what to probe for you have lost your way.)
- If you feel lost, revisit your hypothesis and play devil's advocate, by questioning your previous stage assumptions; this way, you hinder yourself from derailing during the interview, or coming up with an interview that can't be scored.
- Don't feel shy when attempting to stand in the client's shoes. You can always ask for permission or, if that doesn't suffice, for forgiveness!
- Five minutes before the interview time is up, let the client know about it, asking "is there anything in addition to what we have talked about that you would like to say, something I haven't asked you about and you yourself haven't brought up?"

- Close by thanking the client for giving you an opportunity to "better understand where you are coming from," and repeat the assurance of complete confidentiality of the interview.

Contributions of Developmental Interviewing to Interventional Practice

As this point, let us ask ourselves what the exercise of developmental interviewing, once learned, would contribute to a process consultant's feedback sessions and coaching conversations generally. Even if, after having studied this kind of interviewing, you would *never* do another developmental intake, how would you have benefited? Here, from my experience, is what you would have learned:

1. To focus completely on clients' verbal as a medium in which they make meaning, defining testable hypotheses.
2. To appreciate clients' body language – tone, certainty, pauses, pitch, speed of articulation, gestures – as a way of underscoring, or with-drawing, explicit meanings (doubt, guilt, developmental conflict, espousal, etc.).
3. To focus completely on clients' desires *as they get constructed in reference to a particular Center of Gravity*, in front of your very ears and eyes.
4. To pay attention to what is <u>not</u> said because it cannot be said, being beyond the client's present developmental ceiling (reachable upper stage).
5. To empty yourself of all pre-meditated intentions, good or bad, and become a receptacle of clients' stream of consciousness.
6. To stop your habitual *satisficing* by which you go with intuitively persuasive assumptions that you have never checked out.
7. To ask low-risk questions that will not derail clients' train of thought, but keep them focused on their own internal process.
8. To strengthen your ability to ask for implications of answers given (stories told) without engaging in interpretation, but rather by drawing inferences that can be checked out on the spot instead.
9. To avoid any *show and tell* that contaminates the boundaries between you and the client.
10. To shift from persuading and showcasing yourself or your skills to understanding others in their own terms (hopefully from a developmental levels above theirs).

IN SHORT, YOU WOULD HAVE LEARNED TO FULLY ENGAGE WITH OTHERS.

I think this will even benefit your discussions with your children!

Four Important Strategies

Given that there is a lot of detail in what we discussed in this chapter, here is a summary of four most important points made:

Never interrupt the client's flow of thought. This is a capital requirement of developmental intervention. Why? With a lot of precautions and care, you have set up an environment in which the client can be utterly him- or herself. You have removed the barriers to full trust on the part of the client. You are now encountering the client's mental process of meaning making directly. To stick to the client's agenda, it behooves you not to disturb the object under investigation. You are, after all, a researcher at work.

This entails that any arbitrary comment on your part, any uncalled-for opinion or the like is immensely distracting to the client. All you would achieve is derailing the client's flow of thought, and thereby yourself.

Let's take, for example, WHY questions. (Yes/No questions are even worse). What would you gain from having the client construct answers to Why questions, just for you? Nothing. What would happen if you invited the client to think about some 'Why' would be the following: the client, in order to please you (especially at S-3), would leap out of his or her present flow of thought, and would construct something fanciful to satisfy your curiosity. The client would be totally free to give you any answer s(he) pleases to construct. That's not what you want. You want the client to stay with his or her own thinking, without any rationalization of why, or yes or no.

Empty yourself out as much as you can, especially of internalized others who want to take the reigns away from you. These 'others' could consist of:
- Coaching rules or clichés derived from identifying with the coaching community.
- Any kind of result your coaching sponsor (another internalized other) wants to see.
- Any kind of recipe you might have learned or made up yourself.
- Premeditated 'coaching plans' that have 'worked well.'
- Ways of saving face or showing off.
- A focus on your own little 'personality' instead of on the conceptual framework you are working from (your personality rather than your *Persona*)
- Your past experience rather than your being in the moment (flow)
- Any contents you are 'interested in' that, by definition, stand in the way of your Persona
- And so forth.

Don't feel shy when attempting to stand in the client's shoes. This much is true in the ICF definition of active listening: that you want to understand what the client says in the context "of the client's desires" if this means "of the client's emotions." After all, the stage interview is about the *social-emotional profile* of the client. This profile answers the question: what does the client think/feel s(he) should do, and for whom? And this is an emotional and axiological (value) issue. So your task as an interviewer is clearly concerned with emotions, – how they are conceived, generated, framed, conceptualized, verbalized, and so forth. Only when you can replicate the client's emotions from your gut will you be able to stand in his or her shoes. The test of whether you succeed in doing this is, however, not an emotion, but a **confirmed hypothesis**. That is the difference between conventional (content- and belief-based) and evidence (structure) based interventions.

REMEMBER ALSO: You cannot repair what you have failed to do in the interview itself when evaluating (scoring) the interview! This is the harsh truth. Garbage in, garbage out, as they say in software engineering. Although you will get a real chance of evaluating your interview only once it is transcribed (or you have listened to it from the recording), you ought to be cognizant of your questions and probes while the interview is going on. You must, in a way, always "look over your own shoulder." Once the interview is over, it is too late. One important way to stay on track is to play "devil's advocate," by asking yourself: "could what I just heard be said from a different stage than I am presently assuming?" This is hard to do while conducting the interview, but the more of it you manage to do, the better an interviewer are you.

An Amplified Definition of Active Listening
We are now ready to amplify the definition of listening that we started with at the beginning of this chapter.

Active Listening – Ability to focus completely on what the client is saying and is not saying, to understand the meaning of what is said in the context of the client's desires, and to support client self-expression.

Reflecting, throughout the chapter, on all of the elements, above:
- what the client is saying and not saying,
- understanding the meaning of what is said
- in the context of the client's desires
- to support client self expression,

we introduced the following additional, new elements into the above definition:
- Listening as the testing of consciously formulated, rather than 'intuitive' hypotheses (beliefs).
- Active listening based on hypothesis formulation and testing.
- Limits of what clients can know about their developmental whereabouts.
- 'What is said' as the projection of a Center of Gravity.
- Clients' desires as a function of their Center of Gravity.
- Self expression as articulations of clients' train of thought, a medium for probing meaning making.

On account of this, let me propose an amplified definition of listening as *developmental listening*:

Developmental Listening – Ability to focus attention on what the client is saying and is not saying *while testing a developmental hypothesis*, by probing the client's train of thought in order to understand the meaning of what is thought, felt, and said in the context of the client's **Frame of Reference**, and to support client self-expression to the fullest extent possible.

What makes this definition of Active Listening *evidence based* are the following elements added to the ICF definition:
- Linking the focusing of attention to a stage hypothesis.
- Specifying that the relevant context is the client's *Frame of Reference* (not directly his or her desires which flow from it).
- Specifying that the client's train of thought is the medium of exploration.
- Specifying that 'self expression' equates to *expression of a Center of Gravity*.

As the reader will increasingly understand, the evidence based definition of Active Listening, above, changes the entire coaching enterprise, and requires many significant changes and unlearnings in working with clients. In particular, it embeds coaching within the framework of process consultation as defined by Schein, referred to in the Introduction (Schein, 1999, 20):

Process Consultation is the creation of a relationship with the client that permits the client to perceive, understand, and act on the process events that occur in the client's internal and external environment, in order to improve the situation as defined by the problem.

It is now probably much clearer to the reader:
- in what sense 'coaching' is process consultation;
- that in *developmentally deepened process consultation* (DPC) as presented in this book, there is no direct way for a client "to perceive, understand, and act on" process events in his or her environment.

In developmental process consultation, we DON'T make a distinction between what Schein calls internal and external environment. We assume in a constructivist way that the so-called *external* environment is a secondary phenomenon, more precisely, that it is a *mirage* constructed internally as a function of the speaker's developmental stage (and/or cognitive profile).

This being the case, the client, "in order to improve the situation as defined by the problem," not only needs to be made aware of why s(he) is construing the issue or problem the way s(he) is. Through developmental feedback, the client also needs to be made to understand how her present Frame of Reference (manifesting a particular Center of Gravity) colors *everything* that is important about the problem she is bringing forward. Such feedback is crucial, and is methodologically separate from the developmental interview on which it is based.

From this deliberation we begin to see that developmental process consultation has a different time flow compared to traditional process consultation as well as coaching. The difference lies in the fact that the developmental interview becomes the foundation of all subsequent communications between process consultant and client. This fact also highlights the emphasis that is put on the art of developmental feedback, and ways of interweaving feedback with "discussions of the problem." **The way feedback is received by the client acts as a further test of the developmental hypothesis that has been formulated.** The reader finds more information about this issue in Appendix B.

***

Now that we have introduced a definition of developmental – i.e., hypothesis based – listening, we have implicitly introduced notions of *coaching research*, especially notions focused on what empirical evidence consists of. It is worth spelling this out briefly:
  1. Coaching research following an adult-developmental methodology is based on listening, centrally *developmental listening*, and regards the nature of the coaching

relationship as well as developmental patterns characterizing different client groups.

2. The purpose of such research is to gather *evidence*, either about the client, the coach, or the coaching relationship.
3. There is no evidence without formulating hypotheses that can be confirmed or rejected.
4. Evidence is thus another word for "confirmed hypotheses."
5. In this sense, evidence is always relative to a particular hypothesis and shares its limitations.
6. When we introduce hypothesis testing into coaching, we are basing coaching on 'coaching research.'
7. When we use conclusions from coaching research in practical coaching work, we engage in 'evidence based coaching.'
8. In the case of developmental coaching – coaching based on developmental listening – the hypotheses we formulate derive from developmental stage theory.
9. By using the tools of developmental stage theory, we promote professionalism in coaching through the use of semi-structured interviews – (social-emotional interviews in volume 1, cognitive interviews in volume 2 of this book).
10. After tape recording, transcribing, and evaluating ('scoring') interviews, we are able to provide feedback to clients on their developmental profile as a foundation for all subsequent coaching interventions and outcome studies.
11. Knowing clients' developmental profile underlies coaching conversations proper, as well as the formulation of coaching plans and any coaching outcome report.
12. **Determining coaching outcome in terms of developmental shifts from one stage to another is a precise way of determining CROI – both individually and for an entire coaching program.**

CHAPTER SUMMARY

In this chapter, I have introduced the reader to an evidence based form of Active Listening. Starting from the conventional ICF definition of listening, I have shown that focusing attention based on research hypotheses is an extension of traditional listening techniques which deepens the professionalism of process consultation generally, and coaching in particular. In the process of clarifying the definition of listening, we have seen that *understanding what the client is saying in the context of the client's desires* is not a scientifically adequate way of defining listening. This is the case because the crucial question in listening for interventions is: *how clients' desires get generated based on their Frame of Reference in the first place*. We have shown that desires as reported are just CONTENT and cannot serve as guidelines for understanding clients, except very superficially. **What is required is to understand the *meaning generator* that provides clients with desires in the first place.** (Without meaning making, the client would not have any desires, and even if s(he) had any, s(he) couldn't communicate them other than perhaps silently, through gestures – a very limited, though dramatic way of doing so.)

In the foregoing, I have implicitly indicated the steps that comprise developmental coaching. It is worthwhile, however, to spell out these steps in greater detail. We can say that the process has six sequential steps, the first two of which are directly tied to Active Listening:

1. Intake assessments.
2. Evaluation and 'scoring' of assessment findings.
3. Feedback to client.
4. Use of findings in negotiating (data-based) a coaching plan.
5. Use of findings – and confirmation of findings – in subsequent coaching conversations.
6. Repeat of assessments to assess coaching outcome (CROI).

What remains now is to summarize in some more detail the actual process of interviewing that takes place in developmental interventions.

Once you have introduced the client to the stage interview and received a signed agreement, you begin by handing the client the ten index cards on which the individual prompts are written. You follow this up by going through the index cards with the client, explaining what the individual prompts mean. Thereafter, you give the client a few minutes to review the prompts, in order to let you know what prompt to begin the interview with.

Let's say the client has chosen the prompt 'Control' to start the interview with. The client is thereby giving you a chance to elicit developmental information in the context of what 'Control' may mean to him or her. Obviously, the client feels that control is an important issue. The client is also indicating that s(he) can think of a recent incident in which the control issue – in whatever form – has come up in a memorable way. We can say that the client is now ready for a PROJECTIVE TEST REGARDING THE MEANING OF *CONTROL* IN HER LIFE OR WORK.

By *projective* is meant that the client has chosen 'Control' as a prompt into which to project his or her own meaning making. This is exactly what we need the client to do! As interviewers, we now have a chance to witness, document, and probe the client's meaning making process as exhaustively as necessary to confirm a stage hypothesis. The goal of this process is to research (find out) from what specific stage the client is actually making meaning of control.

The interview process typically lasts about 60 minutes. This includes the time needed to introduce the interview, explain the prompts, and have the client search for the first prompt to converse about. When these preparations are completed, we can begin to record the interview. Without such recording, it would be very hard, even for an expert, to provide a correct SCORE about which to give feedback to the client.

CHAPTER HIGHLIGHTS

Listening takes many forms and can be conducted in a more or less evidence focused way. Conventional, content-based interviews are not suitable for evidence based process consultation. To engage in developmental consultation, the consultant is charged with the mandate to understand "where the client is coming from developmentally," having at least an inkling of his or her own developmental level (and thus coaching level). By fulfilling that mandate, the consultant positions him- or herself as a helper who can refrain from premature 'helping,' basing the consultative work on precise knowledge of the social-emotional issues that impede solutions to the client's problem. The consultant is on even more solid ground when s(he) also assesses the client's cognitive grasp, in a way fully explained in volume 2 of this book.

From this chapter, the reader might want to take away the following insights regarding *benefits of the client*:

1. In being actively engaged with the consultant's interviewing process, the client becomes the focus of attention of a helping process that is based on empirical evidence articulating his or her own meaning making process.
2. This process provides an objective 'mirror' in which the client can 'see' the presenting problem in greater objectivity, and this makes the client becomes an equal partner in the joint diagnosis of the problem stated.
3. Through the interview, the client gains a deeper awareness of his or her own meaning making as the root of the problem initially presented to the consultant.
4. Through the consultant's developmental feedback, the client learns to fully own the problem, to the extent that s(he) is able to developmentally (and this extent is known to the consultant).
5. Through feedback, the client begins to understand external process events as the *mirage* that they are, realizing that all of her problems are a function of her ascertained Center of Gravity (and cognitive profile).
6. Since the client's developmental potential is also assessed and given feedback on, the client may be helped to make an internal, developmental shift that can be more important and impacting than 'solving' the problem initially formulated.
7. Through such a shift, the client may become able to position herself toward peers and reports in a new way that casts the so-called problem in a form more amenable to a 'solution' (if one exists).
8. As a consequence, the client is better equipped for working on the *real* problem, using some of the techniques conveyed to her by the consultant during the developmental intake and feedback process.

From the perspective of the <u>process consultant</u>, the following aspects of developmentally deepened consulting work would seem to be most relevant:

1. The use of a unified conceptual, empirically validated framework frees the consultant from using a theory of helping that is out of touch with where the client is developmentally (thus with how the world shows up for the client).
2. By formulating and testing explicit social-emotional and cognitive hypotheses about the client (and/or her environment), the consultant gains objectivity, not only regarding who the client is, but also regarding his/her own theory of helping and its applicability to particular clients.
3. Based on empirical knowledge of how the client, from her particular Center of Gravity, generates problems, observations, reactions, judgments, and goals helps the process consultant to generate more realistic action plans.
4. The more the consultant knows about his or her own Center of Gravity substantially improves the chances for success with clients.
5. In developmental process consultation, the consultation proper is preceded by an 'intake' phase where data are gathered about what interventions with the client are promising, and which don't make any sense.
6. Concretely, developmental intake is based on focusing and supporting attention in all of its forms:

  a. attention directing questions
  b. probing
  c. rephrasing
  d. reminding
  e. summarizing
  f. (empathic) acknowledgment
  g. asking permission (to insist, to repeat, to keep probing)

7. When crossing over into evidence based practice through structured, stage-specific listening, the notion of *process consultation* is methodologically deepened and practically refined in the sense of a research-based enterprise in which the consultant functions as the evidence gathering instrument.

Practice Reflections

- What, for you, is *active listening*?
- How do you enter and leave it?
- What new aspects of active listening has the chapter made you aware of?
- In terms of what you have read so far, what aspects of the client and the client's situation seem to have up to now escaped your attention?
- How do you typically *make up your mind* as to what as your client's 'main issues,' and how would you critically look at that process from the perspective of this chapter?
- As you have matured as an adult and professional, how would you say have you deepened your listening (be precise)?
- When you imagine that what produces your client's verbal content is a *thinking and feeling generator* different from your own, how does that change your way of listening?
- When you begin to separate out *content* from *structure* in what you hear from your client, what kinds of structure emerge?
- What kinds of hypothesis would you say you typically formulate in your practice, and how do you go about testing them in the absence of developmental knowledge?
- How does the probing for content you typically carry out differ from the probing for structure that this chapter is focused on?
- Which of the requirements of developmental listening are the most novel to you?

5
How Spread Out Between Risk and Potential is Your Client?: Making Finer Distinctions Between Stages

The reader now knows at an elementary level what developmental stages are, why they are important to know about in any kind of intervention with people, and how to go about eliciting correct information about them in conversation with a particular client. Before we practice the interviewing process more assiduously, we need to know a little more about the journey from one main stage to another.

In particular, we need to acquire a vocabulary and a notation to make finer distinctions as to "where a client is developmentally." It is the task of this chapter to bring this about. We are going to talk about INTERMEDIATE STAGES, the pattern they form, and the RISK-CLARITY-POTENTIAL INDEX their knowledge permits us to compute. Once we have absorbed this additional information, we will be better prepared to understand illustrations of intermediate stages.

To begin with, it might be good to recall that stages are modes of functioning in the social world, and that each of them is characterized by a certain *psychology* or mind set. This is made clear by a quote from Clare Graves (1981), a developmental researcher:

Briefly, what I am proposing is that the psychology of the mature human being is an unfolding, emergent, oscillating spiraling process marked by progressive subordination of older, lower-order behavior systems to newer, higher-order systems as man's existential problems change. Each successive stage, wave, or level of existence is a state through which people pass on their way to other states of being. **When the human is centralized in one state of existence (center of gravity), he or she has a psychology which is particular to that state (**bolding by O.L.**).** His or her feelings, motivations, ethics and values, biochemistry, degree of neurological activation, learning system, belief systems, conception of mental health, ideas as to what mental illness is and how it should be treated, conceptions of and preferences for management, education, economics, and political theory and practice are all appropriate to that state.

What Graves calls 'a psychology which is particular to that state' might equally be called an 'epistemology' or way of knowing. We already know quite a bit about, say, the epistemology of S-2, a self-centered state of mind in which others' thinking and feeling is not internalized but remains external to, and separate from, the individual concerned. We also know about the consequences of such a self-world perspective, briefly summarized below:

Orientation	S-2	Intermediate Stages	S-3
View of Others	Instruments of own need gratification	?	Needed to contribute to own self image
Level of Self Insight	Low	?	Moderate
Values	Law of Jungle	?	Community
Needs	Overriding all others' needs	?	Subordinate to community, work group
Need to Control	Very High	?	Moderate

Communication	Unilateral	?	Exchange 1:1
Organizational Orientation	Careerist	?	Good Citizen

Table I.1. Changing orientations across adult stages

The interesting question now arises: how is an S-2 way of knowing transformed into that of a subsequent stage? This much we already know: the change occurs in stages, thus discontinuously, through little jumps whose timing is hard to predict since it depends on the developmental potential available to an individual. We also know that age and education are weak predictors of when and how this might happen. Interestingly, though, there is PATTERN to such changes, or rather developments, and these patterns are recursive, meaning they re-occur between all main stages.

In order to understand what I mean by *pattern*, let's have a bird's eye view at the entire journey from S-1 (infancy) to S-5:

Trajectory of Social-Emotional Stages

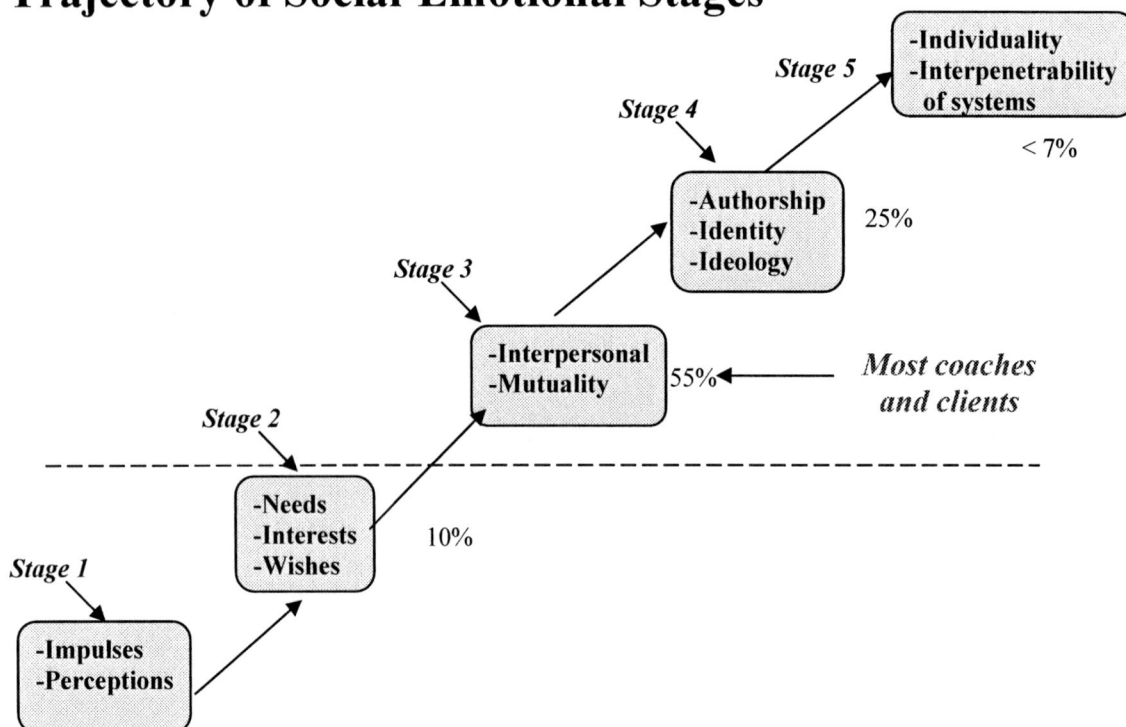

Fig. 5.1 Trajectory of social-emotional development in adults
(Courtesy James Brits)

Given that research has found (at least) four *intermediate* stages to occur between each of the main stages – which between S-2 and S-5 altogether yields 16 – it would be clarifying if we could assume some kind of *pattern* according to which the journey between the main stages is made by individuals. This would potentially provide us with a conceptual framework within which movement to and between intermediate stages could be understood regardless of the particular range of stages.

Orientation	S-2	Intermediate Stages	S-3
View of Others	Instruments of own need gratification	?	Needed to contribute to own self image

Table I.1 Changing orientations across adult stages

What, in other words, are the steps by which an individual who can take only a single perspective – his or her own – will transform this stance or *epistemology* into one where others are valued as community members who can act as guarantors of their own self-identity and self-cohesion?

One would surmise that when one steps away from a main stage, such as S-2, one would do so very tentatively. After all, in a step beyond any stage, not only the View of Others, but EVERYTHING in the individual's world view is going to change. We can say with R. Kegan that the individual's 'subject-object relations' are then in a state of transformation. This term is useful for reminding us that the changes we talk about here regard what an individual is "subject to," and what the individual "can take as object," or reflect upon (and thus can be responsible for). In short, we are talking about changes in the ability of taking responsibility for oneself. These surely are transformational changes that pervade everything else in the individual's life.

Distribution of stages: Nobody makes meaning on a single level, but acts from a <u>Center of Gravity</u> (S), risking regression (S-1) and open to surpassing self (S+1)

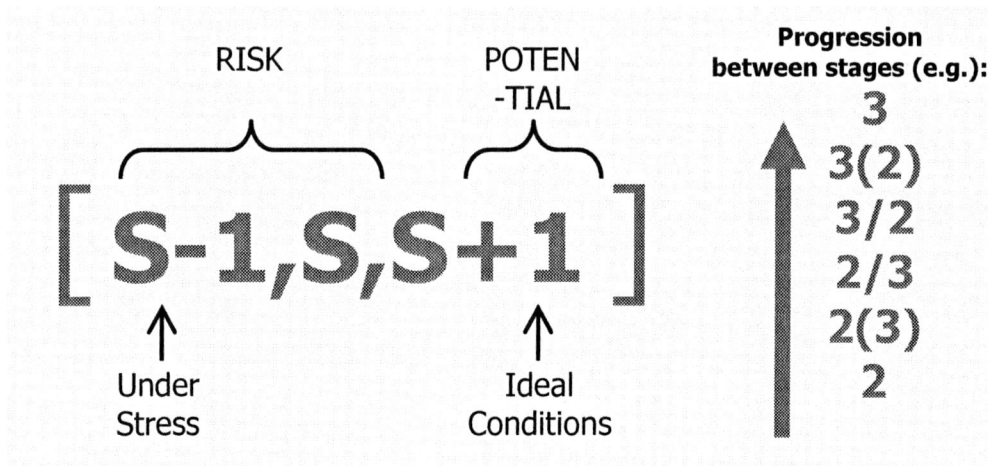

Fig. 5.2 Intermediate developmental stages

The diagram above introduces another consideration worthy of our attention. Given the complexity of consciousness, it is unlikely that people live at a single stage and only that stage. It is more persuasive to assume that they live within a certain RANGE of stages, say from S-2 to about halfway up to S-3. Another way to conceptualize this might be to say that individuals act from a single, most important stage that serves as a **Center of Gravity**, and that surely they may at times act from a 'lower' and a 'higher' stage, depending on the strength of their developmental potential. In other words, the CLARITY of the Center of Gravity may shift depending on how much the individual lives at a lower stage, and how much on a higher one.

Using the notation on the left side of Fig. 5-2, we can say that, at any time, individuals live at a certain stage serving as a Center of Gravity (S) from which they can 'regress' to a lower stage (S-1), and equally can 'transcend and include' (Wilber, 2000) their present Center of Gravity by acting from a higher stage (S+1). By saying so, we are introducing the terms of RISK and POTENTIAL, – risk for acting from the lower stage(s), and potential to act for a higher stage. This conceptualization leads us to the following two conclusions:
1. Adult development occurs between Main Stages such that nobody "jumps" from one Main Stage to another; instead, people make little steps one at a time.
2. While most people are *spread out* over no more than three stages at a time, namely S-1 (risk), S (clarity), and S+1 (potential), it does happen that an individual's present functioning is stretched out over four or perhaps even five stages. (The latter case is very rare, in my experience, and either points to a mistake made in scoring an interview, or to a developmental issue of its own kind (e.g., fragility).

I have now introduced a way of thinking about the progression through stages that will help us become very precise about where exactly an individual presently makes meaning of her life and work. As said, individuals, rather than living at a single stage, live within a RANGE of stages, where the typical range comprises three stages: S-1 (the lower stage), S (the center of Gravity), and S+1 (the higher stage). I have implied that to proceed from S to S+1 requires the existence of DEVELOPMENTAL POTENTIAL, and that regressing from S to S-1 is a matter of DEVELOPMENTAL RISK.

The question now arises whether, through the evaluation of interviews, we could arrive at a kind of **index** that would signal in a short-hand notation what are the proportions in terms of which an individual presently lives at S-1, S, and S+1, respectively. Such an index would be highly welcome in coaching and other interventions, because it would spell out the amount of developmental risk and potential a person's Center of Gravity is presently associated with. For instance, if a client's developmental risk (to act from S-1) is much higher than his or her potential (S+1), our intervention might have to be more remedial than being focused on enhancing and realizing the client's potential.

In order to arrive at what I will call the *RISK-POTENTIAL-CLARITY INDEX*, -- where 'clarity' refers to the Center of Gravity (S), we need to return to the issue of how an individual might 'step away' from one stage and 'move toward' another.
Going back to the Trajectory diagram, above, we can formulate:

- When initially stepping away from a Center of Gravity (S), an individual has only just begun to disengage from a world view that up to now has defined for him or her 'who I am.'
- Consequently, the individual is experiencing a certain *loss of self*, which means s(he) is no longer as strongly embedded in S as s(he) has been previously, and therefore may be at a loss as to knowing 'how the world has changed for me.'

Since nobody can step backwards into an old self, except temporarily and at some psychological cost, the individual's journey will have to continue. If we notate the pattern of intermediate steps between main stages as a➜b➜c➜d, what happens when an individual gets from stage 'a' to stages 'b' and 'c'? Here are some suggestions:

- Having left behind safe harbor S, by moving to S(a), and aiming for the next higher Main Stage, when moving to S(b), the person will not only feel uncertain about him- or herself, but will actually get into a conflict. Why? Because s(he) is now under the influence of two different stages simultaneously, for instance, of S-2 and S-3.
- Consequently, the conflict in consciousness is one between acting according to S-2 or S-3.
- This conflict will be confusing the person because the safety of S-2 has vanished and the certainty of S-3 has not yet been attained.

There is, of course, a difference in thinking and feeling between arriving at S(b) and at S(c), simply because S(c) is closer to the next higher main stage than is S(b). If we are talking about the journey from S-2 to S-3, for instance, the person at S(c) will be more likely to act according to the higher stage, here S-3 (other-dependence) than at S(b). However, both S(b) and S(c) define developmentally conflictual states since at both positions both stages in question equally influence the individual. The crucial difference between S(b) and S(c) is that S(b), the individual resolves the stage conflict in favor of the *lower* stage, e.g., S-2, while at S(c), s(he) will for the first time act in a manner one would expect from an S-3 individual.

What is going to happen at S(d), the last intermediate stage before reaching, e.g., S-3? Clearly, the individual will talk up a storm about being at, and acting from, S-3, because anything that reminds him or her of S-2 is just unacceptable at this point. Not only to convince others, but mainly to convince him- or herself, the person will have to hammer home that S-2 is passé, and that the only way to act authentically is now S-3. In short, we will hear a lot of *espousal* about being at a higher stage from this individual simply because that's not where the person is right now! If the person had already reached the higher stage, such espousal would be unnecessary.

To sum up, when you leave a Center of Gravity such as S-2, – think of a person in late adolescence, – you pass through the following phases:
- S(a): strong inclination to act from S-2
- S(b): conflict between S-2 and S-3, resolved toward S-2
- S(c): conflict between S-2 and S-3, resolved toward S-3
- S(d): shaky grasp of S-3, with a lot of espousal of already being at S-3.

Adopting Kegan's precedent, we can refine our adopted notation. The notation we will adopt will change according to where along the stage trajectory we are, that is, whether we are moving from S-2 to S-3, S-3 to S-4, or S-4 to S-5. For the case of S-2 and S-3, we will write:

- S(a) = 2(3): strong inclination to act from S-2
- S(b) = 2/3: conflict resolved toward S-2
- S(c) = 3/2: conflict resolved toward S-3
- S(d) = 3(2): shaky grasp of S-3.

The information above is summarized in the following diagram:

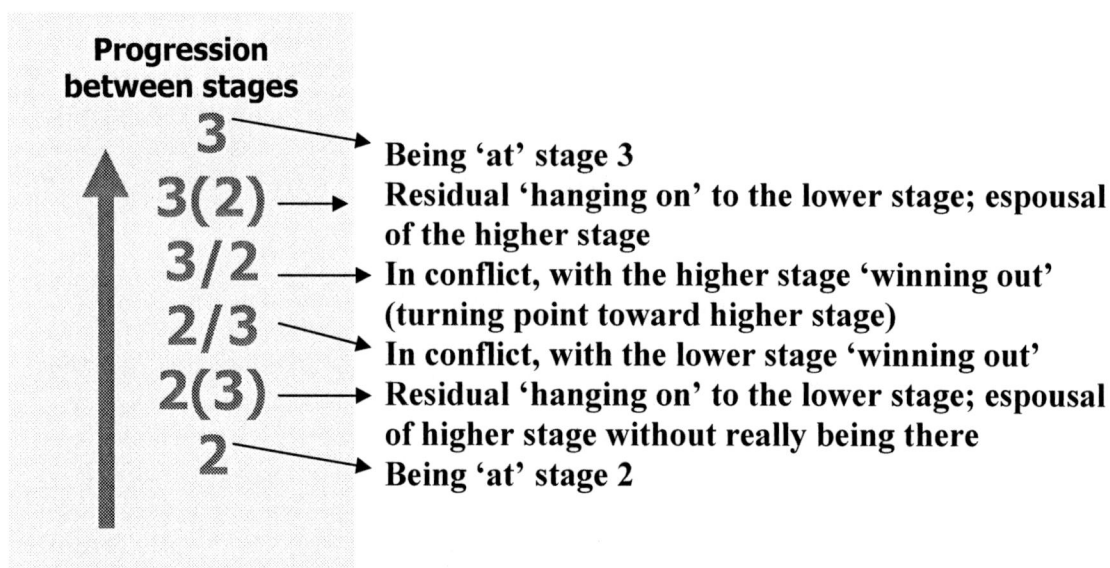

Progression between stages

3 → Being 'at' stage 3

3(2) → Residual 'hanging on' to the lower stage; espousal of the higher stage

3/2 → In conflict, with the higher stage 'winning out' (turning point toward higher stage)

2/3 → In conflict, with the lower stage 'winning out'

2(3) → Residual 'hanging on' to the lower stage; espousal of higher stage without really being there

2 → Being 'at' stage 2

Fig. 5.3 Progression from S-2 to S-3

As seen above, round brackets signify either a first step away from a Main Stage [2(3)] or a last step just prior to reaching a subsequent Main Stage [3(2)]. Thus the brackets indicate something like "a little distance from the Main Stage." In the case that the integer in brackets is higher then the integer in front of the bracket – 2(3), 3(4), 4(5) – we are at the beginning of the journey towards the higher stage. By contrast, when the integer in brackets is lower than the one in front of the bracket – as in 3(2), 4(3), 5(4) – we are at the end of the journey towards the higher stage.

This notation holds true for all stages. Therefore, we can say that the pattern of progression from a lesser to a higher stage is *recursive*. The meaning of the steps forming the progression is, of course, specific to the particular range, and is thus different for the journey from S-2 to S-3, S3 to S-4, and S-4 to S-5.

We have now moved halfway toward understanding the *Risk-Clarity-Potential Index* (RCP). This index will enable us to describe a client's present Center of Gravity with precision. In addition, we will be able to specify what kind of *developmental risk* – to act from a lower stage – the client is encountering, and what kind of *developmental potential* – for stepping up to a subsequent stage – the client is presently harboring. Clearly, this is important information, not just about individuals, but entire groups, and not just for coaching clients, but for any intervention we may want to undertake to boost a person's mental growth (see Appendices B, C, and D).

To understand the Risk-Clarity-Potential Index still better, let's consider what an interview looks like that has been recorded and/or transcribed. A 50-minute interview, when transcribed, can occupy between 12 to 15 (or more) single space *pages*, depending on the skill of the interviewer and the verbosity of the client. Our task as readers of the interview is to read through it and identify those interview sections or paragraphs that have 'structural relevance.' By this is meant those sections that, regardless of content, clearly reveal a stage, main or intermediate.

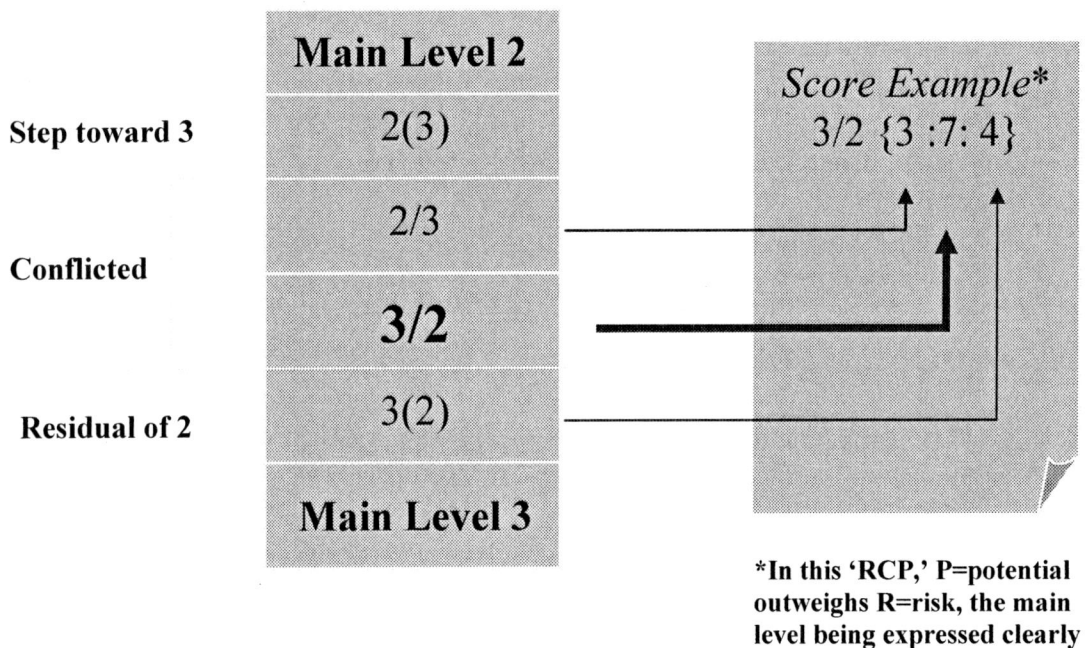

Fig. 5.4 Computing the Risk-Clarity-Potential Index (RCP)

The reader will ask: How can such sections be determined? Clearly, to do so presupposes knowledge of stage theory, developmental listening, and developmental interviewing – just what we will study further in subsequent chapters. For now, let's complete the discussion of the RCP.

Let's assume that a developmentally schooled reader of an interview (or listener to an interview tape) has found 14 structurally relevant sections, and has scored them according to their respective levels. The reader has found that the range of the interviewee's stages lies between S-2/3 and S-3(2). The diagram above makes this more clear.

As the right part of the diagram indicates in curly brackets, half of the scored interview sections (=7) articulate S-3/2, 3 indicate the lower level S-2/3, and 4 indicate the higher level S-3(2). In short, the client's Center of Gravity (S) is S-3/2, her risk level is S-2/3 (S-1), and her potential is S-3(2) (S+1), and these three aspects are weighted just as shown by the RCP on the right.

Concretely, we have before us a client who is presently conflicted between acting according to constraints of S-2, on one hand, and S-3, on the other. In the majority of cases, the client is acting from a Center of Gravity of S-3/2, and is thus able to resolve the developmental conflict in favor of S-3 (7 times), while in a minority of cases s(he) resolves the conflict in favor of S-2 (3 times). Also, there are 4 cases in which the client indicates an ability to think, feel, and relate in terms of the higher level of S-3(2). Since there are fewer indications of risk than potential, we can say that the client's developmental potential outweighs her developmental risks (although only slightly, and within the margin of error). This is important information since it suggests the type of intervention or coaching that promises to be most effective.

We can write this interview scoring result in a compact form. To do so, we first state the Center of Gravity, and then, in curly brackets, specify the relative weight of the three adjacent levels in the form of the **Risk-Clarity-Potential Index,** or RCP. Using a compact notation, in this case we would write:

Center of Gravity	Risk	Clarity	Potential
3/2	3	7	4
Notation: 3/2 {3: 7: 4}			

Table 5.1 Example of the spread of stages

We speak of 'clarity' to indicate the clarity with which the Center of Gravity is expressed in relation to risk and potential. If we spell out this compact SCORE, we find:

S-1	S	S+1
Risk	Clarity	Potential
2/3	3/2	3(2)
3	7	4

Table 5.2 Example RCP

Let's recall the title of this chapter: *How Spread Out Between Risk and Potential is Your Client?: Making Finer Distinctions Between Stages.* This is indeed what we have ascertained: the client is 'spread out' between risk and potential with a clarity index of 7 which shows that she is *strongly embedded* in her present Center of Gravity. Depending on how long the client has been at that stage, this could either be a natural result of having just reached the S-3/2, or if she has been at this stage for some time, it could indicate some kind of developmental arrest (stuckness). As we can see, the client has a potential to proceed to S-3(2) that is larger than what is holding her back, – or makes her regress to her risk level of S-2/3.

What kind of a person do we have before us? Briefly – the subsequent chapters will help you greatly in getting more of a perspective on this – the person before us is on a journey that we can now describe more clearly.

Orientation	S-2	Intermediate Stages	S-3
View of Others	Instruments of own need gratification	3/2 {3: 7: 4}	Needed to contribute to own self image

Table 5.3 RCP defining the transition from S-2 to S-3

To focus on the most important social-emotional aspect, the person's view of others, we can say that she is presently centered on (embedded in) a conflictual state where both S-2 and S-3 are determining how she views others outside and inside of herself. Most of the time, she is able to view others as 'needed to contribute to her self image,' where they are the guarantors of her self cohesion (S-3/2). However, there are also situations where she tends to see others rather as instruments of her own need gratification (S-2/3), thus remaining bound to what is essentially an S-2 behavior and outlook. When she is at her best, she can actually do better than S-3/2, and, proceeding to S-3(2), can talk up a storm about being part of her community, serving that community, and defining herself in terms of it. This is her potential. She has obviously learned to adopt conventions even if they contradict her immediate needs and desires. She is beginning to become a valuable member of civil society who has the strength to override her own need gratification when required. However, to do so still takes a lot of effort.

In the example above, the client is 'spread out' over three stages: 2/3, 3/2, and 3(2). This is described by her RCP, in curly brackets. What is the RCP like should a person be more spread out, say, over five levels? For example:

S-2	S-1	S	S+1	S+2
2(3)	2/3	3/2	3(2)	3
1	2	7	2	2
Notation: 3/2 {3: 7: 4}				

Fig. 5.4 Example RCP #1

As you can see, the RCP has not changed, but the distribution of stages over the person's range has been altered. All we have done is to sum the two lower and the two higher stages, to indicate risk and potential, respectively. This is entirely legitimate, because both S-2 and S-1 together indicate risk, while S+1 and S+2 together indicate potential. However, should the scoring of the interview be correct, there is now an additional factor of developmental uncertainty (fragility) that is expressed by the larger spread of the scores. The following example indicates even more uncertainty:

S-2	S-1	S	S+1	S+2
2(3)	2/3	3/2	3(2)	3
2	*1*	7	3	1
Notation: 3/2 {3: 7: 4}				

Fig. 5.5 Example RCP #2

As you will note, here the lowest stage scored – S-2(3) – is more strongly represented than the next higher one (S-2/3), while the Center of Gravity has not changed and the potential has been unevenly split between S-3(2) and S-3. The person concerned has actually fully reached S-3, but only quite faintly (=1). She has major issues to work out, giving how spread out she is between S-2 and S-3. To judge from the score, she must be very confounded, both in her life and her work. As developmental experts, we can see that right away.

As you will agree, the notation demonstrated above is very subtle and flexible. It is actually not only a problem-solving, but a *problem-posing*, device! This is so since the notation indicates with precision not only the range of developmental spread but also the proportions to which intermediate stages within the person's range are present. Once we are competent scorers, we can notate shadings of risk and developmental potential that are very helpful when thinking about how to approach a particular client.

A word of caution is also in order here: PEOPLE 'ARE' NOT THEIR DEVELOP-MENTAL SCORES OR EVEN STAGE! This cannot be said often enough. Developmental scores are simply a short-hand for describing very complex findings about Self and Other in a concise way, especially for communicating between developmental experts. There is no real need to communicate such precise scores to clients. Rather, it belongs to the art of process consultation, to use such scores as a conceptual framework for approaching client problems based on estimating developmental risks and potentials. This especially holds for giving feedback on the interviews.

For example, let's compare two clients, both having a communication problem:

- Client 1:

S-2	S-1	S	S+1	S+2
3(4)	3/4	4/3	4(3)	4
2	1	7	3	1
Developmental Score = 3/2 {3: 7: 4}				

Table 5.6 Example of large developmental spread

- Client 2:

S-1	S	S+1
3/4	4/3	4(3)
3	7	4
Developmental Score = 3/2 {3: 7: 4}		

Table 5.7 Example of small (more typical) developmental spread

As seen, both clients have the same RCP, except that client #1 is spread out over 5, and client #2 over 3, stages. Also, both clients' score shows a potential that is higher than their risk to act from lower levels (3<4). In regard to 'communicating better,' what might this entail?

Here are some suggestions:

- Both clients are embedded in their present level (S-4/3) to an equal degree, such that they have made a developmental shift that supports them in coming to grips with their internalized others, and to be more solidly able to act from their own integrity.
- For both clients, communication is fraught with conflicts since they are enmeshed in the struggle between being defined by others' expectations and their own values and principles, respectively.
- Although client #1 'reaches higher' in developmental level, namely fully to self-authoring, the solidity of this reach is weak, and is compromised by the stark risk to act from two levels below the Center of Gravity (S-3(4)).
- Client #1 is also developmentally more fragile, since more spread out, and thus less predictable for others than client #2.
- In terms of communicating with others, this would seem to entail that client #1 is more likely to be attached to communicating as member of a group, with the goal of remaining 'in synch,' valued, boosted, supported, and helped by the group, and more unlikely to risk being ostracized than client #2. Therefore, client #1 is likely to 'play it safe' to a higher degree than client #2, and is therefore potentially a less forceful communicator and less effective change agent.
- As a result, the communication issues of both clients, despite the same RCP, would seem quite different developmentally, regardless of the specific content of what they are communicating about.
- In terms of intervention, it would seem easier for the process consultant to work with client #2 whose narrower developmental range and non-diffuse potential promises better outcome.
- A coach taking on client #1 would have to be solidly at S-4 to encounter the likelihood of success, whereas a coach of client #2 might 'get away with' being at S-4(3) where a lot of espousals are still heard.

Given the richness of the compact RCP scores, how is feedback to be given by the process consultant? Concretely, how would feedback on social-emotional findings differ for the two clients above, regardless of their behavioral and cognitive issues?

In my practice, I give feedback to clients in accordance with my assessment of their ability to appreciate findings they themselves could not surmise, given that they are subject to their developmental level. I am aware that feedback to clients in the range from S-3 to S-4 is fundamentally different from feedback to clients in the range from S-4 to S-5, due to their different ability of being objective about themselves. By 'objective,' I mean the degree of freedom from internalized others and the attendant ability of grasping one's present strengths and challenges. I know I prefer clients who have made it beyond S-4, simply because that is the point where they have themselves begun to 'de-construct' their splendid success story, so that the burden of doing so is no longer entirely mine. Another issue that determines my feedback to clients is their cognitive profile (see volume 2). Clients who can think systemically are better able, of course, to put their own life and limits in perspective within whatever system they choose as the set of coordinates to work within.

Since S-3 clients define themselves by the expectations of others, it is easy for them to be engaged in some internal *entanglement* with the coach, especially if the practitioner's coaching level is also S-3. In that case, both parties constitute for each other internalized others that are hard to sort out for both of them. In this context, feedback regarding a developmental finding, given by a practitioner who does not know his or her own Center of Gravity, is certainly risky for the relationship. The way the entanglement works out for both parties can take many forms. Essentially, though, what is missing in the relationship is the ability of the intervening practitioner, to take the client's Center of Gravity as object, rather than either identifying with it, or feeling responsible for (or guilty about) it in some way. The need for the practitioner, to function at a higher developmental stage could not be more obvious.

The above considerations also apply to S-4 if client and practitioner share that particular Center of Gravity. In this case, entanglement is replaced by *detachment*. The closer the respective centers of the parties are to each other (in the range around S-4), the higher is the risk that a kind of defensiveness creeps in where one or the other party feels like being 'on top' of the other. Cognitive and behavioral aspects of the parties' developmental profile will decide how exactly and to what extent such defensiveness may erode the helping relationship.

As far as the two clients discussed above are concerned, here are some hunches as to what kind of feedback and coaching plan might be more appropriate for each of them:

- Since client #2 is developmentally less fragile (less distributed over the range of levels), I would see feedback more straightforwardly geared to realizing the client's potential, rather than focusing feedback on remedial action.
- In terms of improving behavioral issues such as 'communicating better,' I would, to explain the RCP, elicit information from the client about communication issues that occur at S-3/4; at that level, clients need to make a major effort to assert themselves as to being master in their own house.
- I would also want to find out what is the meaning of the fact that the client's developmental potential (for acting from 4(3)) is higher than the risk of communicating from a lower, less self-authored level.
- I would therefore deliver my feedback in steps, not in a single session, since initially I don't have enough information about the actual scenarios in which communication problems occur for the client, and how they are perceived by her.
- Regarding client #1, I would ponder the fact that the weight of risk and potential together is equal to the client's degree of embeddedness at S-4/3. I would do so because the wider the spread around a Center of Gravity, the less secure or 'clear' can such a center be, both for the client and the process consultant.
- In the case of client #1, I would expect a sense of being *confused* on the client's part (and therefore mine), given that the 'wings of the bird' (the developmental spread) can, in this case, barely support the bird itself that wants to fly.

- With regard to communication problems that arise I would predict that the client's internal mental space when communicating with others is criss-crossed by numerous contradictory paths (predictions) of what the other party wants to (or will) hear, which predictably leads to confusion in the recipients of the communication as to "what is really meant" by the speaker.
- In short, rather than give comprehensive but abstract feedback, I would wait for the client to tell me – demonstrate to me would be even better – what communicating with others 'feels like,' so as to have some behavioral evidence based on which I can develop a coaching plan using role plays focused on 'communicating better.'

6
How to Understand Developmental Conflict

By now, the reader has absorbed the information in Table 1.1 of Chapter 1 to the extent possible without actually practicing how to discern individual stages on his or her own. We have moved *between* the different columns of the Table but not *within* them, except for indicating the general patterns that the 'within column' changes typically follow (chapter 5). In short, the foundations for a deeper understanding of what happens within each of the columns have now been laid.

Orientation	S-2	S-3	S-4	S-5
View of Others	Instruments of own need gratification	Needed to contribute to own self image	Collaborator, delegate, peer	Contributors to own integrity and balance
Level of Self Insight	Low	Moderate	High	Very High
Values	Law of Jungle	Community	Self-determined	Humanity
Needs	Overriding all others' needs	Subordinate to community, work group	Flowing from striving for integrity	Viewed in connection with own obligations and limitations
Need to Control	Very High	Moderate	Low	Very low
Communication	Unilateral	Exchange 1:1	Dialogue	True Communication
Organizational Orientation	Careerist	Good Citizen	Manager	System's Leader

Table I.1. Changing orientations across adult stages

The next step we'll take is to go into more detail about what the intermediate steps between the main stages, those 'within' each of the columns, really look and feel like, and what sets them apart from each other in each of the different ranges (S-2 to S-3, S-3 to S-4, S-4 to S-5).

At this point, it is important to distinguish between learning from ILLUSTRATIONS of stages, and ACTUAL INTERVIEWS. In actual interviews there are, as you will surmise, no indicators at all of what range of stages is involved. The developmentally unschooled listener/reader therefore finds herself in a 'no man's land.' It is this no man's land that this chapter is meant to lead you out of.

The first step in listening to, or reading, interviews consists of defining the range over which an interviewee is *spread out*, as we called it in Chapter 5. But even this is initially too difficult, since one and the same content can be spoken (made meaning of) at more than a single stage. What is needed is an illustration of the (four) intermediate steps between a main stage and its follower, say S-2 and S-3. Once we understand the gradual transition from one end of the range to the other, we can apply this knowledge to all possible ranges. In line with this, the present chapter will assist the reader in learning how to move through the full range from S-2 to S-3, and on to S4 to S4-5, by way of illustrations.

Before going into detail, let's consider one general finding we have already ascertained. We have seen that when you leave a main stage at x(y) – where x is the lower and y the higher stage – you are on shaky ground. You are leaving a safe haven for the unknown, and you are likely to encounter increasing LOSS OF SELF as you proceed. When you get to x/y, you are basically still at x. You have gone as far as you can go without letting go of x (the lower stage), and this has brought you into deep conflict between x and y (the higher stage). You escape that conflict by resolving it to x, your 'home,' as it were.

But there comes a time when resolving conflicts in the accustomed to manner becomes impossible for you. The losses mount, and the gains begin to be seen in moving to y/x, where the lower stage is beginning to be left behind. This first bridge head is also embattled, and it takes decisive action to hold it and move on. You may need support, as troops do that have just crossed a strategically important river, or landed on some enemy coast. When you finally reach y/x, you have for the first time reached the territory of the higher stage, namely y. You have shown that you are able to distance yourself internally from your S-2, S-3, or S-4 personality, whatever it may be. You have achieved a decisive victory!

Now what? You must go on, regardless of the losses incurred. When you are in the range from S-2 to S-3, the social surround will help you. There are, after all, *social forcing functions* that make people adopt conventions even if they don't like them (or else they may end up in jail, if they are caught, or be punished publicly in some other way). This, however, does not hold for the range of S-3 to S-4, and certainly not for the range from S-4 to S-5. There are no or few social supports. Essentially, YOU ARE ON YOUR OWN!

So you go on, somewhat battered but proud, so to speak, persevering on your path toward the higher stage. What is shifting in this journey has been described by Kegan abstractly as *subject-object relations*. This is a helpful concept. Let's explore it further.

Kegan means by 'subject' what you are subject to, and thus not in control of, while 'object' is what you can make into an object of reflection. Since people are not in control of their present stage, they are subject to it. You know this since you have learned that it is only by hindsight that you discovered aspects of yourself you were previously not aware of. This is the universal truth. Do you recall the separation from your 'family religion' and family conventions you didn't know you were subject to before you divorced yourself from them? At that point, you made an object of them and moved on. YOU CHANGED YOUR SUBJECT-OBJECT RELATIONS!

More generically, a newborn is totally subject to itself, without any object to 'know,' – no other, mother, brother, or what have you. However, as the newborn grows it becomes a child, an adolescent, and adult. What happens in terms of stage, essentially, is that the subject shrinks and the object grows on the person. Consequently, in later adulthood, the person will have shed much of her subjectivity and acquired a larger and larger object, including a deeper understanding of self. In short, the teleology – the direction – of adult development is one of self-discovery, self-development, surpassing older notions of self, and thereby revolutionizing what is 'other than you,' or the world at large. From a developmental vantage point, life is a discovery procedure.

Let's keep this overall tendency in mind as we proceed through the intermediate stages. In all cases, we are dealing with **self discovery through self loss**, as paradoxical as that may seem. Take as an example the aspect of View of Others:

Orientation	S-2	S-3	S-4	S-5
View of Others	Instruments of own need gratification	Needed to contribute to own self image	Collaborator, delegate, peer	Contributors to own integrity and balance

Table I.1 Changing orientations across adult stages

To go beyond using people as instruments of your desires you need to find out which of these desires are YOURS, and which may be shared by others. You need to realize that there are habits, needs, ways of thinking shared by all people of your community, and learn to think and feel as they do (S-3). Having done so, you may discover that the conventions adopted by you do not properly reflect your own unique voice. What is more, you need to bring that voice out into the open as yours. You will be on your own in doing this, because only you can know your voice (S-4). But even finding your own voice is not the end of life's journey. When you have 'promoted' others to fully being your peers, and learnt to respect them for who they are, however different, you may need to go still further and leave behind that self authoring splendor of yours (S-4) entirely. You may want to surrender it for a still larger self that not only 'respects' others, but works with them in order to know itself still better (S-5). Of course, less then 10% of people have as long a breath (or as large a developmental potential), but to reach S-5 remains a goal of humanity nevertheless.

Let's start with a summary of all levels in the range from S-2 to S-3. The entries are necessarily short and somewhat cryptic. So, bear with me.

Level	Characteristic
2	Ruled by needs, desires, wishes; 'two world hypothesis'
2(3)	Beginning to be influenced by physical and imagined others
2/3	Conflicted over risking exposure to others' feelings and thoughts; resolution to level 2
3/2	Conflicted, but with more detachment from own needs and desires, resolution to level 3
3(2)	Able to be influenced by imagined others and their expectations
3	Made up of others' expectations; 'our world' hypothesis

Table 6.1 Range characteristics between S-2 and S-3

As you can see, the gist of the S-2 to S-3 journey lies in 'internalizing others' perspective.' Since an S-2 person can hold only a <u>single</u> perspective – his or her own – this means that a SECOND perspective, that of others, has to be absorbed by the person. When this has been achieved, the person ends up defining herself by the *second* perspective. What has happened to the first perspective? **It is still there, but has been thoroughly identified with the second one,** to the extent that you can 'regress' to it but don't feel comfortable doing so. The first perspective (of S-2) is now outside of your comfort zone. It will take reaching S-4 before the first perspective, centered on the self, emerges again with full autonomy (which it does in about 25% of all cases, according to research). That may happen in a decade from now, or less or more. Nobody can predict it. (Certainly not you yourself.)

From Stage 2 to Stage 3: Discovering Yourself as a Social Being

We are now ready to consider an illustration of S-2 (adapted from Lahey et al., 1988, 94-95):

Client: I'm really sad that my colleague lied to me regarding his salary raise. Now I can never be sure when he's telling me the truth. Like if you know a person has lied to someone else or to you before, then you know you just can't count on them.
Interviewer: What do you mean by 'count on them'?
Client: You need to know who the people are that you can turn to when you need truthful information or help.
Interviewer: Like what kind of help are you thinking of?
Client: Like if you're new to a workplace and working very hard to increase your salary, and you don't know whether that would make any difference in the company, you need to know who you can ask to give you the right answer. You need to know whether that person will tell you the truth.

Above, we formulated:

Level	Characteristic
2	Ruled by needs, desires, wishes; 'two world hypothesis'

In what way is the speaker above 'ruled by needs, desires, wishes,' and holds a 'two world hypothesis'?

A two-world hypothesis says that there are two worlds, the speaker's own and the world of others, and the two never coincide or even meet. More than that, I the speaker, don't really care about what your world is like at all. It's MY world I am 'into,' so why should I care about what yours looks like! You can stay with yours, and I'll stay with mine, period.

This stance has certain consequences for living, but also for the concept of truth, as shown by the above illustration. Somebody, a colleague, has lied to the speaker, and this is upsetting. Not so much because lying is not a nice thing to do – as convention tells us – but because it puts the speaker and the gratification of her desires in jeopardy. If I (the speaker) can't be sure that people tell me the truth – and there is only ONE truth – then I can never be sure of anything. And since I can't hold a second perspective, not to be sure of anything is just terrible because it means I CANNOT COUNT ON ANYBODY TO HELP ME OUT.

Counting on somebody is spelled out like this: *"You need to know who the people are that you can turn to when you need truthful information or help."* Truthful information translates to helpful information – information helpful to me – because 'truth' has to do with what I, the speaker, need. So, unless I, the speaker, am all powerful and don't need help, I am in a tough spot. One solution to this situation is to concentrate as much power as I can and tell others what to do, namely to help me when I am in danger. The other is almost impossible to achieve: to make sure that I am never vulnerable, and therefore never need help. Therefore, individuals like the speaker tend to strive for absolute control. The truth for them is black or white. And the world is a dangerous place because there are worlds 'out there' that they know they don't control, that they may not ever be able to control, and that is highly upsetting.

It is timely here to recall our caricature of S-2, discussed previously:

> S-2 is an 'I' stage, characteristic of late teenage and early adulthood, although in our own culture, private sector profit concerns often drive many adults to revert to this stage, at least in their 'world of work.' Persons on this stage are highly, if not totally, steeped in their own wants or needs. They are impulsive, seek immediate gratification for those needs and wants, pay little attention to what others say about them, but will vehemently deny feedback that is not concordant with their own rigid self-perception. Above all else, they are interested in preserving the image they have established for themselves, regardless of how accurate it might be. When challenged, they can be very emotionally explosive and abusive to the feedback's source(s). S(he) readily understands others' perspectives, not out of empathy, but for the sake of knowing how to manipulate them to satisfy their own needs and ends. They will follow socially established (S-3) community rules and conventions when beneficial to them, or as long as they believe they will not be caught or punished. Thus, cheating, lying, deception, and falsification will be used, as necessary, to achieve self-set goals. They can work effectively and productively, if working alone and if their objectives happen to be aligned with those of the organization. In a Leader role, they will tend to micro-manage, exploit others, create ill will and mistrust, and misunderstandings will abound within the team or work group. Unbridled 'careerism' typifies this stage, for those individuals who manage to work their way into positions where they are given any degree of social authority.

The reader will now understand why there exists a *social forcing function* for bringing S-2 individuals into the community, whether they are normal adolescents, gang members, or what not. Civil society would be ruined if S-2 behavior was not kept in check. If there are no moral imperatives S-2 individuals can be taught, at least there have to be legal constraints that do the job. (Remember Enron?).

SUMMARY OF S-2:
- **Instrumentalism:** In the fragment above, the ultimate concern is with whether the speaker will lose a source of help for herself. The speaker's own interests constitute the ground from which she attends to her colleague's perspective. So far, there is no evidence that the speaker attends simultaneously to her own and to the colleague's needs. Consequently, there is not even a beginning of an evolution to S-3.
- **Essence of this stage:** As a self subject to my needs, wishes, and interests, I relate to another person in terms of possible consequences for my world view. I 'know' you in terms of how helpful you can be to me, and am thus unable to consider your independent view at the same time that I am taking my own into account.
- **Pervasive limitation:** A 'split universe,' where each person's knowing is separate from others' way of knowing.
- **Distribution:** about 10% of adults.

You might say that each stage carries within it the seed of its own destruction. That would be quite to the point. Life is ceaseless change, and staying where you are is an illusion. How, then, do people move on from S-2? Here are some highlights.

HIGHLIGHTS OF THE JOURNEY TO STAGE 3:
- **Journey toward stage 3:** This journey is about bringing others' perspective inside yourself. Your new perspective now includes your ability to imagine others taking a perspective on you, and to bring inside yourself the mediation of these separate perspectives, – which previously were seen only as a matter of social consequence in the external world.
- **Developmental risk:** loss of imagined self containment
- **Meaning of 'internalizing another's perspective':** Ability to hold more than a single view:
    - First, a bringing inside the self another's or others' perspectives.
    - Second, an ability to derive your own thoughts and feelings as a direct consequence of how others are thinking and feeling, rather than solely as a consequence of what others will DO in response to your actions.

***

Regardless of how S-2 individuals come to grief, there comes a point where they have to move on. The essential step for them to take is to OPEN THEMSELVES UP TO OTHERS, to become 'empathic,' or be influenced by others' perspective.

Let me use an example I remember from studying with R. Kegan. If your teenage kid does not call you, the parent, when staying out beyond the agreed upon time, you can be sure that the move to 2(3) has not occurred. For that telephone call to come in, the kid would have to realize that you, the parent, is possibly worried about his or her safety. This means to acknowledge internally that there is another human being living in his/her own world of thought and feeling that I can no longer ignore. Not because I will be punished if I don't call. Rather, punishment and other consequences aside, I call because I have begun to absorb other people's perspective, and have my feelings and thoughts influenced by them, or rather by what I imagine them to think or feel. I am beginning to relinquish the *split universe* which, so far, has provided for me my safety and strength.

Level	Characteristic
2(3)	Beginning to be influenced by physical and imagined others

Let's see what beginning to be influenced by another's perspective might sound like when put into words (adapted from Lahey et al, 1988, 104-105):

Client: It really makes me sad that my colleague lied to me. Now I can never be sure whether he's telling me the truth.
Interviewer: What is that sadness about?

Client: It's that he let me down. We've became friends, and as friends promised to tell the truth to each other, and he didn't follow through with that. So now I don't know whether I can count on him. And I don't know why he did lie to me, or why and whether he might do so again.
Interviewer: It seems to be important to you to know why he lied?
Client: Yes. Like maybe he lied because of something I did that made him angry at me.
Interviewer: In what way would it help to know that that was the reason?
Client: Well, I wouldn't have provoked his anger by speaking about him to others had I known that that would make him lie to me. Like if he told me: "Don't call me unreliable toward others, or I'll start lying to you." Then, of course, I wouldn't do that, and keep my mouth shut toward others.
Interviewer: Why wouldn't you talk about him to others in a bad way?
Client: Because I'd remember when I was about to complain about him to others that he'd get angry at me and start lying to me, and so I would keep silent. I really want to know I can count on him.

In what way is the speaker of this fragment beginning to be influenced by others, whether they are physically present or only imagined? The speaker says: "*I wouldn't have provoked his anger by speaking about him to others had I known that that would make him lie to me.*" However opportunistic this may sound, it's a fact that the speaker is now beginning to wonder about his colleague's STATE OF MIND. The speaker is beginning to take a second perspective, however self serving this perspective may initially be. This would not be a generalized attitude of the speaker, but an ad hoc procedure. The speaker would "*remember when I was about to complain about him to others that he'd get angry at me and start lying to me.*"

This sounds very concrete, as if the speaker's memory were a tool for reminding him not to do certain things that are risky. The other's act of lying sounds equally much like a physical event. This fixation on physical events as well as concrete objects is a typical feature of S-2 thinking. Such thinking is all about objects that can be manipulated, people included. The holding of another perspective is just beginning to take hold, and consequently is still very fragile. The physical and mental worlds are still very close, and the latter haven't gained their independence of the former. This is, in part, a matter of brain physiology, and in part a matter of mind set, inextricably interwoven. Not only social-emotional, but cognitive, development is involved here.

So, when all is said and done, what ultimately keeps mattering is "I really want to know I can count on him," which returns us from S-2(3) to S-2. The tiny step beyond S-2 that was made has been entirely self serving, very awkwardly physical, with no great forays into the other person's mental world. The acknowledgement of the other is purely pragmatic. It goes only as far as is needed to keep safe, and keep one's need gratification on track. That's because the split universe – the two-world hypothesis – is still in force, and has been suspended only for pragmatic reasons. The second perspective has not been internalized yet, but is has, to so speak, been 'tried out.'

As I previously indicated, the progression in consciousness humans experience is such that you can't return to an earlier position. (As Heracleitos said, you can't step into the same river twice, neither your own internal or an external river.) Having made the first step out of S-2, the client we listened to above is likely to get to feel more pressure due to being caught between two main stages, S-2 and S-3. This in-between position can be an uncomfortable place to be: wanting to protect oneself from risk or danger, and beginning to realize that one may oneself contribute to the risk or danger. Let's gain a clearer picture of what this developmental conflict is about and feels like.

Level	Characteristic
2/3	Conflicted over risking exposure to others' feelings and thoughts; resolution to level 2

Imagine you don't really know the other person who is your friend. (It could be a lover.) You are very bonded to him or her, but neither do you have a clear understanding of yourself, nor have you cared to investigate what the other person is really about. You are linked to the other mainly by your own neediness or yearning and insecurity. Also, you are probably not very schooled in letting others know your own true feelings and thoughts, either because you don't have the language for it (you don't understand them yourself), or it is frightening, or both. (Just read your early love letters.) That's the situation the client is in right now (adapted from Lahey 1988, 102-3).

Client: It makes me really sad that my colleague lied to me. Seeing him as my friend, I was counting on him to tell me the truth. We've always promised to tell each other the truth, and he didn't follow through with that. He lied to me.
Interviewer: Tell me more about your sadness.
Client: Well, I am sad because I don't know whether I can count on him to tell me the truth. Is he going to lie to me all the time? I guess it also makes me sad that he felt he *had to* lie to me. Maybe he was angry about something I did, and so he didn't feel like he could trust me anymore, or something like that.
Interviewer: What, for you, would be sad about that?
Client: Well, it's like maybe he lost a friend. Like he himself couldn't count on me. I'd be sad if he was upset because he thought that I let him down. So, I really wish I knew whether that was the reason why he lied.
Interpreter: How would it help you to know that was the reason?
Client: Well, because then I could let him know I was sorry, and he'd feel better knowing I really want to be his friend, and that I didn't mean to let him down.
Interviewer: How would that change things for your colleague?
Client: Well, because he'd feel better. And then, feeling better, he wouldn't be mad at me anymore. Then, in turn, I could count on him again, like if I needed help or something.

The conflict we are witnessing here plays out in the domain of feeling, specifically *sadness*. The client is sad about not being able to trust his colleague, but is also beginning to surmise that his own behavior may have something to do with what is perceived by him as lying. This inner conflict sets in motion a new kind of imagination. It initiates a thought experiment focused on: "perhaps he lied to me because I unwittingly let him down, and so he had no choice?" This is a nagging question that now overtakes the client as he further investigates the possible reasons for having been lied to. Suddenly, the world outside of the client is no longer independent of him or her. Rather, the awful truth is that the client may actually be responsible for it, at least in part.

Thinking through the possibility of having himself been the cause of the colleagues lying to him, the client now realizes that if his assumption holds he would have to apologize to his colleague. That would indeed change everything, because then the colleague "would feel better knowing I really want to be his friend, and that I didn't mean to let him down." In short, the client would not shy away from apologizing to his colleague if only this would make the latter feel better and bring him back into the client's orbit where he could continue to be of help to him. And being able to trust that his colleague would help him out if need be is really the apology's main purpose.

What has happened for the client internally here? He has begun to build a theory (model) of another person that would tell him how the other feels and thinks, and how s(he) might act. This fragile second perspective enables the client to formulate hypotheses that can explain things about other people's behavior. The theory is not very deep. It is strictly limited to a one-to-one relationship with the client focused on the client's own benefit. The fact that the colleague would feel better if apologized to is a by-product of the more important result that he would be willing to help out if help was needed. Clearly, this stance, while it indicates a move beyond S-2(3), does not leave the range of S-2. The ulterior motive is not to know how the other person really thinks and feels, or to apologize, but to secure future assistance. In other words, the conflict between S-2 and S-3 is being resolved to the side of S-2. (We notate this state of affairs as S-2/3)..

***

What would it look like if the client were able to resolve the developmental conflict in favor of S-3? It could only mean to let go of one's own needs and desires as the principal raison d'être of one's relationship with others. The step toward S-3/2 would also entail a higher level of curiosity about the other person, her thinking, feeling, and behavior generally, and this curiosity would come 'with fewer strings attached.'

Level	Characteristic
3/2	Conflicted, but with more detachment from own needs and desires, resolution to level 3

Let's see what this would sound like in this particular case (adapted from Lahey et al., 1988, 108):

Client: I am really sad that my colleague lied to me. I was counting on him to tell me the truth. We've always promised to tell each other the truth, and he didn't follow through with that. He lied to me.
Interviewer: Tell me more about how his lying to you is making you sad.
Client: Well, because I don't know whether I can count on him to tell me the truth, and whether he can actually follow through with promises. Of course, I am also asking myself whether he going to lie to me all the time. I guess it also makes me sad that he felt he had to lie to me. Like maybe he didn't think he could count on me.
Interviewer: What makes you sad about that?
Client: Well, it's like he lost a friend. Like maybe he was angry about something I did, and so he didn't feel like he could trust me anymore. So, in a way I guess I must have let him down. That makes me sad because he must have been upset that I let him down.
Interviewer: How might you have let him down?
Client: Well, maybe he felt he couldn't count on me, and so that's why he lied. I wish he would have told me if that's what he felt.
Interviewer: Tell me more about why his telling you is so important to you.

Client: Because then I could have let him know that I was sorry. He'd feel better, and I'd feel better too, because I wouldn't be worried about whether he was feeling let down, and then if he wasn't, I'd know he wouldn't lie to me either, and I'd know I could count on him.

You probably noticed in the illustration above that, overall, we are moving deeper into a reciprocal relationship. That is a state where I wouldn't do anything to somebody that I wouldn't want him or her to do to me, regardless of any material benefits attached to it. I would adhere to the ethical convention that keeps people at peace with each other and lets them work together, no favors asked. (I would do this not in the sense of an S-4 person who has internalized Kant's *categorical imperative*, but because I've picked up this idea in my social surround, and that's what I am identifying with at the moment.) However, that would mean I would have to let go of the priority of having my needs met first and foremost. I would have to take the risk that my trust in others would ultimately remove my suspicion that nobody would help me out should I be at risk.

This step does not only demand a leap of faith, it also requires that I scrutinize what I am habitually doing, or have done in some particular case. I have to investigate my own motives, and thereby gain more of an understanding of others' motivation. The internal processes I am capable of get strengthened thereby.

The change of heart that's going on here is most clearly seen in the lower half of the illustration of S-3/2. The client now says that, in a way, he is making himself sad because it is what he himself did, not what the colleague did, that makes him sad. A new complex hypothesis now follows. In the client's view, the colleague:
- must have felt that he couldn't trust the client any more and therefore lied to him (this puts the colleague at the same stage as the client in the client's eyes);
- must have been upset that the client let him down;
- must have felt that he lost a friend.

In short, the client is here building a replica of himself, a person just like him with the same feelings and misgivings as he has experienced. Taking himself as a model, the client designs a model of the other person. If I can understand my own feelings – sadness, misgivings, – then I have a key by which to understand others. Thus expressing the social nature of feeling, the client has entered into a rather deep internal process. He is *internalizing* another, second perspective, one that is generated from his own self experience, it is true, but is freed from the priority of need that so far has dictated the client's behavior. Clearly, the stakes are turning in favor of a stance we expect an S-3 person to hold. Given this turn of events, the client now experiences a heretofore unknown urgency to communicate more closely with his colleagues: "I wish he would have told me if that's what he felt." And further:

Because then I could have let him know that I was sorry. He'd feel better, and I'd feel better too, because I wouldn't be worried about whether he was feeling let down, and then if he wasn't [feeling let down], I'd know he wouldn't lie to me either, and I'd know I could count on him.

This is more than a person at S-2/3 can muster to think or say. This reciprocity of feeling – "he'd feel better, and I'd feel better too" – is not open to a person clinging to strictly material outcomes. What's in focus here is mutual trust and comfort. BUT, here comes the catch:

"and then if he wasn't [feeling let down], I'd know he wouldn't lie to me either [as I wouldn't], **and I'd know I could count on him."**

Too bad! We are apparently still in the grip of S-2. That's expressed clearly by the score of S-3/2. This stage indicates that, yes, I can detach from my interests and needs, but only so much and so long. I remain in conflict. And while I have managed to resolve it – temporarily – in favor of S-3, I am not yet beyond the grip of *instrumentalism* (where I use other people as tools for my need gratification). However, I have the POTENTIAL to eventually get to S-3, – if I continue the journey!

It is of interest, at this point, to revisit the notion introduced earlier, of a consultant's MODEL OF THE CLIENT. The reader will realize that formulating such a model is not really a possibility for an S-2 individual. As we have witnessed, such an individual only very gradually escapes the grip of instrumentalism, where any kind of 'helping' is out of the question since the individual overwhelmingly wants to be helped. We rightfully surmise that developing any kind of a model of a client would minimally presuppose an S-3 stance.

As Schein rightfully formulates, culture forcefully enters into how we communicate with others, especially in helping relationships. However, culture and developmental level are closely intertwined. In addition, both are hidden dimensions hard to make explicit. For relationships to be perceived as equitable, and certainly for them to be perceived, on that basis, as 'helpful,' certain developmental as well as cultural preconditions have to be met. An analysis of how individuals grow out of S-2 into S-3 reveals what it takes to be able to formulate a *minimally acceptable* model of another person (who may be a 'client').

As Schein sees it (1999, 117-118), the following 'filters' are involved in establishing helping relationships:
- My self-image.
- My image of the other person or persons.
- My 'definition of the situation.'
- My motives, feelings, intentions, attitudes.
- My expectations.

When we inspect these five filters, it becomes clear that even an S-3/2 individual cannot truly be credited with the ability of formulating and holding an objective model of a client. The reasons are as follows. At S-3/2:
- My self image is still constrained by my inability of 'bracketing' my own needs and desires, despite the fact that I have just begun to be motivated by others thoughts, feelings, motivations, as far as I can imagine them
- Despite my newly won *conventionalism*, my image of the other person or persons is still 'contaminated' by my own interests in having them support me in situations of need, or boost my self image
- My definition of the situation I share with another person is still one-sidedly weighted toward my own needs and desires, and is thus not 'objective' enough to grasp what the other person's needs might be, especially should they deviate from my own

- My motives, feelings, intentions, and attitudes are all still caught up in the 'two-world hypothesis' where my world is mine, and yours is yours
- My expectation of you, the client, is that I need your help as much as you may need mine, and who needs more help is hard to say.

The reader will agree that from S-3/2 onward the distant possibility arises of being able to act as a 'consultant' or 'coach' who, given sufficient cognitive resources, may – once S-3 has been reached – have at least the potential to develop a community-based model of a client. Aware of the distance that separates S-3 consulting from professional consulting at S-4 and beyond, the reader will begin to appreciate how developmental level plays into the Persona, and thus the effectiveness, of a helper.

***

We have seen so far that much more is involved in the journey from S-3/2 to S-3 than resolving internal, ethical or other conflict. As s(he) proceeds to deeper levels of insight into self and other, the (young) adult's thinking and feeling get revolutionized. A kind of social imagination comes into being where the person can develop hypotheses about others' behavior based on own experience. You might say that a rudimentary *social theory* gets created which stipulates what is the best way for us all to live and work together. The keyword is TRUST, and trust leads to a situation where I derive my own feelings from somebody else's whom I trust. An internal force is created that lets individuals forgo their anxiousness about their vulnerability and helplessness, and simultaneously relaxes their need for control. This state of mind is even more clearly expressed in the subsequent step.

Level	Characteristic
3(2)	Able to be influenced by imagined others and their expectations, feelings & thoughts

One might say that, moving toward S-3 via S-3(2), the individual becomes internally *enlarged*. That's what is meant by *mental growth*. Her social world grows to the same extent that she grows in insight into herself as a social being (and beyond). This is the essential equation of adult development: subjectivity (ego-centricity) decreases, objectivity – ability to take oneself and others as object – increases.

Here is what this state of mind sounds like (Lahey et al. 1988, 106-7):

Client: I am really sad that my colleague lied to me. I was counting on him to tell me the truth. Not, you know, that he has to [tell me the truth], but that he should want to.
Interviewer: What is it in his not telling you the truth that makes you sad?
Client: Well because, why would he want to lie? Maybe he didn't think he could count on me.
Interviewer: What is sad about that?
Client: Well, I'm sad if maybe he felt I let him down, perhaps he couldn't trust me. I wish if he thought he couldn't trust me he would let me know his feelings.
Interviewer: What would his telling you do for you?

Client: I could then reassure him that he can count on me, and help him feel he can trust me. I'd like us to work this out so I don't feel bad about him lying, and so he doesn't feel he can't trust me.

Interviewer: Tell me more about why that's important to you.

Client: Because it's not right he should be feeling bad because he can't trust me, and I should be feeling bad because he lied. I shouldn't even be feeling bad because he lied. I shouldn't even be thinking of, or wondering whether, he's somebody I can count on, because really, we should both just be wanting to let the other one know that we can trust each other.

Interviewer: Why is that?

Client: Well, that's just what friendship is.

You will agree that this exchange goes a long way toward a Center of Gravity defined by mutual trust. The client shows himself to be capable of taking another person's point of view and making it the source of his own thinking and feeling. What once was an external other has become a fully internalized other. Protecting one's self-interest is no longer at the center of attention. Rather, the S-3(2) self is clearly able to hold a second perspective – others' points of view – internally, and make it the source of his own behavior. Making others' point of view – including their needs, desires, likings, concerns – the source of one's own actions is the hallmark of the S-3 Frame of Reference.

This being so, the client releases the colleague from having to tell the truth: "Not, you know, that he has to [tell the truth]." Rather, it is now a matter of WANTING TO TELL THE TRUTH, given the trust that was established between the two parties. As we continue to read the excerpt, the concern is more and more solidly about the other person, rather than the speaker. The reason for being sad or upset switches from the colleague's behavior to that of the client's. The speaker is no longer upset that his colleague lied, but rather about the possibility that he, the speaker, may have prompted the colleague to lie. Linked to this reversal is the urgent wish to know the other's state of mind: "I wish if he thought he couldn't trust me, he would let me know his feelings."

This strongly implies that the two-world hypothesis of S-2 – you are in your world, and I am in mine – has broken down. No longer is the client in splendid isolation from the other, but depends, for his own actions, on knowing what is going on in the other's thoughts and feelings. Given the trust that should prevail between them, it's not okay that the other party should feel bad, as little as the speaker himself should feel bad:

It's not right he should be feeling bad because he can't trust me, and I should be feeling bad because he lied. I shouldn't even be feeling bad because he lied. *I shouldn't even be thinking of, or wondering whether, he's somebody I can count on, because really, we should both just be wanting to let the other one know that we can trust each other.*"

"What, then, separates this illustration, scored at S-3(2), from S-3?" the reader will rightfully ask The short and simple answer is that for a person at S-3, there is no need to make so much fuss about trusting others, and having others' thoughts and feelings inform one's own. At S-3, these things can simply be assumed. They don't have to be talked about so emphatically any longer (so, what matters is more to be found in what is NOT said). This becomes clear in the somewhat cryptic statement at the end: "that's just what friendship is."

The statement is a rhetorical flourish espousing S-3, to signal how uneventful (normal) the situation discussed really is: given that the two individuals are friends, all that has been so emphatically spelled out can be rendered by a single term: FRIENDSHIP. In short, the fact that so much fuss is made about being trusted and wanting to be told what is on the other's mind is an indication that S-3 is still a mirage, and thus has not been reached.

SUMMARY OF THE JOURNEY FROM S-2 TO S-3
- Starting from a focus on own needs and desires, a young adult increasingly opens mind and feeling to the world of others, to the point where the adult's own feelings are generated by internalizing others' feelings.
- This process of internalization is initially fraught with conflict between defining others as instruments of my need gratification, on one hand, and defining them as the origin of my feelings and guarantors of my internal cohesion, on the other.
- To resolve this conflict – played out in S-2/3 and S-3/2 – requires the ability to imagine how others think and feel and, in particular, how they may think and feel about ME who is their 'Other.'
- In this way, a full exchange of Self and Other takes place, where Self becomes Other – assuming others' viewpoints – and Other become Self – a social likeness "like myself."
- The loss of self that occurs is that of an *asocial* self that cannot let go of its own sacred needs, adhered to in one-sided urgency and with non-negotiable relentlessness.

We have completed the journey from S-2 to S-3. The reader might now expect that the journey from S-3 to S-4, and S-4 to S-5 is going to turn out to be a very similar one, given the PATTERN we have spoken about:

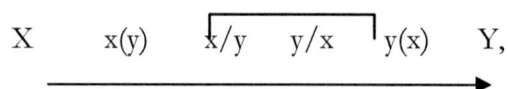

$$X \qquad x(y) \qquad x/y \qquad y/x \qquad y(x) \qquad Y,$$

Fig. 6.1 Generic notation of developmental progression (Kegan)

where X is the lower, and Y the higher, stage, and where '( )' means "hanging on," and "/" means "conflict between two stages." While the above mentioned expectation holds true for the notation itself, the reader should consider that the flavor of the journey, its overall spirit, and the content it entails are going to be much influenced by *where the journey starts*. Since the overriding concerns of a person are different at different stages, what makes the journey salient is likely to be different as well.

With regard to the journey from S-3 to S-4, dealt with below, it's clear that if defining oneself by others' expectations no longer works, a substitute for the internalized others – in whom the person is now fully embedded – has to be found that can guide thoughts and actions. This substitute, most likely, is going to have to be the person's own self. As a result, SELF DISCOVERY is emphatically what the journey from S-3 to S-4 can be said to be about.

***

Imagine you are defining yourself entirely by internalized others – viewpoints stemming from your family, work environment, professional community, etc. – and you have no idea that you are doing so. **That is the reality of S-3.** Everything seems to be 'alright' with you. In fact, you may be flourishing, esteemed and supported by your colleagues, and so forth. So why should you proceed with the journey, hard as it has been anyway, and leave the comfort of what you know best? You are, after all, a 'good citizen,' of moderate self insight to be sure, but able to subordinate your needs to requirements of community. Might not the fact that there is no social *forcing function* for growing up beyond S-3 deter you to take another step in your self development? (As you may know, the main character in G. Grass's <u>Tin Drum</u> refuses to grow up into his teenage, at S-2).

Orientation	S-3	Intermediate Stages	S-4
View of Others	Needed to contribute to own self image	???	Collaborator, delegate, peer
Level of Self Insight	Moderate		High
Values	Community		Self-determined
Needs	Subordinate to community, work group		Flowing from striving for integrity
Need to Control	Moderate		Low
Communication	Exchange 1:1		Dialogue
Organizational Orientation	Good Citizen		Manager

Table I.1 Changing orientations across adult levels

What is this motivation to become the author of one's life, paid for by the loss of the safety of being held by community? As Kegan would say, we are never outgrowing the tension between wanting to be autonomous and to be included in a community simultaneously. One and the other yearning are linked, and this link constitutes the human condition. In this sense, humans may have little choice, or at least less than they think.

Most likely, there will be incidents in your life and work through which the contrast between S-3 and S-4 becomes more or less painfully clear to you, even through observation of others. You may have noticed that you often feel very uncertain about 'what to do' (or for those who are always doing something, 'what to do next'), thus relying on advice from others. When such advice fails you may regret not to have followed your own gut feeling and made a different decision. If you are a woman, there might also have occurred issues like abortion where the matter of having a child or not squarely settled on YOU. You had to decide about life and death. To do so, you would have to begin searching for a solution within yourself, to *hear you own voice*. It is that kind of situation that is at issue here.

Let's look over the journey we are now entering upon, that from S-3 to S-4. It is one of the most momentous and consequential of all developmental transitions.

Level	Characteristic
3	Made up of others' expectations; 'our world' hypothesis
3(4)	In need of 'handholding' by physical others to act on own behalf
3/4	Conflicted over, and unsure about own values, direction, worth, capability
4/3	Conflicted, but with more detachment from internalized viewpoints, resolving to Stage 4
4(3)	Nearing self-authoring, but remaining at risk for regression to others' expectations
4	Fully self-authoring decision maker respecting others; 'my world' hypothesis

Table 6.2 Range characteristics between S-3 and S-4

According to the table, **it seems that what the journey from S-3 to S-4 is centrally about is taking some personal risks.** They might be risks such as losing the support of a group, perhaps even of your family; being ostracized by co-workers; being avoided by friends, things like that. Are you up for dealing with that? You might ask: "what would be the rewards of going it alone?" This is an S-2 stance, don't you think? So how are you going to move on from your 'our world hypothesis' to a 'my world hypothesis' as it is associated with S-4?

To clarify where the journey begins, let's briefly recall here the caricature of S-3 from a previous chapter:

> S-3 is a 'We,' or a sense of community, stage. Self-image is determined entirely by what others think, whether these others are internalized or external others. Thus, people at this stage are highly, if not completely, identified with an external socially established norm or standard that has been internalized. If rank, position, power, etc., are viewed as being important by the system that defines them, then they are important to this individual, as are appearances – social correctness. Obtaining status, in whatever terms the external reference is based upon, makes them highly competitive, but they will not stoop to the stratagems Stage 2 persons will in order to achieve their ends. They 'follow the rules,' and are 'above board' about winning and losing. It is very unlikely that they will 'see' or think beyond the established operational principles and values of 'their' organization. Because their image is so caught up in the status quo, they will be unwilling to take the risks necessary to change it, even if they can stand apart from their unit, group, or organization far enough to objectively assess what could make it operate more effectively. Hence, they do not make good change agents, either in the sense of seeing what needs to be done or in actually doing it. Any change they believe might be beneficial will be whatever is being echoed by the majority. In a leader position, this person will follow what they believe the norms are and will try to establish a climate accordingly. Yet, they may have a very tough time doing so, unless those norms lead them to simultaneously gain recognition, or credits, within the broader social structure. What contributes to the climate first is how it will affect their stature. Hence, the climate will be focused as much on individual achievement as it is on the group's collective effectiveness.

Here are some highlights of S-3 (as you already know, neither age nor education are good predictors of any stage):

- An S-3 individual is made up by expectations of others, especially internalized others (that by definition can't be seen), but initially also by physically present others who are referenced internally.
- Appearances and social correctness are of high importance (the advertising industry found that out!).
- Going with the status quo is the name of the game.
- Change is not welcomed, and since maintenance of the status quo highly matters to the individual, s(he) is not a good change agent.
- An S-3 individual can be a 'leader' of sorts – in the eyes of others – but the capacity to lead will be small since the individual is adverse to risks (and cognitively, may not have the wherewithal to think systemically).

Now think back to the client whose colleague lied to him. When we left that client, he was living at S-3(2), emitting loud espousals about having arrived at S-3. We now begin to see how this client would have developed to S-3 and would have acted from that Center of Gravity. Predictably, he would have:

- let go of his fixation on getting his needs met first and foremost;
- found it most important *to fit in*, to gain the support of important individuals and groups;
- diligently avoided betraying other's trust, both to follow established conventions and *to get ahead;*
- become a good observer of others, to know what the rules are;
- become an expert in using connections (a "networker" without a core of his own);
- acquired at least moderate self knowledge, although only little systemic knowledge of the environments in which s(he) works.

Perhaps making the journey to S-4 sounds a little bit more inviting now? Being part of civil society is not quite good enough for many people with developmental potential. Not that there is anything wrong with being at S-3, as I've said. (Society needs all stages.) It's just that in many circumstances, the S-3 individual is going to feel as if s(he) was *in over their head in modern society*, to speak with Kegan (1994). This is because many (especially well-paid) professional positions these days require more than an S-3 stance. In fact, to be a PROFESSIONAL really means acting from S-4, period.

SUMMARY OF STAGE 3

- **Distribution:** Between 50 and 60% of adults.
- **Advance over Stage 2:** My theory of self now includes others' perspective.
- **Essence of this stage:** My self is made up by the expectations of physical or internalized others (family, religious or peer group), and I lose myself when losing membership in, and the support of, the group.

- **Conventionalism:** The ultimate concern is with whether I am adhering to what is expected of me. Being 'good' means following the rules of an institution larger than myself that I have strongly internalized, and without which I will be *at a loss*.
- **Pervasive limitation:** I cannot distinguish my internalized points of view from those of physical others. Consequently, I have no 'theory of self' independent of what I have absorbed from the social surround, whether by adherence to, or strict negation of, existing conventions. My guilt is about not being sanctioned by others, not about failing my own standards (which I haven't acquired yet).

HIGHLIGHTS OF THE JOURNEY TO STAGE 4
- **Journey toward stage 4:** Starting with the distinction between physical others, internalized others, and 'myself,' individuals inch toward a sense of what is 'other than me;' they don't get social help in doing so, and are thus on their own.
- **Developmental risk:** Loss of imagined safety as member of a physical and/or internalized group, thus loss of the communal or shared self.
- **Meaning of 'forming a theory of self:'**
  - First, people must internally distance themselves from their need of being acknowledged and accepted by community; they must be able to 'go it alone' if their own inner voice tells them to do so.
  - Second, people must develop a better and better notion of their uniqueness, of what makes them different from others, and find the courage to make that difference known to others while respecting others' otherness.
  - Third, people must develop an ethical theory of integrity of self.

Let's see, then, what the steps of the journey sound like, as we did when making the journey from S-2 to S-3.

Level	Characteristics
3	Made up of others' expectations; 'our world' hypothesis

We start with an illustration of S-3. The excerpt regards a work situation, specifically making decision in an organizational environment. (S-3 to S-4(3) illustrations adapted from Lahey et al., 1988, 46-71):

I have just been gathering data for the decision I and my boss have to make, rather than going ahead with the decision on my own, or waiting for the boss to come in. He really prefers to delegate, and I just didn't take up the challenge to make a decision on my own. But now I realize that he really doesn't mind if I make a decision that has to be made, and that he really likes me to do that because then he doesn't feel as if he's depriving me of authority, or as if he really should be making the decision. Before, it really was a strain between us, because we didn't get to make decisions as much as I really found necessary and wanted to, or else I harassed him about making the decision, and then felt guilty about it. Making the decision by myself occasionally makes both of us happier, and even makes things between us a lot smoother.

The speaker seems to be able to distinguish her own take on things from that of her boss, and can hold both her own and her boss's point of view as a part of herself.

However, the distinction between herself and her boss is a very tenuous, physical (not internalized) one. We notice, in particular, that "I and my boss" form a unit here, both in the sense of the boss as a physical other and an internalized (invisible) other. As we saw before, the individual designs a model of the other person – who could be a coaching client – that is taken from her own understanding of herself. There is no struggle, no conflict, only a complete (though temporary) equilibrium between what the person is subject to and can reflect upon as an object, as we would find at any other main stage.

Something like the following seems to be going on in the excerpt. The speaker has recently come to the realization that her boss does not seem to mind when she makes decisions without him, in fact, the boss seems to prefer to delegate decisions to her. (This is of course her construction of the boss, not the real boss.) This realization is important to the speaker, since when acted upon by her, there is less of a strain between the two parties, and less guilt on her part is coming up. The lessening of guilt strengthens her self coherence. **However, what she does not realize is that <u>not</u> she herself, but the (internally constructed) boss is presently the guarantor of her internal self coherence!**

> But now I realize that he really doesn't mind if I make a decision that has to be made, and that he really likes me to do that because then he doesn't feel as if he's depriving me of authority, or as if he really should be making the decision.

This theory of the other is self-soothing, one might say. It confirms for her that she is 'alright' in doing what she does. No reason to worry or feel guilty. What she experiences, then, is a socially guaranteed harmony that has nothing whatsoever to do with her own principles, or her own theory of self (of which there presently is none). In fact, she could be 'anybody.' ("We are all a member of this wonderful community!"). It sounds a little bit like Rousseau's state of natural innocence, only transposed into the speaker's present social context.

Let's note here the important capability of the speaker to hold multiple perspectives. This is really a great advance over S-2. Without that capability, the speaker could never succeed in the journey to S-4, simply because she would remain fixated on her own perspective. Therefore, she certainly has the POTENTIAL to proceed further toward S-4. This potential is both a social-emotional and cognitive one, and while I am here disregarding the latter, it should be kept in mind that the two go together.

To summarize: the S-3 individual:
- is defined by others' internal or external presence;
- can hold multiple perspective within herself, her own perspective and that of others;
- is being shadowed by the psychology of one or more imagined others who guarantee her self coherence;
- consequently, lacks her own *identity generator* that could release the accompanying other(s) from their burden of having to guarantee her identity (a fate they suffer silently).

Clearly, then, if this journey is to go on, the following things have to happen:

- The S-3 individual will have to distinguish herself from physical others who guarantee her self identity.
- She must detach herself from the invisible internalized others who do the same – and that is the hard part.
- She must discover in herself elements of contradiction between herself and others that can serve as *hooks* for her own declaration of independence.

What might a first step in the direction of self-authoring look like?

Level	Characteristic
3(4)	In need of 'handholding' by physical others to act on own behalf

Interviewer: Tell me a little bit about how you presently make decisions in your job.
Client: Things have changed recently. My boss used to make all decisions. But now I am making decisions at work on my own if that's what I want to do.
Interviewer: How does that work?
Client: It's not good for me to be so dependent on my boss. He himself helps me to see that. He keeps saying I have to make more of the decisions at work by myself, and I really do feel that it's important for me to decide myself.
Interviewer: In what way is that important to you, making decisions on your own?
Client: I'm an adult, and I think it is time that I started making my own decisions, don't you think?

"Espousals, espousals!" the reader might say. No adult at S-4 would have to say "I am an adult!" It would be understood. But here, the espousal serves the useful purpose of having the S-3 individual wake up to her potential. She now makes decisions on her own "if that is what I want to do," – which sounds pretty self authoring. But when it comes to presenting a theory of her self authoring, she falls flat: "It's not good for me to be so dependent on my boss," a statement that she probably picked up in her social surround. What's more, she is asking the interviewer for re-assurance regarding her newly acquired adult conviction!

Formulating as she does, the speaker articulates her insight into the state of dependency she is presently in. She acknowledges that she needs the boss to hold her hand and support her – as any good boss would – in making more of her own decisions. (A boss who micromanages her could be fatal for her at this point.) It is HE who keeps saying "be more self authoring, don't always wait for me." In short, a small step beyond S-3 has been made here, but with the help of a physical other.

What has not happened here is a detachment from internalized others that crowd out own authentic voices. Only the physical, hand-holding other has been spotted. There is no distance yet "between the self and its internalized points of view" (Lahey et al., 1988, 59). It is this distance which we will have watch as we proceed, since that distance will tell us how far removed from S-4 the individual really is. Let's listen to the music of the subsequent step.

Level	Characteristic

| 3/4 | Conflicted over, and unsure about own values, direction, worth, capability |

Interviewer: Tell me more about the way you presently make decisions in your job, please.
Client: I have recently changed in this. I used to wait for the boss to come in. But now I just make a decision by myself, and don't wait for his. When I need to solve an important problem, I'll tell him about it and say: "Boss, I'd like you to support me in this, else I am going ahead." Of course, he finds no time for me, and I'd enjoy work more if he did, but at least, I get to decide.
Interviewer: How does that work out for you?
Client: To tell you the truth, sometimes I wonder whether doing it this way is much better than delegating, because even though he doesn't say that much, I can see that it hurts his feelings that I just go ahead without him, and I feel like I'm being a bad employee. Why don't I just wait for him to make the decision? It's not so bad, and he is so busy!
Interviewer: What happens then?
Client: I often get really angry and think: "Don't I have the right to act on my own judgment? It isn't fair of him to make me feel guilty." And so go ahead, but I end up feeling guilty about it.

Has the distance between self and internalized others increased here? Yes and no. It is not that "things" have changed, but I have changed. The speaker has taken initiatives that confront the internalized (and physical) other with decisions she has made on her own. However, she remains ambiguous, 'torn,' regarding making decisions by herself: "I would enjoy work more if he did [support me directly]," but "at least I get to decide." This way, at least she can get used to the flavor of being a self-authorer. Nevertheless, she remains in conflict about it:

Sometimes I wonder whether doing it this way is much better than delegating, because even though he doesn't say that much, I can see that it hurts his feelings that I just go ahead without him, and I feel like I'm being a bad employee. Why don't I just wait for him to make the decision? It's not so bad, and he is so busy!

Clearly, she is taking responsibility for the feelings of physical and internalized others, just as she burdens the other with having to guarantee her self cohesion (either be being there, or by telling her that she is alright). This conflictual state is often a source of anger for her: "It isn't fair of him to make me feel guilty." While this sounds as if some physical other was making her feel guilty, is really her own projection by which she makes herself feel guilty. She is really making herself feel guilty given who she is, in a classical S-3 fashion. And what is the guilt about? It's about acting on her own, as if she shouldn't be doing such a thing.

So evidently, the self, the views it has internalized, and the other are still not clearly differentiated here. Although the distance between the self and internalized others has grown somewhat during the journey from S-3(4) to S-3/4, it has not grown enough for the speaker to let go of her guilt. One thing is certain though: the self has ventured more and more deeply into her internalization of others, and thereby has set the stage for a "show-down" where the truth will come out: that she really doesn't need her boss to make decisions, nor the espousal that she is actually capable of doing so, for that matter.

Level	Characteristic
4/3	Conflicted, but with more detachment from

When that show-down happens, she will have arrived at a turning point in her life (adapted from Lahey et al., 65)

Interviewer: Tell me a little more about how you relate to your boss when it comes to decision making.
Client: I used to wait for him, but now I just make the decision on my own. I feel guilty about it sometimes, because I know my boss would rather be consulted, and would want me to wait for his input. I can see him feeling upset about my decision, and I feel myself changing my mind, right on the spot, that's not right for me to make my decision, and that just stops me in the tracks.
Interviewer: So what happens?
Client: Sometimes I make the decision, and sometimes I don't.
Interviewer: How are you able to make decisions under these circumstances?
Client: I remind myself that it doesn't make sense to wait for him, because then I only end up punishing him for my decision not to make up my own mind. We both end up unhappy then.

Why is this stance to be scored S-4/3 rather than S-3/4? In what way is the speaker here more distant from internalized others (more herself), especially since she remains conflicted?
Here are some suggestions:

- Although the boss – the internalized other – is still considered the guarantor of her self identity as a decision maker, and although the need for his permission to act still has the power to stop her in her tracks, she can *sometimes* make the decision and stand by it.
- The client has come to see that "it doesn't make sense to wait for him," because she then ends up "punishing him for my decision not to make up my mind."

In short, she is beginning to see the futility of the situation: "We both end up unhappy then." For her to see this, she must be able to see clearly her own role in making both herself and the boss unhappy. This insight into the vicious circle of her self doubts and uncertainties is a very liberating and healthy one, however painful it may be.
The speaker is now forced to consider her own doing as the origin of what, up to now, she has projected onto her boss. She is beginning to externalize her internalized other, thereby detaching herself from the other. She has 'enough' of the inner ruminations of what the boss might think or feel, and she is loosening her grip on him as a guarantor of her identity. She is getting ready to relieve the other, now that he has become fully external to her, of this burden, which properly speaking should be her own: "I remind myself that it doesn't make sense – for me – to wait for him." This developmental advance of the speaker will have the further beneficial consequence that she no longer has to take responsibility for others' feelings. He will finally have his feelings (restored to him), and she will have hers (for the first time)!

But what has the speaker really discovered about herself up to this point? She has scrutinized the way she operates at work, and has gotten an inkling that all the ambiguity about decision making she has been in is her own doing. What a mess! In taking ownership of this ambiguity, she is getting to see the real source of her doubts. As yet, she has no well developed theory yet of who she is herself, not even as a decision maker. But at least she has put enough distance between self and other now to proceed to getting more clarity regarding herself.

Level	Characteristic
4(3)	Nearing self-authoring, but remaining at risk for regression to others' expectations

The speaker has arrived at a turning point, not only in her career but in her life. (People are not split up within themselves enough to act one way in life, and another way at work, as Kegan would say.) She still needs a lot of espousals to make self authoring work for her, but so what! At least, she has tasted how it feels to make decisions on her own.

Let's see what the espousals look like (adapted from Lahey et al. 1988, 67):

Interviewer: Tell me more about how you make decisions in your work these days.
Client: I used to wait for my boss's approval, but now I just decide by myself. My boss doesn't like it a lot of the time, but I think it's not only better for me but better for our relationship.
Interviewer: What do you think provoked this change in you?
Client: I have just had to accept the fact that there are some things I am not going to get from him, and he has to do the same thing. He's working with somebody who has certain expertises, and though he does not fully share them, he has to understand that I am competent in what I do, and will thus make decisions on my own.
Interviewer: Are you still concerned about his reactions to how you proceed?
Client: I know he doesn't like it, but I try not to dwell on that. And I'm aware that there's a part of me that doesn't want him to dwell on it either. I find it much easier when he doesn't dwell on our different competences.
Interviewer: What makes it hard when he does dwell on that?
Client: Well, I just have to work harder to remember that although I can be sad about his not helping me decide, I do think it's very important for me to honor my own interests. **Interviewer:** You said "it's very important?"
Client: Yes, because I'm not me if I don't.

Above, I spoke about the meaning of *forming a theory of self* as a requirement for reaching the turning point of S-4/3 and proceeding to S-4(3) and beyond. Let's review that statement here.

- **Meaning of 'forming a theory of self:'**
    - First, people must internally distance themselves from their need of being acknowledged and accepted by others, the community; they must be able to 'go it alone' if their own inner voice tells them to do so.
    - Second, people must develop a better and better notion of their uniqueness, of what makes them different from others, and find the courage to make that difference known to others while respecting others' otherness.
    - Third, people must develop an ethical theory of integrity of self.

How far has the speaker come regarding these requirements?

To judge from the excerpt above, the speaker now makes her own decisions because she thinks it is "not only better for me but better for our relationship." That is, she is beginning to see a way to satisfy her own self identity needs without doing harm, or impeding, relationships like those with her boss. She can to some extent stand away from relationships, and consider whether they converge with her identity needs or not. In short, the distance between her own self and her internalized others (like her boss and other people) has sufficiently grown for her to make them into an OBJECT, – so she can reflect upon them from a distance. In short, she has fulfilled the first requirement, above.

What about the second and third requirement?

I have just had to accept the fact that there are some things I am not going to get from him, and he has to do the same thing. He's working with somebody who has certain expertises, and though he does not fully share them, he has to understand that I am competent in what I do, and will thus make decisions on my own.

The reader might say that this expresses a 'two world hypothesis,' and it does, but not in the sense of S-2. The two worlds are seen here as two entities that relate to each other, **such that each has its own Center of Gravity**. Importantly therefore, this form of the two world hypothesis does not clash with a "my world hypothesis" – referred to by the third requirement – which states that I am my own person, and you are yours, and that's okay.

So far so good. But what about the ways in which the speaker still 'hangs on to' S-3:

I know he doesn't like it [that I make decisions on my own], but I try not to dwell on that. And I'm aware that there's a part of me that doesn't want him to dwell on it either. I find it much easier when he doesn't dwell on our different competences.

This statement is a clear give-away regarding S-4(3). It conveys the speaker's need to disregard that place in herself where she is still wedded to her internalized other (the boss). To do so is a requirement for her at this point in her development since she knows that she could be 'devoured' by this inner place in her, and therefore needs to disown it. More than that, she also cannot permit herself to dwell on the misgivings of her internalized other. To do so would have the same effect: it might take her back – make her regress – to an S-4/3 stance, and this she wants to avoid at all cost. She has had enough grief with relationships like the one to her boss, and she surely does not want to provoke any temptation on her part to glide back into that. So, in a way, the show down of which I have spoken is a show down involving her, rather than her boss. This is entirely appropriate, because she is now beginning to be her own self.

Asked how she manages not to dwell on her remaining misgivings, she says:

Well, I just have to work harder to remember that although I can be sad about his not helping me decide, I do think it's very important for me to honor my own interests, … because I'm not me if I don't.

The expected espousal has come in here. Interestingly, it is linked to her ability to distance herself from a feeling of sadness about being on her own. The importance of honoring her own interests now overrides her sadness, which is about losing a self protected by internalized others. These others are now dissolving, and she is on her own. Life is a risky place to be. Espousal will lead her on, toward the now nearly inevitable S-4 – should she have the potential to go there: "because I am not me if I don't honor my own interests."

SUMMARY OF THE JOURNEY TO STAGE 4

- Although the S-4(3) individual still holds on to a "3-ish" stance, essentially her internalized others are no longer the determinants of her own self's organization.
- As one could say (Lahey et al. 1988, p 69), internalized others now become *mediated by the self's organization.*
- Initially, this is a very precarious situation, to sustain the distinction between the self and its internalized views. It takes practice and learning – or perhaps coaching by a developmentally more advanced individual – to solidify the self authoring capability.

***

What has the speaker gained, and what was lost? The speaker has lost the protection of her internalized – and potentially also of her externalized – others. She is 'stripped naked,' in a way, and has to stand up for herself. The consequences of marching to her own drummer are hers to deal with, and hers alone. However, the gains are considerable. The speaker has done what only about 25% of adults ever accomplish: arriving at S-4. She has opened up for herself a niche where she is likely to be able to manage not only herself, but others.

Orientation	S-4	Intermediate Stages	S-5
View of Others	Collaborator, delegate, peer	???	Contributors to own integrity and balance
Level of Self Insight	High		Very High
Values	Self-determined		Humanity
Needs	Flowing from striving for integrity		Viewed in connection with own obligations and limitations
Need to Control	Low		Very low
Communication	Dialogue		True Communication
Organizational Orientation	Manager		System's Leader

Table I.1 Changing characteristics across adult stages

But she has accomplished more than that. She has reached a higher level of self insight, where her values are self-determined, and her needs flow from her striving for integrity. Having been very uncertain about herself and thus in need of a large amount of control, she now can relax that need and enter into dialogue with others, rather than remaining capable only of a 1:1 exchange. She has become a Manager in the developmental sense of the word.

Level	Characteristic
4	Fully self-authoring decision maker respecting others; 'my world' hypothesis

It might be a good exercise to understand slightly more academic language when speaking about this developmental stance. Learning to follow such language will serve you well. Lahey et al. 1988 (p. 79-80) characterize this developmental position as follows [punctuation, O.L.]:

The stage 4 self constructs a system, or psychological organization, which generates its own values, administers itself by regulating and evaluating its values in accordance with its own standard. The stage 4 self is identified with ("subject to") the system which generates its values and goals. It cannot consult itself or others about that system in ways which could lead to its modification or transformation because it cannot take its fundamental organizational principles as an object of reflection.
The evolution beyond stage 4 (consequently) involves a gradual differentiation from this embeddedness, or dis-identification within the system-as-constructed. Just as the stage 2 self gradually evolves toward taking the other's perspective inside the self, so the stage 4 self gradually takes as object its own and others' self-systems, *and thus brings other whole systems and forms inside the new self.* The new self becomes a context for the interaction of whole psychological self-systems, both with others and within the self. Because the stage 5 self is no longer ultimately invested in any one system or form as it is, interaction among forms and systems can result in modifying such systems or creating new forms. To the stage 4 self the product, i.e., the effect on the system itself, is ultimate. The new stage 5 self, however, creates a context for a PROCESS of forming and transforming ideas, theories, and systems.

While abstract, this formulation shows you that what this books talks about in more concrete and popular terms is ultimately a *complex internal process.* The process has to do with the evolution of consciousness over the adult life span. Not only does an individual over the duration of this journey increasingly succeed in making an object of his or her own self system. The individual is also able to reflect on other people's system. This creates in the individual an *enlarged mental space* where "ideas, theories, and systems" generally get formed and transformed. Concretely, this means that the S-4 individual can take a perspective on the way in which others define themselves, and can relate him- or herself to other systems that have become an object of reflection. However, the S-4 self cannot yet create *the context for a process that is as open to self transformations* to the extent an S-5 individual is capable of.

Let's think for a moment about what might happen in this *enlarged mental space.* (This space also matters in terms of cognition which is correlated with social-emotional stages at about 0.6). Since I can take a perspective not only on my own system of values but also on that of others, I can certainly compare systems and also coordinate them with full knowledge of their content. I can consequently understand the fragility of my own and other systems, and also the limits to which I can separate two systems from each other. In addition, since other systems are transparent to me, I can discern the degree of embeddedness in themselves of the systems I am involved with, including my own. As a result, I can engage in more than merely transactional processes – where other systems remain external to me. I can actually engage in *transformational processes in which my own system modifies itself in consensus with, or under the influence of, another system or systems.*

Since at this time in the history of science, we cannot avail ourselves of any empirically proven mind-brain correlation, and thus do not know about constellations of elements in the brain specific to S-4 – if we ever will –, we can be grateful to have available in Kegan's notation a rather precise SYMBOLIC SHORT-HAND. By way of this short-hand, we can CONVERSE with some precision about rather minute differences in world view that determine much of what is otherwise explained through endless studies of "performance" and "motivation," including "emotional intelligence." We can therefore replace the endless trait lists of behavioral research with a compact notation, such as S-4 {3: 7: 4}! (What's even more, once the scoring of developmental interviews is either automated with inclusion of *artificial intelligence* or is approximated by questionnaire simulations of psychometric validity, we will be in the possession of methods applicable to larger number of individuals, especially for use in organizations. See Appendix D of this volume.)

***

Before proceeding with the journey from S-4 to S-5, let's briefly review what the abstract characterization of the S-4 stance is telling us (final wording by Steve Stewart):.

S-4 is an 'I' stage, but one much different from Stage 2. These individuals, rather than trying to become someone, have found themselves or 'come of age.' They have been successful while pursuing Stage 3 goals and have, in their eyes, earned the 'right' to stand above the crowd and be noticed. Consequently, they are highly, if not completely, identified with the value system that they have authored for themselves, yet they are very respectful of others for their competence and different values and beliefs. They find great difficulty in standing away from themselves to discover their own voids, but they will accept them when they are discovered. In this sense, they can be more self-accepting, relative to those less well developed. They can stand back, however, from the institution that previously defined them far enough to be objective about what they 'see.' Since they are far more objective, they can be good at apprehending what could be done to change the system of which they are a part and, once doing so, will have enough strength in their own center-of-gravity to weather the storms that may come about in actually instigating a change or transformation process. The changes they author, however, will, more likely than not, be directed towards making the organization more responsive to themselves, authoring and moving it in directions approximating their own personal 'institution,' rather than one more universally self-sustaining. The climate they create will be one that follows the status quo, but taking on their own idiosyncratic values and operational principles as time passes. Since they are caught in their own Frame of Reference (FOR), they fail to appreciate the value of other FORs that are just as much, if not more, developed. This, by definition, limits the extent to which 'their' organization can learn-to-learn, grow, and further develop.

Here are some highlights of this characterization. S-4 individuals:
- do not 'have,' but 'are' their value system – they cannot make their values an object of reflection;
- are more self accepting than individuals below S-4, and seek to understand their failings through input from others whom they open themselves to;

- are better change agents than any individual below S-4, although the changes they bring about and support are those that support their own self system first and foremost;
- have a hard time appreciating another frame of reference that does not derive from own values and principles;
- have the potential to become transparent to other individuals, the more so the more they journey toward S-5;
- have the ability to make others' self system an object of their reflection, and thus be 'objective' about others.

The above description suggests, at least in part, what it will take for S-4 individuals to journey to higher stages. Predictably, the theme of their journey will center on the ability to 'stand away' from their own self system, and come to see, with humility, the stark limitations of their idiosyncratic way of viewing the world and themselves. In terms of intermediate steps, this is what the journey looks like:

Level	Characteristics
4(5)	Begins to question scope and infallibility of own value system; aware of own history
4/5	Conflicted over relinquishing control and taking risk of critical exposure of own view
5/4	Conflicted, but increasingly succeeding in 'deconstructing' self; committed to flow
5(4)	Fully committed to deconstructing own values, benefiting from divergent others
5	No longer attached to any particular aspect of the self, focused on unceasing flow

Table 6.3 Range characteristics between S-4 and S-5

Let's now look at an illustration of what an S-4 individual might do when engaged with an intimate who is requesting his or her help (adapted from Lahey et al, 1988, 131-132). This illustration will further clarify the theory of 'helping' presented in this book:

Last week a close colleague of mine was telling me about his feelings about a superior that were evidently very painful to him. I was mainly trying to listen and understand what was important to him in this. I believe that's the way I can be most helpful to him, by being an understanding, sympathetic listener, rather than, you know, trying to fix things up, or lay my own stuff on him regarding what I am thinking or feeling. So, I encouraged him to talk, and I asked him some questions to try to understand better. And basically, he did describe his experience, but I didn't really get a chance to respond at all, since he immediately asked me whether I would have felt hurt if I had been in that situation myself. From what I understood of the situation, I was pretty certain actually that I wouldn't have. But I couldn't tell him that, because that would have indicated to him that I was ignoring how he much he was actually hurt. I would have felt like I was no longer staying with his take on things, thus kind of abandoning him. And that was exactly what I didn't want to do! What I really wanted to do was just to let him know that I understood how he must have felt.

Evidently, the speaker in this illustration embraces a theory of helping that says s(he) shouldn't get involved in another's internal process more than necessary, – just enough to remain an objective listener who can simultaneously signal that he "understood how you must have felt." To engage more closely with the other's story might, in the speaker's view, *contaminate* the objectivity owed to the other person as a peer, and transcends the limits of S-4 empathy. The S-4 individual needs to stay clear of the risk of 'laying my own stuff on him' or 'trying to fix things,' thereby perhaps failing to fully honor what is involved for the other party. As this shows, at work here is kind of 'two world hypothesis,' as we found in S-2. Except now, the other's world is fully considered as sacrosanct in itself, and an objective perspective is taken on it. Nevertheless, the other's world is considered external to one's own process. "I respect you, but don't want to meddle with your process," which is the hallmark of a professional.

So, when it comes to making the link between the other's experience (feelings) and my own, the S-4 person chooses not to intervene, – or rather his self system chooses for him not to intervene. One might say: I intervene with the client (as an 'other'), but not with my relationship with the client as far as it implicitly defines me.

The difference that emerges between the two partners is thus a fundamental one that concerns how they generate feelings. (Lahey et al. speak of different *feeling generators*.) An entire life history goes into how feelings get generated. At S-4, I have my way, and you have your way, and that has to be accepted. I can make a judgment about your reactions, but your reactions will always differ from mine. And in any case, whether they are or not, I am going to keep that to myself. For, how can I impose my standards on you, given that they are mine, and thus by definition different from yours?

There is great consistency here that we have to admire. A certain Prussian rigor, you might say (if you were born into German culture, as I was). I know what my values are, and if my values clash with yours, too bad, I will stick to mine. And when you ask me to evaluate my value system and feelings, I cannot do so because your values are sacrosanct to me, and I am not going to mess with them 'imposing my stuff on you!'

Organizationally, this seems to entail that I can not only manage myself, but also other people, at least if I can keep them at some distance from myself. I can manage others because I am certain of my own values. In order to manage other people, especially at S-4, I only have to appeal to their integrity. Otherwise, I will appeal to 'community.' That usually works. And rather than telling them what to do – as I would have to do vis a vis S-3 individuals – I am trusting that they hold themselves to the same standards of excellence as I do. If the respect I show them is not rewarded, then obviously I need to manage by other means (such as control), since their own value system is not up to the level of my own. In any case, I'll get the job done.

In summary:

- **Distribution:** 20 to 25% of adults.
- **Essence of this stage:** Individuals are identified with their own value system as the root of their 'integrity' (which is their highest value).
- **Respecting others:** Others are respected for what they are, but only to the limit of one's identification with one's own value system and identity formation.

- **Self management:** Individuals are able to manage themselves, and thus can manage other people.
- **Limits:** Individuals cannot step away from their own value system and identity or 'integrity,' and therefore do not 'see' how protecting that identity is limiting their ability to rise beyond their own limitations.
- **Developmental risk:** Letting go of one's self constructed identity toward a position of 'no self' is the most arduous step in human self development, given that our functioning in society is based on ego identity. The positive sign of dealing with the risk of 'losing oneself' is the ability to be 'in the flow.' The essential risk one is taking, well known from other stages, is loss of self (to gain a more highly developed self).
- **Developmental advance toward level 5:** Given the potential to do so, individuals steadily advance toward a self-aware (S-5) position, by first realizing that their own value system and identity is limited and idiosyncratic, something they cannot impose on others. This S-4 stance shows in the following way:
  - **Personal history:** the S-5 individual is fully aware of his/her own history and value system as a determinant of his/her present identity.
  - **Construct awareness:** the S-5 individual is fully aware of the limitations of language in rendering the concreteness and depth and flow of human experience.
  - **Penetrability:** the S-5 individual lives in a transparent, inter-individual self system
  - **Self identification:** the S-5 individual increasingly abstains from identifying with particular parts of the self, realizing the diversity, complexity, and wholeness of self experience, including of parts so far disowned.

I have already indicated that the ensuing journey will center on moving out of the splendid isolation of one's integrity. Let us see how this might happen in steps we can clearly notate:

Level	Characteristics
4(5)	Begins to question scope and infallibility of own value system; aware of own history

Evidently, the first step is making an object of one's own value system, to reflect upon it. We can see this happening in the following illustration (Lahey et al. 1988, 144):

Last week a close colleague of mine was telling me about his feelings about a superior that were evidently very painful to him. I was mainly trying to listen and understand what was important to him in this. I believe that's the way I can be most helpful to him, by being an understanding, sympathetic listener, rather than, you know, trying to fix things up, or lay my own stuff on him. But then he asked me how I would have felt had I been in his situation. I didn't feel that I could really respond to his question, because I didn't think I would have felt hurt, and I thought that my focusing on that would be abandoning how he really was hurt. But then I felt later that my not telling him more about how I felt really deprived both of us of an opportunity. Maybe the way I even come to decide what is helpful cuts us off from another kind of experience, but I don't know how helpful it would be if I did let him know my reactions.

Initially, the speaker is not swayed by the other's feelings of hurt, although fully acknowledging them. With hindsight, however, reflecting upon his stance, the speaker feels "that my not telling him more about how I felt (or would have felt) really deprived both of us of an opportunity." What this opportunity might be remains somewhat unclear from the evidence we have. But what is clear is that the speaker is turning critical toward his or her own splendid isolation from the other, surmising that it cuts him or her off from a valuable experience. The speaker feels on shaky ground with this, not sure "how helpful it would be if I did let him know my reactions."

We can say that some self doubt has crept in here and, consequently, the splendid isolation is gone (or in any case less splendid). Although the speaker cannot say exactly what opportunity is being missed by his respectful acknowledgement of the other's hurt, there is an inkling here that s(he) is perhaps holding herself too safe for her own good. After all, the speaker's theory of helping may be too self-serving. In short, the speaker has moved a little bit out of the boundaries of the classic S-4 position.

If this journey continues, what would it yield?

Level	Characteristics
4/5	Conflicted over relinquishing control and taking risk of critical exposure of own view

If the speaker is going to go beyond the boundaries of her sacrosanct self, opening herself to the risk of discovering new or unwelcome aspects of herself, she might really get herself into trouble. As on the journey between S-3 and S-4, this step leads to self-discovery. However, in contrast to what happened before S-4 was reached, here the self has already been constituted – it exists, as in existentialism – and now has to be undone, "de-constructed," to so speak. (Will this undoing of one's recent gains ever end?)

We have a little bit of a clue of how this might happen, namely, by generating some doubts about one's own splendid theory of helping (Lahey et al. 1988, 138-139):

Last week a close colleague of mine was telling me about his feelings about a superior that were evidently very painful to him. I was trying to understand what was important to him, because I felt my being an understanding, sympathetic listener would be the way I could be most helpful. But then he asked me how I would have felt in his situation. I found myself not wanting to tell him, because I felt telling him about how I actually would not have felt hurt would be abandoning how he was hurt, and preventing me from letting him know I understood. **And yet, my feeling quite stuck prompted me to consider whether I might be wrong that he would feel I was ignoring his being hurt, or wrong that just listening was the most helpful thing to do.**
So I said, 'you know, I really feel that if I answer your question that will take us away from my really being with you and sympathizing with how you felt.' And he said, 'but that's not what I really want from you. I know how I feel, and **I'm really wanting to understand whether there's another way I could be putting this experience together.'** Well, we ended up talking a long time about different ways we each might have responded, and I really saw how that experience could help both of us to be closer, and to learn from one another. He saw that maybe his being hurt was based on assumptions he might be wrong about, and I saw how letting him in

on my ideas of how to be helpful could really help me to think about them, to improve them, and to be more helpful.

What is the conflict here? Is it one between the speaker and her interlocutor, or within the speaker? And is it a conflict of stages, or a personal one? Also, how is this conflict, if it is one, created?

It would seem that the essential conflict is created *within* the speaker by the consideration that she might be wrong in her assumptions about her interlocutor. Perhaps the theory of helping she has so far endorsed is limited. It could be, for instance, that her colleague would not feel ignored in his hurt as her present theory of helping assumes. Also, 'just listening' might not be the right thing to do in this circumstance. This is one side of the situation.

The other side of the situation is that the interchange between the two self systems now tends toward transparency on both sides. The interlocutor struggles with the issue of whether there are perhaps better ways to understand the hurt he felt coming from the superior. In this way, both parties are beginning to move from their moorings. The speaker throws doubts on her theory of helping, and the interlocutor throws doubt on whether his initial interpretation of the experienced hurt was justified.

In this way, both parties are opening up one to the other, sensing that **together** they might be able to come to more satisfactory conclusions in their inquiry about hurt and helping. However, that is how far they get, and no further. The grip S-4 holds on them remains too strong. And consequently, the conflict between the stages they are in is resolved by both to the side of S-4. While the conflict is one of stages, it is clearly at the same time a very personal one. But no full renunciation of each party's own position occurs. Therefore, the conflict leads to a kind of standoff between the two parties who keep respecting each other highly, but are not ready to embark on real soul searching. However, their appetite to do so has been wetted.

What, then, is needed beyond what has been risked by the two parties? Let's see what might happen in the next step toward S-5 (Lahey et al. 1988, 145-147):

Level	Characteristics
5/4	Conflicted, but increasingly succeeding in 'deconstructing' self; committed to flow

Last week a close colleague of mine was telling me about an important feeling he had that was evidently very painful to him. I was trying to understand what was important to him, because I felt my being an understanding, sympathetic listener would be the way I could be most helpful. But then, he asked me how I would have felt in his situation. I found myself not wanting to tell him because I felt telling him about how I actually would not have felt hurt would be abandoning how he was hurt, and preventing me from letting him know I understood. And yet, my feeling quite stuck prompted me to consider whether I might be wrong that he would feel I was ignoring his being hurt, or wrong that just listening was the most helpful thing to do. So I said, 'you know, I really feel that if I answer your question that will take us away from my really being with you, and sympathizing with how you felt.' And he said, 'but that's not what I really want from you. I know how I feel, and I'm really wanting to understand whether there's another way I could be putting this experience together.'

Well, we ended up talking a long time about different ways we each might have responded, and I really saw how that experience could help both of us to be closer, and to learn from one another. He saw that maybe his being hurt was based on assumptions he might be wrong about, and I saw how letting him in on my ideas of how to be helpful was a wonderful thing.

For one, then he was able to tell me that wasn't what he wanted or needed. So, that prompted me to pause and consider my own frame of help might not be helpful at all! That helps me to improve my ideas, and make them more helpful as a result. **This can be hard, because I do get very attached to my convictions, and sometimes it's one kind of painful or another being open to having to change these convictions.** Still, I realize that's silly no matter how exciting the ideas are, **my holding them so dearly actually deadens my vitality; it drains the juice that makes me alive, even though it's me who invents the ideas to begin with!**

That's why what was even more wonderful was that in telling him what was going on for me, **the planful and contained quality of my way of being with him broke open. My intent to "help" him really got acted on in my being able to be with him.** There the line between helper and 'helpee' dissolved: instead of my being the helper, and my close colleague being the 'helpee', each of us became both of those for one another and ourselves.

You will agree that the speaker is very eloquent here. That is part of the business of being at 5/4. After all, without forcefully espousing a more 5-ish position it might be really difficult to get away from old beliefs, especially if one gets, as she admits, very attached to 'her' convictions.

What the speaker above realizes is centrally that it does not serve her well to identify with any particular idea or theory absolutely – even one created by her. Ideas are just that, ideas! What can be missed in this way is life itself, the ceaseless flow of change that is occurring at every moment. Compared to this flow, "the planful and contained quality of my being with him" had to be left behind. As a result, the relationship between the two parties fundamentally changes. No longer are they external to each other. They are now enmeshed with each other (but not entangled) without therefore losing the clear boundaries each of them draws. They are about to become TRANSPARENT to each other!

For the first time, the speaker has thus gained a foothold in S-5. To do so, she had to abandon old ideas, the conception of herself as an expert helper. This step is of great interest in the context of process consultation. Here is the precondition of leaving behind the expert as well as the doctor-patient model! In fact, the change to S-5/4 might even ready the person to go beyond process consultation in its orthodox form as it derives from Edgar Schein's work!

Does the speaker go beyond the boundaries of consultation here, by becoming a 'transparent other?' What are the professional ethics of this stage (S-5/4)? As a consultant, mediator, or coach, would the speaker have to keep her (S-4) 'Persona' intact, rather than embarking on a quest for further self-discovery, in order not to do harm?

It seems that here, we are entering a realm of professional ethics that has so far not been explored. At least I know of no research on this topic. We are thus left to our own devices in answering this question. What are the limits of a 'planful and contained quality of my being with' the client when in a helping role? Is this perhaps the border that separates 'consulting' and 'coaching' from 'therapy' (aside from Kegan's important distinction between mental growth and mental health)?

One thing is certain: the carefully crafted 'best practices' of the coaching and consulting communities are gone for good at this point (they were already gone upon reaching S-4), and so are the 'coaching competencies' that presently define integrity of coaching for most practitioners. In the present context, they are just another set of ideas that hinder the mutual transparency of self systems to be realized.

Another way of looking at the S-5/4 scenario in the context of process consultation is to say that we are here entering the truly and consciously INTERDEVELOPMENTAL sphere of mutual engagement. Clearly, left to her own devices, the speaker might never have taken the step to abandon her own ingrained theory of helping. One could therefore say **that while the boundaries of conventional consultation are reached here, those of develop-mentally deepened process consultation (and of developmental coaching) have as yet not been reached.** What do I mean by that?

The fourth model of consultation, of DPC, introduced in this book (see the Introduction) is based on the premise **that the consultant's stage of self development is the strongest existing predictor of intervention outcome** (success or failure). If thought through, this premise seems to entail that to set arbitrary limits to self-discovery in consultation – on the side of the consultant – is not conducive to engaging with clients at a deeper level. However, where is the boundary between consultant and client to be drawn?

Level	Characteristics
5(4)	Fully committed to deconstructing own values, benefiting from divergent others

Perhaps understanding the next stage will shed light on this question (Lahey et al., 1988, 140-143; my highlighting):

Last week a close colleague of mine was telling me about an important feeling he had experienced that was very painful to him. I was trying to understand what was important to him, because I felt my being an understanding, sympathetic listener would be the way I could be most helpful. But then he asked me how I would have felt in his situation. So I said, 'you know, I was feeling like really listening to you, creating a space for you talk this through out loud, thinking that would be the most help I could be.' And he said back to me, 'but that's not what I really want from you. I know how I feel, and I'm really wanting to understand whether there's another way I could be putting this experience together.' Well, it really surprised me that my first instinct at helping was one that he wouldn't feel helped by, since I feel like we're so tuned into each other's needs. **But what was really amazing was that when I actually jumped in to exploring right along with him, not just how he felt, *but how I would have felt,* I discovered another "good" reason why I might not have thought to respond to him differently when he asked me whether I would have been hurt.**
I had thought, as I listened to his story, that I wouldn't be. In a way I hadn't wanted to answer his question, because I thought I wouldn't be upset, and I didn't want to restrict him into paying

attention to why I wouldn't, rather than how he felt. But I ended up discovering how by looking at the situation the way he does, by paying attention to pieces I would have ignored but he looked at, I actually would be quite hurt. **He helped me see that what was hard for me was that his situation parallels one that I'm in quite a lot with a colleague of mine; one where I haven't paid attention to all the ways I really am hurt.**

So, I guess I had a lot invested in not paying attention to that hurt (and that's a whole other topic …) – so much invested that I picked, and even rationalized, a way to attend to my close colleague that could keep me distant. You know, I really try not to do that, to get wrapped up in my own ideas of how to respond without giving him some choice. **But I'm a sneaky one, I'll tell you! I've got to be on my toes all the time to keep from controlling everything: him, myself, what's him, what's me, – everything!** I almost have to keep from letting myself get too involved with my first take on things because, whatever actual merit it may have, I'm in danger of making it into the truth. And I also have a tendency not to want to see some other whole way I'm actually operating or feeling, because I might get pulled into making that the truth. That's kind of funny; like it's not that I've got a whole different take in there, too, because it'll make me leave the take I've been going with, but because I'm afraid I'll go too much with the new take. I'm lucky he's someone I can explore those kinds of things with. **We really do help each other not to just take some stand that keeps us from exploring even the hard stuff.**

MUTUAL SELF DISCOVERY might be the term here for 'the really hard stuff.' This kind of discovery is hard for many. Here are some reasons for why that is so:

- My own views tend to get attached to me like infallible 'truths'.
- I have to watch hard to catch myself in this game of subterfuges.
- Unless I can find a partner with whom to catch myself in this way I won't succeed; it's an *interdevelopmental* effect that I myself cannot generate.
- To keep in the flow, I constantly have to watch myself, and this I am helped in doing by the other party.
- This also holds for my watching the other party not getting stuck on loading up on some truth of theirs.

Here, all issues are deeply mutual, having their origin and solution in the inter-developmental engagement of the parties.

In cognitive terms:

- The limits of stability and durability of both self systems have become evident: both are in constant flux.
- Conflict is seen – and is acting as – a source of personal development.
- The value of 'moving on' lies in acquiring a new balance within the self and between selves.
- Self systems can be coordinated, if not merged.
- Each system is a self transforming one that is transparently open to (selected) other systems.
- Taking multiple perspectives is becoming second nature.

In light of volume 2 of this book, on cognitive coaching, it may interest the reader to know that what is involved in achieving increasing self awareness is above all a matter of increasingly fluid thought. Fluid thought is based on *thought forms* characterized as being *dialectical*, meaning that they are ways of knowing that are able to deal with contradictions and apparent paradoxes in increasingly subtle ways. What at first glance appears only as a social-emotional achievement (ED) is not really possible if it is not also sustained by individuals' dialectical thought forms (CD). Because of this, the two aspects of adult development – social emotional and cognitive – are inseparable. This means that cognitive processes may act as a 'motor' for social-emotional development, and vice versa.

As we noticed previously, there is a fair amount of ESPOUSAL   involved in the last speaker's utterances. The 'sneakiness' she refers to here is analogous to what was previously expressed as 'not wanting to dwell on' the differences between the S-4(3) speaker and her internalized other (the boss). Both at S-4(3) and S-5(4)), the individual uses espousal to strengthen her developmental position. She is aware that there are unsafe places *in her* – places she has to keep away from. And this she does in order not to jeopardize her developmental progress. While at S-4(3) this showed us that the speaker had succeeded in separating out from her internalized others, here, at S-5(4), the speaker shows that she has separated out from her orthodox self-authoring self. You can't do the second if you have never done the first.

***   .

At this point, let us briefly return to the question of whether can one consult and/or coach from S-5/4, or even from S-5(4) Center of Gravity. If indeed one can, at what risk, and with what necessary cautions can one do so? This question is not about a shared understanding between consultant and client, but about **the degree to which the consultant can stay *professional* while becoming a transparent equal in the relationship with the client.** If the consultant's professional Persona – almost like that of an actor – is removed, what remains of the consulting relationship?

This is unexplored territory, and no certain answers are available (if there ever will be). We are here at the frontiers of process consultation, and any other social intervention (such as therapy) as well. These frontiers only emerge once we go beyond behavioral interventions where content always overwhelms developmental structure. Although the espousal of *being with the client* can often be heard in coaching conversations and even the popular coaching literature, it is, I would say, not typically uttered by coaches beyond S-4, but by those who have not yet become fully self authoring, and **who therefore mistake their community stance (S-3) for making meaning at S-5.** That's easy to do if you have never reached S-4! This would be my hypothesis. Research that could enlighten us about this issue is non- existent. As for 'therapy,' there is one precious foray into the matter (L. Havens, 1986; 1993).

***

Regardless now of where the limit of professional consultation, behavioral or developmental, lies – whether at S-5/4 or S-5(4) or at S-5 – it might be of interest to explore briefly what an S-5 self report would sound like.

Level	Characteristics
5	No longer attached to any particular aspect of the self, focused on unceasing flow

Taking our cue from the S-5(4) excerpt, and removing much of the espousal embedded in it, we might encounter statements like the following:

A colleague of mine and I have recently become very close simply by closely working together, and I have finally resolved to invite her into my executive team. I have not done this without trepidation, not so much for the company's sake – since I esteem her highly – but because of risks of overstepping personal boundaries. What finally moved me to take the step is that it became clear to me that I couldn't responsibly continue leading the executive team as the only 'highly developed' individual. And this is what in my judgment had been my situation for some time. I was beginning to think about leaving the company. I became sure that to motivate others more strongly, as their leader, I needed to collaborate with an individual who, coming from an entirely different vantage point, would keep me honest vis-a-vis myself, and keep up the learning between us.

After initial trepidations I began to test how this idea would work. I went through many discussions with my colleague about this, and we decided to give it a try, with the understanding that I was not inviting her to join the team simply because of her expertise, but more so since we had shown each other that we could fully take each others' perspective and remain open to the flow of things. What is more, we both agreed that what we were learning from each other had a lot to do with insight into the fragility of our own ability to act from beyond a narrowly self-authoring perspective. We also agreed that if we were together in this, we could better withstand the risk of being 'thrown back' to a control position that would be ever-present in the team, given how it was presently structured. So, I would say, we consciously entered into a pact of complete brotherhood and humility in this, from which we promised to withdraw if we found that we simply couldn't keep up the calm and even-handedness needed when so exposed to each other, and to go our separate ways. And I can tell you, I wake up every morning now, amazed that two human beings can do what we are attempting to do without losing their way! And of course, sometimes I feel, and so does my partner, that the greatest obstacle of succeeding in this resides in the very medium we are embedded in for the duration of our work, which is everyday language!

I have constructed this self report of an S-5 individual to the best of my ability, and can't be sure that it is entirely successful. Let me state, therefore, what was my aim to bring to the surface regarding a fully self-aware developmental position:

- There is some, but not much espousal about *being with each other* left in this illustration.
- The risk of engaging with each other at a self-aware level is taken for the sake of the team as a whole, and of developing the team further (this, of course, could be merely 'espoused,' and would have to be checked out through a scored interview).
- The individuals concerned are acting from humility about their idiosyncrasies and limitations.
- They are fully aware of the risk to their own identity and further self-development that they are taking in the partnership.
- They are doing their best to stay in the flow, shaping themselves into a complete learning organization as best they can.
- They know that the way they use natural language is going to be the real crux of the enterprise.

SUMMARY OF STAGE 5

- **Distribution:** Less then 10% of adults ever reach this stage.
- **Advance over Stage 4:** Individuals no longer identify with a particular part of their self, history, expertise, thus 'being in the flow of life.'
- **Essence of this stage:** I am transparently linked to others that I trust enough to ask for help in questioning my perspective, thus being open to unchartered pathways and unforeseen discoveries (about myself).
- **(My Own) Learning Organization:** The ultimate concern is with expanding my purview to potentials in me I have so far not grasped, or have defended against; I am motivated to support others in their development even where it may impinge on my own immediate advantage.
- **Pervasive limitation:** I am not fully aware of the extent to which my 'languaging' of reality gives me the illusion of 'knowing what is going on' inside and outside of me; while I can represent 'objective reality' with increasing accuracy, I remain blind to much that escapes categorization and formulation, – the constant flux of life.

JOURNEY BEYOND STAGE 5

As far as we know today, – for instance on account of Susan Cook-Greuter's work (1999) – developmental stages extend further to *post-autonomous* stages where maximal subject-object separation is replaced by universal *embeddedness*. Two main aspects of this advanced progression in consciousness are stated below.

- **Developmental risk:** Journey into spirituality beyond existing developmental grounding is fraught with the risk of overextending existing resources
- **Meaning of 'universal embeddedness:'**
  - First, keen 'construct awareness,' meaning pervasive awareness of the limitation of language in capturing what is real.
  - Second, insight into using verbal language as a way of limiting awareness for oneself and others.
  - Third, loss of the permanent object world by further de-centering from self (subject).
  - Fourth, cyclical rather than linear experience of causality.
  - Fifth, immersion in the phenomenal flux, and access to layers and layers of symbolic abstraction.

Discussing both of these topics in depth would amount to another chapter. Here, I will have to be brief.

It is typically assumed that S-5 provides the most solid grounding for a serious venture into 'spirituality.' The idea behind this is that there may be unnecessary suffering if a person's developmental and spiritual potential are out of synch. (This is, for instance, shown by research on individuals in early adulthood that embraced Eastern philosophies subsequently and came to grief because they never developed the self in the first place that they set out to lose.) There are many developmental risks if the spiritual journey is undertaken prior to nearing or reaching S-5 (see Case Study no. 3 on Sarah, Appendix B of this volume). This is the case because your spirituality is always on the level of your adult development, and never lifts you beyond that level but fully reflects it!

Some readers will rightfully object here that there is a risk of thinking of spirituality as exclusive of those individuals not at S-5, which is the majority of people (98%). To think in this way would obviously exclude many people from spiritual experience, and this makes no sense. Therefore, it seems more appropriate to expand the notion of spirituality to all stages, including children (Wilber 2005, 2000; Kornfield 1993). If this is accepted, one needs to observe that **'spirituality' has a different meaning and depth at different stages.** One can rightfully say, with Wilber, that the way spirituality is experienced is entirely stage-specific.

The second entry, above, is meant simply as a clarification of what *universal embeddedness* might mean. Clearly, once OBJECT has overtaken SUBJECT in a person's consciousness, it becomes impossible for a person, to hold herself apart from the world or others, as is second nature at S-4. There is lovely book on the experience of embeddedness in old age by the older Hermann Hesse (2002), entitled <u>Mit der Reife wird man immer juenger</u> (In maturing one only gets younger) that with great clarity spells out the experience of cosmic embeddedness in poetic form.)

CHAPTER SUMMARY

In this central chapter, I have outlined, through self reports, the intermediate steps that serve as milestones along the trajectory from S-2 to S-5. I have demonstrated that similar contents can be spoken from different Centers of Gravity, and that what matters is the underlying meaning making to which content can be traced by a developmentally skilled observer able to play 'devil's advocate.' I have emphasized that the self reports used are *illustrations*, not fragments taken from real interviews, and that they are meant to serve as teaching tools preparing the reader to take on actual interview fragments and/or, eventually, entire interviews for scoring.

The reader now has acquired a comprehensive survey of the developmental landscape through which s(he) him- or herself is presently moving. The illusion that life's journey occurs in some kind of *flatland* (Wilber) should by now be gone, although the social surround continues to reinforce it. The distinction between incremental *learning* and discontinuous *development* should have become clear. It is, incidentally, closely related to that between competence and capability in professional work (see *www.cdremsite.com*).

As you read on, you may want to return to Chapter 6 as a safe haven based on which to understand your own journey and that of your client.

PRACTICE REFLECTIONS
- When you consider the entire range of adult development, where, in your experience, are most of your clients presently positioned?
- This being so, what conclusions as a helper do you draw regarding your practice?
- Given the propensity of the coaching community and its literature, to espouse S-4 if not S-5, what would you want to do to bring some realism into that literature?

- Given the paucity of research on the actual developmental position of coaches, what do you think you can do to contribute to coaching research?

7
The Structure of Powerful Conversations:
How to Listen Between the Lines

Introduction to Semi-Structured Interviewing

I showed in Chapter 4 that the conventional definition of *listening* as a content-focused process takes too much for granted for conventional listening to yield empirical evidence of a developmental nature. From a developmental vantage point, the same can be said about *interviewing*, the topic of this chapter. This is the case because interviewing creates the context in which alone developmental listening can happen. As we saw previously, one cannot expect to gather developmental evidence other than by paying attention to the client's internal mental process, because it is through that process that meaning making centrally occurs. The difference in approach also shows up on the client's side. In contrast to a client feeling "heard," in developmental listening clients feel "understood," sometimes for the first time. There is a world between these two different perceptions of a consultative intervention.

As I showed in Chapter 4, the central tool used in developmental listening is *hypothesis formulation and testing relative to the client*. This tool is unique to developmentally deepened process consultation (DPC). I made the point that in order to gather developmental evidence, the interviewer needs to adopt *explicit*, rather than merely implicit, *hypotheses*. Using explicit hypotheses requires a different kind of interviewer, namely individuals who have experienced, often against their own expectation, a developmental transformation – rather than only having learned 'new skills.' Clearly, only individuals with a certain developmental potential and ability to take risks have the capacity to do so.

In this chapter, I am building on the groundwork laid in Chapter 4, in two steps. In the first step, I review conventional notions of interviewing and contrast them with principles of *evidence based and evidence-gathering interviewing*. Over the course of the chapter, I am spelling out *three generic processes*, one of which, the focusing of attention, receives the greatest share of my attention. In the second step, I use actual interview excerpts, short as well as long, to put the theory of interviewing here formulated to the test. I do so in preparation of Chapter 8, where I score an entire interview fragment and evaluate the quality of the interviewing that led to it, with suggestions for improving it.

As Schein persuasively shows (1999, 60), anything done in consulting to the client's mental process constitutes an *intervention*, even remaining silent. This holds true for all organizational conversations, but particularly for interviewing. By this I mean that interviewing not only gathers data from the client, but also changes the data that the process consultant the client pair will have to work with in the future. On the client's side, these changes occur since a process of *focusing attention* is put in place that is free of the interviewer's internalized others as well as his or her own little personality. This leads to being 'understood' rather than only 'heard.' On the side of the process consultant, these changes take place because semi-structured interviewing is by nature INTER-DEVELOPMENTAL, contributing directly to the self knowledge and developmental capacity of the interviewer.

***

Conservations are not per se interviews, but they may be conducted as such. The switch to interviewing occurs in helping relationships where the process consultant strives to understand the client's mind. Once adopted as a mode of conversation, interviews may have wide-ranging effects ever after, especially if their results are fed back to the client in a systematic way as in CDF, and are used to structure future conversations.

The semi-structured developmental interview introduced in this volume is a 'Rohrschach test' in the figurative sense of the term. It is its purpose to enable process consultants to measure a client's hidden social-emotional dimension. In her role as a developmental interviewer, the consultant is an 'assessor' only once the interview has been completed (recorded or transcribed), not, however, during the interview itself. Although the interview is conducted with a stage hypothesis in mind, no 'scoring' other than that required for instantaneous hypothesis testing takes place during the interview itself. We can thus say that a semi-structured interview in the broad sense of the term comprises **four separate successive interventions**:

1. the building of trust with the client as the *subject* of two developmental interviews (first cognitive, then social-emotional);
2. the tape-recorded interviewing process itself that results in a 'scorable' interview text;
3. the feedback session that presents the results of the scoring, carried out in the context of the client's ascertained developmental profile;
4. *all subsequent conversations* between the two parties (assessor and assessee) that are informed by the developmental feedback given, and the client's reactions to it.

The first intervention, above, is crucial. Where sufficient trust is not established, the client will be unable to tell his or her story *completely*, not so much in terms of content, but in terms of the underlying *thinking and feeling generator* set in motion by interviewing. In the CDF framework, this is achieved by having a more neutral, cognitive *Professional Agenda Interview* and the answering of a behavioral questionnaire precede the more intimate, social-emotional interview. In this way, trust is first built on neutral grounds, based on questions about the work place, before the client's 'Self House' is entered where life experiences may equally be included and focused upon.

As Schein succinctly, although developmentally uninformed, puts it (1999, 43):

Tactically the implementation of active inquiry involves recognition that the inquiry must be managed in such a way that the client's story is fully revealed and that the client begins to think diagnostically himself. If the client's story does not come out in his own words and using his own concepts, the consultant cannot get a realistic sense of what may be going on. It is all too easy to project into what the client is reporting from one's own prior experience. The helper's initial behavior, therefore, must stimulate the client to tell the story as completely as possible and to listen in as neutral and nonjudgmental a way as possible.

While this holds true for all good interviewing, including interviewing for content rather than structure, what the quote says is especially salient from an adult-developmental point of view. In developmentally deepened process consultation (DPC), the client can "think diagnostically himself" only by focusing on his own thought process (mostly unknown to him), supported by the interviewer. This is the case since the client's story has many layers, one of which, the client's developmental *Frame of Reference* (stage), is absolutely **foundational** for understanding the content the client's story superficially consists of. From the vantage point of developmental interviewing, all that the client says, and does not say, paints a picture of SELF and nothing else, even if the conversation is about tasks and tools of the client's trade. The client's story regarding various contents and external situations is relevant only to the interviewee, not the interviewer. The latter knows all too well that behind the mirage of the content lies an entire universe of personal meaning making.

An additional issue regarding the client's story comes into play here, namely the fact that the client is SUBJECT TO his or her own developmental level (as is the consultant). This being so the client's story must be heard by the consultant as the unconscious (and unadorned) expression of the client's present level of meaning making. Of course, this is possible only for a consultant operating on a higher developmental level. (A consultant listening on the same developmental level as the client, since that level is hidden to the consultant, is simply not going to hear what is developmentally salient in what the client is saying.) It is the task of the consultant as interviewer, to propose developmental prompts to the client in order to discern, as best s(he) can, *what the client herself cannot know about*, and what therefore s(he) presently cannot take responsibility for. (Clearly, a client cannot take responsibility for what is unknown to her, as for instance her developmental level, and the same holds for the consultant-interviewer.)

This being the case, what can *fully engaging with adults* mean but **to engage with others wherever they may be developmentally, and from one's own present developmental level**? Since clients can know their present Center of Gravity only once they have transcended (and included) it, only a third party, such as a process consultant, can expertly handle the task of telling them – in whatever appropriate form – where they are presently making meaning from, and how that shapes their issues and outlook. To enable process consultants to do so is in fact the single overriding purpose of this volume as well as the entire book!.

Why would one refer to interviews that are really interventions at times as 'assessments'? Clearly, the term 'assessment' can be misleading, at least to the extent that it implies drawing a clear line between an 'assessor' and an 'assessee.' While this line indicates a detachment on the side of the interviewer (minimally at S-4), and initially suggests an expert or doctor model of consultation, it is in fact an entirely penetrable line. This is so because in a developmental interview, the consultant-interviewer is using him- or herself as the instrument of research, and is thus thoroughly engaged in the assessment process. Only, developmental detachment does not derive from making the interviewee into an object, as happens in conventional interviewing where the client's thought process itself is not researched in depth. In the developmental case, the detachment derives from working from within a consistent conceptual framework that, once mastered, neutralizes the interviewer's "little personality" and bias, to the point where the interviewer BECOMES the carrier of developmental tools.

Keeping in mind the relative sense in which semi-structured interviews can be called *assessments* (as conventionally understood), I will in what follows speak to two different aspects of semi-structured interviewing, namely, interviewing:

- as a method of 'assessment;'
- as a model of structured conversations more generally.

Along the way, I will be discussing the different distances a consultant can chose to adopt between the client's train of thought – or flow of consciousness – and his or her own interviewing process. Specifically, I will distinguish *three generic processes* that by definition entail different distances from the client's mental process:

- Focusing of attention
- Interpretation
- Enactment (modeling of new behavior).

These more theoretical considerations will then be practically demonstrated by analyzing two interview fragments, paying special attention to the behavior of the interviewer as a developmental process consultant.

***

Fully engaging with others in life or in organizational environments is often a crucial matter, not only for the sake of effectiveness but helpfulness. 'Being on the same wave length' is a vague reference to such engagement. In many organizational environments, fully engaging with others has become taboo, and conversations have been replaced by command chain announcements or shop talk. The risks of this development are apparent to those who are focused on managing and helping people realize their adult-developmental potential, and safeguarding the human capital capability organizations are based on.

In this book, I am setting new standards for how helping professionals can learn to fully engage with others, and for what that requires. I have no ambition to turn helping professionals in psychologists, not even *developmental* psychologists. I think there is no need to do so. 'Psychology' is not what process consultation is all about. My interest is rather in offering readers new ways of learning from the social sciences what has been understood about how people communicate. Through this book, I offer methods on which those who want to communicate profoundly and fully can model their own procedure. (I am not promising any S3-recipes, assuming S-4 and higher levels throughout.)

One important way to learn from the developmental sciences is to study how qualitative research interviews are carried out, what their structure is, and what it takes to focus on client's train of thought. The benefits of such study will easily become clear for process consultants whose mandate it is to understand their clients' mental process (Schein, 1999).

***

I have claimed to show in this book that *Fully Engaging Others*, taken seriously, is a function of knowing 'where the client is coming from developmentally.' I suggested that 'being on the same wave length' with an interlocutor may be given a developmental interpretation, such that standards for what is effective coaching and consultation can be introduced, taught, and practiced. In particular, I suggested that process consultants – including coaches – who live at a developmental stage below that of their clients can potentially harm them, but certainly can hope for only limited effectiveness in the long run (when all espousal of effectiveness has vanished). This is so because it is ultimately not knowledge and skills, but the consultant's understanding of meaning making processes in adults that determines effectiveness in engaging with others over the long term.

I have now walked the reader through that part of the adult-developmental landscape that is focused around developmental stages as modes of functioning in the world. I have shown that adults progress through stages throughout their life, and shift from one Center of Gravity to another discontinuously. In subsequent volumes, I will be adding to this material the tools of cognitive coaching based on understanding and practicing THOUGHT FORMS (volume 2), and those of behavioral coaching based on understanding clients' NEED/PRESS PROFILE (volume 3). Therefore, the reader will have available all the information needed to make a judgment about the developmental approach **only at the end of volume 4 of this book**, where I put all these perspectives together through detailed case studies.

Paying Attention to the Interviewer's Process

It may have occurred to the reader that in this volume, I have so far focused on only one of the parties of conversations, namely, the client. It is now time to change direction, and examine the interviewer, or more broadly, the person intervening (to whom I often refer simply as *process consultant*, following E. Schein's usage of the term). After all, it is the consultant who actually leads conversations, or at least is supposed to lead them, in a direction suggested by the greatest possible insight into the client. **It now behooves us to scrutinize more closely what an expert interviewer actually does in order to fully engage with a client.**

Let us distinguish between *interviewing* and *intervening*. Evidently, the second activity is much broader, whether it takes the form of consulting (in the conventional sense) or coaching. Since in evidence based interventions assessments precede the interventions proper –but keep in mind that assessments are a particular kind of intervention in their own right – we need to consider **not only interviewing as a method of assessment, but the influence of disciplined interviewing on powerful conversations generally.** Below, I will therefore distinguish interviewing as a method of assessment from interviewing as a model of disciplined, focused conversations. (Active listening is one thing, focused listening and speaking is another.)

Interviewing as a Method of Assessment

I have demonstrated in Chapter 6 that eliciting developmental information is a skill that can be learned. This skill requires higher levels of awareness than typical interviewing for content, and is therefore a way of stretching developmentally as well as interdevelopmentally. The reason for this is that conventional interviewing only leads to eliciting CONTENTS of many kinds (including *themes*), but not STRUCTURE or stage. The latter is more abstract, and simultaneously more concrete, than the former. It is more abstract, since many more different contents can be captured under one notation or concept. It is more concrete since, ultimately, isolated contents not seen within a consistent conceptual framework are, as Hegel would say, *very abstract*: Knowing only 'facts' or even 'themes' doesn't lead very far.)

I have mentioned two ways of undertaking the process of interviewing, for purposes of assessment and as a model for powerful conversations. One way to clarify the relationship between interviewing for assessment and conventional interviewing is to make a distinction between three *generic* interventional processes a consultant can engage in (see Basseches, 2003):

1. Focusing of attention
2. Interpretation
3. Modeling new behaviors ('enactment' of roles).

These three *generic processes* are taught by all 'coaching schools' under various guises and names, but never clearly distinguished. In fact, these three generic processes are often confounded in pedagogy, which is easy to do since they may overlap in practice. The expert orchestration of these three processes is what professional helping is all about.

Let us begin by clarifying the meaning of the three processes distinguished above – *focusing attention, interpretation, and modeling new behaviors*. We will pay primary attention to how each of them relates to the client's *train of thought* which is the source of all developmental listening, interviewing, and data collection.

***

Focusing attention is a state of mind that can be created by a consultant who is 'emptied out' of all content interfering with active listening. Such content comprises internalized others, premeditated ideas of *helping*, unverified hunches about the client, as well as anything that could focus attention on the consultant rather than the client. In this mental state alone, the consultant is able to use him- or herself as a research instrument, for the purpose not only of listening, but of data collection.

Data collection is the collection of interview data, here for the sake of insight into clients' developmental stage. Data collection can be formal and informal. In conventional process consultation, informal data collection is the rule. The notion is that anybody who calls himself a consultant or coach can ask questions. This is true, but what matters is the quality of the questions, their degree of reflectedness and diagnostic saliency. In developmental process consultation (DPC), the assumption that anybody can ask questions is dropped. The initial step toward consultation is interview based. Data collection thus becomes formal, as signaled by recording. Through explicit recording a set of data is created on account of which the client's social-emotional profile can be evaluated and 'scored' for stage. Although the resulting data set acoustically only includes 'what is said' by both parties, through controlled inferences based on stage theory the consultant can infer, to some high extent, what is 'not said' as well. (What is not said by the consultant as interviewer is also relevant. It is part of the process of hypothesis formulation, probing, and making inferences that the consultant engages in as interviewer.)

Let's reflect for a moment on the difference between the above, research-based notion of listening and the conventional one of listening for content. The notion implied by the former clearly is that content is "just that," and that it has its grounding in something invisible and seemingly ineffable, namely *consciousness*. Also implied is the notion that speech is an action that is partly unconscious and partly premeditated, and that it can be captured by another consciousness to the extent that the latter is free of contamination and follows the strictures of a 'semi-structured' interview. In fact, the only premeditated elements in the interviewer's consciousness are those elements of stage theory that are required for discerning 'where the client is coming from developmentally,' and how to probe for information not explicitly contained in the client's utterances but implied by them. Thus awareness must be focused on both the source of speech in the client, one's own speech responding to it, and the transparency of the balance of the two acoustic streams.

If this sounds forbidding, it is only as forbidding as it appears to people who have never meditated or listened to music. I think that in the present North American and European culture, the number of such people is quite small! One way, therefore, to 'simulate' an empty state of mind in interviewing might be to think of **the interviewing process as a *meditation upon the utterances of the client*** (produced by a source in itself invisible), or else a process of paying attention to a piece of music one is attracted to and wants to 'understand' more deeply, in terms of structure. In both cases, attention is focused on the meaning that emerges from the acoustic stream, either speech or music, and this meaning is grounded in structure, not in contents of one sort or another.

A. Focusing Attention
The first issue to consider is how to go about eliciting a client's attention so one can focus on it and simultaneously keep the client's attention focused on the story being told. This twofold task is not easy. There is a finite number of ways in which, as a consultant, you can engage somebody's attention, whether for the purpose of eliciting content or structure. Here are some:
- asking *attention directing* questions
- probing
- rephrasing
- reminding
- summarizing
- (empathic) acknowledgment.

'Asking attention directing questions' comprises two kinds of question: first, **guide questions**, and second, **probe questions**. Guide questions are defined by the prompts introduced in chapter 4 ('what comes to mind …?') and their explanation, while probe questions are follow-up questions asked during the interview. These follow-up questions are based on comparing what is said by the client to what the interviewer has hypothesized is the client's Center of Gravity. Any discrepancy between the two poses a problem of structured interviewing. Probe questions are searching for missing information that is needed to confirm or reject a stage hypothesis, or else to correct and refine such a hypothesis.

Rephrasing, reminding, and summarizing all are meant to make sure that interviewer and client are both fully engaged and 'on the same wave length.' They are interviewing tools for clarifying and making content more precise, so that it better chimes with, or more clearly rejects, a structural hypothesis. Beyond that structural purpose, these activities also strengthen the bond between the two parties, assuring the client that what s(he) puts out is taken seriously by the interviewer. What is more, when the consultant paraphrases or summarizes, the client typically receives information about new aspects of him- or herself that previously have remained below the level of consciousness.

Often, the consultant will have to ask for permission to repeat questions and keep probing. In conventional social situations, this indicates a desire for understanding, and so it does here. The difference is that the desire for understanding has nothing to do with the content of what is said, but with the source generating the content.

The above varieties of focusing attention have in common that they are all concerned with staying very close to the client's present flow, or train, of thought. For this reason, asking "why" questions or "Y/N" questions is counter-productive in focusing attention because it is a way of sidetracking a client's train of thought. When prompted by such questions, the client will begin to rationalize, rhapsodize, and do anything else possible to please the questioner, or get off a pressing, uncomfortable issue. Clearly, in a developmental listening and interviewing context this is totally unproductive, and thus 'bad interviewing.'

It will have become obvious by now that developmental interviewing and developmental listening are one and the same thing. As I focus attention on the client's speech in order to focus (his or her) attention, I am using myself as a powerful RECEIVER. Receiving what is said by a client from another than a mere content perspective is called LISTENING, and *listening is meaning making in the emphatic sense.* As all meaning making, listening therefore depends on developmental level.

As said, the process of developmental listening is comparable to that occurring in musical listening. In music, we listen for underlying structure, the balance of melody, harmony, and rhythm, and as skilled listeners are aware of modulations, ostinati, contrapuntal weaving, etc. Very much the same is involved here. In focusing attention for the sake of developmental structure, we focus attention on the underlying stage structure of the utterances (acoustic stream) that flow(s) outward from the speaker. As interviewers, we are waiting for *modulations* to lower or higher levels, if you want.

B. Interpretation
Interpretation opens up a wide field of possibilities. It is a procedure by which the process consultant implicitly or explicitly assigns a meaning to what was just heard (or read) by him or her. The outcome of any interpretation entirely depends on the interpreter's *Frame of Reference*, including developmental level and cognitive profile. Interpretation in the conventional sense of hunting for interesting content does not belong to the set of effective developmental tools. There is only a single exception, and

that is **interpretation of what is said in the context of a specific stage hypothesis**. This kind of interpretation is implicit, and is a kind of matching process. The interviewer matches what is heard to his or her guiding hypothesis, and then infers how closely it matches what the hypothesis would lead a developmental expert to expect in terms of stage. When done in a disciplined way, the interpretation will be tentative, simply because no absolutes but rather hypotheses are being tested. More precisely, not a single hypothesis but a *connected set of hypotheses* is involved since stages together form a system. As shown in chapters 5 and 6, single stages always derive their relevance and meaning from being part of a hierarchical system.

There are two major alternatives as to what 'connected set' specifically means here:
- Either the hypothesis presently held is a *range hypothesis*
- Or it is an *'RCP' hypothesis* (which is a range hypothesis reduced to a smaller range).

As you can imagine, changing range hypotheses is dramatic, and typically occurs at the beginning of the interview. The interviewer might say to himself "it seems to me that this client is speaking from a range between S-2 or S-3" (or from a range between S-2/3 and S-3/4). Such a hypothesis extends over six intermediate steps, and is thus very tentative indeed. We can call it a FIRST PASS HYPOTHESIS.

Now let's consider an 'RCP hypothesis.' Such a hypothesis classically encompasses three neighboring steps, such as S-2/3, S-3/2, and S-3(2). We can speak of a SECOND PASS HYPOTHESIS involving a 'zone of inference' whose center is potentially the clarity index of a classical RCP. If the RCP hypothesis encompasses altogether three levels, and thus covers the range from S-1 to S+1, the restricted zone of inference activated by the interviewer extends between S-1 and S+1. If the thrust of what is heard by the interviewer seems incompatible with S (as Center of Gravity) as initially assumed (hypothesized), the interviewer will have to move S either lower or higher, making S-1 or S+1 the new Center of Gravity.

The reader should not be too impressed by these very precise sounding explanations. They are nothing but a verbalization of my own interviewing process, and thus are an attempt to demystify rather than mystify it! I am simply reporting how I work as an interviewer. And what I can do, the reader surely can learn to do as well!

At this point, it is probably clear to the reader that 'interpretation' in the conventional sense has no function in developmental interviewing. The simple reason is that it moves too far away from the client's 'meaning generator', mostly to please the interviewer's ego, or perhaps indirectly the client. Whatever it is, it is simply banished from developmental interviewing!

C. Enactment
While interpretation puts us at risk for stepping away from the client's ongoing flow of consciousness, in modeling new behaviors we are at an even greater risk to disconnect from the client's train of thought. We may, in fact, move to establish a contrast with the client's present thinking, by saying: "let's keep in mind what you just said, and put that

next to a totally different way of seeing this issue ....". Or, "putting myself in your shoes, I could imagine you might think 'why don't I ...?'" Through such a move, we would be only vaguely "referring to" what was said, using it almost as a pretense, without digging very deeply into it. And if conventional interpretation is unhelpful, enactment is even less helpful. (One might say of conventional coaching including 'cognitive coaching' that it rushes to interpretation and enactment without having sufficiently focused attention on the client's train of thought, and therefore can and does not fully understand who the client 'is.')

D. Unlearning What We Know So Well

When you think about what was said about interpretation and enactment, the two other processes used in process consultation outside of focusing attention, you will probably get the feeling that you need to do some unlearning in order to work developmentally. That hunch of yours is exactly right. I am aware that I am transcending the boundaries of conventional coaching and consultation here. I do not do so to antagonize the reader, but to enlarge the concept of process consultation, by integrating into it established evidence based procedures. To consider what this entails in some depth, let's briefly return here to some of the ICF 'core competencies.' Below, I list those relevant in the immediate context of this chapter.

C. COMMUNICATING EFFECTIVELY

5. ACTIVE LISTENING
6. POWERFUL QUESTIONING
7. DIRECT COMMUNICATION

D. FACILITATING LEARNING AND RESULTS

8. CREATING AWARENESS
9. DESIGNING ACTIONS

Clearly, there is no one-to-one correspondence between any of these competencies and the three generic processes named above. However, active listening is not possible without focusing attention, nor is creating awareness possible without interpretation, and designing actions without enacting novel behaviors.

Interestingly, the notion articulated by the description of the ICF core competencies is that you can 'communicate effectively' and 'facilitate learning and results' **with a minimum of knowledge about the client**. We know that this is somewhat true if you count on consultant and client being embedded – or perhaps we should say, stuck – in the social context, as would hold for individuals at S-3. But that's where this truth ends. Critique of this '3-ish' ICF assumption accounts for the principal difference between conventional and evidence based consultation and coaching.

As we already saw in Chapter 4, where the formulation of 'in the context of the client's desires' was assumed to be unequivocal, too much that is an issue of empirical research is simply assumed by the ICF core competencies. (This is, by the way, no different for IAC's 'proficiencies.') From a developmental point of view, the fact that so much is taken for granted in conventional thinking about *helping* puts all present certification procedures in question in a big way.

In short, all of the 'core competencies' are too broad and undifferentiated to hold up to scientific scrutiny. For instance, 'active listening' that is not focusing attention could be interpretive, and 'powerful questioning' could comprise either focusing of attention and/or different types of interpretation. Direct communication, meant to indicate "using language that has the greatest positive impact on the client," could be many things over what is defined by the lists formulated by the ICF Board. Is probing 'direct' or 'indirect' communication, for instance? Developmentally speaking, direct communication, if it means 'to be explicit about one's attempt to understand a client's Center of Gravity,' would most likely be counter-productive, since it would spell out a hypothesis that remains to be tested (for instance). This example just highlights the major issue that exists regarding the above definitions: **ICF core competencies all focus on this or that CONTENT. They were defined without the awareness that there is an *internal client process* that generates that content, and even less that that client process can be precisely understood and evaluated,** as we learn in this book.

Interestingly, the ICF core competency definitions all oscillate between what is meant to keep the coach on track (obeying rules, following best practices) and what is *hypothesized* to be beneficial for the client (an explicit model of whom is never formulated). In full harmony with the underlying behavioristic theory (psychology), the client is conceived as a BLACK BOX that cannot be known, or if it can be 'known,' can be known only as part of the social environment in which s(he) functions. As a result, the fact that the client **makes meaning** of that social environment – and thus actually generates that environment internally – is never considered. (Philosophically, this is the difference between the *intentio recta* – direct intention, on one hand, and the *intentio obliqua* – indirect intention of evidence based coaching, on the other.)

INTERMEDIATE SUMMARY

Our discussion of interviewing has followed a broad sweep over professional assumptions that separate evidence based from conventional consulting. We have reinforced the notion that process consultation centers on the client's internal process from which what is externally 'real' for the client derives. With regard to eliciting scorable information about clients' social-emotional stage ('evidence'), it is important to measure the distance the interviewer and/or intervener inserts between him- or herself and the other party. The essential issue seems to be **how far the process consultant has moved away from the client's on-going train of thought, or flow of consciousness.** Wherever it is a matter of 'understanding where the client is coming from,' or 'how the world is showing up for the client' – it is mandatory to stay with the generic process called *focusing attention.* This procedure also guarantees that – since 'the client knows best' in a deeper sense than is usually realized – we are leaving the agenda and action to the client who alone ultimately has to take developmental steps.

The figure below visualizes what is meant here:

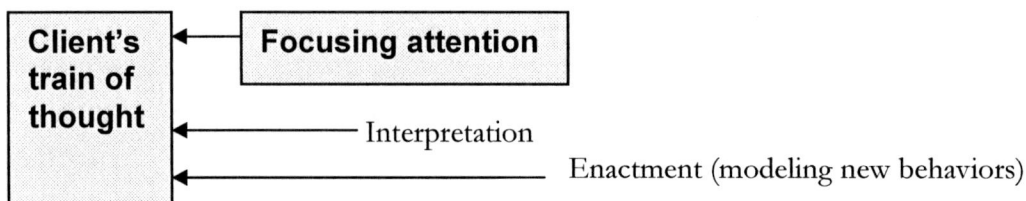

```
┌──────────┐      ┌──────────────────────┐
│ Client's │◄─────│  Focusing attention  │
│ train of │      └──────────────────────┘
│ thought  │◄──────────── Interpretation
│          │◄──────────────────── Enactment (modeling new behaviors)
└──────────┘
```

Fig. 7.1 Distance of the three generic intervention processes
from clients' *train of thought*

Using this distance measure, interpretation is about half way between focusing attention and enactment. Interpretation could entail interpreting client utterances or even those of the coach. Whichever is the case, interpretation does justice to the multidimensionality of most statements uttered by human beings. Something new is "carried into" the existing context in order to shed light on what 'could be meant.' One does not have to be a semiotician to see the complexity.

Structured Interviewing as a Model of Powerful Conversations
Before proceeding to some examples of interviewing as *focusing attention*, let us briefly consider **the value of mastering structured interviewing generally in leading conversations as a tool for process consultation.** The problem to guard against in such conversations, obviously, is total diffuseness, where "anything goes." The ICF core competencies are certainly a first attempt to hinder that from happening. However, as any reflective observer of typical coaching conversations will attest to, the ICF definitions are not powerful enough to introduce structured conversations. In what way, then, does developmental interviewing contribute to powerful conversations that are disciplined far beyond the initial intake?

Let's begin by thinking about this by reviewing the requirements for a developmental intake. Here are some requirements (outside of having the client sign an interview agreement):
   • Make sure you have conveyed that the interview is an 'intake,' thus an intervention, not a test, meant to enable you to be optimally effective.
   • Remain aware that you are doing qualitative research in which you are practicing 'use of self' for the sake of understanding another person.
   • Empty out, leaving behind any pre-defined agenda, and adopt the principle of non-interference with clients' discourse.
   • Become a receptacle for what the client shares with you.
   • Invest constant effort to 'stand in the client's shoes.'
   • Do not ask 'Why' or Y/N questions; they derail the client's associative thinking.
   • Avoid anything deviating from the client's present 'train of thought.'

Clearly, what is going on in evidence-based interviewing is itself a focusing process. The focus shifts from unconscious (implicit) to conscious (explicit) hypotheses, and from 'pop-theories' to evidence-based client models (which are 'theories' of a kind). As a consequence, contaminations are removed from the relationship between consultant and client that either used to serve the purposes of the former, or where assumed to be beneficial to the latter. What actually happens in developmental interviewing could be called *purification* achieved from an S-4 vantage point. As a consultant:

- You open yourself up to a *limited* mental space in which what happens in the relationship can be closely observed and, if ambiguous, empirically probed and tested for verity.
- You make yourself function as a research instrument that 'registers' what happens in the other party, without interference on account of own enthusiasms or impulses (however well rationalized as *professional curiosity*), but nevertheless with empathy.
- You make yourself an object of your own reflection – critical or not – so as not to interfere with important mental happenings in your interlocutor.
- **You don't rush into helping before you know whom you are 'helping,'** and whether your theory of helping is an optimal one for the particular developmental level of your client.
- You model for the client a manner of working that is guided by empathy and thoughtfulness, with a critical edge of self observation.
- Your empower your intuition by testing it against conceptual knowledge – in this case, stage theory – so that higher level intuitions are generated that are not accessible to your *own little personality*.
- You become a better and better observer of yourself who can stand away from his or her own best practices (really habits), and choose them according to insight into the developmental parameters of the situation, or else discard them.
- You constantly convey to the client that the agenda is his or hers, and that you are a sympathetic bystander acting as a midwife at best.
- You practice as a self-authorer, wary of others' 'best practices' that are in contrast to his or her own principles of integrity and awareness of flow.
- You can invent yourself many times over, guided only by the conceptual framework of stage theory which gives you broad leeway as to *who* and *how* you want to be with a client.

The list could go on. I think you get the point.

ELEMENTARY PRINCIPLES OF DEVELOPMENTAL INTERVIEWING
Imagine now you have introduced the prompts (written on index cards) to the client, and want to start the subject-object interview. What should you be keeping in mind as you proceed?

- As soon as possible, develop a hypothesis as to the client's present Center of Gravity, as a guide (compass) for your interviewing. (Initially, this is a challenge, but one that will diminish with practice.)
- Never interrupt the client's flow of thought.
- Probe based on what you just heard, starting with your 'main level' (which in an RCP hypothesis <u>implies</u> the lower and higher levels. (For instance, if your hypothesis is 'S-4', the lower and higher levels implied are S-4(3) and S-4(5), respectively.)

- Stop probing only when sure that you are standing firmly in the client's shoes, seeing the world as does s(he).
- When probing yields a result discordant with your initial hypothesis, REVISE your hypothesis and continue.
- When the client has trouble focusing attention because of discomfort or pain, stop probing and turn entirely *empathic*.

We can summarize these principles by saying: MAKE YOURSELF INTO A VESSEL RECEIVING THE CLIENT'S SPEECH FLOW, AND LOOK FOR SIGN POSTS AMONG THE STAGES THAT COME TO MIND. This entails 'bracketing' all content, and focusing on the structure that gives rise to the content you are bracketing. It also entails conversing with yourself and playing devil's advocate, to be sure you are not deluding yourself. (As I mentioned, this is best learned as member of a small group).

SUMMARY OF DEVELOPMENTAL INTERVIEWING
- **Developmental listening is a form of hypothesis testing.** (Lose your hypothesis, and you are no longer doing developmental interviewing.)
- **Developmental hypothesis testing is achieved through 'probing,' that is, a systematic inquiry into the interviewee's meaning making through language.**
- **Interviewing, when based on an initial hypothesis, is a form of gathering structural evidence (in contrast to an inquiry into content).**
- Evidence based interviewing schools developmental thinking and **listening.**
- Developmental listening means listening for the stage of development at which the client presently makes meaning (generates feelings, etc.).
- Developmental listening is based on understanding clients' language at the level of their unconscious, spontaneous meaning making.
- Developmental listening is about structure (= stage), not content.
- Developmental listening comprises range recognition, hypothesizing stage, stage identification, stage testing through probing, and determining stage through inference and playing devil's advocate.

***

TWO EXAMPLES OF SEMI-STRUCTURED INTERVIEWING
It is now time to turn to the interviewer, and test our knowledge of what evidence-based interviewing is, by scrutinizing the activity of the interviewer in a particular situation. In this chapter, we will stay with short fragments, but will expand them to a three-page excerpt taken from an actual interview in Chapter 8.

We have said that evidence based interviewing is centered on *focusing attention*, rather than interpretation or enactment. Focusing attention typically attaches itself to those interview utterances that were spoken very recently. Let's start with an example we scored as S-2/3 in Chapter 6, focusing on the procedure adopted by the interviewer.

<u>Example #1</u>
Client: It makes me really sad that my colleague lied to me. Seeing him as my friend, I was counting on him to tell me the truth. We've always promised to tell each other the truth, and he didn't follow through with that. He lied to me.
[1] Interviewer: Tell me more about your sadness.
Client: Well, I am sad because I don't know whether I can count on him to tell me the truth. Is he going to lie to me all the time? I guess it also makes me sad that he felt he *had to* lie to me. Maybe he was angry about something I did, and so he didn't feel like he could trust me anymore, or something like that.
[2] Interviewer: What, for you, would be sad about that?
Client: Well, it's like maybe he lost a friend. Like he himself couldn't count on me. I'd be sad if he was upset because he thought that I let him down. So, I really wish I knew whether that was the reason why he lied.
[3] Interpreter: How would it help you to know that was the reason?
Client: Well, because then I could let him know I was sorry, and he'd feel better knowing I really want to be his friend, and that I didn't mean to let him down.
[4] Interviewer: How would that change things for your colleague?
Client: Well, because he'd feel better. And then, feeling better, he wouldn't be mad at me anymore. Then, in turn, I could count on him again, like if I needed help or something.

The reader will probably agree that, overall, the interviewer above is successful in staying as close to the client's train of thought as possible. At [1], the interviewer emits a neutral "tell me more." This reassures the client that what is said is potentially important, and that more detail is needed. It also conveys that the interviewer is focusing on the feeling expressed, here 'sadness.'

At [2], the interviewer seems to want to sort out how the client's thoughts about the other party's 'anger' and lack of trust relate to his own 'sadness.' What is the relationship between these feelings? The interviewer is investigating the client's *hypothesis* that the other party felt s(he) had to lie to the client, which apparently is what induces sadness in the client. This is done from the point of view of stage theory, asking: what kind of sadness is this, S-2, S-3, S-4?

At [3], the interviewer continues his or her hypothesis testing. If the client makes meaning here somewhere in the range between S-2 and S-3, it would be important to understand the reason for why s(he) finds it imperative to know the reason for the colleague's lying to her. The reasons imputed to the other party would convey how far away from S-2 (toward S-3) the client has internally moved so far. This would then allow an inference as to the extent to which the client can take another person's perspective, and hold the other party's perspective within him- or herself.

At [4], the interviewer is asking about the other party's perspective as interpreted by the client, again, to ascertain where the conflict between S-2 and S-3 has taken the client.

In short, neither interpretation nor enactment of a role (e.g., of advice giver) are involved here. Pure focusing of attention prevails. To emphasize the difference of this procedure from conventional interviewing for content, let's now imagine **how this interview could have gone wrong**, in the sense of deviating from the client's train of thought and losing the ability of hypothesis testing. As I will demonstrate, there are many ways in which this could happen.

1.

Client: It makes me really sad that my colleague lied to me. Seeing him as my friend, I was counting on him to tell me the truth. We've always promised to tell each other the truth, and he didn't follow through with that. He lied to me.

Interviewer: I am sorry to hear you feel sad. I know from my own experience that the betrayal of somebody close to you can really get you down.

Misplaced empathy that is not contributing to developmental understanding.

2.

Client: It makes me really sad that my colleague lied to me. Seeing him as my friend, I was counting on him to tell me the truth. We've always promised to tell each other the truth, and he didn't follow through with that. He lied to me.

Interviewer: From what you know or can surmise, why should this have happened?

Pointless 'why' question that can only lead the client to rhapsodize or invent something that will further feed the interviewer's interpretations and enactments. Developmental listening aborted.

3.

Client: It makes me really sad that my colleague lied to me. Seeing him as my friend, I was counting on him to tell me the truth. We've always promised to tell each other the truth, and he didn't follow through with that. He lied to me.

Interviewer: How long have you been friends with your colleague, and why should this suddenly have come about?

Pointless questions about content that derail the client's train of thought. Developmental listening sabotaged.

4.

Client: It makes me really sad that my colleague lied to me. Seeing him as my friend, I was counting on him to tell me the truth. We've always promised to tell each other the truth, and he didn't follow through with that. He lied to me.

Interviewer: How do you think you can find out for sure whether your friend lied to you, and what the reasons for his lying might be?

Pointless modeling of a mode of inquiry that may satisfy the interviewer but gets her not a single step further regarding the question how the client makes meaning of his experience of being lied to.

5.

Client: It makes me really sad that my colleague lied to me. Seeing him as my friend, I was counting on him to tell me the truth. We've always promised to tell each other the truth, and he didn't follow through with that. He lied to me.

Interviewer: 'Lying' is certainly a strong word. Are you sure that's what happened?

Uncontrolled interpretation that interferes with the client's train of thought. 'Powerful question' asking for self reflection completely fruitless developmentally.

6.

Client: It makes me really sad that my colleague lied to me. Seeing him as my friend, I was counting on him to tell me the truth. We've always promised to tell each other the truth, and he didn't follow through with that. He lied to me.

Interviewer: Let's think about what you might do about this, to get an honest answer from your friend!

Disregard of the client's train of thought, with the presumption that the interviewer can be helpful. Misplaced enactment of novel behavior fundamentally unrelated to the issue of the client's meaning making.

7.

Client: It makes me really sad that my colleague lied to me. Seeing him as my friend, I was counting on him to tell me the truth. We've always promised to tell each other the truth, and he didn't follow through with that. He lied to me.

Interviewer: What I am hearing from you is great distress. Don't be shy in expressing your feelings here!

Perverse form of active listening coupled with conventional (S-3) compassion that is far off any developmental focus.

8.

Client: It makes me really sad that my colleague lied to me. Seeing him as my friend, I was counting on him to tell me the truth. We've always promised to tell each other the truth, and he didn't follow through with that. He lied to me.

Interviewer: What do you think would be the best way to clear this matter up between you and your friend?

Perverted powerful questioning attempting to move the client to what is surmised s(he) may desire.

9.

Client: It makes me really sad that my colleague lied to me. Seeing him as my friend, I was counting on him to tell me the truth. We've always promised to tell each other the truth, and he didn't follow through with that. He lied to me.

Interviewer: You are being very clear about how you are feeling! You know your feelings well. This will stand you in good stead when sorting this out with your friend.

Uninvited direct communication in return for the same. Muddling of the internal process of the client.

10.

Client: It makes me really sad that my colleague lied to me. Seeing him as my friend, I was counting on him to tell me the truth. We've always promised to tell each other the truth, and he didn't follow through with that. He lied to me.

Interviewer: Let's think about how you could deal with this event in the most truthful and forceful manner.

Exhortation that does not create any new awareness but dabbles in enactment. Use of a trusting 'we' that reeks of an S-3 client model.

11.

Client: It makes me really sad that my colleague lied to me. Seeing him as my friend, I was counting on him to tell me the truth. We've always promised to tell each other the truth, and he didn't follow through with that. He lied to me.

Interviewer: I can see that your friend might have lied for many different reasons. Tell me more about what you have thought of doing about this incident.
Invitation to the client to rationalize about the event, covered up by a well-meaning attempt to have the client himself find his way with the reported event.

Clearly, this could go on. There is no end to well-meant interferences with the client's thought process. In fact, it is easy to follow voices of your internalized others into any direction that might come to mind!

Most likely, the reader is beginning to see the point I am making here. The point is that an interviewer's reply clearly conveys whether s(he) is working from a developmental hypothesis or not, and if so, whether the hypothesis is clear to the interviewer or has been lost or abandoned. The reply thus says a lot about the interviewer, not just her expertise, but her developmental level ('coaching level') as well. **In fact, the interviewer's reply accurately conveys to the developmentally schooled observer his or her MODEL OF THE CLIENT in all its limitations,** – the way the client is seen and conceptualized is a consequence of the interviewer's own developmental stage!

An S-2 process consultant – if that is not a contradiction in and by itself – might say: "I know exactly how you feel. It's so hard to protect one's interests in this competitive world." This comes down to a perverted kind of empathy dressed up as *camaraderie*.

An S-3 consultant might say: "Well, your friend was clearly not playing by the rules of this community. What a shame that he lied to you! Have you thought of what to do about it? Could you ask some member of your community?" Here, the coach presumes to know that the client is on the same other-dependent level as s(he) her- or himself. There is no higher arbiter than convention here.

An S-4 consultant might say: "I don't blame you. Lying is certainly something no self respecting person would condone. I myself have often encountered people who go after their own advantage first and don't seem to care if they disregard established conventions. Of course you must be upset about it!" This self-boosting intervention also does not get anywhere in the sense of evidence-based interviewing. It just confirms that the coach is completely identified with his own values and principles (S-4).

A consultant nearing S-5 – it that is not a contradiction in and by itself – might say:

"I well understand that you feel hurt. When I am myself in a situation as you describe, I do my best to hinder myself from prematurely assuming that I really have been lied to. Knowing my own failings all to well, I try to give the other party the benefit of doubt. Have you asked yourself what might be your contribution to this lying, or whether your friend might have failed in his attempt to get you to listen to his issues in a more self-revelatory (less self-protective) way? Is it possible that it might be premature to assume that he intentionally lied to you? Let's stand away from our own limited perspective taking, and consider the big picture here. Let's investigate how far we can get clarity on our own (mutual) feelings about this incident of lying, trying to feel the hurt in our own, somewhat different ways."

This response actually conveys some of the difficulties to do process consultation at a level beyond S-5/4. The assumption being made is that the client is at a developmental level comparable to that of the process consultant, and makes sense only under that assumption. If the developmental hypothesis adopted here turns out to be false, the process consultant could get hurt by way of his or her own self revelation that strips away the professional veneer of a neutral helper. The damage done could perhaps be contained if the client is at least at S-4(5) where she is willing to do *model II thinking* (C. Argyris), that is, thinking that investigates its own assumptions.

***

Stepping away from *illustrations* now, let us proceed with an actual short interview fragment. We would like to understand the overall *range of stages* from which the client is speaking (as we will continue to do in the following chapter). For now, let's restrict our attention to the interviewing procedure. This will help us appreciate what is needed to conduct an interview in search of developmental evidence, and truly engage in developmental listening.

Interviewing Example #2 (modified from Lahey et al., 1988, 169-172):
In this excerpt, the speaker is talking about her feelings as a member of a software team putting in place a compiler. The speaker has indicated that she at times get nervous when a flaw in her coding becomes apparent in testing the software the team has built, and her coding errors are thus being exposed.

Interviewer: What is it that makes you nervous and anxious when it becomes clear that a piece of software written by you does not work?
Client: I don't want to embarrass myself. I want to do well.
Interviewer: What would embarrass you?
Client: Well, I am working on the compiler's optimizer as part of a 40 person team, and I am a decent software engineer, although not a great one perhaps. If I were to make an error in what the optimizer does, or misjudge the complexity of the string to be parsed by the optimizer, I would be embarrassed. I just want, you know … I guess it's just wanting to succeed and doing well that's important to me. To be successful at that because I really like my work and think highly of it.
Interviewer: What would be uncomfortable or embarrassing about not performing well?
Client: What about it? Oh, if I were to make a conceptual or coding mistake and no one spotted it, o.k., that would be fine. It's different when the whole team gets to know that I've made an error.
Interviewer: So it's kind of what they'll think of you?
Client: Yes, what they'll think of me kind of thing.
Interviewer: What do you think they might think of you?
Client: That I am a lousy software engineer (laughs).
Interviewer: What would bother you about having them think that of you?
Client: What would bother me? I guess I look at it like if I were to do good work, my colleagues would appreciate me and like me for being such a competent colleague. "You have done a really good job," my team mates would say, "hey, great work!," you know.
Interviewer: So there is some part of you that wants to please them?
Client: Yeah. If I weren't to perform well, I would be concerned they would be unhappy with me. I guess I am torn. I want to do well, too, and I say to myself, "well, what do I care what they feel?" you know. It doesn't really matter.

Interviewer: Are you angry at yourself when you say that?

Client: Yes, I get angry that I can't deal with this situation. It doesn't really matter (what they think). What matters is what I want to feel. If I were to do good work, I should be happy because then I wouldn't be the one who messes up. And that bothers me.

Interviewer: Why do you think you should be happy because you are happy, and not because they are?

Client: Because I want to feel that I am the sole judge of what my competences are, and by extension, who I am. I should be the only judge of my competences.

Interviewer: Let me understand that better. Why do you think you should be the only judge of your competences?

Client: Why I do feel that way?

Interviewer: Yes, why do you think you should feel that way? It seems as though you believe that you should be the judge of your competences, not anybody else. Why would you say you should be?

Client: Because it's me. I mean, why should another person judge me? It's kind of hard to put that into words, the thoughts that I have about it.

What is the Interviewer Actually Doing?

While it is important to ask "what range of hypotheses ought we to test here?," for now, let's simply inquire into, and describe, as best we can **what the interviewer is actually doing**. Focusing attention on the interviewer's procedure will point us to what the interviewer's hypothesis might be.

In response to the client's chosen prompt of *anxious*, the interviewer in this fragment begins by inquiring into the client's feelings of nervousness and anxiousness. She is correctly probing for the meaning making behind these feelings. Interviewer questions are in italics:

Interviewer: *What is it that makes you nervous and anxious when it becomes clear that a piece of software written by you does not work?*

Staying close to the client's mention of 'embarrassment,' the interviewer continues:

Interviewer: *What would embarrass you?*

This leads to a somewhat verbose explanation on the side of the client who speaks to a work situation in which embarrassment could arise. The interviewer probes deeper, asking:

Interviewer: *What would be uncomfortable or embarrassing about not performing well?*

Foregoing the interpretation of some important distinctions the client is making, the interviewer makes a slight interpretation of what the client brings forward, implying that the client is concerned about being evaluated by others. The difference between stating an interpretive inference as a question, on one hand, and interpreting the client's statement is very small in this case.

Interviewer: *So it's kind of what they'll think of you?*

The client adopts this inference, thereby confirming it. (The inference is clearly generated from the interviewer's hypothesis of "the range here seems to be that between S-3 and S-4, but it's not clear how far developed toward S-4 the client is.") The interviewer then probes further, inquiring into the nature of the evaluations by others that the client might be expecting.

Interviewer: *What do you think they might think of you?*

Having provoked a frank statement about the client's apprehension, the interviewer takes note of the expectation the client expresses and asks why, if fulfilled, the expectation would be painful to the client. The interviewer here focuses the client's attention on the community whose internalized voices the client seems to be hearing and listening to.

Interviewer: *What would bother you about having them think that of you?*

Inferring further from what the client is saying, and now testing her hypothesis more forcefully, the interviewer asks:

Interviewer: *So there is some part of you that wants to please them?*, turning an inference into a question to the client (as if to ask the client directly to confirm a hypothesis of other-dependence). The client feels well understood, explaining her feelings further, whereupon the interviewer, inferring 'anger,' asks point blank:

Interviewer: *Are you angry at yourself when you say that?*

This Yes/No question is not beyond reproach, as is also true for the interviewer's previous request to the client, of confirming her hypothesis directly (unbeknownst to the client). However, the interviewer has not lost the client, who goes on explaining her feelings, in particular the circumstances that make her feel angry at herself, and explaining why she thinks she should be happy (with herself). The interviewer now seizes upon the client's comment about 'being happy,' somewhat reproachably changing focus, and asks the client to explain her take on happiness further.

Interviewer: *Yes, why do you think you should be happy because you are happy, and not because they are?*

Not only is this a 'Why' question, but a rather convoluted one that conveys some of the discomfort the interviewer seems to be feeling right now. The interviewer's focus is on the client's being happy because of feelings in the client, rather than in others – in other words, on how 'self authored' this feeling of happiness in the client might be. Because the client is rather erratic in her focus, the interviewer seems to feel she has to change topic going along with the client (a frequent dilemma), in order to stay close to the client's train of thought. Therefore, when the client switches attention to being the sole judge of her competences – rather than the team she is part of – the interviewer follows suit.

Interviewer: *Let me understand that better. Why do you think you should be the only judge of your competences?*

This 'why' question is much too direct for getting at developmental evidence. It presumes that the client actually knows 'why,' and can spell out the reasons for the interviewer. No wonder that the client needs re-assuring at this point, as well as time to think up something that will please the interviewer!

Client: *Why I do feel that way?*

Interviewer: *Yes, why do you think you should feel that way? …*

Apparently, the interviewer feels a need here to interpret and re-direct the client (slightly), converting the client's "I feel that way" into "I should feel that way." This move in thought reinforces the interviewer's focus on issues of responsibility introduced above. By imputing to the client an ethical motive ('should'), perhaps the interviewer is here – somewhat awkwardly – groping for a way to appeal to the client's sense of integrity, to test how far toward S-4 the client may have been able to move developmentally? The interviewer continues her questioning as if she was forcefully aiming to establish some definitive hypothesis. She therefore deviates from focusing attention and presents an interpretation.

Interviewer: … *it seems (to me) as though you believe that you should be the judge of your competences, not anybody else. Why would you say you should be?*
In order to impute to the client her own interpretation of what is going on, the interviewer now uses a direct 'Why' question to establish the developmental situation *as she sees it*. Whereupon the client, unable to fully endorse a self-authoring perspective, replies evasively and somewhat confused:
Client: *Because it's me. I mean, why should another person judge me? It's kind of hard to put into words, the thought that I have about it.*
Let's review what has happened in this conversation, continuing to focus on the interviewer.

It must have become evident to the reader that the quality of the interview – and thus the developmental score assigned to the interviewee – is a function of the quality of the questions the interviewer has managed to ask. This is the stark truth about developmental interviewing. No scoring of the interview after it was administered can make the interview any better than it is. It's truly *garbage in, garbage out*, as they say in software engineering. Nevertheless, interviews have a certain robustness even when the interviewing is mediocre. Of course, in this case the likelihood of high inter-rater reliability – of different interviewers agreeing on the same scoring – is most likely quite low.

Turning Our Attention to the Client
Although the focus of this chapter is on the interviewer and on developmental listening generally, to conclude this chapter let's test our developmental knowledge by asking: 'what is the range of stages involved in the interview discussed above?' As we have seen, an interviewer's schooled intuition regarding the stage a client makes meaning from is a crucial capacity in working developmentally. This intuition is strengthened by conceptual knowledge about adult stages.

***

To answer questions regarding the developmental stage the client is presently making meaning from, let's return to the fragment discussed above.

As we know by now, an individual's perception of how s(he) is perceived by others, whether by single individuals or a group, is of particular salience at S-3. Here, we want to find out whether it is a reasonable first hypothesis to say the client makes meaning from S-3, and if it is, what are the neighboring stages the client may be speaking from. For example, assuming a spread over three consecutive levels, S-3 could be the Center of Gravity, with S-3(2) as a lower stage and S-3(4) as a higher stage associated with it. Alternatively, S-3 could be the *lowest* stage in evidence (S-1). This would then pose the question of whether the client's Center of Gravity lies at S-3(4) (=S) or higher. Our task is to decide these questions based on empirical evidence provided by the interview.
If somebody is nervous or anxious about how others will judge her, clearly that person is demonstrating taking other people's perspective on herself and, beyond that, potentially having their own feelings be influenced by others. In search of clues about the client's adult journey toward S-4, a developmental interviewer will ask herself how much knowledge about her self the individual interviewed can demonstrate, and how far she can articulate her difference from (physical and internalized) others.

Being embarrassed is an indicator of other-dependence. Although a person at S-4 and S-5 could be embarrassed as well, it would most likely be for other, more ego-systemic reasons. For an S-4 individual, these reasons could have to do with the violation of own standards (S-4), rather than with being found out by others. In the case of S-5/4 or S-5(4), a person might be embarrassed about her own attitude of holding back toward others that is suddenly seen as hindering her to fully engage with other's self-probing. In the absence of such indications of higher stages, we would have to assume that the interviewee is speaking from S-3(4), not S-3/4 or S-4/3. Especially in the latter case, of S-4/3 as the Center of Gravity, it would be legitimate to expect a stronger concern of the speaker about who she is in her own eyes, and also how authentically self-authored the values are that matter to the person.

Returning to the interview, we hear the speaker say: *"What about it [i.e., being embarrassed]? Oh, if I were to make a conceptual or coding mistake and no one spotted it,* **o.k.; that would be fine.** *It's different when the whole team gets to know that I've made an error."*

In the present context, this is certainly a weighty statement. How so? Looking for the upper stage range for this interviewee, it seems that s(he) has just ruled out an hypothesis such as S-4/3. In that position, we would rightfully expect some incipient ability to act according to her own standards. We would thus expect more clarity about what sets the person speaking aside from internalized and physical others, as well as some demonstration of her own values. Even then, such values might still be derived from the social environment, rather than having been internally generated, but that could be determined by further probing. Certainly the notion that "It's different when the whole team gets to know that I've made an error" is not an indicator of anything beyond S-3(4).

Given this situation, the issue becomes pressing whether there is some internal place in the interviewee where she makes meaning based on her own idiosyncratic values and principles. The interviewer senses this, and decides to inquire more directly into such values and principles. If these do not fully exist yet, perhaps there is at least some indication of the interviewee being 'torn' between being determined by others' expectations and her own?

This is indeed what seems to be happening, since the interviewee continues by saying *"I want to do well, too, and I say to myself, 'well, what do I care what they feel?' you know. It doesn't really matter."* Enacting defiance here, the interviewee demonstrates some self authoring capacity, however slight. It now is the interviewer's task to determine exactly what this capacity of self determination is and how far it reaches, so to speak, in terms of own self esteem. To test self esteem, the interviewer resorts to focusing on ethical issues, in the sense of obligations, or 'shoulds' that people feel. Anger at oneself and being the sole judge of one's competences are the contents addressed next.

Asking why the interviewee feels she should be the sole judge of her competences, the interviewer is told: *"Because it's me. I mean, why should another person judge me? It's kind of hard to put into words, the thoughts that I have about it."* Hard to put into words it is indeed! Apparently, the interviewee is 'confused' between two kinds of imperative: first, to defy others and insist on her own opinion of herself, without explaining (and understanding) why; and second, to openly question why others should have a right to judge her, given that she thinks highly of her work and typically does not 'mess up.' The *'because it's me'* is a clear indication that some part of the interviewee is reaching for a self directed way of behaving in the world, a way in which she would be the sole arbiter of what should be done and for whom. However, as she significantly adds at the end of the fragment, *'it's kind of hard to put into words, the thoughts that I have about it.'*

The interviewer has certainly done the best she could. She has raised ethical issues for the client, and given the client a chance to *demonstrate* a consistent S-4/3 stance. However, her hypothesis that the client might be able to surpass her other-dependency by confidence in her own identity, have so far been disappointed. In the judgment of a competent interviewer, stage S-4/3 is presently beyond the client's reach.

Here we have arrived at a point that will often be reached in even longer interviews: **We don't have enough information to score a Center of Gravity with certainty!** In the present case, that is so mainly because we are dealing only with a fragment, not an entire interview. If we had recourse to a full-length interview, surely there would be utterances we could go to, to *disambiguate* what we have found out so far about this interviewee's ability to act (or not to act) from S-4/3. Despite our giving her a full chance to demonstrate S-4/3, in what we have heard so far she has been unable to do so. We need to conclude, therefore, that her notion of being the sole judge of her competences is an *espousal* that keeps her at S-3/4. To our present knowledge, the notion of being the sole judge of her competences is not lodged in her but rather derives from her social surround, – namely, the internalized others which at this time determine her being-in-the-world.

What, then, have we found out about the range of stages over which this interviewee is presently distributed? I think it is fair to say that our finding about the interviewee's developmental range is the one indicated below:

Level	Characteristics
3	Made up of others' expectations; 'our world' hypothesis
3(4)	In need of 'handholding' by physical others to act on own behalf
3/4	Conflicted over, and unsure about own values, direction, worth, capability

Table 7.1 Range estimate for a client

While fully able to take other's perspective, to the point of being over-determined by such perspectives, the interviewee seems to have made a first, shy step beyond S-3. Because of this, she is able to entertain the possibility to 'be the sole judge of my competences' and 'to be happy because of how I feel rather than others do.' But that's as far as it goes. There is presently no evidence that she has the ability to consistently hold even an S-3/4 perspective consistently, except in the form of defiance and anger at herself. There is even less evidence that she can consistently hold an S-4/3 perspective where others' opinion is balanced, and successfully refuted if need be, by one's inner voices that support one in standing up for one's own, potentially very idiosyncratic, values and principles. In short, we can only say that the range of this interviewee lies between S-3 as the lower, and S-3/4 as the higher, level, with a Center of Gravity most likely at S-3(4).

***

The reader will recall that, in Chapter 5, I introduced what is called the *Risk-Clarity-Potential Index* (RCP). The idea behind the index is to arrive at a precise measure of the proportions to which a person is spread out over various stages around a Center of Gravity. I noted in Chapter 5, that this becomes possible only when dealing with full-length interviews. When listening to, or reading, such interviews, we have the opportunity of scoring all those text passages ('bits') that clearly reflect a particular stage, main or intermediate. We have seen above that we don't have enough information to do so in the fragment just investigated.

To reinforce that it is entirely possible to be more precise about an interviewee's stage than just discussed, let's suppose we actually had enough data about an interviewee such as the one above. If we had at our disposal a full-length interview, we might have found that out of 16 *structurally relevant* passages (which is as much as may accrue during a 1-hr interview), the majority, 8, were focused on S-3(4), 5 around S-3, and 3 around S-3/4. In that case, we would have scored the interview with an RCP as shown below:

Risk	Clarity	Potential
S-1	S (Center of Gravity)	S+1
S-3	S-3(4)	S-3/4
5	8	3

Table 7.2 Example RCP

Clearly, in this case the interviewee's RCP would have been **S-3(4) {5: 8: 3}**. This would have told us that the interviewee is presently strongly embedded in her Center of Gravity, S-3(4), with a potential to move to S-3/4 of 3, and a risk of regressing to S-3 of 5. As developmental process consultants, this would have told us that we are dealing with a client who is presently emerging from a purely other-dependent perspective (S-3), and has become fairly comfortable with a stance that conveys some incipient independence from other's opinions, judgments, and expectations. It would moreover convey that the client is still burdened by a strong tendency to 'fall back' to a position where the inner need for, and the capacity of, independence are quite weak indeed, despite there being a potential for being in conflict about how to act and for whom (S-3/4). As we have seen, this potential for conflict easily leads to confusion, where it is literally 'hard to put into words the thoughts I have about it.' When properly probed developmentally, language does not lie about the level of consciousness presently embodied in an individual!

In order to understand what this RCP entails for work in an organizational environment, you might want to return to Chapter 6, where we discussed in detail the steps of moving from S-3 to S-4. The speaker in those excerpts was concerned with how to make decisions independently of her boss. She initially needed his physical handholding to dare to make decisions by herself at all (S-3(4)). Gradually, however, she became bolder, more confident internally that she could arrive at decisions herself. By separating out from her internalized others, including 'the boss,' she discovered that her relationship to her boss actually improved once she went ahead making decisions on her own. When having moved to near S-4, she emitted a lot of espousals about being a self authoring person. By contrast, the person described by the RCP above is only at the beginning of this journey. You will agree that she has a ways to go to be able to act from S-4(3).

SUMMARY OF DEVELOPMENTAL LISTENING
- The relevance of developmental interviewing lies in the fact that it schools your developmental *listening*.
- Developmental listening means listening for, *and above*, the level of development at which the client presently makes meaning.
- Developmental listening is based on understanding clients' speech flow at the level of their unconscious, spontaneous verbal meaning making.
- Developmental listening is about 'structure' (= stage), not content; any content can be spoken from any stage.
- Developmental listening comprises range recognition, level hypothesizing, level identification, level testing (probing), and determining level through inference and playing devil's advocate.
- Developmental listening fails if the interviewer cannot, or does not, offer an interviewee all possible opportunities to demonstrate the highest possible stage from which meaning can be made. (It is the interviewer's mandate to make the client *shine* developmentally, and if this is not accomplished, the interviewee is going to be short-changed by the interviewer.)

The reader who revisits Chapter 4 and rereads Chapter 7 at this point has, I think, a lot going for him or her in the direction of trying out developmental interviewing. When doing so, keep in mind that as with all other skills, this kind of interviewing needs practice to develop roots within you. Remember that 'emptying out' is the first requirement, while adopting stage theory as a conceptual framework is a second, related one.

Most likely, without further practice in classes working together in small groups under the guidance of a certified developmental consultant, the reader's interviewing skills will remain unaccomplished. **Espousals of accomplishment at this point would be risky for consultant as well as client.**

Practice Reflections
- When you try out structured interviewing with individual clients using developmental prompts, what happens for you as the interviewer?
- When you use prompts, how does your relationship to your client change, compared to conventional, content-focused interviewing?
- What happens to your content-bound intuitions when you switch to developmental interviewing?
- In what way do conversations become more focused for you when using the developmental prompts introduced in Chapter 4?

- Considering what you've learned in this chapter, how do you evaluate your own interviewing in terms of the *closeness* you maintain to your client's train of thought?
- When you consider your good intentions to *help* others, in what way might they interfere with the very purpose of your helping?
- What do you think are skills you have to *unlearn,* to become successful as a developmental interviewer?

8
How to Test Your Developmental Knowledge

Having come this far, the reader may feel s(he) has scaled a mountain, at least a small one. We began this book with vague notions of what is a stage, and now have been exposed to all the tools needed for going to work on some *actual case study* meant to explore how helping professionals and consultants can fully engage others by using the techniques taught in this book.

Thus far, we have built up developmental knowledge in small pieces – short illustrations of stages. It is now time to find out how what we have learned works within a larger 'text window.' In this chapter, I will use an <u>actual</u> interview rather than staying with illustrations. I will also extend the length of the interview under discussion. Consequently, the reader will be able to rely on a larger amount of information about the client than has been the case so far. It is the purpose of this chapter to provide opportunities for the reader to test his or her developmental knowledge on an extended interview fragment.

When evaluating an interview, one can focus on the interviewer, the client, or both. In this chapter, I will look at both parties, starting with the client, and entertain some hypotheses about their relationship. I will present a full-fledged *coding sheet* as used by developmental experts. The coding sheet (adapted from Lahey et al. 1988) notes with precision what part (excerpt) of the interview a particular score relates to, as well as the reason for why a particular score has been assigned to the excerpt. In this way, interview scorers can hold themselves responsible for the full scope of issues that arise in determining a client's developmental stage. After formulating an overall score for the interview, we will discuss some of the consequences for coaching or mentoring the client speaking in the interview. The three case studies in Appendix B will further assist readers to begin orienting themselves toward developmentally grounded consultation.

Prior to entering into a discussion of the interview fragment, below, there are some general issues to consider that scorers should be mindful of. These considerations have to do with the MENTAL SPACE that we can say a stage score and RCP define.

When you, the consultant, know the range of stages within which a client presently makes meaning of his/her life and experiences, **you have an immediate appreciation of the MENTAL SPACE within which you can expect clients to move about.** Part of this mental space is known to the client, and part of it is lying in the dark for him or her. **The hidden part of the space is that region in which the client is SUBJECT TO his or her own thoughts, feelings, aspirations, and fears.** The client does not 'have' these thoughts, feelings, aspirations, and fears, but rather 'is' them, with no opportunity to reflect upon them. (Here is your chance as a process consultant.)

Thinking of the consulting relationship, it clearly interweaves two mental spaces, – that of the two parties to the consultation. Consequently, one can imagine there to be a smaller or larger intersection in which both parties can *understand* and *misunderstand* each other. As we now know, the extent to which such understanding gets realized largely depends on each party's respective developmental range and level.

The interweaving of two mental spaces can be clarified if we distinguish within the common mental space of the two parties three sub-domains, or *Houses* (Laske, 1999b):

- Self House
- Task House
- Environmental House.

Both parties reside in all three Houses, but in different ways. What is of primary interest here is the way in which clients reside in these houses.

The *Self House* contains all those elements that have to do with the parties' professional agenda, meaning the (often unconscious) assumptions they are making about their work within as well as outside the consulting or coaching relationship. In this House, clients very crisply reveal their social-emotional stage in personal terms, by talking about themselves, their motivation to work, personal values, and how they see their professional career.

The *Task House* is defined by the roles the parties play, and the formal authority they possess. In this House, clients detail the functions they fulfill in the organization, the roles that flow from these functions, and how they integrate the different, potentially conflicting, roles they are playing into their professional self image.

The *Environmental House* concerns the frame of reference within which both parties make sense of their environment, organizational or not. In this House, clients reflect on their experience in an organization, how the organization's cultural climate influences their work, and what elements of the culture are of primary importance to them. For instance, they may hold a strictly neutral, structural view of the organization following the division of labor, or else they may focus on political cliques, cultural rituals, or human resources issues.

Given this subdivision of the mental space the parties to the consultation have in common, we can describe interviews, as well as coaching and intervention sessions as being localized in a particular House, and 'moving' from one House to another. For instance, an interview session might begin in the Task House, move to the Environmental House, and end in the Self House. This would have the advantage that the conversation starts on somewhat neutral ground – the client's tasks and functions –, moves to his or her conception of the environment they live or work within, and finally focuses on the Self House where the client's professional agenda, values, and personal culture are central. The Self House is also the domain that is most directly influenced by the client's social-emotional stage. However, the client's Center of Gravity comprehensively and equally defines all Houses.

I focally employ the sub-domains of the shared mental space, or Houses, in the cognitive interview, to elicit the client's thought forms (volume 2). I mention them here because they introduce **additional structure**, not only into interviews, but into consultative conversations generally. If, for instance, a client's present developmental score is S-3, as a developmental consultant you will know pretty much right away about what to expect the client's Environmental House to feel and look like. The Task House then falls into place as well, since predictably clients are oriented to the peer group with the overriding interest to be accepted, supported, bailed out, and/or boosted by its members. Simplifying things a little, one can predict clients' attitude in the Houses depending on their developmental level as follows:

Center of Gravity	Self House	Task House	Environmental House
S-2	'My needs come first'	'I need to be in control'	'I need to know what they will do'
S-3/2	'I really need to know what others are thinking and doing'	'Knowing about how others feel and think gives me lot's of clout'	'I am learning a lot about my environment'
S-3	'I live in and for the community'	'Let's all work together'	'What a privilege to work with such a community of people'
S-4/3	'There are times when I can't follow consensus'	'It's often hard to get the cooperation I need'	'I have real doubts about the consensus we are working from'
S-4	'My integrity comes first'	'Others clearly look to me when things get tough'	'I stand behind my values for everybody to see'
S-5/4	'I more and more rely on others to keep me honest'	'My collaborators are invaluable for my own self development'	'The more I really understand others, and they understand me, the better for the organization as a whole'

Table 8.1 The Three Houses differentiated according to Centers of Gravity

(Do you see the coaching problems 'pop right out' here?)

Two other aspects should be considered. As we know from the end of chapter 7 where we discussed the *Risk-Clarity-Potential Index* (S-3(4) {5:8:3}):

RISK	CLARITY	POTENTIAL
S-1	S (Center of Gravity)	S+1
S-3	S-3(4)	S-3/4
5	8	3

Table 8.2 Example RCP

there exists, at all times, a burden of 'risk' and a promise of 'potential' in a client's (and our own) life, and this burden and promise have a certain weight. Although the weight determined by a score always contains a margin of error, a client's RCP gives the consultant a certain firm notion – although not an absolute one – of what is to be expected of a client at this particular time. This notion can guide interventions since it defines the client's *mental space*. For the consultant, this space is one of hypothesis formulation and testing.

In the client's mental space defined by the RCP S-3(4) {5: 8: 3}, certain interventions make sense and others do not. Concretely, the following questions arise:

1. In which of the client's Houses is developmental risk most pronounced (Self, Task, Environment)?
2. How does the clarity index manifest in the clients daily life and work?
3. Does the clarity index indicate 'stuckness,' and if so, of what kind?
4. What, given the clarity index, can the client not be expected to take responsibility for?
5. In which of the three Houses is the client's potential, if any, most easily realized?
6. How far can the client be 'stretched,' given his or her developmental potential?
7. What would lead to a 'breakdown,' and should breakdown be risked to happen for its benefit of raising awareness?
8. What are specific situations that send the client into the realm of risk?
9. How can such situations either be guarded against or provoked, to protect the client or raise awareness and stimulate growth?
10. What interpretations, if any, of the client's developmental situation can be understood by him or her – how should feedback be given?

More pragmatic questions can also be generated based on the RCP, such as:
1. How can I show the client through concrete examples – say, by enacting new behaviors – what s(he) presently cannot do or see?
2. How can I interpret client statements so as to highlight present risk and potential for the client?
3. What additional information from the client do I need to assess the kind of 'embedding in the present stage' that is involved?
4. How can I lead the client to investigate what subsequent stage or stages – in this case, S-4/3 – s(he) is poised to proceed to?
5. Is the client's team (family, circle of friends) a hindrance to his or her mental growth? (See Appendix C).

And so forth.

As the reader will have noticed, it does not matter for these questions whether the context of the intervention is life or work. For one thing, people don't act one way in life and another at work. Although life and work may provide different arenas of potential and risk for people, nevertheless people are – as Kegan would say– acting from a single Center of Gravity, here defined by the stage score and the associated RCP.

***

Looking at an Extended Interview Fragment

The fragment under discussion here is based on one of the ten interview prompts introduced in Chapter 4, namely, the interview prompt of OUTSIDE OF. What happens when a client chooses this prompt is a little bit like a Rohrschach test. The client, strictly focused on content, 'projects herself' into the prompt, thereby creating a universe of discourse that can be scrutinized in terms of structure or stage. In this universe, every word of the client counts (as we will see below), and every question asked by the interviewer counts as well. The parties we observe are engaged in *applied qualitative research*.

We will first examine the client, and then the quality of the interviewing. Let's assume that you did not administer the interview yourself, but have been asked to score it as best you presently can.

When you read this excerpt in its entirety, be aware that reading any interview for the first time is a *privilege that will be lost* on subsequent readings. On first reading, you don't yet have acquired any prejudices through previous study, and a first reading is therefore precious. Initially, especially as a beginner, you will be interested in the *content* of what is said. As we know, developmental listening and reading go beyond content, to discern *structure*. Perhaps by now you have developed a feel for this distinction. What we need to do here is 'to put content into brackets,' so to speak.

First, let's state the interview excerpt in full. It is an excerpt relating primarily to the interviewee's life rather than her work, except at the end. The interviewee is actually a coach, as we'll find out. I have numbered passages of client statements *numerically*, and those of the interviewer *alphabetically*. This will allow us to know exactly where in the interview we are at any point during the discussion. The number of client passages also appears in the coding sheet below. The interview excerpt extends over nearly three pages. It is stated below in full.

INTERVIEW EXCERPT

[a] **Interviewer:** Okay, so let start with the prompt you selected, namely 'outside of.' What I am interested in here is <u>what</u> it is you are feeling outside of, internally or externally, and also how that feels to you, to be outside of something or someone. As you look around in the workplace or the family or wherever, where do you see yourself as being an outsider, and how does that make you feel?

[1] **Client:** There are a couple of ways that I am different or have been different over the course of my life. One is that I am an only child. And at the time of my growing up that was not as common a thing as it is today. A second is that I was widowed in my 20's- a pretty unusual time in one's life to be widowed. So I was like about 40 years off the age and the developmental curve. What I am finding these days as a little unusual is that I am an only child without children.

[b] **Interviewer:** *So, when you think of the outsider role, of being an outsider as being an only child, can you say more about that, what that meant for you?*

[2] **Client:** Some of … what I am conscious of at the moment is…, do you mean what it historically meant to me?

[c] **Interviewer:** *However you wish to make sense – perhaps both what it meant then and what it means now?*

[3] **Client:** What it meant then was I would look around and be aware that other kids went home to lots of siblings and lots of conversation, and my house was much more quiet than the norm. At the time I always thought I was missing something. And today what I am most conscious of is being an only child without children. I was at a women's covenant meeting at my church this morning. They are a wonderful group of women. And I am the only one in this group of women without children. Some have grandchildren; there are two infants born in the last month in there. I look around the room and I am only one that does not have children. I am just aware of the unusualness of it. Although [but] I do not feel like an outsider anymore. It's

like a condition of my life that just <u>is</u>. And so I am more curious about it. So when I run into someone who is in that place it's, "'wow,' what is it like for you?"

[d] Interviewer: *When does the experience of, sort of difference, show up for you most pronouncedly? And what is the feeling associated with that?*

[4] Client: The difference will show up when groups of people men or women, mostly women, but men too. We'll introduce ourselves and – tell how many children you have yah da da… I'm 54, and it's not that common for people to not have children. Women especially in women's groups. It's not that common for people not to have children. When people discover I am an only child without children that is really uncommon. I have been more aware the last few years that there are gifts that come to me because of that as well as sadness about that. And I get real curious when I run into people with similar situations. Yesterday for example, I was in a monastery that a local church bought. It was a cloister in a Convent, and in walking through it and seeing all the stuff that was there because people were cloistered, I found myself saying that this was a whole building-full of women who had no children. And wondered what that was like, since so much of our American life is really associated with family and raising family. And I happen to love children. So, it's not like I am childless by choice.

[e] Interviewer: So there is a language… the difference shows up when you are with people who have children and speak about them. When do you …

[5] Client: When they kind of feel awkward, not knowing what to do about my situation. They assume something that is not true, and its like 'Will **Katherine** enjoy holding my baby? It's a funny thing I have observed that in women's groups. And when you do not have children they assume you do not like them. It's that funny kind of ritual that groups go through to figure out what are we going to do with this person?

[f] Interviewer:: *Yes, who is this person?(!)*

[6] Client: Yes, so I have learned to deal with it sometimes by telling people that I wish it had not been this way, or other times that I really like children, and I will be the baby holder during this meeting.

[g] Interviewer: *You spoke about the experience of being different this way as being both a gift and burden. Can you speak to how it shows up as a gift?*

[7] Client: Yes, I am close to my husband in a way that sometimes couples aren't when they have children. We have built our relationship on shared interests that really run deep with us. That is one of the gifts. Another is in my ability to travel, to learn, to really experiment with learning, and to experiment with different ways of being. I did not have like a role of mother that I played. And so I experienced it as both the joys and delights of having to invent something because I did not have a role; I was a wife but it's not quite the same. It's funny how people categorize mothers and working mothers and that sort of thing.

[h] Interviewer:: *What has that freedom of being able to define yourself independently of being a mother meant for you?*

[8] Client: It meant I could align with groups, or be part of groups, I had not chosen or had [not had] the opportunity to do so [choose] before.

[i] Interviewer: *Give me an example, please?*

[9] Client: Ummm, yes, I am trying to give one here. Several years ago I started to take long extended retreats at Gethsemane Monastery and that probably would not have been possible or likely had I had children. I was able to follow my real curiosity about Thomas Merton's life and the way it led me. That was what I was originally curious about, and I was able to discover what it would be like …. (?), or able to see how monks lived in community, in a way I would not have been able to see before. One of the things that was so striking about that first experience was that I learned something different about community. That it is a place where people accept each other and their foibles in a different way than most other groups. It's like a deep acceptance and growth process that people get on. I found that really attractive.

[j] Interviewer: *So that speaks to the groups or community that you choose to be a part of …*

[10] Client: … Or stumble on to. I did not know I was going to find community. I really loved Thomas Merton's work on Buddhism and thought I was going to go down and poke around his hermitage, but instead I got really intrigued by this view of communal life. I did not expect that to happen at all. My husband said he could see me in some other part of my life choosing to become a nun – an Episcopal nun.

[k] Interviewer: *The thing I am really intrigued with is, you framed the gifts of being an outsider- in this case you started as an outsider and with a perspective of not being a parent, a single child without children and framing the gift as a door into community. Can you say a little bit more?*

[11] Client: A kind of paradox …

[l] Interviewer: *Yeah, an interesting paradox. I would like to know what the impact …, when that perspective on yourself had you feel outside of, or apart from others as well …. Perhaps we could go back to the experience of yourself as part of the women's group this morning?*

[12] Client: That is not so true of this group now. It has been operating for some time. It was more when it began. I can feel apart from, lately, meaning the last four or five years. What I am really interested in organizations [for] is faith based organizations. And people's spiritual lives, …. and sometimes in my corporate world, …. that is something I do not hear too many people talking about. So I can feel a little apart from the organization or [from] clients dealing with the surface level conversations that go on. My sense is that there is something deeper that we could be connected with. Sometimes I do not have the courage, or sometimes don't seem to find the doorway, to test that.

[m] Interviewer: *With Clients in corporate environments?*

[13] Client: Yeah, if they initiate it I will go there. But otherwise I have not found a graceful way to explore whether people are interested in those other things the way I am, - like more energy connections…. . And how do people's spiritual [life] and faith operate at work?

[n] Interviewer: *When you feel yourself really restrained from being engaged with people in that way, and it sounds like that is clearly an important part of who you are….*

[14] Client: Yes it is.

[o] Interviewer: *What is the experience you have of not being able to move into that space with them, and not be able to bring them into your world?*

[15] Client: A kind of sadness. Although it's not really …(?). I do not know how to explain it. It's not like a deep emotion. It's more like a universal sadness, like when a child dies and it's out of season. Also, there is a part of me that says 'do not push at it, but allow it to evolve.' (I know) that whatever is developing in the work or in the relationship, it will develop in its own way. So I can get curious about what is going to happen.

I had an experience last week of piloting a course. From something that I said, the key client, the guy at the top who heads this whole power plant, nuclear power plant, came up to me and said, 'from something you said, do you coach around people who find themselves, who seem to find their faith and their work aren't in sync, and where they have to compromise themselves.' I said 'yes, I do coach people about those things.' He said, 'I would like to talk to you.'
Now, I hadn't a clue about his background. And if you had asked me I would have said there is no way we are ever going to have this conversation. And yet there he was …

[p] Interviewer: *Opening that up for you?*

[16] Client: Yeah, and from something I said, and I still do not know what it was. I wonder whether I am holding myself apart, or what is it I have to learn that will bridge a gap that is not really a gap.

END OF EXCERPT

My procedure in this chapter is in five steps, as follows:
1. I first 'eyeball' the entire interview, exemplifying how to hypothesize a *developmental range*.
2. I then go into details about the interview transcript.
3. I comment on the interviewer's procedure, its strength and weaknesses.
4. I present a *coding sheet* for the entire interview excerpt.
5. Since the client speaking in the interview is a coach, I will conclude the chapter by commenting on how to *mentor* her developmentally, rather than coach her.

Let's start with some content clues, in search of an initial structural hypothesis. (Of course, if you yourself have done the interview, you already have such clues, which might, in fact, overwhelm you, since it might be difficult for you to distance yourself from assumptions made during the interview.)

Reading a few statements at the start of the interview, we can't deny that the speaker is focused on herself. This is clearly an artifact of the prompt chosen by the client, as well as the way the prompt is probed for by the interviewer in order to make explicit in what way the interviewee is feeling herself to be 'outside of' something or someone.

Although the speaker is focused on herself like an S-2 person might be, the way she is using natural language suggests that she has no problem standing outside of community in a reflective way, thereby taking community (as well as her own life as a community member) as *object*. We would thus surmise that the speaker is minimally at S-3(4) where expressions like "I am the only child" not only describe her own experience, but also the way she is thinking of society looking at her from a conventional 'our world' perspective.

[1] Client: There are a couple of ways that I am different or have been different over the course of my life. One is that I am an only child. And at the time of my growing up that was not as common a thing as it is today. A second is that I was widowed in my 20's- a pretty unusual time in one's life to be widowed. So I was like about 40 years off the age- the developmental curve. What I am finding these days as a little unusual is that I am an only child without children.

The above hunch seems to be confirmed by the client's further elaborations of how she is 'different' from others, in which she takes her own as well as society's perspective on her unique life history. Even her choice of interpreting 'outside of' as *different from* suggests that she is not simply unconsciously embedded in her social surround, but knows where society ends and she begins. (Of course, at this point, we have no way of telling whether what she calls 'difference' is borrowed from the social surround or is based on her own authentically generated values.)

In fact, reading on, it seems that most of her discourse is spoken from relatively strong 'I' perspective where the speaker, standing outside of community, observes what is going on in the social world with herself as a member. The speaker's discourse is a delicate mix of conversations located in her Self House and Environmental House, as is often the case in life coaching. (It is true, she sometimes takes responsibility for people's feelings (see below), but that is to be expected within an S-3 to S-4 range.)

Think, for instance, of the speaker's fourth statement:

[4] Client: ... It's not that common for people not to have children. When people discover I am an only child without children that is really uncommon [for them, OL]. I have been more aware the last few years that there are gifts that come to me because of that [being childless, OL], as well as sadness about that. And I get real curious when I run into people with similar situations.

In this statement, the client explicitly takes a perspective on the community she is part of. Speaking as a member of that community, she declares that it is uncommon for most female persons not to have children, – whether they are an only child or not. She then goes to a place in her mental space where she finds certain "gifts that come to me" exactly because of not having children.

To be aware, and speak of, such gifts deriving from deprivation, an individual clearly has to be aware of the complexity of their own inner landscape. To some extent, the individual needs to have weighed what is lacking in her life against the gifts bestowed on her by the very lack she deplores. We are witnessing a considerable internal process through which the speaker makes meaning of her own life in a somewhat autonomous fashion. (Exactly what is the extent of her autonomy is still unclear.) It seems reasonable, then, to surmise that there is more going on here than being totally embedded in community, as we would expect at S-3. There never really was a justification for us to locate the speaker's train of thought within an S-2 to S-3 range.

Level	Characteristics
3(4)	In need of 'handholding' by physical other to act on own behalf

3 /4	Conflicted over, and unsure about own values, direction, worth, capability
4/3	Conflicted, but with more detachment from internalized viewpoints, resolving to level 4
4(3)	Nearing self-authoring, but remaining at risk for regression to others' expectations
4	Fully self-authoring decision maker respecting others; 'my world' hypothesis

Table 8.3 Suggested range for interview excerpt

As proposed, since the speaker can be credited with being able to take a perspective on community, we might want to put her minimally at S-3(4). That's a cautious stage estimate. In that position, she has just begun to move out of being totally embedded in others' expectations. The question now arises: **what is the ceiling of the speaker's range?** Concretely, how able is she internally to construct her own psychological organization that, in turn, generates the values and principles from which she is acting, community notwithstanding?

Reading to the end of the excerpt below, we might begin to entertain doubts that S-4 is the limit here. Speaking of her coaching work, the speaker says:

[12] **Client:** I feel a little apart from the organization or clients dealing with the surface level conversations that go on. My sense is that there is something deeper that we [my clients and I, OL] could be connected with. Sometimes I do not have the courage, or sometimes don't seem to find the doorway to test that.

Thinking about this statement in terms of the journey from S-4 to S-5, are there indications here that the speaker has begun to stand away from her own self authoring system? Might she not, by distancing herself from the organization and from clients, also be demonstrating her capacity to stand away from her own professional and self-authoring self, and if so, in what way? How is she actually constructing this 'something deeper' that she and her clients 'could be connected with'? Is this an espoused *higher realm* taken from some community's ideology and internalized by her, or is it based on authentic values and judgments generated by her as distinct from others? And where in the journey from S-4 to S-5 might the speaker begin to wonder about this 'something deeper,' frankly admitting that, at times, she does not "find the doorway to test that" [hypothesis; OL] in a client?

Level	Characteristics
4(5)	Begins to question scope and infallibility of own value system; aware of own history

Perhaps one could summarize at this point that we don't exactly know what the lowest and highest stage of the client's range are. However, we surmise that we are moving somewhere within the range between S-3(4) – where a perspective on physical and internalized others begins to be taken, on one hand, – and S-4(5), – where embeddeding in something 'deeper' than one's own self can be felt, on the other.

Having now 'walked through and around' the excerpt as a whole, let's go to work and study it systematically, from beginning to end, beginning with the client. (Remarks about the interviewing are sometimes interspersed. They are summarized at the end of the excerpt.)

***

Following the interviewer's brief explanation of the chosen prompt, the client interprets the prompt ('outside of') as meaning *being different from others*. In [1], she begins to enumerate some of the ways in which she has felt different from others. More recently, this feeling has come to be associated with "being an only child without children." We can say, then, that she seems to construct difference as a kind of lack, a place she feels is somewhat unusual from the community's point of view. She initially frames her relationship to community in a way that certainly demonstrates S-3(4) as a minimal point of departure for interpreting this interview.

For some inscrutable reason, in [b], the interviewer uses the original prompt ('outside of') to reinforce the interpretation of 'outsider.' As a result, the client is made uncertain of what is asked for, and requests a clarification [2]. The interviewer loses some professional autonomy by suggesting "however you wish to make sense [of it]." The client starts afresh in what she construes as her past. (What is being construed by speakers as falling into the past is structurally always part of the present, – the time in which the past is being constructed.)

[3] The interviewee continues with the motive of 'something missing.' In her growing up, it was a lack of others, while in the present it is rather her awareness "of being an only child without children." Clearly, this is an important content in her life, and we will have to see how exactly she is construing it in what follows. We might surmise that this content is *structurally potent*, in the sense that, first, it helps her define a boundary between herself and others, and second, it turns her inward and lets her ask herself about how she might be different from other people from a vantage point of self-authoring. We might also surmise that conflicts between S-3 and S-4 that arise in this speaker's discourse have to do with whether she feels more as a victim of her situation (S-3/4), or rather as being more highly in charge of her life compared to others (S-4/3).

Continuing in [3], the client describes a recent situation at a women's covenant meeting:

[3] … They are a wonderful group of women. And I am the only one in this group of women without children. Some have grandchildren; there are two infants born in the last month in there. I look around the room and I am only one that does not have children. I am just aware of the unusualness of it. Although [but] I do not feel like an outsider anymore. **It's like a condition of my life that just is. And so I am more curious about it.** So when I run into someone who is in that place, it's "'wow,' what is it like for you?"

Here, feeling of lack has given way to curiosity. Being an only child without children, – what kind of human condition is that? Would it help to know what it is like for others? Although the client here deeply engages with community, she does not seem to do so in order to learn from others how to feel about, or act upon, her own condition. She maintains her somewhat defiant (and resigned) stance of "it's like a condition of my life that just is." This attitude conveys a certain objectivity, both toward herself and others, that keeps internalized others at bay (S-4/3).

The interviewer does not seem to be quite in tune with the client's mental process. He is rather in his own mental space, and now moves a little bit away from the client's immediate train of thought, asking: "When [under what circumstances, OL] does the experience of, sort of difference, show up for you most pronouncedly?," but (thank God) finally harks back to the client's feeling state that may accompany her curiosity. In [4], the client's feeling state is once more marked by how uncommon it is for people not to have children: "When people discover [that] I am an only child without children that is really [something] uncommon [for them]." While this insistence on the uncommonness of her condition tends to keep her apart from others, reinforcing that and how she is different, the difference she is constructing is one taken over from the social surround. It is not one based on her own authentic values, at least not in a way we have evidence of. Paradoxically, then, she considers herself as different on grounds that are those of her internalized community, not strictly her own (S-3/4). In short, she "buys into" her community's conventions.

However, the speaker's feeling of difference also has aspects that lend themselves to a grounding in her own incipient authenticity. These aspects come to the fore as soon as one perceives one's own human condition as based on choice, rather than fate:

[4] I have been more aware the last few years that there are gifts that come to me because of that [being an only child without children, OL] as well as sadness about that. And I get real curious when I run into people with similar situations. Yesterday for example, I was in a monastery that a local church bought. It was a cloister in a Convent, and in walking through it and seeing all the stuff that was there because people were cloistered, I found myself saying that this was a whole building full of women who had no children. And wondered what that was like, since so much of our American life is really associated with family and raising family. And I happen to love children. **So, it's not like I am childless by choice.**

The last sentence seems to be spoken with some relief ("at least it's fate, not my personal choice [as holds true for women who have chosen a monastic life], and I can therefore not be held totally responsible for it!"). This realization – that she is childless by fate – seems to strengthen her perception of her difference from the community. However, she continues to strongly adopt the conventional view that not having children is "uncommon." She also feels inclined to protest her love for children as something that is expected by the community, especially mothers. By so doing, she identifies with feelings prescribed by her internalized others. Protesting that she loves children fully identifies her with motherly conventions, however much she seems to try to convey her own values by stating that love.

In [e], the interviewer has lost his hypothesis, if he ever had one. It is not clear what his take is on what was just said. (This is a risky situation for any interviewer to be in.) To find a way out, he comments on "when the difference shows up." In [5], the client makes an observation about the awkwardness of others when they learn that has no children. For her, this awkwardness signals a difference between her and others. She takes responsibility for their feeling awkward, and for their uncertainty as to "what to do," as any person at S-3/4 is likely to do.

Taking a critical perspective on others, the client then infers that some wrong assumptions are being made about her that she needs to correct. These assumptions lead to very physical issues in her conversation with others, such as "Will Katherine enjoy holding my baby?" The assumption to be undone is that if you do not have children, you don't like them either, and therefore holding them would not be enjoyable for you (or others). This assumption brings her into a conflict where communal reality contradicts her own feelings about children as well as about herself. (Clearly, she encounters the risk of being "ostracized" by others, especially mothers, for not liking children, especially "my baby.") The client keeps her bearing, however, seeing what is happening as a kind of 'ritual' that she is – expectedly – submitted to, to find out how she really feels about children (and thus, who, in the mothers' eyes, she really "is.").

In [f], the interviewer mimics the client's audience, by spelling out the question its members are all asking themselves: "who is this person?!" This is an empathic response without much structural clout, but at least it keeps the conversation going at this point. It makes the client feel understood, so she can renew her effort to speak to how she herself feels, and how she has learned to react to mothers' rituals.

There are two, in some sense contradictory, responses the client has learned to give in order to cope with mothers' ritual. These responses might be seen as illustrating an S-3/4 and an S-4/3 stance, respectively. The first is to declare herself a victim of circumstances – "telling people I wish it had not been this way" – while the second overcomes the conflict between S-3 and S-4, at least mildly, by her asserting herself as a somewhat self-authoring member of the community (S-4/3): "telling people … that I really like children." It is true, in order to envision the latter score, we would be entitled to expect more of a real insight on the side of the client into who she is on her own terms, regardless of community, and this may be forthcoming during the remainder of the interview. So, as interviewers, at this point we should be looking out for opportunities for the client to express her self-authoring stance, if any. (We can't correctly score the upper part of the client's range if we don't manage to give her the opportunity to shine as a self authorer. In fact, that's our mandate as interviewers.)

In light of this mandate, the interviewer might have asked something like: "You just said that one of the responses you often give is to assert that you really like children. Can you say more about what that response does for you in the way of relating to a group of mothers?" But the interviewer is still "out to lunch" on where the client is developmentally, and, seeking a safe harbor, returns to an earlier spot in the interview where the client addressed being without children as entailing gifts [g]. The interviewer slightly generalizes this remark as one regarding "both a gift and a burden" (sadness=burden), and asks the client to focus on "how it shows up as a gift." Overall, then, the interviewer seems to have formulated a hypothesis for himself that says that there is more to the client than the S-3/4 stance of victim.

The client now turns from the community of mothers to her relationship with her husband [7]. In her eyes, the closeness of her relationship with him is a real gift: "We have built our relationship on shared interests that really run deep with us. That is one of the gifts." Another gift is the client's "ability to travel, to learn, to really experiment with learning, and to experiment with different ways of being." Here again, the client's response is two-pronged. One response points to a physical and internalized relationship, while the other points directly to herself. As interviewers, our ears would perk up, of course, upon hearing of the 'ability to experiment with different ways of being,' because that remark could provide an entry for us to probe the client's mental space more deeply in an S-4 direction.

For now, the client continues [7] stating that because she did not play the role of mother, something else had to fill her life: "I experienced it – the childlessness – as both the joys and delights of having to invent something, because I did not have a [social] role."

This is a stark statement worthy of our attention. The notion here seems to be that if a women is not a mother, she doesn't really have a role in society (which sounds like "pre-women's liberation"). Although the client acknowledges the role of wife, she feels that "it's not quite the same," for reasons that are not disclosed. Again, the client finds it "funny" [which conveys both perplexity and distancing at the same time] how the community categorizes "mothers and working mothers and that sort of thing." She could have said that she finds it "curious," as she has before expressed being curious about what others whom she separates out from experience. It's not entirely clear what 'funny' means to her other than 'strange.'

At this point, the interviewer comes back with a voice of his own [h]. Generalizing somewhat from what has been said, and missing the chance of inquiring into what is meant by "having to invent something because I did not have a role," he now asks about "that freedom of being able to define yourself independently of being a mother."

The client goes along with this question [8]: "It meant I could align with groups and be part of groups I had not chosen or had (not had) the opportunity to do so before." From our vantage point as developmental listeners in search of clues to the strength of the client's S-4 potential, this is an interesting statement. The 'freedom of being able to define yourself independently of being a mother' is here specified as being one of freely choosing groups, rather than being part of a pre-ordained group, that of mothers (if not of family). There is no reason to assume that focusing on groups necessarily conveys a "3-ish" stance, although this is often the case. What matters is how the relationship to groups is experienced and made meaning of by the speaker. Choosing groups freely could be a rather self authoring way of relating to community. At least it could be a fine bridge for becoming self-authoring in the safety of a self-selected, more highly developed group.

Wisely, at [i] the interviewer asks for more information: "Give me an example." The client thinks for a moment, going back in her memory, and then provides an example [9]:

[i] Several years ago I started to take long extended retreats at Gethsemane Monastery, and that probably would not have been possible or likely had I had children. I was able to follow my real curiosity about Thomas Merton's life and the way it led me. That was what I was originally curious about, and I was able to discover what it would be like, or able to see how monks lived

in community in a way I would not have been able to see before. One of the things that was so striking about that first experience was that I learned something different about community. That it is a place where people accept each other and their foibles in a different way than most other groups. It's like a deep acceptance and growth process that people get on. I found that really attractive.

Structurally speaking (bracketing content here), where does it get us? What comes up for her is, as once before, focused around *curiosity*, this time curiosity about "Thomas Merton's life and the way it led me." Thomas Merton is an internalized other, for sure, but one that can be named and thus held as object. He is a writer that "leads" the client, apparently not in the sense of somebody the client is subject to. He could, through his writings, function as her model of self-authoring. We will have to see. In any case, the curiosity playing out here concerns different kinds of groups, and what happens in those groups where deep acceptance (rather than competitive scrutiny) prevails.

What the client initially had a great deal of curiosity about was the way in which Thomas Merton's writings led her in her life, and what discoveries 'he' – that is, her interpretation of his writings – readied her for. As she says: "I was able to discover what it would be like … (to live a monastic life?]), … or able to see how monks lived in a community, in a way I would not have been able to see before." The discovery Thomas Merton's writings readied her for was being able to 'see' a new kind of community. What she found really attractive in what she discovered in the monastery was:

That it is a place where people accept each other and their foibles in a different way than most other groups. It's like a deep acceptance and growth process that people get on.

We might surmise here that our fledgling self-authorer is choosing to find herself through the membership in groups of a special kind, those in which acceptance outdoes competition. We might further surmise that this choice, to work through groups, is based on a theory of self of an idiosyncratic kind, or on a 'value generator' of a special kind. Right now, we can only speculate. What we really need at this point is for the interviewer to help us out with a forceful probe. For instance, the interviewer might ask:

- Can you say more about why this is attractive to you at this point in your life?

Or, in a more demanding way:

- In detail, what does the deep acceptance and growth process you just spoke about mean to you in your own life?

However, the interviewer is not up to the task. In [j], he meekly comments "so that speaks to the groups or community that you choose to be part of," – which leaves the initiative to the client, rather than setting a direction for the client to proceed in. In short, the interviewer is certainly <u>not</u> leading a "powerful conversation" in the sense of this book at this point.

Left to her own devices, the client in [10] just 'stumbles on.' She "did not know that I was going to find COMMUNITY" written large, and while very interested intellectually in Merton's 'work on Buddhism,' she derives an even stronger experience from actually witnessing a communal life of a kind she had been seeking but had not found: "I did not expect that to happen at all." And looking for an internalized (and perhaps also physical) other who could reinforce her unforeseen experience regarding community, she says: "My husband said he could see me in some other part of my life choosing to become a nun." You notice that the interviewee here speaks of herself through another person's mouth, that of her husband, as if it was too much for her to surmise what her future might look like, or else for indicating the close relationship with her husband she mentioned before (who might know her better, almost, than she herself does).

The interviewer, if he had been as struck by the last remark as I, the writer of this book, am, could now have summarized what he heard, and paraphrased it in some way, such as: "So it seems that stumbling upon that monastic community really hit you, unforeseen as it was, and you began to see a part of yourself that would like to live that way, now or sometime in the future. Can you say more about how that would dovetail with your values and your vision of yourself at this point in your life?"

Instead, the interviewer is off on his own little ego-trip (thus unable to follow a stage hypothesis), and speaks about what 'intrigues him' at this point [k], never mind the client whom he is supposedly trying to understand at a deeper level. He goes back to 'the gifts of being an outsider,' a very abstract paraphrase of what the client had said a while ago. In fact, the interviewer now provides an interpretation of the core of the interview as he understands it, – an abstract rendition of what he has understood, by saying:

[k] The thing I am really intrigued with is, you framed the gifts of being an outsider – in this case you started as an outsider and with a perspective of not being a parent, a single child without children and framing the gift as a door into community. Can you say a little bit more?

The risk the interviewer runs using such broad brush strokes in reviewing the interview is, of course, that it leads the client off track. Especially an S-3 client will most likely follow *any* direction the interviewer points to, and if the direction is a mistaken one, important opportunities will be missed and interview time will be wasted. (An interview only lasts about 50-55 minutes!), and we are still on the first prompt!. Here, the interviewer presents a high level, condensed summary that starts with being an outsider and ends with "framing the gift – of being without children – as a door into community."

Wow! So, expectedly, the client is a little confused at this point, and can only emit [11]: "A kind of paradox …," without us learning what she might mean. This is made worse by the interviewer now picking up the term "paradox," and trying to make it stick. Not being ever very comfortable with attending to what was just said, – the client's train of thought, – the interviewer in [l] gets more deeply into a muddle by saying:

[l] Yeah, an interesting paradox. I would like to know what the impact …, when that perspective on yourself had you feel outside of, or apart from others as well … Perhaps we could go back to the experience of yourself as part of the women's group this morning [thank you, Spirit! O.L].

Having gotten into two incomplete sentences here, the interviewer finally withdraws (perhaps with some embarrassment) and asks the client "to go back to the experience of yourself as part of the woman's group this morning." The assumption here is that the interviewer's (incomplete) summary of the entire interview could be helpful to the client when she returns to something she said a while ago – which, to the interviewer, now feels like a last resort. The interviewer is strictly following his own agenda, not the client's! In some way, he is trying to manipulate the client into saying something that falls along the lines of his own interpretation, without giving her any implicit guidelines as to what is meant by "the experience of yourself as part if the women's group this morning."

The client now follows the interviewer's directive and begins speaking about the group initially commented upon by her [12]. She makes a distinction between how the group started and how, after "some time," it operates at present. The client admits to feeling apart from the group lately (the last four or five years)

[12] What I am really interested in organizations [for] is [the nature of] faith based organizations. And peoples' spiritual lives … and sometimes in my corporate world … that is something I do not hear too many people talking about. So I can feel a little apart from the organization or [from] clients dealing with the surface level conversations that go on. My sense is that there is something deeper that we could be connected with. Sometimes I do not have the courage or sometimes don't seem to find the doorway to test that.

It seems the interviewer has, unfortunately, been successful in getting the client off her original train of thought, and has readied her to talk more in abstractions ("faith based organizations"). However, she manages to recover, and to return to a self-referential posture from which she speaks to "something deeper we – she and her clients – could be connected with." Clearly, it would be highly informative for structural reasons to know more about what the client means here. The interviewer does not give her the opportunity to reveal that, and thereby perhaps sabotages insight into where, from a self authoring point of view, the client might be, – what might be the ceiling of her present range.

The interviewer really fails pretty badly here. It would have been natural to ask at the end of [12]: "You just talked about the spiritual aspect of the life people lead, pointing to 'something deeper that we (?) could be connected with.' Could you say a little more about what you meant by that? Who, for you, is this 'we,' and what it is that, in your view, is that 'something deeper' that connects people?"

No such powerful conversation happens here, however. Clinging to the last sentence as if it were detached from the rest of the utterance, the interviewer simply asks for a Y/N clarification [m]: "with clients in corporate environments?" This not too difficult to make inference is confirmed by the client, who now takes for granted that the interviewer knows what she is talking about (which is not the case), calling that "it" [13]:

[13] Yeah, if they initiate it I will go there. But otherwise I have not found a graceful way to explore whether people are interested in those other things the way I am, like more energy connections … And how do people's spiritual [life] and faith operate at work.

Where are we here with regard to any kind of hypothesis regarding the client's uppermost stage (developmental ceiling)? That is hard to say. What we can surmise is that the interviewer does not have access to a clear hypothesis himself, and therefore also does not know what the missing information is, and how to probe for it. This leads to failed opportunities for both the client and the interviewer, especially the client. It is clearly the mandate of the interviewer in powerful conversations, to give clients as many opportunities as possible to demonstrate their presently uppermost stage (ceiling), and thus their potential. In this case, we would like to know whether the ceiling is an S-4/3, S-4(3), or even S-4 and beyond. We determined some time ago that the lowest scorable stage is most likely S-3(4). We now have to be content with what the client, insufficiently prompted, provides us with.

The client tells us that, with her corporate clients, she will not initiate a conversation in a spiritual direction if her clients "don't go there themselves." Although her values seem to tell her that there is something deeper "that we could be connected with," she chooses to leave the initiative "to go there" to her clients. She gives two disparate reasons for that. The first is that she simply has not found a 'graceful way' to explore whether people "are interested in those other things the way I am." The client – who is a coach – says:

Sometimes I do not have the courage, or sometimes don't seem to find the doorway, to test that.

In sum, it is not only that she has not found a graceful way of initiating such a conversation. She also finds that sometimes she has the courage to do so, and sometimes not (clearly a conflictual stance), and even if she has the courage "does not find the doorway to test that."

What a superb opportunity it would have been for the interviewer at the end of [12], to say: "That's really interesting that you should bring up the term 'courage' here, aside from the issue of not finding a doorway to test a corporate client's spiritual leanings! Can you say more about why you think it takes courage to engage clients in what you see as 'something deeper' that connects you with them, please?"

Without such a probe, we are left to having to puzzle out what the client means when she says at the end of [13]:

Like more energy connections, and how do people's spiritual [life] and faith operate at work.

As a coach, then, the client (speaker) is looking for 'energy connections.' She feels that, in part, to develop such connections depends on her, both on her courage, and her finding a graceful way to lead clients in a direction that is important to her. Just as Thomas Merton 'led her' to discover community of a different kind, she is – relying perhaps on this internalized other – now emulating his work in herself as a carrier of energy she is yearning to be linked to. Compared to this inner yearning, "how people's spiritual … and faith operate at work" is really an intellectual issue.

Apparently, the speaker is one of many coaches who have chosen coaching as a way of self development, by using her spiritual inclinations (that, as we know, can occur at many different levels). The hidden assumption underlying this choice is that coaching is inter-developmental, as we say at the Interdevelopmental Institute, – in the sense that both parties to the coaching potentially develop. Here, we are listening to a person of strong spiritual yearnings connected with community, trying to find out how she herself defines what transcends her own values (spiritual or not).

The interviewer partly understands that the client is striving for spiritual community not only in her social life, but also in her coaching work. At least, he is groping for understanding something of the kind. In [n], he asks, somewhat tentatively:

[n] When you feel yourself really restrained from being engaged with people in that way, and it sounds like that is clearly an important part of who you are,…[what happens to you???]

The interviewer's notion here is that, at this time, the interviewee is 'bigger' than she permits her corporate coaching self to be, and that to feel less 'restrained' is important to her for her self development, not just as a way of becoming more effective with clients. The client jumps to the implied Y/N question at the end, and confirms the hunch. Whereupon the interviewer asks one of the best questions he has so far been able to formulate [o]:

What is the experience you have of <u>not</u> being able to move into that space with them, and <u>not</u> [to] be able to bring them into your world?

Why is this a good question? The question is based on interpretations such as "moving into that space with them." It also considers the opposite 'energy flow,' of "bringing them [that is, <u>others</u>] into your world." The image here is one of leading into another's space and back into one's own, as "something deeper that we could be connected with" [12].

Now, it's not clear what exactly being able to do so would do either for the coach (speaker) or the corporate client. We could expect the client to now reveal something of her self-authoring capacity, given that she has been prompted to answer to her spiritual experience and its function in her professional work. Unfortunately, the interviewer has prepared her for looking at her coaching experience in a negative way, as having to do with being "restrained from being engaged with people in that way." The interviewer has emphasized this somewhat negative perspective by asking about her experience of NOT being able to move together into a spiritual space, thus NOT being able to "bring them into your world." In addition, the client has previously stated a sense of sadness about there being something missing in her life [4], indicating the inseparability of gift and sadness, – or as the interviewer put it [g], "gift and burden." So, we are somewhat prepared for what the client says next [15]:

A kind of sadness, although it's not really …. I do not know how to explain it. It's not like a deep emotion, its more like a universal sadness, like when a child dies and it's out of season. Also, there is a part of me that says do not push at it but allow it to evolve … that whatever is developing in the work or in the relationship, it will develop in its own way. So I can get curious about what is going to happen.

Apparently, the client is confused here about how she experiences not being able to enter spiritual realms with (most of) her corporate clients: "I do not know how to explain it." Her sadness is 'not really' sadness, but rather a kind of 'universal sadness,' "like when a child dies and it's out of season," – like when a development that ordinarily would have been possible is suddenly aborted. The client's inability to explain clearly what she experiences is, I would say, an indication of the difficulty she presently has to articulate **her own self experience and self definition**. She can point to it, but she cannot articulate it.

There is also another part worth noticing to the client's response. As a coach, she feels it is better not to push, but allow 'it' to evolve, "that, whatever is developing in the work or in the relationship, it will develop in its own way." We see the client here taking a perspective on a relationship, that of coaching, and the process that is ongoing between coach and corporate client. The IT here is something that the client, speaking as a coach, subordinates herself to, wanting to let it evolve, and trusting that it will. If this is a correct interpretation, it would mean that the client is – in some way to be explored – standing away from her own self, and looking at the interaction between two different selves (or systems) that stand in a helping relationship. The client's present theory of helping says not to push, but to trust that 'it' – "something deeper we could be connected with" – will emerge of its own accord.

If we now had more ample information to justify that this client makes meaning of herself as a self-authorer (S-4), we would be on much firmer ground in interpreting the speaker's "something deeper we could be connected with" [12] than we actually are. The client is not taking the lead in making something happen in a coaching relationship, she is only "curious about what is going to happen" more or less independently of her intervention. That is, she is waiting for permission coming from outside of her, to go into a mental space larger than her own.

In [15], we get another chance to hear the client speak to her coaching work as a manifestation of her values and principles:

I had an experience last week of piloting a course. From something that I said, the key client, the guy at the top who heads this whole power plant, nuclear power plant, came up to me and said, 'from something you said, do you coach around people who find themselves, who seem to find their faith and their work aren't in sync, and where they have to compromise themselves?' I said 'yes, I do coach people about those things.' He said, 'I would like to talk to you.' Now, I hadn't a clue about his background. And if you had asked me I would have said there is no way we are ever going to have this conversation. And yet there he was …

Interestingly, this passage follows the one at the beginning of [15] where the client was speaking about a 'universal sadness' that befalls her when unable to bring clients into the spiritual space in which she functions (or at least strives to function). Apparently, she is at times astonished when this sadness is lifted. This happens when clients take the first step to ask for being helped with synchronizing faith and work (which may be a spiritual issue, or may not be). When this happens, the client's assumption, that "there is no way we are ever going to have this conversation," is shown to be wrong, or misleading, and her faith that spiritual conversations can happen is restored. In a way, then, the client's self definition as a person, the ceiling of her present potential, is intrinsically linked to her spiritual 'edge' in her coaching.

Again, the interviewer is not up to the task of developmental listening here. The excerpt ends with a somewhat cryptic, ambiguous question on his part: [p] Opening that up for you?

[END OF EXCERPT]

This question is not really a probe, but an inference converted to a question. Questions like the above remain cryptic (even if they are stated as complete sentences), and are therefore not of much use in developmental interviewing. Since this is all we know about the client, we will have to come to some kind of conclusion about her developmental profile as it now stands, a topic I will address below.

***

Before drawing some conclusions about the structure – range of stages – of this interview, let's briefly review the strengths and failings of the interviewer. Clearly, the interviewer – who is a beginner in developmental listening – tried to do the best he could, knowing as much as he then knew about developmental interviewing. I did not select this particular interview to present a bad example of interviewing. Knowing what it takes to learn the craft of developmental interviewing thoroughly, I am full of compassion for people who make the leap. This also holds in this case. I simply selected this example to show *e contrario* (by contrast) what good interviewing is, thinking it would be pedagogically more productive to do so than to present a 'perfect' interview. Besides, there is really no perfect interview! There are only more or less good interviews, and to administer good interviews is a matter of practice, nothing else.

So, what can we say about the interviewing process we have witnessed above? If the interviewer tried his best, what were his strengths? Here are some:
- The interviewer shows courage by attempting the interview in the first place; without that courage, practicing it cannot begin.
- He is analytically savvy – perhaps too savvy – in looking for a conceptual kernel that he could foist his next question on.
- Despite his lapses, he keeps the interview going, sometimes, but not always, confusing the client.
- He often understands the gist of what was being said, without being quite able to get at the essence of it right away.
- The interviewer is groping toward questions by which to clarify the interviewee's present developmental potential compared to the risks.
- The interviewer studiously avoids 'WHY' questions (but nevertheless asks some unproductive Y/N questions).

Thinking about the challenges the interviewer could not successfully handle, what comes to mind is this:
- The interviewer's greatest weakness is his difficulty to stay close to the client's train of thought, – just focusing attention.

- The interviewer does not start out with a clear hypothesis, then to work from that hypothesis – say S-3/4 – in order to test for the stage below and above the assumed Center of Gravity (as he should have done).

- The repertory of options the interviewer has for staying close to the client's train of thought is very limited (his paraphrasing is at too abstract a level, his commenting is awkward, and his direct questions are often too distant from the client's train of thought to be effective).

- Since abstract thinking comes easily to the interviewer, he often (almost unconsciously) *interprets*, and thus reframes, what the client is saying, – as when he speaks of "a gift and a burden," where the client had only spoken of gifts (thereby putting a negative spin on the client's utterances).

- Many of the interviewer's questions are not powerful probes aiming to substantiate an hypothesis, but rather comments or inferences converted to questions that, essentially, maintain the status quo of his level of insight into the client.

If the interviewer had started with a hypothesis such as S-3/4, he would have had to say to himself:

"The issue here seems to be how far the client can separate out from her internalized others (husband, group of mothers, Thomas Merton, etc.) and articulate to some degree her own independent values and principles. Since she seems to attempt to do so by addressing issues of community, she is not making her task easy for herself. I should make her aware of that through my questions, and present to her as many opportunities as I can for having her demonstrate her self-authoring capacity. I could probably best do this by linking myself to everything she says about her gifts in life, what they mean to her, and perhaps also by paying close attention to what she says about the ideal, monastic, community. I would then see whether her values are borrowed from the social surround, or rather are authentic values generated inside of herself, in contrast to, or at least surpassing, conventional community values."

In the above interview, there were many opportunities for the interviewer to follow these directives. The fact that he didn't do so makes me surmise that, at the moment of the interview, his cognitive profile – the ability to think abstractly – was more highly developed than his social-emotional capacity. I would hazard the guess that his own developmental level – or coaching level – was slightly higher than that of the interviewee, but not much (S-4(3)). Despite this, the interviewer may have followed what came easiest to him, namely to think abstractly, and therefore he did not make sufficient use of his insight into his own life and work. However, these are speculations. I cannot provide proofs for them, and so they simply fall outside of evidence based education.

***

At this point, what remains to be done is to arrive at a succinct summary of how the above interview might be evaluated or *scored*. Let us follow the procedure that is used with full length interviews.

In professional developmental assessment, it is customary, – following Lahey et al.'s (1988) example as well as my own practice and courses of instruction – to use a CODING SHEET. This coding sheet has several different purposes:

- Collecting the interview reader's (or schooled listener's) evaluations in a succinct manner, to streamline the evaluation process
- Collecting data for a systematic comparison of different individuals or groups (data mining)
- Collecting data on the quality of a coaching program and criteria of coach selection in organizations
- Documentation of the ROI (or Coaching ROI = CROI) of a coaching process for individuals or groups

The format of a coding sheet for scoring social-emotional interviews is as seen below.

Interview ID and page number	Bit number followed by the scoring hypothesis	Three questions to ask yourself when deciding about a score. 1) What structural evidence leads you to these hypotheses? 2) What evidence leads you to reject other plausible counter-hypotheses? 3) If you have a range of hypotheses, what further information do you need to narrow the range? (Below, I mainly address question no. 1, regarding structural evidence. I sometimes use a question mark to indicate a counter-hypothesis or range, without deciding the issue.)

Table 8.4 Format of social-emotional stage Coding Sheet

As seen above, the coding sheet comprises three sections (columns). The first lists the anonymous "interview ID" (rather than the name of the interviewee), as well as the page number of the text fragment (or number of the running tape) that is scored in columns 2 and 3. Column 2 states the number of the interview 'bit' [passage or fragment] that is being scored, and the scoring hypothesis attached to it. Column 3, finally, is where the real work gets done. In this column, the user typically answers three questions (Lahey et al., 1988, Appendix F, 423 f.):
1) What structural evidence leads you to these hypotheses?
2) What evidence leads you to reject other plausible counter-hypotheses?
3) If you have a range of hypotheses, what further information do you need to narrow the range?

The third column easily accommodates a quote of the crucial sentences, at least in outline, that are meant to be scored as *structurally relevant*. In my experience, lifting out one or more sentence(s) from the interview (by placing them into column 3 of the coding sheet) is in itself commensurate with 'framing' or 'highlighting' the text so that attention can more closely focus on it. This is a welcome aid in deciding how to score a text fragment.

The best way to look at the coding sheet is to consider it as a record of all *structurally relevant* passages of an interview that were scored. As such, the sheet represents the EVIDENCE that is available to justify the scoring. However, there is more to it than that. **The coding sheet guides your thinking as you engage with the interview, and is thus itself an evaluation tool and tool for professional self reflection.** It challenges you to do the following:

- Select a text passage that has structural relevance beyond its content.
- Decide how long that passage is going to be (1 sentence, more sentences, half a page, several pages, etc.).
- Isolate and go into depth in your thinking about what is said in the text fragment, and debate the best, most justifiable stage score for it (column 2).
- Justify underneath the quote your reasons for scoring it this way and no other
- If possible, also state what 'counter-hypothesis' you are rejecting, thereby activating your ability to play devil's advocate.
- Finally, having justified your scoring, ask yourself what information is missing in the interview that would aid you in choosing a more appropriate scoring or refine a present scoring..
- To achieve some degree of *inter-rater reliability*, get together with a group of colleagues who can score the interview independently of you.

What is the outcome of the coding sheet? Based on this author's modification of Lahey et al.'s scoring procedure of 1988, the outcome of the coding sheet is twofold:

1. Information about the interviewee's Center of Gravity.
2. Information about the proportion – in terms of number of text 'bits' – of scorings of stages 'below' and 'above' the Center of Gravity.

The second part of the scoring outcome makes it possible to formulate not only a stage score but an associated Risk-Clarity-Potential Index (RCP), as introduced in Laske's dissertation on developmental coaching (1999a). To understand how the RCP is arrived at, I need to remind the reader of the following facts (see also Chapter 5).

A full fledged 50 minute interview, when transcribed, typically covers between 15 and 20 8.5 x 11 pages single spaced. (It may be longer, depending on the verbosity of the client and the style of the interviewer). When one expertly distinguishes content from structure, one finds that interviews typically contain at most 16 to 18 *structurally relevant* text passages. I call these passages 'bits' that it makes sense to score. Since most interviewees are 'distributed over' no more than three levels (S-1, S, S+1), the sum of all passages, say 16, would in the coding process be partitioned into three distinct subsets:

- Passages at the center of gravity (S).
- Passages below the center of gravity (S-1).
- Passages above the center of gravity (S-2).

If more than 18 (or so) bits are scored, *over-scoring* occurs (that is, too many bits are scored). For a learner, and for pedagogical reasons, it is sometimes advantageous to over-score. This is done in order to arrive at a first overview that can later be 'cleaned up' to focus on the 'really important' bits. This procedure will be exercised below.

The interview excerpt quoted above comprises exactly three single-spaced 8.5 x 11 pages. Counting a full fledged interview at fifteen pages, on three pages no more than at most 15/3=5 'bits' should be scored, to avoid over-scoring. Over-scoring entails that the line between content and structure has remained too blurry, too many contents being considered as *structurally relevant*. In the present case, I will deviate from this rule for pedagogical reasons. I do so in order to demonstrate how clarifying – especially for beginners – using the coding sheet can be. In fact, I will score as many 'bits' as possible, to alert the reader to shadings of meaning. After all, having before us only a partial interview, we cannot expect to arrive at a definitive score and RCP anyway.

Before we begin, let's remind ourselves of what was said about the RCP in Chapters 5 and 7.

Risk	Clarity	Potential
S-1	S (Center of Gravity)	S+1
S-3	S-3(4)	S-3/4
5	8	3

Table 8.5 Example RCP

There, we dealt with the score: **S-3(4) {5: 8: 3}**. As the reader knows, the RCP score (in curly brackets) indicates that 8 'bits' or passages of the interview transcript (or tape) were scored at the Center of Gravity S-3(4), 5 passages at the lower level, of S-3, and 3 passages at the higher level, of S-3/4. Accordingly, altogether 16 passages in the interview were found to be structurally relevant, whether they were confined to a single interview page, or stretched across two pages. As you can see, the RCP simply sums up the passages that were evaluated as being at one or another stage.

Let's now go back to the interview excerpt discussed at the beginning of this chapter. As you see, the interview has the ID #046, and comprises 3 pages. In the example below, also listed in column 1 is the number of the text passage (spoken by the interviewee) referred to, in '[ ]'. In column 2, altogether thirteen bits were scored (#1 to #13). In the third column, one finds a quote of the individual text passage scored (in quotation marks), and underneath, in italics, the justification for the scoring. Also, enclosed in '< …>' underneath the justification of the scoring, I sometimes suggest a further probe the interviewer could use to obtain missing information.

Chapter 8 Interview Excerpt; Prompt 'Outside of'		
Interview ID #046 & Page	Bit Number & Score in Teleological Range 1 1(2) 1/2 2/1 2(1) 2 2(3) 2/3 3/2 3(2) 3 3(4) 3/4 4/3 4(3) 4 4(5) 4/5 5/4 5(4) 5	Questions to Ask: 1) What structural evidence leads you to these hypotheses? 2) What evidence leads you to reject other plausible counter-hypotheses? 3) If you have a range of hypotheses, what further information do you need to narrow the range?
1 [1]	[not a bit, but an indication of the lower range boundary] > 3(4)	"There are a couple of ways that I am different or have been different over the course of my life. One is that I am an only child. And at the time of my growing up that was not as common a thing as it is today. A second is that I was widowed in my 20's- a pretty unusual time in one's life to be widowed. So I was like about 40 years off the age and developmental curve. What I am finding these days as a

		little unusual is that I am an only child without children." *The client takes a perspective on her difference from others, reflecting on her position in society. She does so by embracing conventional notions of what is 'unusual' for a woman. Her perception of her difference from others defines her present world view. What remains unclear is how far she can transcend this position based on her own authentic values. The score above simply indicates the lowest scorable position of the speaker's range.*
1 [3]	#1, 4/3	"I am just aware of the unusualness of it [my social position]. Although I do not feel like an outsider anymore. It's like a condition of my life that just is. And so I am more curious about it." *The client assumes a neutral stance of curiosity regarding her condition, presumably based on her ability to stand away from the crowd and make her own judgments.* <Tell me more about your curiosity.>
1 [4]	#2, 4(3)	"I have been more aware the last few years that there are gifts that come to me because of that [childlessness] as well as sadness about that. And I get real curious when I run into people with similar situations." *Demonstrably maintaining her stance of curiosity – rather than feeling like a victim of her condition and of community judgments – the client introduces the positive, self-sustaining side of her condition, its gifts to her.* <Can you say more about the gifts you have in mind that come to you?>
1 [4]	#3, 3/4	" … And wondered what that was like [to be a monastic woman without children] since so much of our American life is really associated with family and raising family. And I happen to love children. So, it's not that I am childless by choice." *The client here defers to convention and community, making a point of her love of children, relieved to be able to conclude that she is childless by fate, not by choice. Whether she could actually make the choice not to have children is an open question.* <In what way does that matter for you, to be childless by fate rather than by choice?>
1-2 [5]	#4, 4/3	"It's a funny thing I have observed in women's groups … when you do not have children they assume you don't like them [children]. It's that funny kind of ritual that groups go through to figure out what are they going to do with 'this person'." *The client again adopts a 'neutral' stance of curiosity, referring to what women in groups do as "a funny ritual." Since it is a 'ritual,' the client can stand outside of it, rather than feeling she is subject to it. Based on her incipient value system, she clearly views others and community with a critical eye.* <Can you tell me more about what it feels like to be 'this person'?>
2 [6]	#5, 3/4	"So I have learned to deal with it [my childlessness] sometimes by telling people that I wish it had not been this way, or other times that I really like children, and I will be

		the baby holder during this meeting." *In social situations, the client wavers in her answers. She sometimes publicly regrets her situation of childlessness, at other times declares herself 'the baby holder' to put others at ease. Whatever the case, she certainly takes responsibility for others' feelings.* <In terms of your feelings, what is the difference for you between these two answers?>
2 [7]	#6, 4(3)	"I am close to my husband in a way that sometimes couples aren't when they have children. … That is one of the gifts. Another is my ability to travel, to learn, to really experiment with learning, and to experiment with different ways of being. … And so I experienced it as both the joys and delights of having to invent something because I did not have a role [as a mother]." *The client here names some of the gifts of living her condition. These gifts are based on self-generated values. She identifies with her marriage relationship in one breath with the 'joys and delights' of inventing (composing) her own life. Her self-authoring stance is more espoused than positively demonstrated. There is no sign of wavering or conflict as to the gifts that come to her.* <What would you say it is that you are having to invent?>
2 [8]	#7, 4(3)	"It meant I could align with groups, or be part of groups I had not chosen, or had the opportunity to do so [i.e., choose] before." *The client herself chooses the groups to which to belong, based on her values. She defines herself by her own preferences, using groups as a medium through which to express them.* <So, choosing a group to belong to is really important to you. Can you say more about that?>
2 [9]	#8, 4/3	"One of the things that was so striking about that first experience [of monastic life] was that I learned something different about community. That it is a place where people accept each other and their foibles in a different way than most other groups. It's like a deep acceptance and growth process that people get on. I found that really attractive." *Inspired by Thomas Merton [an important internalized other for her], the client has found a type of community she is strongly attracted to. This community stands in contrast to women's groups in which she has to declare her love of children to put others at rest, and has to take responsibility for others' conventional thinking about motherhood. (A more positive counter-hypothesis here would be S-4(3), but I find the evidence for such a score to be too slim.)* <What, would you say, is the attraction for you of the monastic group compared to the group of mothers?>
2 [10]	#9, 3/4	"… but instead I got really intrigued by this view of communal [monastic] life. My husband said he could see me in some other part of my life choosing to become a nun – an Episcopal nun." *The client uses her husband, a physical as well as internalized other, to indicate an aspiration she might one day want to follow. She does not use the opportunity to spell out why she might eventually want to become an Episcopal nun.*

		\<Would you say that your husband's voice is much like your own?\>
3 **[12]**	#10, 4/3	"I can feel a little apart from the organization or clients dealing with the surface level of conversations that go on. My sense is that there is something deeper that we could be connected with. Sometimes I do not have the courage, or sometimes [I] don't seem to find the doorway to test that." *The client feels apart from others and their conversations, aware that she is following values they do not share, and wondering how to make these values public. Sometimes she does not have the 'courage' to do so, and sometimes she does not find the 'doorway' to introduce them to others, or share them with others. The 'something deeper' she refers to remains unelaborated.* \<Could you say a little more about what you mean by 'courage' in this context?\>
3 **[13]**	#11, 4/3	"If they initiate it I will go there. But otherwise I have not found a graceful way to explore whether people are interested in those other things the way I am – like more energy connections …" *In her search for more energized relationships, the client will follow others' lead in "going there" (i.e., something deeper), but will not invite or prompt them to do so.* *A counter-hypothesis might be that she follows here the strictures of a classical S-4 theory of helping, to honor and thus not to interfere in others' internal process. I rule out this hypothesis since the conflict regarding deeply felt beliefs that she is in seems to overshadow any strongly self-authoring stance here.* \<Can you say more about these 'energy connections'?\>
3 **[15]**	#12, 4	"A kind of sadness. … It's not like a deep emotion, it's more like a universal sadness like when a child dies and it's out of season. Also, there is part of me that says 'do not push at it, but allow it to evolve.' … So, I can get curious about what is going to happen." *Curiosity about others' spiritual life here combines with her sadness of the premature death of spirituality in people she is around in her work and life. To respect others in their ways and not to 'push them' is a major principle of her theory of helping. At the same time, she speaks here from a sure knowledge of her own values, however little elaborated.* \<When you say 'don't push it,' what for you is this IT that you are speaking of?\>
3 **[16]**	#13, 4(5)	"Yeah, and from something I said, and I still do not know what it was. I wonder whether I am holding myself apart, or what it is I have to learn that will bridge a gap that is not really a gap." *The stance here expressed seems to indicate how far she can presently stretch developmentally. She surmises that she might be 'holding herself apart' from others to her own disadvantage for mental growth, but also how she could take a position outside of herself 'to bridge a gap that is not really a gap' at all.* \<When you call the gap 'not really a gap,' can you say what's behind that for you?\>

4	#14	...

Table 8.6 Sample Coding Sheet

Cognizant of the fact that the excerpt has been 'over-scored,' let's take stock of what we found (not counting the first score which simply states the lowest level of the client's range):

Risk	Clarity	Potential		
S-1	S (Center of Gravity)	S+1	S+2	S+3
3/4	4/3	4(3)	4	4(5)
3	5	3	1	1
3	5	5		

Table 8.7 Interviewee's RCP

Putting together all of the bits on the coding sheet, we find that the client's present Center of Gravity is presently **S-4/3**, and that her RCP is **{3: 5: 5}**. We can thus say that the client is *distributed over 5 stages*, and that her developmental Potential is larger (=5) than her developmental Risk (=3), to act from a lower stage than her present Center of Gravity.

Of note in this result is the relative proportion of weights assigned to the Center of Gravity and the Potential. The proportion of Risk to Potential indicates that the client has strong resources for 'moving on' to the next higher, S-4(3), Center of Gravity. This can be a stressful position to be in, given that the gradual weakening of the present Center of Gravity induces a loss of (old) self.

If this is the developmental profile of a coaching client derived from a full length interview, we can begin to entertain ideas about:
1. the mental space in which the clients moves in terms of her feelings, thoughts, obligations, responsibilities taken and not taken, decisions;
2. how to give feedback to the client;
3. the nature of the most effective coaching agenda (including whether coaching would have to be primarily 'remedial' or 'potential boosting');
4. how to approach behavioral issues (of life or work);
5. how the client's cognitive profile (CD) might relate to her social-emotional one (ED);
6. how to appropriately assess coaching outcome (CROI) if the period of coaching is shorter than a year (which is the minimal period for a developmental switch to occur).

Since in the present case the client is herself a coach, we would want to entertain thoughts about **developmental mentoring,** most likely in relation to one of the client's most difficult clients.

Although the score obtained for the client may be a procedural artifact of less than competent interviewing as well as of partial scoring (excerpt only), let's here presume *for pedagogical reasons* that it is the correct score of a full length interview. **How, under these**

circumstances, would we describe the developmental profile of the client (S-4/3 {3: 5: 5}? Here is a suggestion:

The client is presently at a stage of her development where she is regularly taking the initiative to assert her own world view, thereby increasingly distinguishing herself from others. Defining herself largely by her own value system, and following perceptions of her own integrity, she is somewhat weakly embedded in her present Center of Gravity (S-4/3). This center defines a conflictual stance where she is at times uncertain of how to act and manage herself autonomously. In the present case, the Center is associated with a sizable potential of moving to the subsequent stage – S-4(3) – where conflict between S-3 and S-4 is nearly overcome. Her strong potential shows that she has largely outgrown her tendency to accommodate others. The overall score indicates a somewhat turbulent phase in her social-emotional development, in that she is readying herself to leave the safe moorings of S-4/3 and cross over into an (initially espousal-supported) self authoring mode.

In terms of intervention, the consultant is encouraged to make use of existing opportunities for boosting the interviewee's capacity for self authoring. If this is done in mentoring,, rather than coaching, and regards difficult coaching clients (especially if they are equally or more mature than the interviewee), the consultant should be aware of the strain that leaving the safe moorings of S-4/3 could put on the mentee, both in her personal life and her coaching work. The consultant should be especially watchful regarding the expectable need of the mentee, to circumvent S-4/3 confusion about self by heaping upon herself bigger and bigger espousals. A fruitful area of stabilizing the stressful move to S-4(3) as the new Center of Gravity is that of the mentee's spiritual energies. These energies are a potential source of self determination that is presently somewhat difficult for her share with others. Cognitive resources (here not taken into account) could also be used in work with 'mind openers' for the mentee's thinking.

Considering now that the client shows a good potential for "moving on" to the subsequent stage (S-4(3)), we might want to rewrite the above score into an equivalent form in order to highlight *the difficulties ahead.* Instead of:

(1) ED score = **S-4/3 {3: 5: 5}** [RCP sum = 13]

we could write:

(2) ED score = **S-4(3) {8: 3: 2}** [RCP sum = 13], by shifting the client's Center of Gravity from S-4/3 to S-4(3):

Risk		Clarity (Center of Gravity)	Potential	
S-2	S-1	S	S+1	S+ 2
3/4	4/3	4(3)	4	4(5)
3	5	3	1	1
8		3	2	

Table 8.8 Interviewee's RCP rewritten

While this scoring is clearly 'out of kilter,' it illustrates the hypothesis that, right now, the client is "somewhere between S-4/3 and S-4(3)," although with greater force in S-4/3 than S-4(3). Clearly, if we adopt S-4(3) – the subsequent stage – as a Center of Gravity, the client's Risk factor is going to grow, and her Potential is going to shrink. However, there might be some benefit to highlighting that the client has already gained a 'foothold,' although a fragile one, in S-4(3), although this Center is associated for her with a large risk of regression to lower stages.

In coaching and/or mentoring, this second, alternative perspective on the client alerts the consultant **that before further boosting the S-4(3) Center of Gravity, the large developmental risk of the client – to act from two lower stages (S-3/4 and S-4/3) – has to be attended to first and foremost.** This will keep the consultant's enthusiasm for 'helping the client grow' properly in check, and will make it easier to focus primary attention on how to make the client aware of the existing developmental risk, and the ways in which it manifests in her life and work.

In sum, while the first scoring above suggests 'developmental boosting' as a general coaching goal, the second suggests 'remedial' action. This is no contradiction at all, since in both cases the Center of Gravity in question is different. Thus: boosting for the lower (S-4/3) and remediation for the higher (S-4(3)) Center of Gravity. As this example clearly shows, social-emotional stage scores give the consultant crucial guidance in designing interventions! They suggest a set of possible interventions. Outside of coaching and mentoring, these scores alert the consultant to what the client is not going to be able to take full responsibility for, namely, her own self-authoring and follow-through with (largely espoused) plans for action.

Recommendations to the Mentor or Coach
    (1) S-4/3 {3: 5: 5}
    (2) S-4(3) {8: 3: 2}

Based on the first social-emotional score, above, let's now define some recommendations for the mentor who might work with the client (as above we have already begun). Without wanting to reduce developmental scores to practice recommendations in a simple-minded one-to-one fashion, there is at least some pedagogical sense in 'translating' social-emotional scores into suggestions for developmental interventions. This only misfires whenever the cognitive and behavioral scores – provided in volumes 2 and 3 of this book – are either not available or are entirely disregarded. Even with additional information, it would make a caricature of developmental findings if they were to be converted to 'best practices' or recipes. **This is because the entire enterprise of developmental PC is one requiring a self-authoring stance. On account of such a stance, the professional would, by definition, shy away from S-3 derived 'best practices.'** (Such practices are by definition not specific enough for the need of individual clients.) Cognitively, the professional would also understand that there is no one-to-one relationship between developmental scores, on one hand, and behavioral client descriptions or intervention procedures, on the other (as beginners in developmental thinking frequently assume; see the IDM Newsletter vol. 1.4, June 2005).

When formulating recommendations for practice, it makes sense to distinguish between *mentoring* and *mentor-coaching*. In the developmental perspective, the former primarily concerns working on the self development of the coach (as key to success in coaching), while the second, mentor-coaching, regards working with the coach [assessed beforehand] *in relation to a specific client whose developmental profile has also been assessed.* Below, I make some recommendations for these two different uses of developmental information.

ED score = S-4/3 {3:5:5}

It is recommended that the *mentor*:
- assist the client in understanding her propensity to feel responsible for physical or internalized others;
- help the client see more clearly the 'gifts' of her condition (which define her idiosyncratic self), and act upon them;
- support the client in formulating a coherent 'theory of self' acted upon in stretch assignments, including spiritual self exploration;
- facilitate the client's transition to a professional stance where her forays into using spiritual notions in her coaching work are becoming more deliberate and systematic. (The client may oppose this exactly because she is moving toward a self authoring stance (S-4) where, as we saw in Chapter 6, the boundaries between people are very clearly drawn, and to keep them so drawn may be difficult for anybody but a spiritually experienced mentor. See Kornfield, 1993).

It is recommended that the *mentor-coach*:
- role play for the mentee ways of finding "that doorway" to test clients' spiritual needs and resources;
- demonstrate to the mentee ways of addressing the balance of work and faith, by engaging in cautious self revelation (commensurate with the developmental profile of the mentee);
- require that the mentee's client be assessed developmentally;
- introduce the mentee to basic principles of developmental feedback;
- encourage the mentee to experience an assessment herself. (Through such an assessment, the mentee will learn her own *coaching level,* and become able to improve her sense of the extent to which "something deeper that we could be connected with" is open to a particular client.

CHAPTER SUMMARY

In this chapter we proceeded as follows. After a general introduction, we 'sized up' the range of the excerpt to be scored, from lowest to highest stage in the range, and then undertook a detailed analysis of both the speaker (client) and the interviewer.

We found that the relationship between interviewer and interviewee is a mutually enabling one, and that opportunities missed in the interviewing cannot be made up for in the scoring. We also found that the oscillation of the client's consciousness is quite fragile when exposed to inferential or interpretive leaps made within the interviewer's mental space, and that it is therefore best if the interviewer keeps as close to the client's train of thought as possible. This is especially true in the S-3 to S-4 range where the interviewee is by definition wide open to suggestions not properly connected to her own principles.

More specifically, we have followed the scoring of an extended interview fragment using a formal *coding sheet*. Using a coding sheet has the advantage of 'framing' text passages outside of the context in which they originally appear, and thereby objectifying the scorers thinking about them. This in itself is liberating and propels the process of scoring forward, in my experience. Even if the coding sheet needs to be 'pruned' (cleaned up) at a later time, in order to focus on the really important bits, having the documentation of one's scorings clearly before one's eyes adds to the professionalism of the scoring process.

With regard to the coding sheet as a device for forcing precision, rather than staying with mere *hand waving* (e.g., "this text passage seems to lie somewhere between S-3/4 and S-4(3), etc."), we saw that the coding sheet is the principal medium for **making oscillations of consciousness between different stages visible** to the developmentally discerning eye. When used to document coaching outcome, the coding sheet is clearly superior to any verbal suggestion that the coaching has been 'very successful.' This is so since it calibrates coaching outcomes at a level of precision not otherwise attainable.

To briefly demonstrate the last mentioned point, imagine that the coach interviewed in this chapter were mentored by a developmental expert for the duration of one year. Imagine further the post-test outcome of the coach to be:

Pretest [at the start of mentoring]   S-4/3 {3: 5: 5}
Posttest [at the end of mentoring]   **S-4(3){5: 7: 2}**

In this case, CROI would consist of four elements:
- the developmental shift from S-4/3 to S-4(3);
- the maintenance of a strong Center of Gravity;
- an expectable growth in developmental risk (compared to the original S-4/3 score);
- a expectable weakening of developmental potential (to proceed to the next following stage), compared to the original S-4/3 score).

Considering the pretest score of the mentee, the posttest outcome is a success to be proud of. While the Potential has expectably diminished and the Risk has grown because both are now pointing to a different, higher stage (S-4), embeddedness in the new Center of Gravity (S-4(3)) is solid (=7), indicating that a developmental shift has taken place. This outcome presumably manifests as a greater capability on the side of the mentee, to use forays into spiritual territory with her clients more effectively, and thereby strengthen the mentee's own self authoring identity. Not only may the 'doorway' have been found to showing clients "what we could be connected with", but the courage to work with clients on spiritual grounds, and thus tap new "energy connections," may have been strengthened.

When you imagine undertaking outcome research such as described above for *an entire coaching program*, it becomes evident that the quality of the entire program can be precisely assessed in terms of available coaching levels. Also, the coaching team can then be mentored based on solid data rather than hand-waving (opinion surveys etc.). When you proceed to aggregating coaching results over a sizable number of coaching relationships, you enter the realms of CAPABILITY MANAGEMENT.

Capability management is geared to assessing the capability of entire groups. However, the methods of Capability Management are identical with those for determining CROI. The only real difference lies in the fact that you are going beyond single coaching or mentoring relationships. You thereby make it possible for management to act upon aggregated outcomes while keeping the confidentiality of individual results intact. For more details, see Appendix D.

PRACTICE REFLECTIONS

- How are you presently mapping – making visible for yourself – your client's mental space in the Self House, Task House, and Environmental House?
- How are you intuitively determining your client's developmental range?
- What is the nature of the hypotheses about the client, if any, that you are testing?
- In what House are you typically spending most of your time with the majority of your clients?
- Is there a House – or 'floor' of the House – you consistently avoid, or find the client is consistently avoiding?
- Where do your intuitions as to the client's developmental risk and potential come from, and how evidence based are they?
- Are you keeping up a consistent 'devil's advocate dialogue' with yourself when interviewing clients?
- As a thought experiment, make an attempt to estimate one of your client's *Center of Gravity*, – even the RCP that might be associated with it. What suggestions for coaching would you be able to derive from such an experiment?
- If you are coaching teams, think of the benefits of having a concise profile of team members before you when you set out to work with them. For more details on the benefits of such insight, see Appendix C of this volume.

9
What It All Means for Coaching:
The Developmental Foundations Spelled out for Practice

In the preceding chapters, I have introduced new perspectives on understanding what professionals who want to be of assistance to individuals called *clients* have to know about how their clients, as adults, make meaning of their life and work. (I focus on teams in Appendix C, and on larger groups in Appendix D of this volume.) I have addressed issues of human resources or *human capital* of equal concern to HR professionals, OD experts, process consultants, coaches, social workers, career counselors, mediators, line managers, and psychologists, even lawyers.

As the reader will have realized by now, the lessons of this book are not limited to a single modality of consultation, but are relevant to all varieties of *process consultation* in the enlarged, developmental sense of the term. Relative to E. Schein's perspective (1999), I have introduced a **fourth model of consultation** that extends process consultation to its roots, namely, the adult-developmental foundation of interventions, whatever their specificity.

As E. Schein defined process consultation, the term refers to a **consultation to the client's mental process**. This is in contrast to consultation focused on simply delivering solutions or diagnoses. Process consultation applies to all situations where neither the problem nor the solution is well defined (ill-structured problems). It is meant to yield solutions based on understanding how a client thinks, constructs problems, and on how much responsibility s(he) is able to take for consultation outcomes.

In this concluding chapter of volume 1, I am drawing conclusions that are specific to the field of coaching, a field that presently has **no theoretical foundations**. This does not mean that what I point out for coaching is restricted to this young field, but only that coaching at this time seems to have the greatest need for adopting a theoretical, evidence based foundation. Since my general approach is **foundational,** I intend to spell out the most important practical consequences of thinking developmentally in coaching. I fully agree with Kurt Lewin who said that "there is nothing more practical than a good theory." A 'good theory,' in my view, is one that allows strong hypotheses to be formulated and tested about the client system.

This chapter is structured in four sections. In the first section, I highlight the ideas and practices this volume has taught, and what the reader might have learned. In the second section, I reflect on what the approach taught in this volume means for the process consultant generally, while in Section 3, I turn to benefits of the developmental approach **for the client** (whether in life or business coaching, and more generally when being helped by others). Lastly, in Section 4, I address the issue of what developmental coaching contributes to coaching as a knowledge-based profession of the 21st century. I do so by reflecting upon seven hypotheses (I to VII) that flow from the coaching model stated in Section One.

SECTION ONE

Some Highlights of What We Have Learned

Coaching grew up during the 1990s as a branch of behavioral consulting to individuals and teams. Despite the – continuing – lack of a shared knowledge base marking it as a *profession*, coaching has made great strides during the 1990s as an *industry service*. Emerging from a 'seat of the pants' and pragmatic 'self-help' mentality inspired by influential individuals serving as gurus (often needed by S-3 individuals), the industry has developed numerous approaches and ways of 'training' that to this day determine how coaching is thought about, viewed, marketed, purchased, – even researched. Although 'coaching researchers' have begun to investigate coaching from diverse angles (too diverse, one might say, to actually create a consistent knowledge base), they are largely following behavioral theory. They are not venturing into the Vertical of adult development as a source of behavior. As a consequence, so far they have not been successful in centering on **the development of consciousness that feeds and upholds all they are, in various guises, investigating.**

As this volume has at least implicitly demonstrated, if one wants to create a consistent and shared *knowledge base for coaching as a profession* (rather than a mere 'industry service'), gathering facts, however telling and interdisciplinary they may be, is insufficient. What is primarily needed is a consistent and cross-referenced VOCABULARY in which the knowledge base is clearly expressed. Such a vocabulary is best derived from a consistent conceptual FRAMEWORK, such as a developmental one. As we are all aware, behavioral vocabularies are typically formulated as an endless list of variables that have no straightforward relationship among themselves. What coaching researchers presently seem to be building, then, is a virtual *Tower of Babel*, following the notion of 'the more the merrier.' As a beginning, this might be all that can be done outside of a comprehensive and consistent framework such as CDF.

Coaching research aside, in this volume I have introduced a form of evidence based coaching practice that markedly deviates from accepted notions of what coaching is. I have done so, not to leave behind what the field has so far accomplished, but to extend the field both in form (standards) and content. Frankly, I have wanted to introduce FOUNDATIONS that could contribute to making the 'coaching industry' become a *profession*, and move it out of the ghetto in which it presently finds and nurtures itself. In addition, I have wanted to raise standards of coaching ethics, now in its infancy. I have approached this task by focusing on the development of adult consciousness that happens regardless of what humans DO, or at least think they do, to 'develop' others.

***

In contemporary English, the term *development* has two entirely different, but related, meanings (Laske, 1999):

- The development that happens by nature, and is part of *being* human
- The development of others that humans engage in as *agents (helpers)*.

As the reader realizes, the second notion is the one conventionally most used. I refer to this conventional, behavioral notion of development as 'agentic' because it points to human agency. I refer to the first as 'ontic,' or pointing to <u>being</u> (Greek 'on' = being;

Laske, 1999a). Acknowledging development as something that regards 'being' (human) – rather than doing something – says that whatever we do as developmental agents is secondary to what naturally and lawfully happens anyway, without our doing. In short, **doing flows from being, not the other way around!**

Clearly, in this volume I have used the *ontic* meaning of the term 'development' as a foundation for conceptualizing *agentic* development (e.g., coaching). My concern has been to show that the agentic meaning of development, situated on the Horizontal, remains ineffective if not informed by the ontic meaning of the term, which refers to the Vertical, or to **what humans ARE at a specific point in their life journey.** If this point has come across with some clarity, this volume has fulfilled its purpose.

We have seen in the preceding chapters that the Hidden Dimensions of process consultation generally are those pertaining to the oscillations of consciousness as it is revealed by human speech. When we capture such oscillations with the help of a conceptual 'grid' of stages (as first proposed by Kohlberg, Loevinger, Kegan and synthesized by Wilber), we discover that these oscillations have a Center of Gravity from which they extend outward, both in the direction of 'lower' and 'higher' stages. We also discover that these oscillations have different kinds of DEPTH, and that the depth is commensurate with the SCOPE of the individual's object of reflection that the oscillations focus around. The scope of the object of reflection an individual is capable of precisely measures the 'subject-object relations' (Kegan) that, at any time, determine an individual's thinking, feeling, social relating, decision making, and actions generally. As Kegan formulates, being a person and being a meaning maker is the same thing.

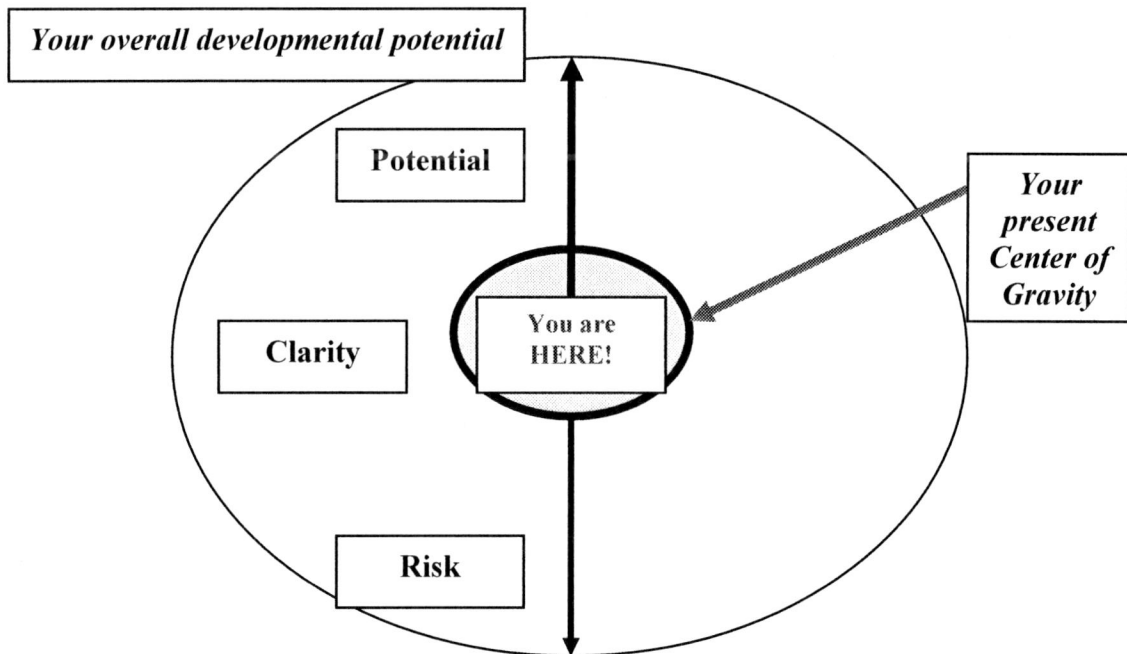

Fig. 9.1 Illustration of RCP dimensions

As shown in the illustration above, the premise of the foundations of coaching (and helping generally) introduced in this book is that every individual acts from a developmental resource and potential that can be precisely assessed. To what extent this potential will become realized is an empirical question with no predefined answers. (You may realize it in your fifties or sixties or later, and you may die before it is realized.) The potential is focused around a center that (following Clare Graves, 1981) we have called a *Center of Gravity*. This term well expresses that, like in Newtonian physics the apple falls from the tree following laws of gravity, individuals predictably act from a social-emotional center that defines their present *Frame of Reference*. This Frame of Reference is a manifestation of their Center of Gravity that determines their position on the vertical dimension of development. As a consequence, learning and development, as well as change and development, are different notions. Some aspects of learning and change may qualify as *developmental*, others may not.

In regard to the central topic of this book, to reveal the hidden dimensions of adult conversations, we have found that no matter what you do, whether as a consultant, coach, or client, you can only act from your present Center of Gravity. (Even denying that you have such a center would derive from your present Center of Gravity.) The center defines where you are developmentally, and to be there fully is your <u>only</u> guarantee of being able to advance further toward some ultimate (open-ended) developmental ceiling. Thus, to deny or ignore your Center of Gravity is clearly mere folly. In fact, you are only 'free' to the extent that you know and accept your Center of Gravity! There is nothing you can 'DO' about it.

From this vantage point, what we have established in this volume is a MODEL of individuals' life's journey. The model is a *conceptual framework* that makes it easier to think about your journey and, what is more, measure your or others' steps along the way. We have learned that measuring adult development is not child's play since developmental insight is not delivered to humans 'on a platter.' Such insight stems from two sources. In life, it comes about through own experience, successes – and more likely – failures, while in research, it is only by learning sophisticated interviewing techniques, and sufficiently emptying out to use them expertly, that you can help others – and indirectly yourself – to understand where others presently are developmentally.

At the beginning of this book, we oriented ourselves with the help of a table meant to spell out some of the stark differences between different Centers of Gravity adults act from:

Orientation	S-2	S-3	S-4	S-5
View of Others	Instruments of own need gratification	Needed to contribute to own self image	Collaborator, delegate, peer	Contributors to own integrity and balance
Level of Self Insight	Low	Moderate	High	Very High
Values	Law of Jungle	Community	Self-determined	Humanity
Needs	Overriding all others' needs	Subordinate to community, work group	Flowing from striving for integrity	Viewed in connection with own obligations and limitations

Need to Control	Very High	Moderate	Low	Very low
Communication	Unilateral	Exchange 1:1	Dialogue	True Communication
Organizational Orientation	Careerist	Good Citizen	Manager	System's Leader

Table I.1. Changing orientations across adult stages

After reading Chapters 1 to 8 of this book, we begin to understand that the differences between Centers of Gravity (stages) are in no way as abrupt as they appear to be in the above table. That is so because developmental differences are based on subtle oscillations around a shifting Center of Gravity that define *temporary truces* (Kegan 1982) between opposing tendencies (such as wanting to be *independent* and wanting to be *included*). We have learned to summarize such oscillations by way of a simple score associated with an RCP index such as **S-4/3 {3: 5: 5}**. Evidently, such a compact score has wide-scoped ramifications for any form of process consultation we might want to engage in.

Let's keep in mind at this point that the social-emotional Center of Gravity is not the only, or all-defining, developmental marker relevant in process consultation of any kind. As I demonstrate in subsequent volumes, there are other, complementary, markers, and consequently methods, for capturing oscillations and fluctuations in adults' mental spaces. These oscillations equally exist in the cognitive and behavioral domains, as focused upon in volumes 2 and 3 of this book, although in a different modality. In the cognitive realm of development, these oscillations are those between THOUGHT FORMS capturing what is *real* for individuals, and used to make sense of the world. In the behavioral realm, the oscillations are those between 'subjective need' and 'environmental press,' or ENERGY FORMS we can measure along Likert scales to compose an individual's behavioral profile in life and at work. (See the case studies in Appendix B.)

As the reader will gradually come to understand by delving into subsequent volumes of this book, there is a natural closure around oscillations of consciousness when we move away from using a single method, as introduced in this first volume. By joining to the social-emotional tools cognitive and behavioral instruments, we strongly increase the cogency of our investigations into consciousness, – and thereby our practice. For instance, we begin to see correlations, and similarities or differences, between social-emotional and cognitive, and cognitive and behavioral, evidence about a client. **Through these similarities or discrepancies we are led to new and richer HYPOTHESES about why a particular client manifests the behavior that can be observed.**

SECTION TWO
Defining a Developmental Coaching Model
We can view the so-called 'coaching community' (a term reflecting S-3 thinking) as a subset of the total population that is unified by a certain mission and certain goals. How is this sub-population structured developmentally? (Age and education will not tell the whole story.) As any population, this subpopulation is no *flatland* (Wilber), but rather constitutes a stratified universe organized in terms of developmental stages. If, as a

coach, you are part of this sub-population, where do YOU think you are? To discuss this topic, I will introduce a new term, that of COACHING LEVEL. **'Coaching level' simply means the developmental stage from which you are presently coaching, whether you know it or not.**

Orienting ourselves predominantly along 'main stages' (S-2 to S-5), this is what we see:

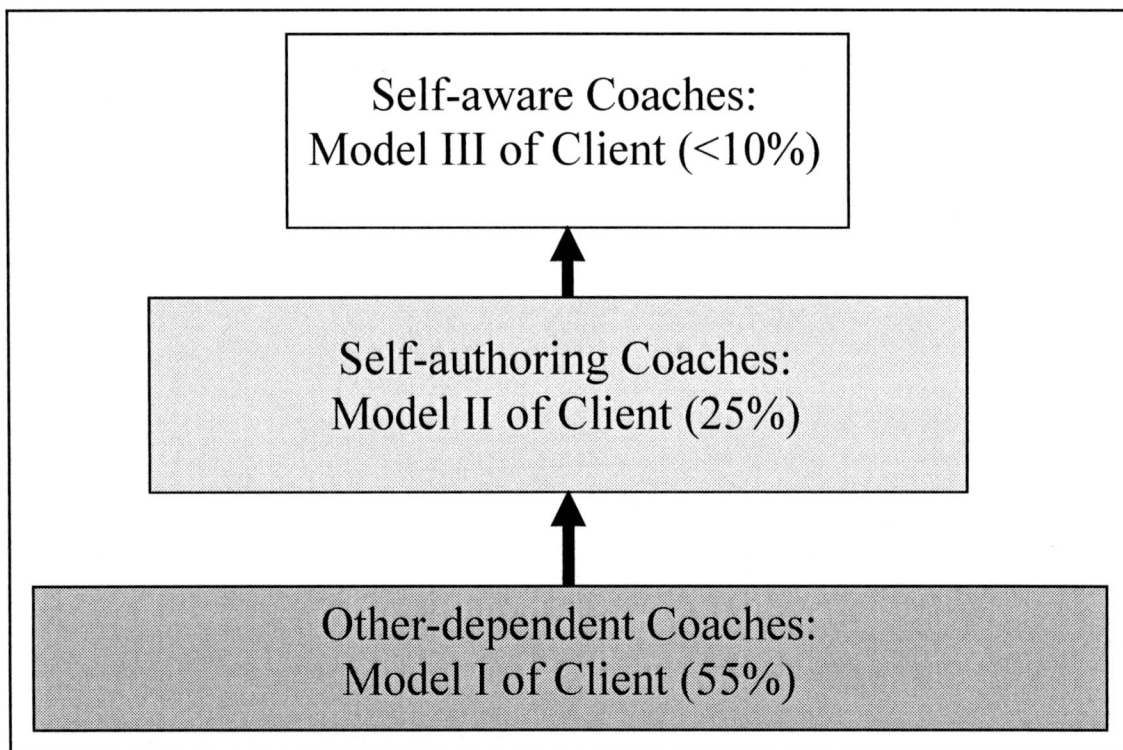

Fig. 9.2 Three distinct Coaching Levels

As shown above (see S. Cook-Greuter, 1999, 35), the constructivist-developmental hypothesis would say that the coach subpopulation of the general population is partitioned into three subsets. These three subsets comprise coaches at S-3, S-4, and S-5, respectively. We can therefore call these coaches *other-dependent, self-authoring, and self-aware*, respectively. These coaches differ in many ways, as shown in Table 1.1, above. In particular, they differ in terms of the depth of the CLIENT MODEL (I to III) they are able to develop based on their own Center of Gravity. By 'model' I mean the extent to which coaches can developmentally understand clients, limited as they are by their own Frame of Reference.

A relatively challenging issue comes up when we consider that the above model is also a PEDAGOGICAL MODEL. The model says that coaches who begin their work in S-3 need to be educated to proceed to S-4 and S-5 if possible. The model also suggests research hypotheses for 'coaching research' meant to investigate the effects of coach training (compared, for instance, to coach education in the sense of IDM). The model furthermore provides important instructional criteria for structuring curricula. In my view, it even provides certification criteria and foundations for an ethics code, – topics beyond the scope of the four volumes of this book.

When we think further about the content of the above model of coaching levels, we are led to formulating the following seven *coaching research hypotheses*:

A. Foundational Hypotheses:

I.   Assuming that the distribution of different national and cultural populations over adult stages indicated above equally applies to coaches, most coaches are working from an S-3 vantage point of other-dependence.

II.   To the extent that adult-developmental attainment in coaches exceeds that of the general population, the percentage of coaches at S-3 could be smaller than 55%; in this case, adherence to S-4 standards by coaches would by definition exceed 25% of the coach subpopulation.

   B. Corollary (Derived) Hypotheses:

III.   In order to move coaches from S-3 to S-4, – or from other-dependence to self authoring beyond what 'life' does anyway – more than 'coach training,' namely, *coach education*, is required.

IV.   Coaches have an ethical responsibility to know their developmental stage, given that 'DO NO HARM' is the uppermost principle of coaching. (Harm is done when one is coaching clients who are beyond one's own Center of Gravity; harm is done even when acting from the same Center of Gravity [as the client], since in that case the realization of the client's developmental potential cannot adequately be supported by the coach.)

V.   Coach education carries the social mandate of moving coaches from other-dependent to self-authoring capacity. This is best done by focusing coach education on coaches' self development.

VI.   Developmental mentoring of coaches extends far beyond the reinforcement of skills, best practices, etc., in that it centrally concerns the meaning making capacity that underlies the ways in which coaches build *client models*.

VII.   Ethics standards for coaches ought to include guidelines for coach training and certification based on developmental stage (or at least, range), which implies that developmental assessment needs to become mandatory in the process of coach certification, as well as prior to beginning coach training or education.

I have on purpose divided the hypotheses above into two classes: foundational and corollary (derived). The first two hypotheses underlie all others. Clearly, these hypotheses concern not only the coach, but the client, and the profession of coaching as a whole. Coaching research can be employed to operationalize these hypotheses to a point where empirical evidence becomes available.

Before entering into a discussion of these hypotheses (in Section Four of the chapter), let's understand better how we might be able to characterize different **coaching levels.**

***

Coaching Levels

The notion of *coaching level* straightforwardly follows from evidence that individuals act from a single, unified Center of Gravity on account of which they function as 'persons' and make meaning of the world they find themselves in. Experientially, while on a 'good day' you may perform at a higher level, and accordingly at a lower level on a 'bad day,' both of these levels are a natural part of your range which is centered on your Center of Gravity. Given this fact, we can therefore make distinctions between four developmental types of process consultation, including coaching: **instrumental (S-2), other-dependent (S-3), self-authoring (S-4), and self-aware (S-5) consultation.** As we know by now, there exist intermediate steps between these main types, but this fact doesn't impinge on the present argument.

A. Instrumental Coaching

Recalling the information presented throughout the book and particularly in Chapter 6, the reader will probably agree that S-2 individuals do not make acceptable process consultants (including coaches). Such individuals can only hold in mind a single perspective, their own, and therefore cannot truly intervene with another person as a 'client' (who is, rather, seen as an instrument of one's own need gratification). In fact, the instrumental perspective on clients, as held by S-2 individuals, could be called the absolute anti-thesis of consultation and coaching. By definition, the minimal level of consultation, and thus of coaching as well, is S-3. (Henceforth, I will use the term 'coach' to strengthen the focus of this chapter on coaching as a profession.)

In terms of central abilities of the coach, here are the reasons why an S-2 individual cannot impersonate a coach:

- **In general:** An S-2 coach is focused on preserving an unquestionable self image. Since the practitioner cannot take a perspective different from his or her own, the model of the client formulated – the way the client is 'seen' – is a mere replica of the coach's own self image.
- **Coaching Presence:** The coach has no presence other than that of a solicitor
- **Active Listening:** The coach is focused on being rewarded for his or her expertise by clients' success, and on being boosted by such success.
- **Attentional support:** The coach's attention is limited to immediate perceptions of clients and self, and these perceptions cannot be made an object of reflection.
- **Interpretation:** The coach has no access to a *model* or *theory* of the client, and therefore cannot interpret clients' statements, except for mimicking or contradicting them (on behalf of own coaching successes), or playing some other kind of game.
- **Enactment:** The coach (slavishly, and depending on cognitive profile, cynically) follows best practices that happen to coincide with his or her personal need and advantage at the time.

B. Other-Dependent Coaching

Having ruled out S-2 coaching as unethical (or at least ethically dubious), let's see what might define an S-3 coach. Recall the caricature of S-3, restated below from Chapter 3:

S-3 is a 'We,' or a sense of community, stage. Self-image is determined entirely by what others think, whether these others are internalized or external others. Thus, people at this stage are highly, if not completely, identified with an external socially established norm or standard that has been internalized. If rank, position, power, etc., are viewed as being important by the system that defines them, then they are important to this individual, as are appearances – social correctness. Obtaining status, in whatever terms the external reference is based upon, makes them highly competitive, but they will not stoop to the stratagems S-2 persons will to achieve their ends. They 'follow the rules,' and are 'above board' about winning and losing. It is very unlikely that they will 'see' or think beyond the established operational principles and values of 'their' organization. Because their image is so caught up in the status quo, they will be unwilling to take the risks necessary to change it, even if they can stand apart from their unit, group, or organization far enough to objectively assess what could make it operate more effectively. Hence, **they do not make good change agents, either in the sense of seeing what needs to be done or in actually doing it. Any change they believe might be beneficial will be whatever is being echoed by the majority. In a leader position, this person will follow what they believe the norms are and will try to establish a climate accordingly.** Yet, they may have a very tough time doing so, unless those norms lead them to simultaneously gain recognition, or credits, within the broader social structure. What contributes to the climate first is how it will affect their stature. Hence, the climate will be focused as much on individual achievement as it is on the group's collective effectiveness.

What is emphasized in this caricature is the extent to which S-3 individuals are wedded to the *status quo* – including the status quo of how they define themselves. They are therefore not good change agents, given that *change* is risky to their social and psychological position, – in fact, to the very way they define themselves! (If you define yourself by others' expectations, you better make sure their expectations are consonant with your goals. You will therefore have to reinforce others' expectations as best you can, and they will define the status quo for you.)
Lacking inner standards, an other-dependent coach derives expectations most easily from the social surround that 'we are all part of.' Whatever change is advocated or pursued has to affect S-3 individuals' stature *positively*, and that means, the change should reinforce a safe, socially supported, self image. This self image is never submitted to the individual's own self-authoring scrutiny which has yet to be developed.

A pedagogical remark is in order here. From the above it is clear that the crucial ingredient of 'coach training' for S-3 individuals is the development of the coach's own self-authoring scrutiny (e.g., independence from 'best practices' and other recipes.) Where this goal is not envisioned or achieved, the training remains one of mere skills without any developmental effects. It simply misses its mandate.

What, in brief, is an S-3 coach capable of? Here is a summary.
- **In general:** S-3 individuals make 'good coaches' to the extent that they can follow the rules defined by the coaching community, and respect the client for what s(he) is. The latter is hard to do for them because of the contamination they experience from (unsorted out) internalized others. For this reason, the danger of colluding with the client under the guise of being helpful is great.
- **Ability to act as a change agent:** S-3 coaches are not good change agents since their internal standards for change in a positive developmental direction derive

from internalized community standards (that remain unquestioned), not from self authored values and principles.

- **Coaching Presence:** S-3 coaches have no presence other than that bestowed on them by community acknowledgement (certificates, license) and identification with community-derived best practices and recipes.
- **Active Listening:** S-3 coaches are focused on being *in synch with* the client, but unable to (seriously) challenge the client's values, principles, and self construction based on the coach's own integrity.
- **Attentional support:** Coaches' attention is limited to keeping the client in his or her group or community even if that is developmentally harmful to the client.
- **Interpretation:** S-3 coaches have no *model* or *theory* of the client other than that bestowed by their internalized community, and this model or theory remains unquestioned to the extent that self authoring capacity is missing in the coach. Therefore, interpretations tend to uphold best practices even where that is harmful to the client developmentally.
- **Enactment:** S-3 coaches unfailingly follow those communal practices that safeguard their own membership in the coaching or other community.

In a nutshell:

– other-dependent coaching level (approx. 55 % of coaches): the coach defines him-/herself by dependence on the external or internalized social environment, such as the coaching community, client goals, corporate culture, best practices. *Low level of coaching presence in terms of developmental self-awareness.*

C. Self-Authored Coaching

The reader will recall that the journey from S-3 to S-4 is centrally about sorting out, and separating out from, the *internalized others* that S-3 individuals are entirely made up of. This is a challenging task! You first have to single out those physical others that presently guarantee your self-cohesion, and subsequently, have to extend your search to others that have *sneaked into* your picture of the world and of yourself. The first step in this search would have to be becoming inquisitive about yourself and your own certainties borrowed from the social surround. Many questions come up that no variety of self-help practice can ultimately answer. (In fact, 'self help' is a misnomer, and should be called 'other-dependent help.') Is what others believe in really what you believe in and want to stand for? Are others' challenges congenial enough to be adopted as your own? What will you lose if you deviate from others' expectations? What would being on your own look like? Where do you begin to dissociate yourself from the social surround to find your own voice?

If we translate the core of these questions into terms of a developing coach, and of coach training, the following issues would seem to arise:

- Am I ready to embark on my own search for coaching principles that fit my view of clients and clients' predicament independent of my professional community?
- What in my present coaching work do I need to question in order to take the next developmental step (since the mere acquisition of more 'skills' will not suffice)?

- To what mentor can I turn without becoming hooked on him or her as just another physical and internalized other? (Clearly, this is a mentor who sets me free, rather than enslaving me to his or her ideas and practices, by making me into an independent thinker rather than an embodiment of skills.)
- Is what I am learning about coaching convergent with the values I am beginning to form for myself?
- What dubious assumptions are hidden behind the so-called 'core competencies' and 'proficiencies' – assumptions about the coach, the client, and coaching itself?
- How are my values and principles different from the common lore of the coaching community (and coaching literature)?
- How can I experiment with the coaching principles I have learned even if I risk jeopardizing acceptance by my peers?
- How can I escape the *ghetto speak* of conventional coaching (obvious from any seminar on coaching)?

These are important questions on the way to self authored coaching! I have heard many of these, and variants thereof, in the 2004-05 Free Teleforums and Ambassador Groups of the *Interdevelopmental Institute*. In my experience, sometimes these questions block the individual's access to advanced teaching, sometimes they promote it. What happens depends on how far an individual has progressed to self authoring, and that has little to do with 'interests,' 'skills,' 'experience,' or 'life style.'

Below is a summary of the limitations of S-3 coaches (consultants):
- S-3 coaches define themselves by the community they are part of, and loss of community (consensus, etc.) is therefore experienced as loss of self, and much feared.
- The community in question may be an external or internal one, or both, and is not (or not highly enough) differentiated from the self.
- The coach's model of the client is one of identification and collusion.
- The coach's procedures are typically 'best practices' that fit *any* client. They are neither based on the coach's own principles or research evidence, nor do they do justice to the individuality of particular clients.

***

Let's assume now that the above questions of an S-3 coach have been posed and answered, and that through an arduous self-inquiry some progress in the direction of self-authored coaching has been made. What, then, do we expect of a self-authoring coach? Let's recall the caricature of S-4, restated below, to see the limitations that come up for the coach at the subsequent developmental level:

S-4 is an 'I' stage, but one much different from S-2. These individuals, rather than trying to become someone, have found themselves or 'come of age.' They have been successful while pursuing S-3 goals and have, in their eyes, earned the 'right' to stand above the crowd and be noticed. Consequently, they are highly, if not completely, identified with the value system that they have authored for themselves, yet they are very respectful of others for their competence and different values and beliefs. They find great difficulty in standing away from themselves to discover their own voids, but they will accept them when they are discovered. In this sense, they can be more self-accepting, relative to those less well developed. They can stand back, however, from the institution that previously defined them far enough to be objective about what they 'see.' **Since they are far more objective, they can be good at apprehending what could be done to change the system of which they are a part and, once doing so, will have enough strength in their own center-of-gravity to weather the storms that may come about in actually instigating a change or transformation process.** The changes they author, however, will, more likely than not, be directed towards making the organization more responsive to themselves, authoring and moving it in directions approximating their own personal 'institution,' rather than one more universally self-sustaining. The climate they create will be one that follows the status quo, but taking on their own idiosyncratic values and operational principles as time passes. Since they are caught in their own frame of reference, they fail to appreciate the value of other frames of reference that are just as much, if not more, developed. This, by definition, limits the extent to which 'their' organization can learn-to-learn, grow, and further develop.

The reader will agree that the individual that comes across here sounds *more professional.* It is important to note that this aura of professionalism is a hard-won achievement. (Only 25% of people ever succeed in getting as far, and who knows what percentage of coaches succeeds on this journey.) On the positive side, the coach can no longer hold others responsible – neither the client, the organization, the untimely end of the coaching, the interference of the coaching sponsor, the limits of coach training etc. – for whatever happens in the coaching. Equally positive is that, to the extent that self authoring is in effect, the coach has become a better change agent. Why should that be?

For one thing, S-4 coaches are by definition *more objective,* in the sense of being able to sort out 'where others end and I begin.' This is a very helpful thing to be able to do. It means that as I de-center from community and its conventional views, best practices, and assumptions, I am becoming aware of my own inclinations and strengths to a much higher degree than previously. For instance, I begin to be able to formulate in my mind my own idiosyncratic coaching MODEL of the client that tells me 'what is going on here.' Having distanced myself internally from what my training taught me, I begin to reflect more autonomously on what the hidden assumptions of that training have been, and why I initially 'bought' those, now dubious, assumptions not based on evidence. Looking closely at my clients, I see things going on that I never learned about and never noticed before. (My S-3 lenses were hiding large parts of the client.) I begin to ask myself: 'Is this best practice really 'best' in the present case? Might it not do more harm than good? Can I take a stand against this course of action? What are my own convictions, and how should I make them known? What are the standards I alone am responsible for?

In this context, it will be evident to the reader that coach education that instills idiosyncratic *question generators* – critical thinking – in learners is far superior to coach training, even if the training should happen to include "critical thinking skills." **In fact, the overriding task of coach education is to promote two abilities:**
- **Critical thinking**
- **Hypothesis testing**

These two are related, in fact, one might say they are identical. You can't think critically without suspending belief and testing appropriate hypotheses – about clients, yourself, coaching, etc.

What does it take to engage in critical thinking by which to distance yourself from ideas pre-digested for you by others? You need to formulate CONCEPTS of your own devising that you can test empirically, as hypotheses. The best way to do this is to move within a consistent CONCEPTUAL FRAMEWORK that has been tested by social science research (as the one used in this book). Not because such a framework is ever one of absolute truths, but because in working with it, you strengthen your own intuitions of how it might be tested!

Interpreting the S-4 caricature, above, with regard to coaching as a professional activity, the following highlights of an S-4 coach emerge:

- **In general:** While self authoring coaches stand their own ground, working from a clearly articulated *Persona* beyond communal best practices, they cannot easily, if at all, step back from their own value system, and thus are not open to potentials or propensities in themselves (and therefore in clients) that challenge that system.
- **Ability to act as a change agent:** On account of their greater objectivity in seeing themselves (and therefore others), S-4 coaches are better change agents. Their internal standards for what is a positive change to aim for are not derived from best practices, but from their own critical evaluation of how such practices relate to the client, their assessment of the client's environment, and from their analytical understanding of the client's developmental potential. This understanding is based on values and principles of their own idiosyncratic meaning making.
- **Coaching Presence:** The presence of S-4 coaches is that bestowed on the relationship by their own theory of integrity (on which a perspective cannot, however, be taken).
- **Active Listening:** S-4 coaches are focused on being successful in 'helping' clients based on their own, idiosyncratic values and principles, – but without a comprehensive grasp of the client's potential that might require self-aware methods to be fully revealed.
- **Attentional support:** The attention of S-4 coaches is limited to confirming their own unquestioned 'theory of helpfulness' that determines what is heard from the client.
- **Interpretation:** S-4 coaches, caught in their own frame of reference, cannot truly appreciate the meaning of statements made by clients who make meaning beyond the coach's present developmental level. (This is the main reason for why you can't successfully help a client who makes meaning beyond your present coaching level.)
- **Enactment:** S-4 coaches unreflectively follow their own values and principles, and cannot stand back from them to make room for substantial 'otherness' (contrariness) of the client (although you may still be able to bring about some behavioral change that, however, may be purely cosmetic).

In a nutshell:
- — "self-authoring" level (20-25% of coaches): the coach defines him-/herself by a consistent system of values and principles, 'marching to her own drummer,' and is able if necessary to deviate from best practices and expectations of others in order to safeguard integrity. *Medium level of coaching presence.*

D. Self-Aware Coaching

We debated at some length at the end of Chapter 6 where to draw the line for coaching as a professional activity viewed within Kegan's framework of developmental stages. Our thoughts had to do, not merely with what the journey to S-5 entails, but with whether successfully liberating oneself from a (hard-won) self-authoring stance might not become counter-productive in professional coaching. Although we ended up saying that this question seemed to be one of empirical research, ultimately no such research can decide how far to take the craft of 'coaching,' this being a matter of principles, not primarily of data.

In particular, where coaching begins and ends is a matter of coaching ethics (not primarily of coaching skills etc.), and it is thus ethics we need to explore further.

In this context it is helpful to remember that we are in this book thinking about coaching as moderns, not the way the great Greek thinkers of antiquity would have done. Ethical issues, for us, have to do with obligations (shoulds), while antique thinking saw ethics as having to do with *excellence* (virtue). The primary ethical notion originally was that all things, including humans, embody an ideal FORM (enteleicheia), and that 'being ethical' means striving to approach the ideal human form as closely as possible.

In Plato's writing, Socrates served as the quintessential mentor who, through inquisitive as well as supportive dialogue, would help bring the human form to life, propelling it on its way. (The modern notion that this form might be a 'developmental one' is beyond antique insight, although Aristotle on principle might have been ready to adopt it since he understood 'form' as lawfully developing across time.)

At this point, two questions arise:
1. was Socrates a 'coach'?
2. what changes are introduced into the notion of 'coaching' when we move from an ethics of *virtue* to an ethics of *obligation*?

The first question, "was Socrates a coach?", is intriguing from a developmental perspective. Socrates apparently thought that self-questioning was a primal but undeveloped virtue of young adults, and of adults generally. He also assumed that the individuals he questioned already knew the truth but somehow couldn't get at it, being too 'confused' (by internalized others). Therefore, they needed help. **His theory of helping was developmental in the perspective of an intellectual as well as social-emotional *midwife* who wants to bring 'reason' to life.** And once reason is alive in a person, excellence (virtue) is not far off. In short, while Socrates somewhat one-sidedly focused on reason (cognition), he might indeed be seen as the first developmental coach. What the Greeks called 'reason' was not the disembodied and instrumental *intelligence* of our time, but something that pervasively informed the human form (entelecheia). In short, reason was once a Capability, not merely a competence!

Today, our thoughts about excellence are more pragmatic, to say the least. 'Excellence' has lost its strictly ethical meaning, and has become reduced to a matter of performance (which, for Greek thinking, flows from the extent to which the ideal form has been realized in an individual, and is thus a secondary phenomenon). However, even in 'self-help,' the notion remains that every individual essentially 'knows best' (or embodies his/her own ideal 'form'), and therefore essentially can help him- or herself. As a consequence, we view coaching as the next best practice outside of self-help. Coaching begins where the insight dawns on people that individuals are limited in how much they can understand about, and thus help, themselves. That is the opening through which professional helping and process consultation enter social life.

The second question, as to an ethics of coaching 'obligation,' is equally fascinating. The central notion here is that the helper – coach or consultant – has certain obligations to fulfill, and that 'excellence' of performance as a coach depends to a great extent on whether the obligations are indeed fulfilled. The question then arises: obligations toward whom? In a way, that is a secondary question, considering **that nobody can fulfill obligations toward others s(he) has not fulfilled toward her- or himself.** Thus, in coaching nobody can fulfill obligations toward clients that, as a coach, s(he) has not fulfilled toward the self. What this says is that nobody can be a coach in the strict, professional sense of the term who is not at least acting from S-4. And that is indeed a central tenet of developmental coaching as presented in this book!

***

It is important to realize that developmental stages are also *stages of ethical thinking*. We could easily rewrite Chapter 6 as an introduction to ethics. As a result, the 'ethics' coaches are capable of at different stages differ from one another – or, as Socrates might have said, the degree of excellence adults (including coaches) at different developmental stages are capable of differs between individuals. If we maintain – as does the ICF, for instance – that there is only one 'coaching ethics,' we have to say that people are at various stages of fulfilling the obligations of that ethics. This is to be expected in a world that is a stratified universe, not some kind of flatland.

In this book, I have often asked the reader to consider (following Kegan) what a client at a particular stage CANNOT take responsibility for. This is an ethical as well as an epistemological question (question regarding ways of knowing). Clearly, nobody can take responsibility for obligations s(he) becomes accountable for only at a higher developmental stage. And differences in *feeling accountable* are clearly central to determining what developmental stage somebody is making meaning from in coaching (and otherwise). Not feeling accountable for knowing one's coaching level is an example.

I indicated above that developmental and ethical stages are one and the same thing. Following the ethics research of Lawrence Kohlberg (www.allpsych.com/psychology101/ego.html), we can in fact map developmental stages to the following four stages of ethical thinking and self-awareness (S. Cook-Greuter, 1999, 35):

Developmental Stage	Attainment
IV. Transcendent	<1%
III. Postconventional (S-5): self-aware	9%
II. Conventional (S-2 to S-4): instrumental, other-dependent, & self-authoring	80%
I. Preconventional (S-0 to S-1)	10%

Table 9.1 Overall distribution of adult developmental attainment

To quote Cook-Greuter (ibid.): "The conventional tier (II) represents the stages most commonly found in adolescents and adults. These are the stages most representative of the conventions (the practices, beliefs, norms and values) of what it means to be an adult in a given culture, hence the label 'conventional.' This is also, therefore, the tier in which differences in local socialization most likely play the biggest role in individuals' differing self-perceptions, both within and across cultures."

Apparently, then, when discussing 'coaching ethics,' we are moving away from pre-conventional ethics, such as the self-focused morality of children and young adolescents, for whom morality is defined as obeying rules and avoiding negative consequences. Instead, we are focusing on the *conventional* level where fulfilling obligations, based on following expectations of others and the community at large, are seen as moral law. However, as we have learned, there are important differences between the ways in which individuals at the conventional tier, comprising S-2, S-3, and S-4, fulfill ethical obligations. Which of these ways, then, should we assume are ethical obligations we need to consider?

It seems to me that the crucial assumption regarding ethical obligations in coaching is this: that nobody can fulfill obligations toward others s(he) has not fulfilled toward her- or himself. This epistemological principle is equivalent to the notion **that coaches cannot fulfill ethical obligations toward those who are fulfilling obligations to themselves at higher stages than does the coach.** This, in turn, leads to the conclusion that to coach clients who reside at higher developmental levels is either unethical or at least ethically questionable. Which inference, in turn, leads to the notion that it is an ethical obligation of the coach to know his or her own developmental level (coaching level).

Considering what I said in the Preface – that in my experience **readers cannot *use* knowledge about developmental stages before they have applied it to themselves,** – it is evident that in order to map the journey of the developmental coach, we need some kind of model of the milestones involved. This is relevant especially since the conventional notion is that learning is linear, rather than being based on stages of capability which determine what can be learned in the first place.

The table below is meant to serve that purpose.

LEARNING TO THINK DEVELOPMENTALLY	
Ego-centric Pitfalls *S-2 & S-3 Errors*	*Mature Professional Approaches* *Stage 4 & Above*
1. Coaches ignore or deny developmental differences ("We are what we are; it's inborn.") [S-2 & S-3]	4. Coaches recognize and accept developmental differences ("I think my client must be in a developmental transition which I don't fully understand yet.")
2. Coaches recognize developmental differences, but evaluate them negatively ("S(he) is not as developed as I am.") [S-2 & S-3]	5. Coaches analyze developmental differences, thereby moving out of their developmental blindness or comfort zone ("Like it or not, my client is not at the developmental level I thought s(he) was," or "think this client is developmentally over my head.")
3. Coaches recognize developmental differences but minimize their importance ("We may be at different points in our development, but we share a common personal culture.") [S-3]	6. Coaches begin to think and listen developmentally through training and case studies. ("I am much helped in my coaching by doing a developmental intake that shows me how the world shows up for my client.")
	7. Coaches actively leverage developmental differences between clients, to make the most of existing potential, and to minimize its obscuration ("My interviews show that this client is presently developmentally overstretched; I need to lighten that burden by embedding her more deeply in her present developmental level, using the very good cognitive resources assessment has shown she has.")

Table 9.2 A seven-step model of developmental thinking in professional interventions

The seven-step model above is one of coaches' waking up to developmental differences between their clients, as well as to their own developmental journey. Both processes are intertwined; they cannot be separated. The model flows naturally from the evidence presented in this book. Its entries move from ego-centric pitfalls to mature professional approaches, thereby defining a path of **maturation of coaching level.** Essentially, pitfalls listed in the Table can occur at all coaching levels, but they are more easily overcome at S-4 than S-3, and at S-5 than S-4. Although, as I have pointed out, coaching level is not well predicted by age or education, – without education that has developmental effects the path outlined by this model cannot be completed.

As shown, coaches (and people generally) naturally start from ignoring or denying developmental differences between individuals, between themselves and their clients, as well as within themselves at different points in their life. More appropriately put, they are simply blind to it. This blindness can easily be prolonged if one is not sensitive to one's developmental journey (which requires a systemic view of life). Once these differences are recognized, one can still play them down and minimize their importance. Some coaches I have known stop short of moving to mature professional approaches that include developmental assessment. For reasons having to do with their own coaching level, they never make it to coaching work in which developmental stages are consciously leveraged.

***

Above, I have discussed the ethical implications of coaching level. We have reflected upon some important notions regarding coaching ethics. We are now ready to return to the question posed initially as to the nature of self-aware coaching. In particular, we have posed the question of whether one's coaching practice can properly extend beyond S-5/4.

Let's recall here what the journey from S-4 to S-5/4 and beyond entails:

- **Journey toward stage 5:** Starting with the distinction between my own identity and that of others, and feeling a keen need to work with others as 'midwives' of my own development, I gradually begin to see the limits of my own character, history, assumptions, certitudes, and self-constructed identity, and therefore the limits up to which I can impose my values and perspectives on others.
- **Developmental risk:** I begin to risk exposure of my own limitations to critical and intimate others who participate in my self development, resulting in the gradual loss of my self-authoring self.
- **Meaning of 'abandoning my self-authored self' ['being in the flow']:**
  - First, I must be shaken out of my unconscious identity with my life history and 'successes,' to grasp the limitedness of my own universe.
  - Second, I must embrace knowledge sources other than intellect, such as 'heart' and 'spirit,' thereby bringing the sacrifice of mere rationality, – however, I can give up only as much rationality as I possess which depends on my cognitive profile!
  - Third, I must extend what is 'real' for me to comprise a multi-faceted view of the world in which my many certainties can be balanced against each other in a search for the authentic action required of me at a particular moment.

What, then, is self-aware coaching? Let's summarize some of the ethical obligations of that kind of coaching:

- As I free myself from *being*, rather than *having*, my values and principles, I begin to take responsibility for the limited universe that I represent vis a vis my clients and others generally.
- I can only accomplish this by putting my own self development first, and abandoning any one-sided identification with this or that aspect of my own personality, or this or that 'expertise.'
- As I acquire an ever-larger object of reflection – and thus shed more and more of my ego-centricity – I become ready to serve others in the way of giving myself up and away for the sake of others, trusting, that my gifts to others will be returned to me. (Expect espousals!).
- As I relinquish my own 'strengths' to embrace all of myself (including my failings), I revise my theory of helping to let go of those boundaries I previously have needed to define myself as different.
- In my now *self-aware* coaching, my work becomes strictly *inter-develop-mental*, as I owe my transparency – the extent to which I am transparent to myself – to my clients' interaction with me.

- When I am ready to relinquish my coaching Persona (rooted in S-4, and on the brink of collapsing at S-5/4 and certainly S-5(4)), it is my obligation to relinquish coaching as a way of helping others.
- **If (for some reason) I do not relinquish coaching, I must hold myself responsible for maintaining a professional level of work that lies below the developmental stage I have reached as an individual. In this work, I take responsibility for NOT FULLY sharing what I understand about myself (and perhaps the client).**
- This margin of knowledge defines my *wisdom* that cannot be shared other than indirectly, with those ready to absorb it.
- As a mentor, I am now ready to refocus coaches' work on their self development as the most potent predictor of their coaching success.

We might say, then, that coaching as well as consulting has a beginning and an end in a person's life, and that it comes to a close when I can no longer pretend that I am an independent other in relation to my client. I have become a mentor (but in a sense not anywhere near to what today is called a 'mentor-coach'). All that remains then is to thank my clients for the journey beyond myself that they have afforded me!

For this reason, I am suggesting in this book that coaching as a profession ends for an individual when reaching S-5/4 or S-5(4). However, since few individuals ever reach this point in their adult development, there is no reason to fear that the profession will ever lack practitioners!

Let's conclude this discussion with a reminder of the caricature of S-5:

> At this stage, people are no longer strongly identified with any particular aspect or asset of their own Frame of Reference. They know that no matter what they do it will be limited. Consequently, they have come to realize that learning-to-learn, life long learning, is not just a platitude, but becomes their life. Collaboration and collegiality become the means for exchanging Frames of Reference openly, where exposure of self-limitations is routinely accepted as the only means to learn increasingly more about the self and others. This makes them potential unifiers – consensus builders at their level – and an invaluable resource for rethinking corporate goals, operational principles, and values that combine to create culture. **Such a person is best positioned where visionary risk taking and development of others, their organization, and the broader social context are called for.** Such a person is often highly self-critical, even humble, seeing clearly the limits to which s(he) can impose their perceptions and convictions on others, as suggested. The climate they will create will be one that is open to exploration, risk taking within reasonable limits, and the emphasis, above all else, will be on promoting and sustaining growth and continued development of others and the organization as a whole.

I think this caricature speaks for itself. There is no need to rhapsodize about it in the style of much of contemporary coaching literature espousals.

***

Above, I have drawn some conclusions regarding what is self-aware coaching. I have suggested that *coaching* in the orthodox sense of the term becomes extinct at or beyond S-

5/4, except if one is able to hold oneself responsible for not acting out, in the coaching, all of one's self-awareness. This is possible because one can always act at a lower developmental level than one is presently holding, however precariously and uncomfortably so. It entails no particular risk professionally if we consider that most coaching clients are living at developmental stages far below S-5/4, and therefore cannot function as transparent partners of the kind that individuals at and beyond S-5/4 require and thrive on.

Granting, then, that self-aware coaching is the highest form coaching can take in terms of adult development, we might initially think that no limitations of such coaching exist. I think otherwise.

- **In general:** S-5/4 individuals make an acceptable coach to the extent that they can take responsibility for operating at a lower developmental stage than is their accustomed modus operandi. This especially holds for relinquishing the need of relying, for the coach's own development, on a transparent other who makes meaning within the same frame of reference as does the coach. This developmental self sacrifice is ethical only to the extent that it heightens the practitioner's ability to be compassionate in relation to, and insightful about, the client's particular struggles and challenges. This ability is an extension of what is required for ethical coaching at lower coaching levels: that of operating at a higher developmental stage than the client is presently capable of doing.
- **Coaching Presence:** S-5/4 coaches may be tempted to impose on the client a level of meaning making the client is incapable of, which might do harm to the client in ways the client cannot detect, does not understand, and cannot fathom.
- **Active Listening:** S-5/4 coaches may be engaged in their own journey in a way that precludes total openness to that of the client, espousing, for instance, "something deeper we can be connected with," configured in terms of one's own spirituality. Between the Scylla of selflessness and the Charybdis of selfhood, the coach must find his or her own most potent way of listening.
- **Attentional Support:** The attention of S-5/4 coaches inevitably veers beyond the social-emotional (and cognitive) horizon of most clients. Because of that, S-5/4 coaches may find it taxing to have to restrict their focus to what clients at lower levels are capable of constructing as *reality*.
- **Interpretation:** S-5/4 coaches may overextend the client's capacity to follow interpretations requiring loss of internal others at S-3 and of self beyond S-4, unable to remember the painfulness of such loss.
- **Enactment:** Adapting to the client's lower developmental stage, the coach may unconsciously continue to follow strictures of self authoring that hamper a free unfolding of the flow in which alone coach and client can meet to the *mutual* benefit of their developmental capacity.

In a nutshell:

- *self-aware* level (< 10% of coaches): the coach is no longer defined by any part of him-/herself (such as 'expertises') but is *in the flow*, able to risk self exposure, and open to whatever otherness and contrariness the client may present. *Highest level of coaching presence.*

SUMMARY OF SECTION TWO
In the second section of this chapter, I have discussed some general consequences of the developmental model introduced in this volume, specifically geared to coaching. In particular I have asked: what is the relevance for professional coaches of being able to formulate developmental hypotheses? To illustrate answers to this question, I introduced the notion of COACHING LEVEL, assigning to each level a set of pertinent practice characteristics. However crude these assignments may be, the named characteristics facilitate understanding better what are the strengths and challenges for coaches at different developmental stages.

Considering now that coaches and clients alike are subject to developmental stages, and thus are unable to see the limitations of their present stage before having transcended it, it might be instructive to fashion a **Typology of Coaching Relationships** that takes this fact into account. Such a typology is required for answering the question: what return on investment (ROI) can be expected when coach and client operate at different developmental stages? More precisely, we might want to ask: what is the *coaching ROI* (CROI) that can be expected when coaching level and the developmental level of clients diverge? Naturally, what this typology tells us also holds true for other forms of process consultation as well.

Coaching Level	Client's Developmental Stage	Predicted Coaching ROI (CROI)*
S-3	S-3	Developmentally minimal but mutual; behaviorally positive depending on measured client potential
S-3	S-4	*Developmentally counter-productive;* behaviorally ephemeral or negative (harmful)
S-3	S-5	*Developmentally counter-productive;* behaviorally negative (harmful)
S-4	S-3	Developmentally positive; behaviorally positive depending on measured client potential
S-4	S-4	Developmentally minimal though mutual; behaviorally positive depending on measured client potential
S-4	S-5	*Developmentally counter-productive;* behaviorally harmful
S-5/4	S-3	Developmentally boosting, but behavioral effects may be transitory due to overstretching
S-5/4	S-4	Developmentally mutual; behaviorally lasting depending on measured client potential
S-5/4	S-5/4 or higher	Developmentally mutual, but fraught with developmental risk for both, depending on developmental balance; behaviorally unpredictable

* See O. Laske, "Can Evidence Based Coaching Increase ROI?" Intern. J. of Ev. Based Coaching and Mentoring, vol. 2.2, Fall 2004.

Table 9.3 Typology of coach-client relationships

As shown in the table, coaching effect (positive or negative) varies lawfully with the relationship between the developmental stages of coach and client. In the table, a distinction is made between developmental and behavioral effects. By this distinction is meant that wherever developmental effect is non-existent or minimal – no developmental shift being possible –, behavioral effects can still be achieved, but their long-term robustness is in doubt.

To understand this fully, recall the three-dimensionality of **human capability** discussed in Chapter 1 (CD, ED, & behavior):

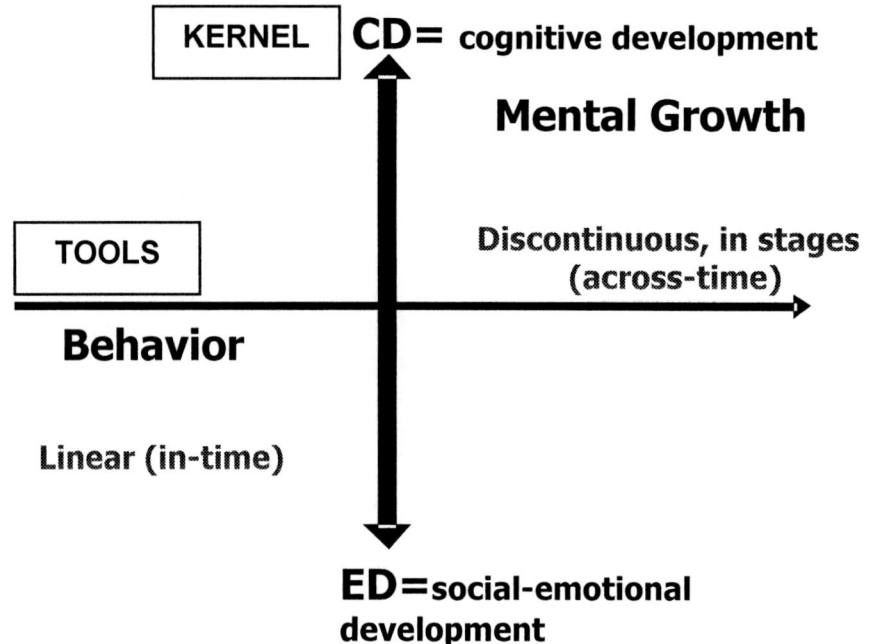

Fig. 9.3 Intersection of vertical and horizontal developmental dimensions

On the horizontal axis of this diagram are located all those behavioral coaching interventions that do not take developmental stages into account. These stages are part and parcel of the Vertical, specifically the ED-pole of the vertical axis. Since both axes are inseparable in life and practice, developmental effects may still be achieved when working strictly behaviorally, although those effects might be slighter and might not be recognized as such by either party. Conversely, developmental effects achieved in professional developmental coaching may not instantaneously become evident in coaching outcome, but may manifest themselves only after some delay.

(The term 'ROI' assumes an instantaneous effect of coaching interventions, and is therefore a developmentally *inappropriate* term. We have replaced it in the table by CROI – the ROI of developmental coaching, which is defined in terms of the *developmental risk-potential balance achieved*, rather than in merely behavioral or outcome terms. However, this runs counter to 'balanced' score-card and HR thinking, and companies presently pay a heavy price – inability to strategize the future – for that).

When we inquire into the position of client and coach along the vertical axis, in order to compare developmental stages between coach and client, interesting differentiations result. These are listed in Table 9-2 above as *hypotheses* for which evidence can be expected from future developmental coaching research. We invite the reader to study the table in detail, and to design a research study for testing these hypotheses assembled in Table 9.3).

The table makes a distinction between interventions that are either 'developmentally counter-productive' and/or 'behaviorally harmful.' **Interventions are developmentally counter-productive wherever the coach resides at a lower stage than does the client.** In this case, actual harm may also be done, since the coach is not in a position to appreciate the developmental potential of the client (even if s(he) has learned to assess it using CDF). Even if the client's potential could be intellectually appreciated, the coach cannot actually embody it in him- or herself (except by espousal).

In some cases to be researched, what is developmentally counter-productive may in addition be behaviorally harmful. This happens when unawareness of the client's developmental stage leads to behavioral suggestions that overtax or overstretch the client, or are otherwise unhelpful to the client at his or her present developmental level. Another kind of harm is done when clients whose developmental potential is not considered or understood are not challenged in the proportion their resources would permit or suggest. Whenever behavioral or developmental harm is done, one can ethically speak of **client abuse** by coaches. Not knowing about developmental stages does not excuse abuse! (Clearly, in the future, clients will increasingly learn about their adult-developmental rights as clients.)

SECTION THREE
Readers of this book who are coaching clients, having come this far in the book, might ask themselves certain orientation questions. They might want to decide whether engaging a developmental coach is worth their time and expense. Foremost, they might wonder what it is that is different in developmental coaching in comparison with conventional (behavioral) coaching. The table above will have given them a foretaste of the ethical issues made visible by a developmental approach.

In order to orient readers who are actual or potential coaching clients, I briefly address in this section the benefits of engaging with evidence based developmental coaching. To keep this section free of marketing spirit and jargon, I will concentrate on those *structural benefits* that are the basis of *client benefits*.

Above, I have already alluded to the most important structural benefit: **finding a coach at a developmental stage above your own!** There is simply no other structural benefit that is ultimately more relevant than this one. The client may ask: How do I know whether my coach is operating at a higher developmental stage? The answer is simple: find out whether your coach can knowledgeably talk about your own developmental level once it has been assessed by her or a third, mentoring party.

Overall, it would seem that for clients, developmental coaching involves a major re-orientation (1) in what to expect of coaches and their training, (2) how to make use of coaching, and (3) what to require of oneself as a client. A fourth issue might be (4) how the client can help him- or herself by getting the coach mentored developmentally. These four issues will be at the center of the following discussion.

What to Expect of Developmental Coaches

R. Kegan has rightfully pointed out that therapy is about *mental health*, while coaching is about *mental growth*. (One might add that *developmental* coaching is about mental growth that is actually measured as a precondition of the coaching process.) This distinction will put to rest the assumption that developmental coaches are really 'therapists.' While there are, in fact, therapists working within a developmental framework (called *clinical-developmental psychologists*), their work is 'coaching' only to the extent that it is 'enactment' of novel behavior, a generic process that is not the sole privilege of coaching.

What, then, should clients expect of developmental coaches, especially those certified through the *Interdevelopmental Institute*? This entails the related question of what developmental coaches expect of clients. Here are some suggestions:

- Developmental coaches expect clients to be sensitive to the fact that they are engaging in coaching at a particular point in their journey across the life span, and consequently begin coaching "somewhere in the middle" (J. Flaherty, 1999). This entails that what clients developmentally bring to coaching is of the greatest relevance for the formulation of coaching goals and for coaching outcomes.

- Developmental coaches expect of clients that they are curious about how they presently make meaning in their life and work, and that they are sensitive to developmental changes that have recently occurred in their life.

- Developmental coaches also expect that clients understand that their 'performance,' 'behavior,' and use of competencies, etc. are all dependent on their present developmental level.

- Developmental coaches work based on developmental (and other) assessments; they are evidence based professionals. (Of course, there are, strictly speaking, only evidence based professionals, or else amateurs).

- Developmental coaches work on the basis of insight into 'who the client is developmentally,' rather than assuming that they already know who the client is.

- Developmental coaches use behavioral methods and assessments, but do so in combination with developmental assessment findings. This approach amounts to working based on explicit hypotheses able to *explain* client behavior, rather than simply observing and describing or 'changing' it without any developmental effect..

- Developmental coaches view behavioral coaching as an incomplete profession since all behavior is ultimately developmentally determined; if this fact is ignored, the coaching process is distorted as one focused on mere *performance*, or else on spiritual issues that are kept out of touch with developmental ones. (To developmental coaches, both of these approaches make little sense.)

- Developmental coaches distinguish between *developmental intake* and *coaching proper*. Only when the intake assessment has occurred can coaching proper begin. This simply follows from the fact that developmental coaching is data- or evidence-based. In short, developmental coaches eschew mere *hand-waving*; they require proofs of who the client is, achieved through assessment.

Another issue for clients encountering developmental coaching for the first time is the flow of developmental compared to behavioral coaching, diagrammed below:

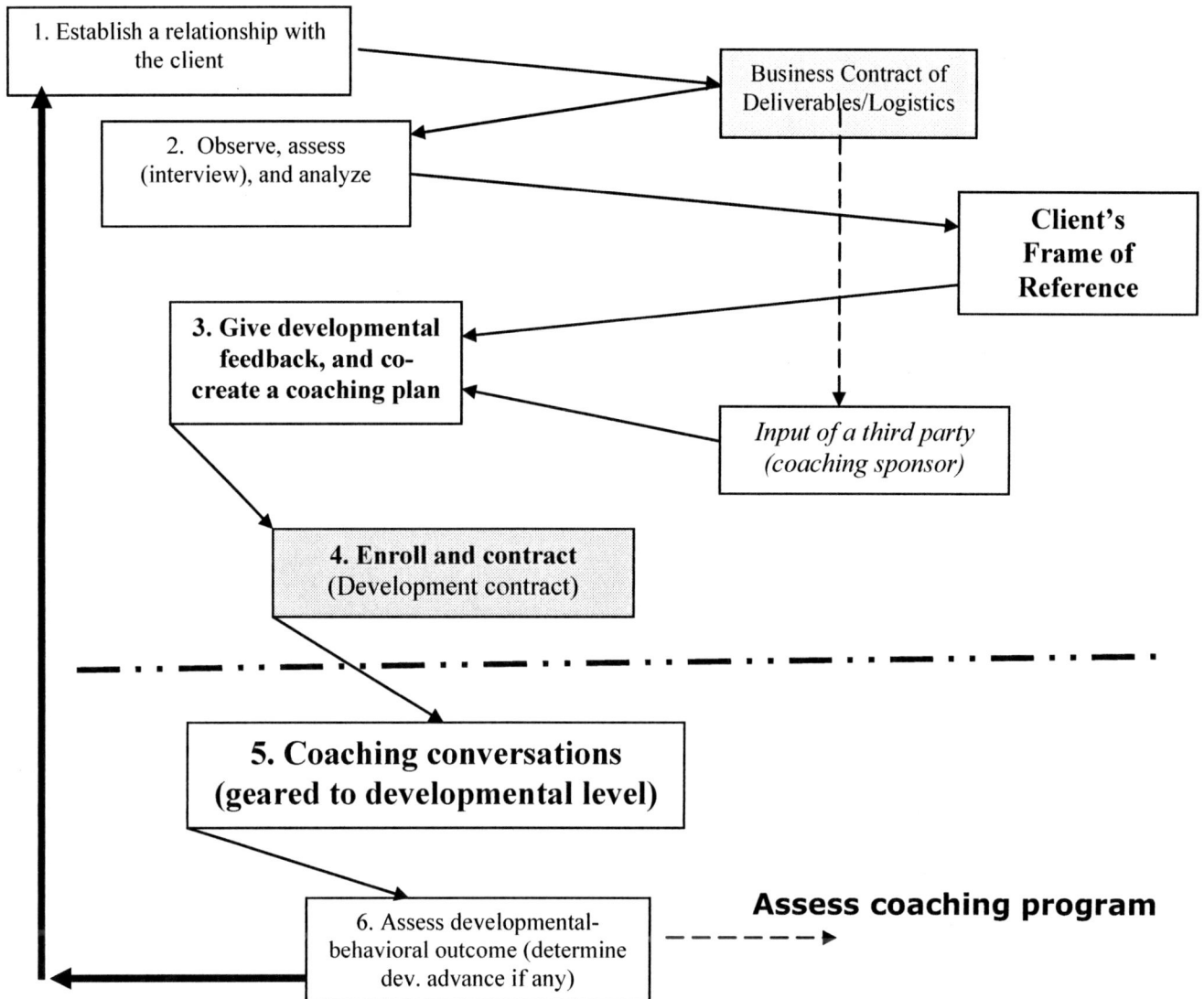

Fig. 9.4 The flow of developmental coaching

Since, as shown above, evidence based developmental coaching is based on prior assessments, coaching as an intervention is divided into two main phases:

1. Developmental intake
2. Coaching proper.

In phase 1, the coach assembles data about the client's developmental and behavioral whereabouts – the evidence the coaching is going to be based on. In phase 2, after having evaluated the assessments and determined the findings, the coach gives feedback to the client and, based on the client's understanding of the feedback, negotiates with the client a realistic coaching plan. 'Realistic' in this context means a coaching plan that is commensurate with the developmental potential and risk of the client that has been assessed. I speak of coaching plans based on the client's present FRAME OF REFERENCE.

Figure 9.4 depicts the flow of coaching when it is based on the client's FRAME OF REFERENCE which, in turn, derives from the client's present developmental level. Say, for instance, that the client comes to coaching with the goal of "becoming a better communicator," prompted by 360 degree feedback or informal observations of peers and supervisors. The meaning of this goal is initially unclear, and is therefore best made the topic of process consultation. What does the client mean by 'communication?' Becoming a better communicator at S-3 is starkly different from the same goal at S-4 or S-5. (At S-3, becoming a better communicator could mean nothing more than staying in tune with crucial collaborators so that one is more likely to be accepted as a member of some group or culture. At S-4, the same goal is most likely related to holding an idiosyncratic point of view in matters of one's own and others' work, and attempting to relate this point of view to others more effectively, etc.).

As shown in the diagram, there are two contracts being put in place, a *logistic contract up-front* and a *developmental contract* following assessment feedback. The two contracts are independent of each other. The second contract may never actually be 'signed' if the client is not internally ready or willing to learn and develop. This is not the coach's, but the client's, responsibility.

The argument in developmental coaching is that **merging the logistic and the developmental contract is sub-optimal in terms of coaching effectiveness**. While behavioral coaches may be able to offer clients a behavioral learning contract, a developmental contract can only be offered by a coach who actually knows **the client's developmental profile,** and consequently is aware of what learning and development can be expected of the client in the first place. Where this matter is left to 'intuition' or 'hand-waving' (lack of empirical evidence), full professionalism of coaching is not attained.

There is still another benefit to developmental coaching, namely that the coach has the capacity to *determine coaching outcome* much more succinctly than is presently thought to be possible. This is because the initial intake that precedes coaching can be matched to a *post test* once coaching ends, to determine CROI (coaching ROI). Although this only makes sense when the coaching period has a duration of at least one year, behavioral assessment at the end of coaching can be equally beneficial. (Since all assessment findings are confidential and therefore 'do not leave the room,' post tests are ideally suited to wrapping up a coaching period, or else to plan ahead for future coaching sessions.) As this shows, developmental coaching introduces important new information about what has happened in the coaching, and what might be set as a goal as coaching continues.

In conclusion let's briefly think about the *systemic ramifications* of the developmental approach to coaching. Once every coaching relationship in a company is based on a separate logistic and (assessment based) development contract, comprehensive data collection can occur based on which the quality of *entire coaching programs* can be assessed, and the quality of the coach team explicitly managed. To achieve this effect, a <u>double</u> data base needs to be established: first, an *anonymous* DB for management to act upon, and a *confidential* DB for HR to act upon in 'developing' coaches along with the workforce.

In the anonymous DB, all markers identifying particular individuals (coaches or clients) has been removed, so that misuse of confidential information cannot occur. This confidential information is fully accessible only in the confidential DB, where developmental experts in charge of developing human capital are at work. Both DBs must be kept separate to avoid management decisions that violate the confidentiality of assessment.

Evidently, only certain corporate cultures (beyond at least S-4(3)) lend themselves to this approach, namely those where confidentiality has a value that derives from respect for the individuals in the work force, in contrast to the manipulatory practices of short-term firing and hiring. (Respect for human resources varies with national culture, and is typically greater in Europe than in North America, especially the U.S.).

How to Make Use of Developmental Coaching

Both *therapy* and *coaching* have in common that the beneficiary needs to learn how to best make use of them. This burden falls on the client, not the coach, but the coach can certainly help the client achieve making optimal use of sessions. Making optimal use of coaching, behavioral or developmental, presupposes not only a willingness to engage with the coaching, but also the potential for doing so. This potential can be assessed objectively, either by observation or, better still, by way of developmental assessment. There are a variety of reasons why clients may not make optimal use of coaching. Here are some:

- They are developmentally not ready for the coach.
- The coach is developmentally not ready for them (functioning at a lower developmental stage).
- There is resistance that neither the coach nor the client really understands (although it could be explained by making a developmental assessment of both parties).
- The coach has not properly prepared the client for the benefit of coaching, having failed to present to the client a comprehensive set of findings about who s(he) is developmentally.

In this regard, too, developmental coaching makes important contributions to the coaching field. Since clients at different developmental stages make use of coaching differently – the S-3 client to become more embedded in, or remain within, a group; the S-4 client to get a firmer grasp on his/her own value system, for example – insight into the developmental whereabouts of clients helps the coach to teach the client how to use coaching sessions optimally. For instance, if the coach knows s(he) is dealing with an S-4/3 client, the client's efforts to make progress in acting in a more self authoring way can be made an explicit goal of the coaching (rather than wasting time finding out the hard way that the client can't do), and this goal can then guide the client in using coaching sessions.

What to Require of Oneself as a Client in Developmental Coaching

The issue of the hidden demands of developmental coaching is perhaps the most significant facet of the developmental, compared to the conventional

(behavioral), approach to coaching. What clients require of themselves is entirely a matter of their developmental profile, cognitive and/or social-emotional. It is also a matter of their professional aspirations, that is, of the internal pressure they impose on themselves, in contrast to the external pressure of the environment.

For instance, an S-3 client cannot be expected to require of her- or himself taking total responsibility for his or her decision making (as a self authoring client would). Such a client will largely rely on internalized others that show up in some physical form, to be able to function properly. If the coach does not help clients see that what they require of themselves lies at the core of possible coaching outcomes – not just performance, but developmental outcomes – clearly the coaching is not going to work out in an optimal way. **In choosing between a behavioral and a developmental coach, it thus behooves the client to decide what s(he) requires of him- or herself in the first place.** To make this choice effectively in most cases will require the help of a developmental coach to begin with, since such a coach has better insight into what the client can be asked to take responsibility for than any other professional. In working with such a professional, the developmental level the client objectively requires on the part of the coach can be determined.

How to Help Yourself by Getting Your Coach Mentored Developmentally
If I am to judge from my own experience in working with a personal coach, I would say that I have typically felt 'not quite understood.' More precisely, I have had a distinct feeling that the coach only partially understood what really motivates me and what my developmental resources are. (This has typically surfaced clearly in the third session when the 'welcoming package' has worn off.) I do think that this experience is a very widespread one on the side of clients, even those whose developmental sensitivity is not overly well developed.

At the Interdevelopmental Institute, I have developed a way out of this dilemma. (The reader will excuse me for briefly lapsing into marketing speak.) **The client can require the coach to be mentored by a developmentally schooled expert.**
The IDM mentoring program is based on the notion that, as an alternative to learning to assess clients themselves, coaches can learn developmental assessment by being mentored in giving developmental feedback to clients, based on assessments carried out by the mentor. Through inclusion of a developmental expert in the coaching work, the client is better served since the behavior at issue in the coaching can now not only be observed and described, but also *explained*, and the potential of improving the behavior in question can be determined. As the coach continues to be mentored, the benefits for the client are not far off. (A model for this procedure is found in clinical supervision where a supervisor guides a student clinician who is the mentee.)

SECTION FOUR
In this concluding section of Chapter 9, I give a brief summary of what, in my view, is the contribution made by developmental coaching and its theory to the coaching field at large. I will address the seven hypotheses, foundational and derived, that I introduced at the beginning of this chapter. As the reader will probably agree, most of the issues addressed by the hypotheses could not even be thought up and formulated outside of a developmental framework as presented here.

Below, I describe the developmental contributions to coaching by discussing the seven hypotheses in some depth, one after the other.

    I.   Assuming that the distribution of different national and cultural populations over adult stages indicated in Table 9.1 equally applies to coaches, most coaches are working from an S-3 vantage point of other-dependence.

For the reader of this book, "working from an S-3 vantage point" has acquired a very precise meaning. It entails that coaches at that stage are too entangled in internalized others to be fully aware, either of their own self authoring resources or that of their clients. Since internalized others take a multiplicity of forms, some of them shaped by current coach training, it is evident that such training needs to be more closely scrutinized. Especially the *coaching essentials* of present coach training, as well as the *core competencies* and *coaching proficiencies* – together with the assumptions they are based on – need to be better analyzed and understood. Hopefully, this book will prompt a research program into coaching competencies to come into existence despite the existing commercial pressures to maintain the status quo of conventional coach training, – in the future increasingly adorned with some nods toward "coaching research."

    II.   To the extent that adult-developmental attainment in coaches exceeds that of the general population, the percentage of coaches at S-3 could be smaller than (the typical) 55%; in this case, adherence to S-4 standards by coaches would by definition exceed 25% of the coach subpopulation.

It stands to reason that the majority of coaches are presently making meaning between S-3 and S-4. This can be easily inferred from the general coaching literature as well as coach community communications generally, where the tenor is emphatically on the mental "WE" state that S-3 is based on. (For this reason, much of the literature sounds like *ghetto speak*.) This inference includes those more 'spiritual' coach circles where espousal of vantage points transcending S-4 is practiced. (Such espousal would not be necessary or natural at stages beyond S-4/5). This inference is not in conflict with the fact that ICF 'core competencies' as well as IAC 'coaching proficiencies' are formulated "as if" coaches were acting from S-4. Ethical stipulations above one's own developmental stage – thus espousal – typically emerge wherever a pedagogical need is felt to improve professional standards, without actually taking action to bring improvement about through appropriate pedagogical opportunities and quality control based on developmental insight.

For this reason, it appears that the greatest challenge to present coach training, whether commercial or academic, lies in developing curricula that can assist coaches in making the journey from S-3 to S-4, which is presently *over their head*. It seems to me that this requirement is the single most significant and urgent requirement regarding the future of coach training, especially its commercial branch. Without getting into an endless list of 'eaches' that would circumscribe the outcomes of pedagogical offerings needed – 'attendees will be able to …' – the easiest way to define such outcomes is to point to the capability of S-4 individuals. Quoting from the S-3 caricature stated in this book will suffice for understanding what needs to be done:

They 'follow the rules,' and are 'above board' about winning and losing. It is very unlikely that they will 'see' or think beyond the established operational principles and values of 'their' organization. Because their image is so caught up in the status quo, they will be unwilling to take the risks necessary to change it, even if they can stand apart from their unit, group, or organization far enough to objectively assess what could make it operate more effectively. Hence, **they do not make good change agents, either in the sense of seeing what needs to be done or in actually doing it. Any change they believe might be beneficial will be whatever is being echoed by the majority.**

It seems to me that this description of the S-3 mind set gets to the core of the pedagogical issue that is on the table. It is easy to say that what is needed most is 'critical thinking.' Such thinking alone, however, will not suffice, since the issue is not a purely cognitive, but also a social-emotional, one. (Critical thinking can also be used defensively.) It might be more apt to say that since there is no social forcing function for proceeding to S-4, educational ventures are needed that assist S-3 coaches to put the focus of their training not on skills but on *self development*. There are many ways to do so, one of which might be to become familiar with conceptual frameworks such as presented in this book, and the educational courses based on them (Laske, 2005).

III.   In order to move coaches from S-3 to S-4, – from other-dependence to self authoring – beyond what 'life' does anyway, more than 'coach training,' namely, *coach education*, is required.

We have already left behind strictly foundational issues, and entered into the fray of pedagogical ones. While coach training is only INFORMATIVE, what is needed is coach education that is truly TRANSFORMATIVE. To demonstrate the difference, consider a lengthy quote from the August 2005 IDM Newsletter, below (permission by Antoinette Dawson):

Finally! I have begun to overcome my own **bottleneck(s)…** I no longer stand in the way of my own thinking, or being, or coaching, or organizational perspective as I used to do! How did this happen? When did it happen? How do I know? What's next?

Well, for me, like for many of you, it has been an **arduous** journey. I venture to say my readers will have many questions as to what it is like to really go the developmental path, compared to all of the other kinds of development they have invested in.

Could I have overcome these bottlenecks on my own (that is, without engaging in IDM offerings)? I certainly have tried. Since early in my young adult years, I have been a seeker of how things work, I have been asking myself a multitude of questions. Here are some of them:

'what makes people tick, what makes me tick, why don't we tick the same way, how do I change the way I tick, can someone else help, where do I find them, what do I tell them…will they know when they meet me, what skills are required, what questions are required, what perspective is needed, where did they get it, can they pass it on to me, what will it look like on me, what will it sound like coming from my voice, who should I tell, how will they know, how will they test it, will it make them more aware, will it make them more fulfilled, will it help them overcome their own bottleneck?'

I think now that all of these questions occurred because I did not have access to a consistent conceptual framework within which to ask the <u>right</u> questions, – those having to do with my meaning making. Although, clearly, the IDM framework is a MODEL, it is a model validated through research over the last thirty years. And that helps asking the <u>right</u> questions, in my experience!

There are, of course, many ways to ask questions about oneself. It strikes me that I have been asking question in a multitude of ways, too many to enumerate. Some of these stand out:

- Self talk, journaling, self-help, reflection, self-care, exhortation, reflection, changes and shifts.
- Relationships, conversations, formal education, training, coaching, counsel, 360 feedback, strength indexes, value inventories.
- Positive psychology, prayer, meditation.

to name a few.

What I've learned is that as long as you don't attend to the tacit assumptions you are making – about oneself and others – you are SUBJECT TO THEM, that is, not in control of them. This is, in fact, the human condition, as one learns at IDM: We can only look at our assumptions once we have revised them!

The other thing I've learned is that one cannot provoke a shift through mere learning or "changing," however radical. One has to be ready for it! Also, one has to have the developmental potential needed to proceed on life's journey. Some of the learning I have done has been just that, learning. It has not been development. **I've learned that neither learning nor change is by itself *development* in the emphatic sense of IDM.** Development happens discontinuously, not incrementally. You wake up some day and you find yourself sporting another world view. You are in a trial situation, trying on the new world view like a new dress or suit. How far can I reach in it? What did I lose to gain this new self? How can I recover from my risk to fall back to earlier stages?

In particular, I have learned that **developmental shifts work!** I know this since my formerly 'hidden' dimensions are no longer hidden to me. What I have finally realized is that most of the intuitive, innovative inklings, and all of the 'evidence' presented to me…about me…, was research gathered, packaged, and presented about 'research.' **It was NOT research about me, about how I think or how I tick, or how I presently make sense of my own journey!**

What developmental thinking and evidence-based coaching has offered me is a glimpse, a look, a snapshot, an inward glance at how I am making meaning with myself, with my experiences, with life purpose up to this point. Developmental thinking and developmental mentoring has introduced me to MYSELF, – the hidden dimension that mediates between me and my own thinking and meaning making. The barriers separating me from myself are revealed and thus minimized, overcome, subject to the perspective and thinking that I have wanted to identify and project, but could not – before now.

How did this happen?

The subject-object interview [taught in the IDM Workshop, Gateway, and Course One Part A] was for me the starting place for tacitly introducing me afresh to my own stage & level, and explicitly introducing me to a frame of reference that showcased for me what my own 'thought forms' are. Through partaking in Program One Parts A and B, I now understand much better how I think about what I think about.

How did I get to this point?
I am a lifelong learner and student of adult development. I selected IDM after meticulously searching and sifting through the various advanced coach training programs on the market. I thought initially that the focus on post-graduate coach education would be a certifiable distinction in my Executive Coaching and OD work. With that in mind, I did not enroll with the expectation that the process would identify and elucidate my own hidden dimensions.

Mentoring was part of what happened!

During the actual study of behavioral and cognitive development at IDM, and through mentorship …, I experienced a transformational breakthrough, I would say. I believe this to be true because I now better understand that there is a relationship between the (informative) assessment data collected about me during my professional career and the three (transformative) developmental tools used in Evidence-Based Coaching at IDM. I have become, so to speak, a product of the product.

This quote speaks for itself. It certainly illustrates that as long as self development, and assessments supporting it, are not adopted as a focus in developing professional coaches, coach training will remain a shadow of what it has the potential to be.

***

> IV   Coaches have an ethical responsibility to know their developmental stage, given that 'DO NO HARM' is the uppermost principle of coaching. (Harm is done when one is coaching clients who are beyond one's own Center of Gravity; harm is done even when acting from the same Center of Gravity [as the client], since the realization of the client's developmental potential cannot adequately be supported by the coach in that case.)

This developmental hypothesis is commensurate with the requirement of functioning at S-4. At this stage, one begins to take responsibility for one's own system of values and its limitations, as well as the roots on which it is based. One fulfills obligations toward oneself first and foremost, and expects the same of others. One also becomes aware of the harm that can be done if one imposes one's own propensities, life history, and idiosyncratic assumptions on others for the sake of 'helping.' Consequently, one's begins to see the risk one runs when one's thinking is not self-critical. Comparisons between oneself and others no longer work. Naturally, then, the need to know 'where I am developmentally' becomes an authentic and imperative need. Indications to the contrary simply indicate a developmental level below S-4.

> V.   Coach education has the social mandate of moving coaches from other-dependent to self-authoring capacity. This is best done by focusing coach education on coaches' self development.

Considered from a societal point of view (as articulated by Kegan in his 1994), the coaching movement seems destined to fill a gap modern society has so far not been able to fill: the gap between the S-3 functioning of the majority of the population, and the S-4 requirements of most professional activities, including coaching. When I adopt a developmental point of view, it is with this destiny of coaching in mind. I am then required to put on the table what one might call *undiscussed mental demands of coaching* (Kegan, 1994, 234 f.), both on the client's side (see above) and the coach's side (see the entire book).

It is important to realize that the **'undiscussed mental demands of coaching [in general],'** to use Kegan's terms, are no different from those of psychotherapy, however distinct the two disciplines might be, one being centered on mental growth, and the other on mental health. As Kegan says of practitioners of therapy (1994, 237-238):

Therapists (substitute: 'coaches' O.L.), for example, must keep their experiences in the often intense therapist-client relationship from governing the course or purpose of that relationship. They must bring these experiences – their longings and their fears, their attractions and their revulsions – under the regulation of a system of belief that will direct the relationship on behalf of its public purpose. ... For the therapist, the distinction between the public and private is not "an established condition of modern life," it is an ongoing fourth order (S-4) claim on the mind to regulate or direct interpersonal relations ...

Given *the undiscussed [mental] demands of coaching* – which in the present cultural climate have begun to sound like 'unmentionable demands,' – where is Coach Training headed? Where is there a discussion of the *mental demands of public life* coaching shares with professional interventions such as psychotherapy? Clearly, a developmental theory of coaching is a first step to bringing these unacknowledged demands out into the open. Such a theory can help the coaching community to begin to grasp its responsibility, to act on behalf of the social forcing function now lacking that would bring individuals closer to the level of S-4 functioning. If there are any models for such functioning, certainly coaches carry a major responsibility to learn to embody them for their clients' sake. (Expect espousals!).

In addition to coach education, rather than training, the **mentoring** of coaches defines another possible avenue of transcending most coaches' need, to derive support "from the identification with the cultural surround, the essence of third order [S-3] consciousness" (Kegan, 1994, 247). As I have shown above, developmental mentoring of the coach (by a developmental expert) is a right of the client whenever there is enough self awareness that one's self development as a human being and professional is at stake. Pursuing this right naturally leads to screening coaches in a much more stringent way that is presently typical, quite regardless of skill certification. **Developmental assessment of coaches is an important tool for satisfying client demands and adult-developmental rights.**

VI.   Developmental mentoring of coaches extends far beyond the reinforcement of skills, best practices, etc., in that it centrally concerns the meaning making capacity that underlies the ways in which coaches build a *model of their clients*.

This is a far cry from what today is called 'mentor-coaching.' Mentoring in the sense of Kegan only begins at S-4, where the above mentioned need, to derive support from the identification with the cultural surround, has ceased. Here again, the coaching community needs to grasp its responsibility "to get out of the way," that is, to address the problem rather than to be the problem.

The crux of coaching and mentoring, in my view, lies in the ability of practitioners, to formulate a MODEL OF THE CLIENT that is free of what Kegan calls *identification with the cultural (and social) surround*. Since coaches and mentors never actually meet with the client him- or herself, but always do so through a MODEL of the client, it stands to reason that the more developmentally apt this model is, the closer the practitioner can move to the client him- or herself.

As I have shown in chapters 4 and 7, since the human mind constantly models the world whether people are conscious of it or not, practitioners *always* act from a model of the client. That is not the issue. The real issue is to KNOW that one is acting from a *model* of the client, and to be able to scrutinize the assumptions of that model. Such scrutiny is not outside of, but is the crux of, coach education in contrast to coach training. It requires S-4 functioning.

> VII. Ethics standards for coaches ought to include guidelines for coach training and certification based on developmental stage (or at least, range), which implies that developmental assessment needs to become *mandatory* in the process of coach certification and prior to beginning coach training.

This hypothesis may be too strong, but it is worth considering. It might be too strong since one cannot legislate a particular developmental stage, nor can one publicly force it to be realized. One can only appeal to the self authoring kernel in individuals. One can, moreover, sensitize practitioners to the need of crafting opportunities for reaching a certain developmental range (such as S-4 and up). The assessment tools needed to make this happen exist; – they only need to be put to use. **Perhaps this is the ultimate justification for teaching and practicing evidence based coaching?** I leave the answer to this question as an exercise for the reader living at S-4.

Chapter Summary

In this chapter, I have derived some practical conclusions from the theoretical foundations of *developmental process consultation* (DPC) specifically for coaching. Wherever one proceeds from theory to practice, potentially explosive issues arise. I have done my best to make them just explosive enough, following Kurt Lewin's dictum that "there is nothing more practical than a good theory."

Since this chapter's concerns have been rather diverse, a short review is in order. I have dealt with four different, but related topics:
1. A review highlighting what volume 1 has (potentially) taught readers.
2. A developmental coaching model.
3. Benefits of developmental coaching for the client.
4. Contributions of developmental coaching to the profession of coaching, in the sense of a professional (evidence based) practice for individuals at S-4 and up.

Section 1 summarized what the volume has shown readers about the oscillations of human consciousness when captured by way of a grid of developmental stages, or discontinuous steps leading to consecutively more differentiated world views. The differentiation in question is one between the 'subject' and 'object' of consciousness or, put differently, between what humans are subject to in contrast to in control of.

In Section 2, I introduced a model of developmental levels applied in coaching practice, or *coaching levels* that facilitated making a distinction between three main types of coaching: *other-dependent, self-authoring, and self-aware coaching.* The model showed us the differences in the (heretofore largely unacknowledged) mental demands of coaching, primarily on the coach but also on the client. Section 2 also presented a *Typology of Coaching Relationships.* The typology both highlighted the harm that can be done when coaching level and level of client functioning diverge, and the expectations regarding CROI (coaching ROI) it is reasonable to entertain from a developmental point of view.

In Section 3 of this chapter we turned to the client. We spelled out what clients can expect of certified developmental coaches, and what are the mental demands on clients' own use of coaching that they should be aware of. In addition, we clarified the flow of developmental coaching, showing that in this approach to coaching the logistic and the developmental contracts are two different things. We also surmised that only a developmentally schooled coach can ultimately offer to the client a true *developmental contract*, and emphasized the client's right to have his or her coach developmentally mentored by a practitioner able to think developmentally.

Section 4 comprised a discussion of seven hypotheses about coaching generally, focused on the future of coaching as a profession (rather than an 'industry service'). We distinguished foundational from pedagogical hypotheses in order to clarify the distinction between coach training and coach education, introduced in this volume (see also Laske, 2005). This distinction was further clarified by a testimonial focused on the benefits of self development through developmental mentoring.

As we near the end of the volume (except for the Appendix), let me mention a topic I have not attempted to introduce, namely, the application of methods of developmental assessment to **human capital management** at large. I give a short introduction to this topic in Appendix D of this volume.

To conclude this chapter and summary, I list below the vignettes of the three main coaching levels discussed in volume 1 of this book.

Vignette of the Other-Dependent Coach (S-3)

- The coach defines him-/herself by the community s(he) is part of, and loss of community (consensus, etc.) is therefore experienced as loss of self, and much feared.

- The community in question, may be an external or internal one, or both, and is not differentiated from the self.

- The coach's model of the client is one of identification and collusion, rather than one made precise by focusing on clients' developmental level.

- The coach's procedures are typically best practices which fit *any* client; they are not based on his/her own authentic principles, nor do they do justice to the individuality of the client.

- Whether 'holistic' or not, approaches to coaching at S-3 fall short of the mandate of coaching, to understand the client before rushing in with one's own little personality to "help" him or her.

Vignette of the Self-Authoring Coach (S-4)

- The coach defines him-/herself by a fully developed value system that grounds his/her self identity and integrity.

- The value system is one that can be clearly articulated, but is difficult for the coach to step away from in a critical fashion; it is centered on the coach's integrity (which is the coach's highest value).

- As a result, the coach IS his/her values and principles, rather than HAVING values and principles.

- The coach's model of the client is typically one of differentiation of 'my' and 'his/her' values and principles, with opening toward 'dialogue' but not true communication.

- The coach's procedures are critical of best practices that under- or misrepresent his/her own principles and values.

Vignette of the Self-Aware Coach (S-5)

- The coach no longer defines him-/herself by reference to any fixed part or ability of the self, and fully steps into the flow of life.

- The flow in question is one which is shared with others who are essential to the self as critical equals.

- The coach's model of the client is therefore one of openness to whatever 'otherness' or contrariness the client may present and evoke in himself.

- The coach let's go of all attempts to bias the model of who the client is in terms of his or her own 'little personality' (internalized others).

- The coach's procedures are typically critical of his/her *own* best practices.

PRACTICE REFLECTIONS
Section 1
- How, in your coaching, do you make visible for the client what s(he) is subject to, and thus cannot see?
- In what way is your coaching focused on enlarging the client's object of reflection?
- How do you deal with developmental conflict in the client, where two different stages are simultaneously exerting their influence?

- What, for you, is the relationship of the skills coaching often focuses on to the underlying self-understanding of the client using the skills?

Section 2

- Do you know your coaching level?
- If not, how do you assess whether you are developmentally (not personality- or otherwise) compatible with your client?
- To what extent have you developed a critical, self authoring view of teaching materials that have shaped your practice?
- Have you discovered inconsistencies and espousals in coaching recipes and best practices that make you wary of them? Spell them out!
- Are these recipes and practices commensurate with your own developmental level, that is, the obligations you are already fulfilling toward yourself?
- What would you do if you learned that your client functions at a higher developmental level than you yourself?
- How would you justify that your coaching has been *successful* if you knew that your own developmental level is lower than that of the client?
- What kind of outcome research on the results of your coaching are you engaged in, and how evidence-based is it?
- Would that research stand the test of developmental coaching research?

Section 3

- Are you prepared to grant the client the right to learn about your coaching level?
- Is your coaching level part of the credentials you feel set you apart from other coaches?
- What are the mental demands on your coaching you honor that transcend conventional (S-3 and espoused S-4) demands for 'excellence' in coaching?
- How do you feel about coaches' espousal of functioning at higher coaching levels than they actually do?
- In what sense do you view the coaching process as being inter-developmental?
- What kind of developmental contract are you offering your clients that is different from the logistic contract?
- In what way is the developmental contract you offer based on your own present developmental level and insight into the dynamics of developmental shifts?
- How do you assure that the client's developmental contract is commensurate with his or her developmental potential?
- What kind of mentoring do you feel yourself drawn to, one that focuses on skills or one that focuses on your own self development, and why?

Section 4

- How would you approach the empirical question of whether the developmental levels of coaches (coaching levels) are typically higher than those of the general population?
- In your opinion, to what extent is the coaching movement honoring its mandate to assist individuals in making the journey from S-3 to S-4? (Take a risk!)
- Are you yourself prepared to accept the mental demands of that journey, and if so, how do you propose to do so?
- How do you see the relationship between coach training and coach education?

- What empirical evidence validated by social science research is your coaching practice based on, if any?
- What part of your development as a coach has been based on coach training, and how much has been true (that is, transformational) *coach education*?
- In your experience, is academically offered coach training any closer to coach education than the training offered commercially? Give examples.

EPILOGUE

It is time to look back.

In this volume, I have introduced the reader to a **new process for understanding others, especially adults, both at work and more generally in life.** I have done so by explaining and exercising a new *vocabulary* that enables practitioners to be more precise about clients' feeling, thinking, decision making, and goal setting over the course of their adult life. The vocabulary makes it unnecessary to use spiritual or philosophical terms wherever precise developmental terms are available, thereby cutting down on espousals of spirituality and keeping it pure. Last but not least, the vocabulary I have introduced in this volume makes it possible to create a scientific *knowledge base*. In this knowledge base, concepts have an agreed upon meaning (see the Glossary), in contrast to the Babel of terms and variables presently created and used in coaching research.

In the nine chapters of this volume, I have presented a developmentally based approach to process consultation, and in the Appendix will demonstrate how to put it to use, and what such application yields. The usefulness of developmental work in intervening with individuals, teams, and entire organizations is just beginning to become public knowledge. Much more awareness of the benefits of the adult-developmental approach is required. The reader is invited to demonstrate the usefulness of the *Constructive Developmental Framework* (CDF) to others, whether clients or colleagues through his or her own professional work.

My goal in this first volume has been to empty some floors of the academic ivory tower where developmental concepts have so far been housed. By teaching methods of developmental assessment, I have set out to demystify the process of adult development heretofore kept under academic wraps.

As this volume has shown, thinking developmentally requires more than learning new skills. It also entails a lot of *unlearning*, and that unlearning may be harder to accomplish than the learning. Properly understood and used, developmental thinking requires *mastering hidden dimensions*, those of human lifespan development. There are no 'easy buttons' for doing so. As especially chapters 4 and 7 suggest, this volume challenges readers to engage in self transformation. In real world applications of what this volume teaches, this is achieved by becoming the reflective instrument of one's own qualitative research on clients. The link between using developmental assessments and self transformation is unique to this book (and the constructive-developmental approach to process consultation generally).

There is something else this volume accomplishes. In the process of demystifying adult development through the teaching of assessments, the reader is introduced to new performance standards for process consultation (including coaching), based on 20th century research in the developmental sciences. These more highly professional standards derive from the distinction that is made between Capability and Competence, as well as that between competences per se and their actual use. As a further result of introducing the Constructive-Developmental Framework (CDF), a new kind of coach education, as well as an extended ethics code, seems to be called for.

Along the way, I have also introduced a host of new research topics. Many of these topics can be addressed by using CDF as the methodology of choice in carrying out applied qualitative and quantitative developmental research. Additional methodologies that take their cue from CDF will doubtlessly be invented as time goes on.

On the more practical side, I have brought to process consultants' attention well defined and validated methods of assessment and evidence based intervention initially formulated and tested in the developmental and social sciences, – foremost skills of developmental listening and analysis. These methods have so far been woefully neglected especially in coaching, but also in mediation, HR management, team building, succession planning, and in human capital management generally. Especially companies pay a high price for bypassing these methods. The time has come to change this state of affairs, both for theoretical and pragmatic reasons.

Since what matters in consultation of any kind is not what practitioners HAVE – skills, expertises, prior experience, credentials – but what they ARE (developmentally, as human beings), thus how they use what they have, no amount of training can substitute for a course of education whose goal it is to transform, not simply inform, adult learners. As this volume has set out to demonstrate, consultation as 'helping' in the emphatic sense is a process that promotes *mental growth*, not performance per se. **This is so since performance is ultimately an outflow of mental growth and nothing else.** The world of work would be a different place if this were more widely understood.

As I have elaborated especially in chapter 9, current coach training programs – whether commercial or academic – *by definition* cannot guarantee the full professionalism required of the field of coaching, nor of process consultation in the broader sense of the term. This is so because these programs are strictly behavioral, not developmental. This inadequacy has many facets. Most crucially it has to do with the requirement of professional work to be carried out at the self-authoring stage (Kegan, 1994). As I point out in this volume, these professional standards are not being fulfilled today by a large, albeit unknown, percentage, of practitioners.

As the Appendix will show, the developmental process of understanding others extends beyond individuals. Once readers have learned to evaluate individual interviews, the door opens to assessments of entire organizations. Until interview scoring is replaced by internet-based algorithms – a project that is in the works – manual scoring remains mandatory. Its remaining relevance is easy to understand: **administering interviews and scoring them 'by hand' is, and will remain, the royal road of understanding and giving feed-back to adult clients**. Pushing a button does not contribute to making developmental shifts!

I invite readers of this volume to do me the honor of letting me know how they themselves feel about, and see, the issues I have raised. I also invite them to let me know what they have begun to do about these issues. This will certainly help me in writing

257

subsequent volumes and improving the present one. More importantly, it will seed new standards of excellence in the domain of professional process consultation.

Otto E. Laske, Medford, MA, USA
December 31, 2005

Appendix A
Exercises

Exercises are arranged by chapter. They fall into three categories:

- An extension of Practice Reflections
- Review of chapter details
- Opportunities for exercising new skills

When an exercise is **marked by an asterisk** (*), it is linked to answers at the end of Appendix A. (Remember that if you look up answers prior to working on the exercise, you are defeating the purpose of the exercise. This is your responsibility!)

For those using this volume as a course textbook, the exercises are meant to prepare you for conducting your own trial interview with a client of your choice during and at the end of the course, and for scoring the interview as best you can, either informally (following the example of Chapter 7) or by using a formal coding sheet (following the example of Chapter 8).

Chapter 1 Exercises

#1   Name some highlights of your life, seen in terms of your ability to manage your life and/or work independently of others.

#2   Over the last decade, what have you become better at, in terms of your thinking, feeling, relating to others, degree of accountability, clarity of self?

#3   How do you experience being *subject to* your present Center of Gravity (developmental stage)?

#4   Are you presently more strongly focused on yourself than on others, and how do you experience that situation?

*#5   What is your definition of 'stage'?

*#6   Write down your definition of ED (social-emotional capability) in contrast to CD (cognitive capability)?

*#7   Write down your definition of 'longitudinal' and 'across time' (in contrast to 'in time')?

*#8   Write down your definition of 'vertical' vs. 'horizontal' assessments?

*#9   In what sense does the Vertical comprise causes, and the Horizontal, effects?

#10   What does thinking in terms of developmental stages contribute to your intuitive notion of 'who the client is'?

#11   Briefly explain the difference between the surface structure and deep structure of adult conversations from a developmental point of view.

#12   Briefly describe the two opposite tendencies of adult life as pointed out by R. Kegan.

#13   Why is 'being a person' and 'being a meaning maker' the same thing?

#14   Explain why people <u>are</u> not their stage.

#15   Explain what is a *social forcing function*, and illustrate it by giving examples.

#16   Why are S-3 consultants and coaches like the proverbial 'blind leading the blind'?

*#17   What distinguishes Kernel from Tools in the *Constructive-Developmental Framework* (CDF)?

#18   Explain why results of a behavioral (horizontal) assessment mean different things at different developmental stages.

#19   Explain why a comprehensive client profile should comprise three aspects or dimensions, as described in the first three volumes of this book.

#20   Explain the difference between answers to questions about 'What Should I Do?' versus 'What Can I Do?'

Chapter 2 Exercises

* #1   How would you define *process consultation?*

#2   In what sense is process consultation based on listening, and on developmental listening in particular?

#3   How is process consultation different from what you do in your own helping practice at this time?

#4   Which elements of process consultation do you need to add to your repertory of methods for consulting to people's mental process?

*#5   Why is developmental interviewing impossible without defining stage hypotheses *explicitly?*

#6   If you were to probe for whether a client is speaking from S-2, how would go about ascertaining that level?

#7   If you step back from your present meaning making and role-play S-2 meaning making – holding a single perspective, your own – how does the world show up and 'feel' for you?

#8   Write down an example of a situation in which you were acting from S-2 in your earlier life, as well as some of the consequences of doing so.

#9   Try to make conscious how you managed to advance from S-2 to S-3 in your own life.

#10   What do you think you can do to make your own way of leading conversations more highly conscious to yourself, especially in interaction with clients?

Chapter 3 Exercises

*#1   Process consultation in the sense of E. Schein is hard enough to accomplish (see the Introduction). What additional difficulties do you think come up for a *developmentally based* process consultant?

#2   If you were to review your professional agenda in light of developmental stages S-3 to S-5, where would you place yourself, avoiding espousals as much as possible?

#3 What Center of Gravity – S-3, S-4, or S-5 – would you require of a consultant or coach you want to work with?

#4 What kinds of help for moving beyond S-3 have you experienced in your own life, and how would you characterize such supports in terms of developmental stage?

#5 Write down some important characteristics of stage S-3.

#6 Write down some important characteristics of stage S-4.

#7 Write down some important characteristics of stage S-5.

#8 With a colleague or your class buddy, discuss a S-3 client in terms of what you have done, or would do, to 'help' him or her.

#9 With a colleague or your class buddy, discuss a S-4 client in terms of what you have done, or would want to do, to 'help' him or her.

#10 If you were coming upon a S-5 or near S-5 client, how would you proceed?

Chapter 4 Exercises

#1 What is missing in the ICF definition of 'active listening' that, if present, would make it evidence based?

#2 What is the minimum developmental level for undertaking process consultation and coaching work, and why?

#3 Why do consultants at different developmental levels generate different models of the client (have different notions of who the client is and how to relate to the client)?

*#4 Why is the self-insight of an S-3 consultant lower than that of an S-4 consultant, and in what way?

#5 In what sense is developmental listening 'active' listening?

#6 What is the difference between formulating implicit and explicit hypotheses?

*#7 Why is a conceptual framework required for formulating and testing hypotheses?

#8 What is probing? How does it differ from simply asking questions about content?

#9 In what way do behavioral issues such as *communicating better* vary according to developmental level?

*#10 What is a projective interview?

#11 What are developmental prompts?

#12 Why is an initial hypotheses required for carrying out a developmental interview?

#13 What are some of the benefits of developmental interviewing for process consultation and coaching even if developmental hypotheses are not used in one's work?

#14 Name four procedures of developmental process consultation.

#15 What is required to understand clients' desires and goals in terms of their feeling and thinking generator?

#16 Where do clients goals come from?

#17 Name some of the benefits of developmental process consultation for the client.

#18 Name some of the benefits of developmental process consultation for the consultant.

#19 Name some of the methods of focusing attention.

#20 What sets focusing attention apart from interpretation?

Chapter 5 Exercises

#1 Write out the entire sequence of stages, main and intermediate, from S-2 to S-5.

#2 What is the Center of Gravity of a person at S-3/2, and what are the lower and higher levels associated with the center?

#3 What might be indicated by the fact that a person is stretched out over more than three, say, five, stages?

#4 If the five stages in question were to be S-2/3, S-3/2, S-3(2), S-3, and S- 3(4), what would be your assessment of the person? Describe the difficulties the person might encounter in making decisions.

#5 How would you characterize a person who is spread out over the range from S-4/3 to S-4/5?

#6 If you had a client assessed at S-4(3), and you were working with the client on 'communicating better,' what would be your coaching plan and approach?

#7   If this same client had a 'time management issue' (not being able to keep track of her time, and not able to plan in an effective manner), what kind of information would you want to elicit from the client in order to work with him in an optimal way?

#8   If your client were assessed by a developmental expert as an S-4(5) individual, and you yourself were presently at S-4(3), how would you proceed?

*#9   Explain why a client at S-4 {5:6:2} who has recently moved to S-4 might feel unsure of his self-authoring stance – e.g., his ability to make decisions that he is fully accountable for –, especially in situations of risk of failure.

*#10   Explain why a client at S-4(3) {2:6:4} who is concerned about not being duly respected as the boss might resort to micromanaging as a way of asserting his expertise and self image.

Chapter 6 Exercises

#1   Why is *loss of self* a universal precondition for gaining a higher level of self-awareness? Think of Wilber's description of 'transcend and include' as the way developmental shifts occur.

*#2   What essentially is the journey from S-2 to S-3 about?

*#3   Why is an S-2 individual unsuited to be a professional helper?

*#4   What essentially is the journey from S-3 to S-4 about?

#5   Why is an S-3 individual a mediocre change agent?

#6   Why is developmental position S-4/3 conflictual, and how does conflict manifest at this position?

#7   Why is espousal ('espoused theory,' to speak with C. Argyris), wherever it occurs, stage specific?

*#8   What do people at different stages do to avoid places in themselves that they feel are presently 'unsafe.' Give an example for S-3(2), S-4(3), and S-5(4)?

#9   How does the *my world* hypothesis of a S-2 person differ from that at S-4 individual?

#10   Describe the enlarged mental space opening up at S-5/4.

*#11   What kinds of behaviors and outlooks on the world does the developmental score of S-4(3) indicate?

#12   What is presupposed by an orthodox – self authoring – theory of helping in the expert, doctor, and process consultation modes, respectively?

#13   How would an S-4 consultant intervene with a client's 'feeling generator' at S-4/3? Think in terms of the distance between both parties' developmental level.

#14   What is the developmental risk when moving from S-4 to S-5/4?

#15   What is at stake for an individual when moving to S-4/3?

#16   What is the meaning of 'transparency' of interpersonal relationships at S-5/4?

#17   In what sense is the consultant's own level of development the single most potent predictor of intervention effectiveness?

#18   Is mutual self discovery possible at S-4/3? If so, what is being discovered, and against what odds?

#19   In what sense does any helping relationship reach a limit at S-5/4?

#20   How would you improve the self report at S-5 at the end of chapter 6?

*#21   What is meant by saying that at S-5 'universal embeddedness' replaces subject-object relations between the individual and the physical and/or social environment?

Chapter 7 Exercises

#1   What is a semi-structured interview?

#2   What can be learned from a semi-structured interview for conversations outside of the developmental approach?

#3   Explain why interviewing is an intervention, not a test.

#4   What are the three generic processes of process consultation?

#5   Which of these three generic processes is furthest removed from the client's train of thought as expressed in conversations?

#6   Distinguish and describe different forms of focusing attention?

#7   State five characteristics of semi-structured interviews.

*#8   What are some characteristics of a process consultant <u>at S-3</u> interviewing and probing clients at the same or a lower level?

*#9   What are some characteristics of a process consultant <u>at S-4</u> interviewing and probing clients at the same or a lower level?

*#10   What kinds of help does a client need whose social-emotional score is S-3/4 {5:8:3}?

#11   Get together with a buddy in the class or a colleague, and try out a 15- minute long developmental interview with him or her as a client. Then reverse roles. Report about your experiences in terms of the following ingredients of the interviewing process:
a. Which stage hypothesis did you formulate at the beginning or during the short interview?
b. How did this hypothesis guide you through the interview?
c. How did you probe for lower levels in relationship to the Center of Gravity?
d. How did you probe for higher levels in relationship to the Center of Gravity?
e. If you did not manage to generate a hypothesis, what did you do to substitute for it?
f. What, for you, was the main outcome of the interview in personal and professional terms?
g. In your role as interviewee, what was your experience over the course of the interview?
h. As interviewee, what did you do when feeling that the interviewer was 'lost' or at his/her wits' end?

#12   Extend the duration of the interview to 30 minutes, and report about it following the questions in Exercise #11. In addition, write a short self-critique of your own, or your partner's, interviewing, and discuss the critique with your partner.

Chapter 8 Exercises

#1   How would you describe that part of the client's mental space that is hidden to him or her?

#2   In what way can developmental interventions shrink the part of the client's mental space that presently lies in the dark for him or her?

#3   In which of the client's three Houses (Self House, Task House, Environmental House) do you typically spend most of your time?

#4   What does your focus in the Houses say about your own mental process?

#5   Elaborate the Task House of an S-4(3) client in the sense of Table 8.1.

#6   What does the analysis of the three-page text fragment discussed in chapter 8 contribute to your knowledge of developmental scoring?

#7   What have you learned from the critical analysis of this chapter's interviewer?

*#8   What is meant by the *developmental range of an interview*?

*#9   Explain the numbers in curly brackets of the *Risk-Clarity-Potential Index*.

*#10   What is the purpose of rewriting a developmental score and associated RCP at a higher or lower Center of Gravity?

*#11   Use the coding sheet below for analyzing the following interview fragment:

Interviewer: Good Morning Marianne. This morning I would like to talk to you about how you make sense of your experience either at work or at home. I have some cards here for you to select a topic to discuss. I believe you have had an opportunity to review the topics and wonder which one you would like to discuss this morning.

Client: Sounds good. I think the topic I would like to discuss this morning is "outside of[1]". This came up for me recently and comes up for me a lot because a lot of the work I do is around inclusion and my life has taken a number of different paths that are non-traditional. This came up this weekend as I was talking to my sister. I come from a family of eight, and in some ways I am very attached to my family and close to them, and I cherish that. In working with my sister it became so apparent to me how different my path has become compared to … so many of my siblings. The question here is where do I see myself as being an outsider and in what way, and what does that make me feel like?

I think what is really important is all the work I have done over the past years, introspective work, that "NF" experience in AU/NTL. That and lots of other things I have done has brought me to a different place. I am very happy about that. So when I watch my sister struggle about blaming people in relationships and I watch my other family members be some-what chained up by beliefs we were raised with, I am aware that my world has opened up to question those beliefs. That is really important to me, and I am happy about it. It is definitely weird. For a long time I wasn't quite sure, I had one foot in one camp and one foot in the other. But now I am pretty clear of where I am, and I like that.

Interviewer: When you talk about being outside of your family relationship, how do you feel when you are with your family? Do you feel like an outsider?

Client: No. I don't feel like an outsider, I feel more choiceful about what I am an insider about. I really enjoy them, and I really enjoy the closeness, and a lot of the things we grew up with. But the way that I think about things and the way that I see things is different. I can look at some of the choices my siblings are making or some of their take on things and I think then, "I used to think that." That is what I mean.

I am also aware of some of the decisions I made around my church situation, for example. For a while I was going to this church here in the Westchester area, and I was leading this anti-racism effort. From our work at AU/NTL and work I have done since then, that is a big thing, and it is a huge issue for me and has become a focus for my life's work. In the church we had all these liberals who claimed to understand racism and the importance of creating a non-racist society, but they were not willing to do any of the *introspective work*. They wanted to go paint porches in

---

[1] Outside of: as you look around you in the workplace, or even in the family, where do you see yourself as not fitting, or being an outsider in some way, and how does that make you feel?

black communities. There is a difference, as we know, in that level of awareness. I used to question whether I was crazy or whether it was just because my kids are kids of color or what. But what I have done in the past year is select a different church and surrounded myself with other people who feel the same way I do about this. And yet, I am aware that other people don't, and it is O.K., I just look at it with curiosity now. I don't have any question that I am happy with the belief that I have. And happy with the choices I have made about surrounding myself and my kids with people who are of like mind.

Interviewer: Well. You chose to change churches to one that was more in liking with your values, is that correct?

Client: Yes, I wanted to surround myself with people who had the same, I don't know that I want to say values, for whom racism was as important as it was for me.

Interviewer: O.K.

Client: For a while it was a *struggle* because I liked the people of the other church but I feel good about having made that decision, frankly.

Interviewer: Is it a more integrated church? I am curious.

Client: Yes.

Interviewer: When you are with your family you can't change family, so how do you work with your family when you find them struggling with relationships?

Client: It depends on the context for which they are coming to me. If they are coming to me to just tell me about it, I listen. If they are coming to me for help about it, then I listen in a way that we have been trained to listen and ask questions that help them to maybe look at their issue in a different way.

Interviewer: So you are in more of a coaching mode.

Client: Yes.

Interviewer: You talked a bit about your family, and you talked about your church. How about within your work relationships? Do you feel more like an insider or outsider?

Client: That is a *struggle* because the people that call me to do OD work, I work quite a bit with IT organizations, so within the IT organization I often feel like an outsider because I have such a different perspective. My perspective is all around human systems. Some of those people look at me like I have three heads. And that doesn't feel good. I know that my perspective is valid. I know the importance of engaging people in systems, and garnering all of their energy and motivation for the mission of the organization. When people articulate that "…this is all touchy-feely stuff, … is it really important?," *I feel like an outsider and I feel that that is necessary.* I am aware that if I were not an outsider then they would not need me. So sometimes I feel good, other times I have to stop and say, "Of course your perspective is different, that is what they hired me for."

Interviewer: Yes, that is the value that you bring to them. Do you work with other consultants?

Client: Sometimes…

Interviewer: When you work with other consultants do you feel like an insider?

Client: Yes, I do. There is always the issue of role clarity and boundaries and that type of thing, but I feel that I am bringing my whole self to it. I feel like we are speaking the same language.

Interviewer: It sounds like you are living outside of the context that some of your siblings live.

Client: It has been a *struggle* because I was brought up to be in harmony, "go along to get along;" it has been a *struggle*. It has only been recently that I have been able to look at my sister not with judgment but with, "…isn't it interesting that she is there…"

Interviewer: What I am hearing from you is that it is a struggle about being accepting of your siblings, and not trying to change them over to your way of thinking.

Client: I wish that were true. I can accept it sometimes, but it depends on the issue. If I look at your (own) sister's struggle with her relationship, … I can step outside of it and look at it with curiosity like, "…isn't that something…" If I look at one of my other sisters who is highly educated and whose opinion I really respect, when she makes a comment that my children, "…if they are loved, should go into the world expecting to be loved," I have a visceral reaction to that, and my visceral reaction is, "…what planet are you on?…this is not going to happen that way!…my son is already being followed at Radio Shack." In those instances I feel like an outsider, and I am not as easily (able) to not judge. I have to check myself and say, "…well they are in a different place…they have different experiences." We were raised to think that the way you treat people will be the way they treat you…and that is not true. I am aware of that because I have had these (opposite) experiences. But I want to grab my sister and say, "…get real!"

Interviewer: You are living between two worlds. You did not grow up in the brown person's world so, you do not know what it is like, but are seeing it with your children. Your children are not going to live in a white man's world. You grew up in a white person's world, so you can understand their point of view also.

Client: Exactly.

End of interview data for Exercise #11.

#12 Write a short description of the strengths and failings of the interviewer of the interview fragment quoted in exercise #11.

#13. Given the interview data and the scoring outcome for exercise #11 (see Answers), how would you characterize the interviewee in terms of where she is developmentally? Focus specifically on the developmental conflict she might be in, and what she lacks in terms of a self-authoring stance.

Chapter 9 Exercises

Section 1
#1 Spell out the two meanings of the English term 'development.'

*#2 Explain the notion of 'developmental risk.'

*#3   Explain the notion of 'developmental potential.'

#4   Spell out how 'need of control' varies across developmental stages by giving some examples.

Section 2

#5   Define *coaching level* in terms of its developmental demands on the coach, by giving examples.

#6   How would you go about finding out the coaching level of some members of your professional community?

#7   Why, and in what sense, is "Do No Harm" the uppermost principle of coaching?

#8   Why is an S-3 coach a mediocre change agent?

#9   What is the relationship between critical thinking and hypothesis testing?

*#10   Why is Socrates a candidate for having been the first coach, if not the first developmental coach?

#11   In what sense do developmental levels simultaneously indicate levels of ethical thinking?

#12   Where in the seven-step model of learning to think developmentally do you presently find yourself, and why?

#13   What is the difference between 'being' your values and 'having' them?

#14   What are some risks of coaching at S-5/4?

#15   Why do coaching relationships in which the coach lives at a lower developmental level than the client predictably yield a low ROI?

#16   What is meant by a coaching relationship being *developmentally counter-productive*?

Section 3

#17   What are some preconditions clients need to fulfill in order to benefit from developmental coaching?

#18   List some of the expectations developmental coaches have of their clients.

#19   How does *intake* relate to *coaching proper* in developmental coaching?

*#20   What is the difference between the *logistic contract* and the *developmental contract* (or developmental contract) in coaching, and why is fusing these two contracts developmentally counter-productive?

#21   Describe how the *Constructive Developmental Framework* (CDF) presented in this book can be used to manage, evaluate, and maintain entire coaching programs?

#22   What are the hidden demands of developmental coaching from the vantage point of the client?

#23   What are the client benefits of having the coach be assessed and mentored developmentally?

Section 4

#24   By what methods would you research whether coaches only espouse acting (pretend to act) from an S-4 vantage point, or are actually conducting themselves as self- authoring professionals? Design a small study.

#25   What is the function of a cohesive, research validated conceptual framework in overcoming one's own developmental bottlenecks? (See A. Dawson's thoughts on this question in chapter 9.)

#26   What is the social mandate of coach education, in contrast to coach training?

#27   What are some of the *undiscussed mental demands of coaching* in the sense of R. Kegan's work?

#28   Describe the limitations of an S-3 model of the client in coaching.

#29   What is the purpose of Capability Management? (Check out Appendix D of this volume).

#30   What is your own contribution to clarifying the theoretical foundations of coaching, if any?

Interdevelopmental Institute
51 Mystic Street
Medford, MA 02155, USA
781.391.2361
Email: info@interdevelopmentals.org
www.interdevelopmentals.org

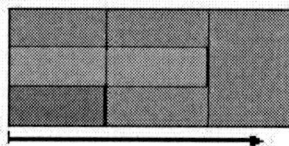

Developmental Interview Agreement

(adapted from Lahey et al., 1988, 426)

I understand that I will be partaking in two developmental interviews, first, a cognitive, and second, a social-emotional, one. These interviews will be tape-recorded for the purpose of evaluation from a structural rather than content point of view. The focus between the two interviews differs. In the first, the focus is on my way of conceptualizing experience, while in the second it is on my present level of meaning making.

I understand that in both developmental interviews I will be in charge of the interview agenda. This takes different forms in the two interviews. In the Thought Form or *Professional Agenda Interview* (volume 2) I will be able to choose topics that shed light on how I presently conceptualize my experiences. In the *Social-Emotional* (Subject-Object) *Interview* (volume 1), I will be able to choose from a list of ten topics called *prompts* that shed light on my present meaning making, whether in life or at work.

I do not have to answer any questions I do not wish to address. Furthermore, I understand that although most people find these interviews engaging and highly revealing, should I feel like discontinuing the interview, or want to speak "off line" for any reasons, I may do so at any time.

I understand also that I will receive feedback from the interviewer, informally or in written form, only once all developmental and behavioral data (the latter deriving from a questionnaire) have been assembled and evaluated. The purpose of this lies in giving feedback based on all three CDF perspectives on which interventions with clients are based at IDM. This procedure guarantees that interventions are strictly *evidence based*.

Most importantly, I have the right to absolute confidentiality of the outcome of the two interviews and the questionnaire. Any excerpts taken from the interviews, written or spoken, will disguise all names of persons and places involved, so as to preserve my anonymity and privacy. None of the information I will share in these interviews and the questionnaire, as well as results obtained through them, will be conveyed, in any form, to any person without my written permission. Therefore, I have no issue agreeing that once rendered suitably anonymous, the interview texts and results, as well as the numerical questionnaire data, can be used for IDM teaching and mentoring purposes.

_____   _____
Client/Volunteer   Date

_____   _____
IDM Assessment Specialist   Date

_____   _____
IDM Director   Date

Interview ID & Page [or no. on tape counter]	Bit Number & Score in Teleological Range 1 1(2) 1/2 2/1 2(1) 5 2(3) 2/3 3/2 3(2) 6 3(4) 3/4 4/3 4(3) 7 4(5) 4/5 5/4 5(4) 5	Questions to Ask: 1) What structural evidence leads you to these hypotheses? 2) What evidence leads you to reject other plausible counter-hypotheses? 3) If you have a range of hypotheses, what further information do you need to narrow the range?
1	#1,	
	#2,	
	#3,	
	#4,	
	#5,	
	#6,	
	#7,	
	#8,	
	#9,	
	#10,	
	#11,	
	#12, ...	

Fig. A.1 Subject-Object interview Coding Sheet
[adapted from Lahey et al., Appendix F, 1988]

ANSWERS TO SELECTED EXERCISES

Chapter 1 (5-9, 17)

#5   Stage is a mode of functioning in the world. It is associated with a *Frame of Reference* based on which people define themselves in their relationship to the world. What people are 'subject to' and can take as object of reflection changes from stage to stage.

#6   ED (social-emotional development) regards the ethical and value issue of what one <u>should</u> do and for whom, while CD (cognitive development) concerns the issue of what one <u>can</u> do, and what one's options are.

#7   'Longitudinal' means 'across time,' implying assessments at successive time points over a longer time period, such as a decade.

#8   'Vertical' assessments and findings pertain to what holds across time, while 'horizontal' assessments and findings pertain to what is in time. More specifically, horizontal assessments yield snapshots of the recent past, at most the present, and thus have no predictive value (although it is often assumed that they do). Every horizontal finding has a different meaning and interpretation depending on where it falls on the vertical (e.g. MBTI or Enneagram types).

#9   Since adult-developmental assessment findings pinpoint the root of a person's behavior at a particular point in time, we say that they encompass the *causes* of that behavior. For instance, somebody's boredom or arrogance has different meanings at different developmental stages (vertical positions), because the meaning making behind being bored or arrogant is different in each case.

#17   The Kernel methodology comprises developmental or vertical assessments, while the Tool methodology concerns behavioral or horizontal assessments.

Chapter 2 (1, 5)

#1   In contrast to expert and doctor-patient consultation, *process consultation* is focused on the client's mental process, not per se on delivering solutions or diagnoses. This approach requires a more reflective and self-aware procedure than does typical consultation.

#5   Since developmental interviewing focuses on the client's present Center of Gravity, without an hypothesis as to such a center the interviewer would be at a loss as to what to ask, comment on, and probe for. The purpose of the interview is precisely to test the interviewer's Center of Gravity hypothesis.

Chapter 3 (1)

#1   In addition to conventional process consultation, the developmentally grounded PC fulfills the following requirements:
      a. awareness of one's own developmental level
      b. insight into the client's developmental level

c. based on developmental level of the client, a determination of how far the client is able to take responsibility for the problem

d. assessment of the developmental underpinnings of the client's presenting problem (the way the client presents the problem)

e. assisting the client in understanding his or her own 'blind spots' that create the problem formulated by her in the first place

f. finding out whether the client, even if s(he) would be given a solution, could follow through with realizing it in the existing environment.

Chapter 4 (4, 7, 10)

#4 An S-3 process consultant unconsciously defines herself by physical and internalized others all of whom obstruct insight into what she herself autonomously stands for. She has not yet sorted out *who is she* in contrast to others, and borrows her self definition from the social surround.

#7 Hypotheses are assumptions that serve the task of gathering evidence. They are always intrinsically related to a conceptual framework from which they issue. While it is popular to speak of stand-alone hypotheses ('It was my hypothesis that going right would get me to the desired destination), research based hypotheses are embedded in the context of a particular methodology. They are never stand-alone, but derive their legitimacy from the methodology they are associated with.

#10 An interview is called 'projective' if the questions asked or prompts followed are verbal stimuli into which the respondent can fully *project* herself. Since when scrutinized by a developmental expert speech reveals a person's Center of Gravity, the verbal content produced by the interviewee in answering the prompt shows the interviewer where the client 'lives' developmentally. The client projects herself into the prompt, and then walks right into that projection. In so doing, she reveals who she is as a member of her developmental peer group.

Chapter 5 (9, 10)

#9 The client in this exercise is clearly on shaky ground since the proportion with which she acts from below and above her Center of Gravity   (4 {5:6:2}) puts her 'off center.' The clarity of her self image is clouded by her strong inclination toward espousal which she is critical enough to discern only in her better moments. Her strong yearning to be self authoring is presently not supported by a high potential for critical self examination. She therefore feels that she cannot be fully responsible for actions whose success (as a badge of her own superiority) is in doubt.

#10 The client in this exercise needs to boost internal voices that tell her she owes it to herself to make decisions on her own (4(3) {2:6:4}). Since the potential for such decisions is still somewhat small, she has taken to telling herself and others that she should be in charge, not only for her own benefit but that of others as well. She therefore perceives her micromanaging as a benevolent gesture of being helpful, mixed up with urges to control the circumstances in which she is judged by others.

Chapter 6 (2-4, 8, 11, 21)

#2   The journey from S-2 to S-3 essentially is about internalizing other people's perspective on oneself, themselves, and the world. One might say that it is the basis of empathy. By recognizing the difference between another person and oneself, one *internalizes* that person's perspective to the point where one becomes able to think, feel, act, and laugh or weep like the other person.

#3   Since an S-2 individual can only hold a single perspective, his or her own, and since helping requires 'standing in the other person's shoes,' such a person cannot truly understand another person, nor is s(he) interested in doing so. As a result, there is no way an S-2 person can be a professional helper. Rather, such a person expects others to help <u>her</u>, and arranges her life so as to use others as instruments that are helpful to her in satisfying her own desires and needs. This may be masked by a pseudo-professional Persona, of course.

#4   The journey from S-3 to S-4 centers on becoming aware of one's internalized others, and thereby freeing oneself of the obstruction to one's own voice that they inevitably bring about. Beyond this negative aspect, the positive aspect consists of acquiring deeper self insight, which leads to a deeper understanding of one's own uniqueness. Lastly, deeper insight leads to, as well as requires, the courage to stand up for one's own unique values, even if one is ostracized by others for acting upon them.

#8   Places in oneself become unsafe when one is transitioning to a higher developmental level. These places regard circumstances to avoid in order not to regress to lower levels. Naturally, such places differ between stages.
a. in S-3(2), it becomes unsafe to be centered on one's own immediate interests and needs, since one is now defining oneself by others' expectations, and these expectations typically do not center primarily on one's own interests and needs.
b. In S-4(3), it becomes unsafe to define oneself by other people's expectation since following others' expectations could induce regression to a other-dependent mode of being in the world, which is exactly what one is trying to leave behind.
c. In S-5(4), it becomes unsafe to think of oneself as being in some splendid isolation from others, and defined by one's successes and specific life history. In order not to regress to an orthodox self-authoring mode, one will talk up a storm about acting from S-5, and is studiously critical of any trace of S-4 in one's life.

#11   An individual at S-4(3) has nearly reached a self-authoring position. At the same time, the individual is still 'hanging on to' significant traces of a previous world view according to which s(he) defined herself by other's expectations. For this reason, while not in conflict about having to march to one's own drummer, the person needs to emphasize that she is now defined by her own values and principles. In this way, she rehearses being a truly self-authoring individual.

#21   Developmental positions up to S-5(4) are all defined by subject-object relations, in the sense that one is subject to one's present Center of Gravity and only partially able to reflect on who one is. Once consciousness is mature enough to suspend subject-object distinctions – strenuously upheld by natural language – and to enter into modes of being embedded in the larger cosmos (experiencing oneself as a particle of it), the subject-object relations one previously acted upon are lifted, even if temporarily, and one is totally *in the flow*. (This experience is often described as *spiritual* or *mystic*.)

Chapter 7 (8-10)

#8   At S-3, a process consultant cannot separate out her own (and the client's) internalized others (voices taken from the social surround), and therefore fails to define a model of the client based on her own authentic values and principles. Consequently, there is high risk of collusion with the client's goals and perspectives, rather than an ability to assess these goals and perspectives objectively. A model of the client formulated by an S-3 process consultant by definition heavily relies on values shared with the client. This precludes the consultant's ability to separate out from the client and approach client issues objectively, that is, from one's own values and principles and within a consistent conceptual framework like, e.g., CDF.

#9   At S-4, a process consultant can objectively assess a client's stance toward the world that derives from levels up to S-4(3). As a result, the consultant can compare his or her own clarity of center with that of a client, and develop an objective view of the   client in terms of her values and answers to questions regarding 'what should I do and for whom?' Since an S-4 individual cannot stand back from her own values but is totally identified with them, an S-4 consultant will steer the client in a direction determined by her own (consultant's) convictions, but at least these will not simply   be taken from the social surround but will be self-authored. Also, acting from S-4, the consultant will be a better change agent than her S-3 colleague, simply because she is more aware of her social embedding, and less anxious about, and preoccupied with, the consequence of changes introduced by way of her own interventions.

#10   A client at this level (3/4 {5:8:3}), with a distribution over adjacent levels as indicated, is presently conflicted between following inner voices borrowed from the social environment and her own authentic voices. Her ability to know, and fully stand by, her own values is minimal, and she will frequently waver about what course of action to take, and will be highly wedded to the *status quo* that she assumes keeps her safe. Given the fact that the client's propensity to regress to S-3(4) is very high, the consultant's or coach's attention will primarily have to be focused on solidifying the client's presently shaky hold on her authentic inner voices that have barely emerged enough to guide her.
In addition, the client will require assistance in solving her conflicts regarding paths to take, and encouragement in listening to her own inner voices. If the Center of Gravity indicated by the weight of {8} has been held by the client for a

long time, she may be stuck at S-3/4, and all resources she presently has to move to S-4/3 should be mobilized. This *stretching* must be carefully calibrated in order not to send the client into even deeper conflicts than she is already experiencing.

Chapter 8 (8-11)

#8   The total range of stages within which the interviewee can be shown to move over the course of the interview.

#9   The numbers represent the proportions by which different stages are represented in the interview. In its *normal form*, the RCP assumes that the client is distributed over just <u>three</u> stages. Broader distributions need to be culled directly from the coding sheet. They are not directly indicated by the RCP which summarizes all lower and higher stages.

#10   The rewritten score highlights implications of the developmental findings that are not immediately evident otherwise. This is so since the shift to a higher or lower level makes an existing risk and potential more clearly visible.

#11

Answer to Exercise 11 of Chapter 8
Subject-Object Interview Coding Sheet 0093

Interview ID 0093 & Page	Bit Number & Score in Teleological Range 1 1(2) 1/ 2 2/1 2(1) 8 2(3) 2/3 3/2 3(2) 9 3(4) 3/4 4/3 4(3) 10 4(5) 4/5 5/4 5(4) 5	Questions to Ask: 1) What structural evidence leads you to these hypotheses? 2) What evidence leads you to reject other plausible counter-hypotheses? 3) If you have a range of hypotheses, what further information do you need to narrow the range?
1	>3(4)	A lot of the work I do is around inclusion and my life has taken a number of different paths that are non-traditional. *Speaker can take a perspective on her life and the community she is part of.*
1	#1, 4/3	For a long time I wasn't quite sure, I had one foot in one camp and one foot in the other. But now I am pretty clear of where I am, and I like that. *Speaker is taking a perspective on a past internal conflict and on having transcended it.*
1	#2, 4(3)	I don't feel like an outsider, I feel more choiceful about what I am an insider about. … But the way that I think about things and the way that I see things is different. I can look at some of the choices my siblings are making or some of their take on things and I think then, "I used to think that." That is what I mean. *Speaker can enjoy other's less dev. perspective and is secure on her own take on things. However, an element of espousal remains.*
2	#3, 4	I used to question whether I was crazy or whether it was just because my kids are kids of color or what. But what I have done in the past year is select a different church and surrounded myself with other people who feel the same way I do about this. And yet, I am aware that other people don't, and it is O.K., I just look at it with *curiosity* now. I don't have any question that I am happy with

		the belief that I have. And happy with the choices I have made about surrounding myself and my kids with people who are of like mind. *Speaker does not care to include other perspective while being very sure of her own. (S-4(3) cannot be entirely ruled out.)*
2	#4, 4/3	It depends on the context for which they are coming to me. If they are coming to me to just tell me about it, I listen. If they are coming to me for help about it, then I listen in a way that we have been trained to listen and ask questions that help them to maybe look at it a different way. *It's not clear whether the speaker identifies with community best practices or can hold them as object*
3	#5, 4(3)	Some of those people look at me like I have three heads. And that doesn't feel good. … I feel like an outsider, and I feel that that is necessary. I am aware that if I were not an outsider then they would not need me. So sometimes I feel good, other times I have to stop and say, "Of course your perspective is different, that is what they hire me for." *Speaker acknowledges the need to be uncomfortable to be helpful, and there is the presence of espousal.*
3	#6, 4	It (i.e., separating from siblings) has been a *struggle* because I was brought up to be in harmony, go along to get along…it has been a *struggle*. It has only been recently that I have been able to look at my sister not with judgment but with, "…isn't it interesting that she is there…" *Struggle is resolved to a fully self authoring position. (S4(3) cannot be entirely ruled out.)*
3	#7, 4/3	I wish that were true but I can accept it sometimes but it depends on the issue. … In those instances I feel like an outsider, and I am not as easily to not judge. *Speaker finds herself regressing to judgment.*

Table A.2 Coding sheet for exercise #11

Scoring Outcomes (Exercise 11)

4/3	4(3)	4
3	2	2

Table A.3 RCP for exercise #11 (4(3) {3:2:2})

Clearly, if the two occurrences of S-4 are only espoused and really belong at 4(3), the RCP will read: 4(3) {3:4:0}. Since the expertise of the novice interviewer makes it hard to sort out *espousals*, this state of affairs is quite possible.

Chapter 9 (2-3, 10, 20)

#2   Developmental Risk is an index of the social-emotional RCP. It indicates the likelihood that a person will regress to acting from a lower level than her present Center of Gravity.

#3   Developmental Potential is an index of the social-emotional RCP. It indicates the degree to which a person has the developmental resources to make a developmental shift to a subsequent higher level, compared to the strength with which the present Center of Gravity is held, as well as the risk that exists to fall below it.

#10   A coach is a professional who consults to the client's mental process. Socrates did just that, by questioning people about their thinking and feeling about things. Socrates assumed that people knew the answer to his questions and/or their problems, but could not locate it because their self definition was based on internalized others, thus on illusions deriving from being defined by other's expectations. Socrates also believed that by 'active listening' and questioning he could develop people's self awareness to higher levels. Therefore one might say that Socrates acted as a coach in the sense of 'process consultant.' He acted as a developmental coach as well, in the sense that he did not put the emphasis on external outcomes and achievements, or even goals, but saw clearly that the latter ultimately depended entirely on the individual's *Frame of Reference*. He argued that if he, Socrates, could change the individual's Frame of Reference, that would be much more effective than to come up with this or that solution (which the person might be incapable of owning, and should come up with herself anyway.)

#20   The *logistic* contract comprises all those matters that pertain to fee, coaching period, coaching goals, expected CROI, and third party involvement. By contrast, the *learning* (or better *developmental*) *contract* is "signed" as a commitment of the client, to actively engage in changing his or her Frame of Reference, and as a commitment of the coach to change the client's Frame of Reference based on developmental insight and techniques (even if moving the client to a higher level of self awareness is not an explicit goal of the intervention).

Appendix B
Three Case Studies

Purpose of the Case Studies

The three case studies below are examples of a wealth of practical experience gathered over the last seven years in using the assessment and consulting methodology presented in this volume. These studies could easily fill an entire small book. Rather than presenting lengthy studies and reports, here I select three cases, to show how developmental thinking in interventions such as coaching can be beneficial to clients and consultants as well.

As the reader now realizes, having one's interventions be informed solely by social-emotional assessment findings is a one-sided affair, however comprehensive the social-emotional score may be. This is because the full power of the ED score only reveals itself when combined with cognitive and behavioral scores. What we observe or are told by clients is of great complexity, not so much in terms of context, but of structure. As we have seen in this book, minimally four ingredients of a complete life or work profile should be taken into account when one is engaged with understanding what ICF calls *the client's desires*:

- Social-emotional stage (ED)
- Cognitive profile (e.g., ability to be objective and hold multiple perspectives; CD)
- Discrepancies between ED and CD
- Behavioral scores from horizontal assessments of self conduct, approach to tasks, and interpersonal perspective (or others, such as MBTI, 360, etc.)

These horizontal assessments can principally derive from many different tools. In this book, following IDM's *Program One*, I am using the *Need/Press Analysis Questionnaire* (NPA, NP for short). In my experience, this questionnaire – anchored in the research done by Henry Murray (2005) – is a singularly revealing instrument since it lays bare minute shadings of human behavior, especially in the workplace (see below).

In Morris Aderman's formulation, the *Need/Press* Questionnaire is focused on work in organizations. (One of its inventories of questions can also be used for life coaching.) As conveyed by its name, the questionnaire generates data centered on the *subjective needs* of a client in relation to the internal and environmental *pressure* the client is exposed to in his or her environment. (In the studies below, the 'Press[ure]' dimension has been omitted entirely, in order to reduce complexity; see volume 3 of this book for a comprehensive introduction to this instrument.) The data assessed through the questionnaire are specific to three related aspects of subjective need, named *self conduct* (SC), *task focus* (TF), and *interpersonal perspective* (IP, which equals emotional intelligence), respectively.

My overriding goal in the case studies is to demonstrate how a developmentally thinking practitioner evaluates behavioral data from the vantage point of the client's social-emotional score. A second goal is to convey suggestions as to (1) what the crucial coaching issues of the respective client might be, (2) how to approach working with the client, and (3) what coaching outcome can be expected. As to outcomes, I limit myself to expectations here, rather than introducing actual post-test results of what transpired in the coaching. (For my empirical studies on this topic, see Laske, 2004b and 2003a).

The Behavioral Assessment Tool NPA

Since the reader is by now well-versed in interpreting social-emotional scores, for the case studies that follow I need only add more detail about the *Need/Press Analysis* questionnaire (NPA). This assessment tool is essentially the work of Henry Murray, a well-known personality theorist who worked at Harvard during the 1930s and 1940s (see the bibliography). Murray's research was adapted to organizational interventions by his student Morris Aderman in the 1960s and 1970s.

In contrast to the majority of horizontal assessments used today, the NPA is based on the notion that the subjective needs of a professional active in an organizational environment are unconscious, or *hidden to the individual*. (This is in complete correspondence with the CDF hypothesis that a person's developmental profile is something the person is subject to.)

When one thinks about subjective needs along Freudian lines, as H. Murray does, one can say that the needs form an 'Id' complex that stands in opposition not only to the assessed individual's Ego, but also the so-called 'real world.' The task of the individual then becomes establishing a livable *equilibrium* between subjective needs and rational control (Ego), on one hand, and between rational control and the real world, on the other. The emphasis in the NPA *directly* falls on the balance of subjective needs and rational control, while in conjunction with developmental assessment data, the NPA is highly useful for investigating the balance between a person's self in relation to the so-called real world, especially the social world.

Concretely, the NPA measures the individual's subjective needs (Need) in relation to the (moral) pressure exerted by the individual on him- or herself, and the behavioral outcomes of this need-press relationship within an organizational framework (when considering how an organization is experienced by an individual). NPA highlights pressure (Press) in two related forms:

- The pressure exerted <u>by</u> the individual on herself, by holding certain ideal notions of what the organizational environment *should be* like, including her own contribution to the organization (ideal Press).
- The pressure exerted <u>on</u> the individual by the actual experience of the corporate culture that defines the organizational environment, or what the environment actually *feels like* for the individual (actual Press).

Measurements of ideal Press correspond to the Freud's *Super-Ego*, while measurements of actual Press constitute a study of the real world, in particular, an organization's corporate culture. In human resource terms, the latter can be interpreted as indicators of *job satisfaction*.

When using NPA data in conjunction with social-emotional scores, we can view the assessment outcome as a set of *symptoms* that describe a professional's more or less hidden professional agenda. These symptoms add to the hidden developmental dimensions that determine professionals' behavior in the organizational environment. NPA data specifically focus on the three behavioral dimensions below:

- **Self Conduct:** The client's relationship to herself, and the nature of her ego needs (Need), as well as how the self is experienced within the organizational context (Press).
- **Task Approach:** The client's ability to deal with challenges in his or her work, set goals, and pursue an agenda (Need), as well as what the organization's task focus should ideally be and is actually experienced as being (Press).
- **Interpersonal Perspective** *[emotional intelligence]:* The client's ability to interface with others, ask for help if needed, and be affiliated with the organization, as well as how the corporate culture is viewed (Need), and actually experienced (Press).

Between these behavioral dimensions many relationships exist. (For instance, a strong need for power under *Self Conduct* may influence the score for empathy under *Interpersonal Perspective.*) However, for simplicity's sake, in the case studies below these relationships will be disregarded. In order to shorten the analysis portion of the case studies, each of the three studies below will moreover take into account the client's assessment outcomes for only <u>one</u> of the three sets behavioral dimensions measured (Self Conduct, Task Approach, and Interpersonal Perspective).

A complete NPA profile of an individual (coach or client) might be considered a statement of client strengths as well as of *issues in need of coaching.* In contrast to a 360-profile, NPA variables regard the client's own unconscious needs and pressures exerted on him or her that largely lie below the level of consciousness. **One can therefore say that NPA outcomes inform the coach about *hidden* behavioral dimensions of the client, just as developmental outcomes inform the coach about *hidden* social-emotional and/or cognitive dimensions of the client.** Consequently, when the coach combines behavioral insights derived from the questionnaire with social-emotional and cognitive insights, a very potent mix of hypotheses and observations becomes available that can be used in evidence-based interventions.

Example of an NPA Need Profile	
Self Conduct	
Self-Concept:	1
Risk-taking:	3
Flexibility:	8
Need for Power:	7
Need for Visibility:	3
Confrontationalism:	2
Task Focus	
Autonomy:	8
Drive to Achieve:	7
Resourcefulness:	8
Endurance:	5
Quality of Planning:	1
Need to Self-Protect	9
Interpersonal Perspective	
Affiliation:	1
Rel. to Power:	4

Empathy:	2
Helpfulness:	5
Dependency:	3
Bias:	8
Summary Scores	
Efficiency Index:	56
Frustration Index:	18
Energy Sink:	47
Attunement:	27
Distortion:	22

Table B.1 NPA empirical data about a client

Concretely, each NPA profile comprises 18 variables, six each for Self Conduct, Task Approach, and Interpersonal Perspective. As shown in Figure B.1 below, these variables are calibrated in terms of steps laid out along a Likert scale from 0 to 9. In addition to individual outcomes, higher-level *summary scores* contribute create a 'big picture' of the respective client.

The summary scores in the table above comprise both Need and Press findings. Specifically, they indicate the client's *Energy Sink* due to gaps between subjective need and ideal press ('shoulds'), as well as the client's *Frustration Index* that derives from gaps between ideal and actual press (pressures exerted on the individual by herself and the organization). The scores also indicate the degree of an individual's *attunement* to the organization's corporate culture, as well as the degree to which the individual has a *distorted view* of that culture based on his or her subjective needs. The overriding outcome variable is the Efficiency Index. This index is from both Energy Sink and Frustration Index. In the present example, it indicates low overall performance efficiency. This result reflects the large amount of energy the individual spends on bringing subjective needs and ethical norms in line (Energy Sink = 47).

The empirical values of the client's variables indicate two important coaching issues, namely the distance of the client's outcomes:

- from *managerial norms* (behaviors of typical managers)

- from *extreme behaviors* (at either end of the scale).

Self Conduct

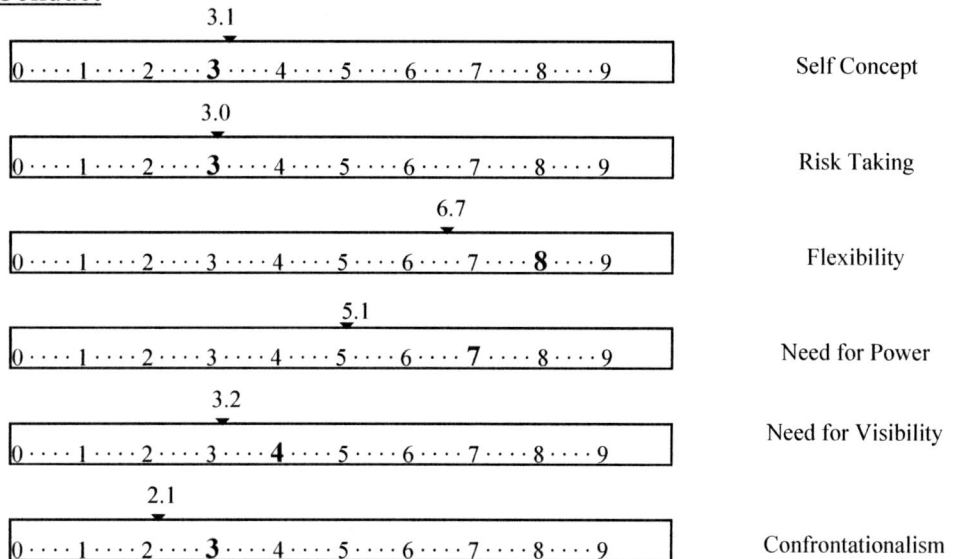

Fig. B.1 NPA outcomes for Self Conduct

Outcome Interpretation

In order to follow the discussion below, the reader needs to keep in mind that the Need/Press Questionnaire measures a client's closeness to managerial norms optimally congruent with an S-4 developmental level. In the Figure above, the norm is indicated above the scale, by way of an inverted triangle. Whenever a client's score (in **bold**) significantly deviates from the norm – taking into account a margin of error of 1, maximally 2 – *a coaching problem most likely unknown to the client* is indicated. In this context, it does not matter whether a client's score lies 'below' or 'above' the managerial norm. **Both cases are equally problematic since scores below the norm indicate having "too little," while scores above the norm indicate having "too much," of what is ideally required of the client in his or her present performance.**

For example, the client in the above example obtains a score of '3' on risk taking, a value that is identical with the managerial norm, and is simultaneously removed from both extremes of the scale (0, 9) which would indicate behavioral danger points (coaching issues). This means that the client is a good risk taker very close to what one would expect from a manager. His or her way of taking risks does not presently indicate a coaching problem.

The Relationship between Horizontal and Vertical Scores

The reader now has an inkling of how relevant behavioral scores can be in evidence based interventions. S(he) will recall the diagram in Chapter 1 by which I visualized the distinction between horizontal and vertical assessments:

CD= cognitive development

Mental Growth

Discontinuous, in stages (across-time)

TOOLS

Behavior

Linear (in-time)

KERNEL

ED= social-emotional development

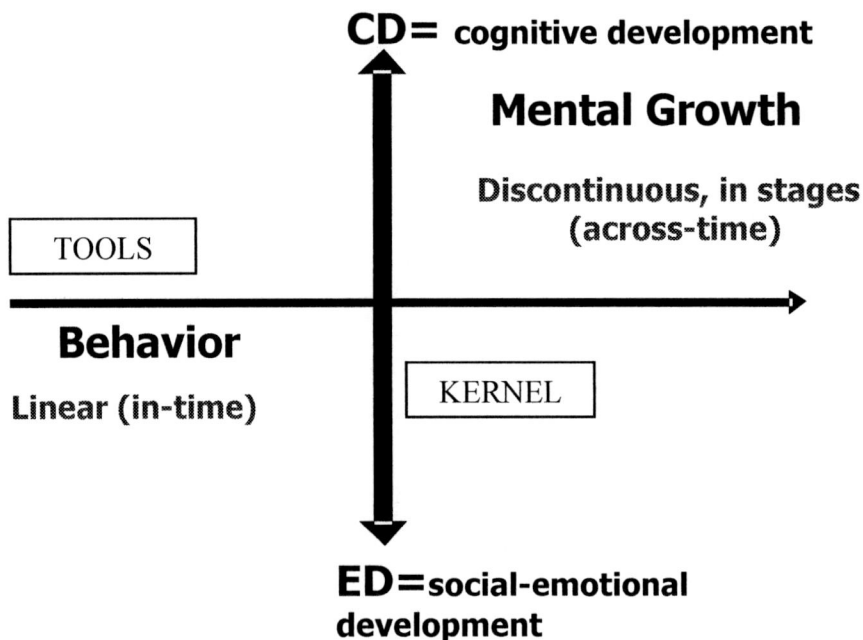

Fig. B.2 Kernel=vertical, Tools=horizontal assessments

As I said in Chapter 1, these two dimensions are only conceptually separable, while in reality they constantly interact with, and inform, each other. It might therefore be best to think of the relationship between the client's developmental and behavioral (NPA) scores as one holding between a rather stable set of *personality traits* (NPA) associated with a dynamic and malleable *developmental potential* (ED). On account of their developmental potential, individuals can over time smooth the hard edges of their personality, increasingly revealing its true essence and limitations at the same time.

For instance, if you have a strong need to control circumstances as well as other people, you will, as you mature, be able to negotiate this inclination with increasing flexibility and subtlety (plus perhaps also cunning). Rather than vanishing under developmental influence, the personality traits will become more easily malleable and socially negotiable, bound up with espousal according to the developmental level reached. **In short, adult development does not completely "revise" your pre-adult personality but, except for cases of developmental arrest or derailment, makes you more adept at *living with* your own little personality.** As we have seen, transcending developmental stage S-4 predisposes the individual to detaching from her own personality in a way that is impossible to achieve at S-2 or S-3. Paradoxically, at the same time, the individual's personality becomes better and better articulated. This apparent paradox can be explained by reference to the *systemic mental space* in which individuals beyond S-4 lead their life and conduct their work.

***

Aspects of the Client's Profile to Consider

Let us now proceed to the three case studies.

Rather than presenting for each an extensive feedback report, I will restrict myself to discussing the following assessment findings:

1. social-emotional (ED) score
2. partial behavioral profile (self conduct, approach to tasks, or interpersonal perspective)
3. client's behavioral strengths
4. client's behavioral challenges
5. client's developmental risk
6. client's developmental potential
7. salient coaching issues
8. remedial vs. growth-focused intervention
9. expected coaching experience of the client
10. expected coaching experience of the coach.

In order to adopt a compact and uniform format, I will discuss the above aspects by commenting on the aspects indicated below. (The reader should remember that the behavioral data I will discuss are a selection from a larger set, and simply serve as examples.)

Format of case study discussion:

A. Client strengths.

B. Client challenges .

C. Summary of client's behavioral profile (coaching issues #1).

D. Developmentally focused summary (coaching issues #2).

E. Intake Feedback.

F. Coaching Strategy.

G. Expectable CROI.

CASE STUDY #1
Rick
4(5) {3:7:3}

<u>Profile and Presenting Problem:</u> Rick is the CFO of a large accounting firm constituted as a partnership. He has been part of the company for 25 years, and has risen from the bottom up. Rick has a strong and fruitful relationship with the CEO but is often at loggerheads with the rest of the executive team. He has been accused by his peers of being 'too close' to the CEO in terms of secret schemes the two are often pursuing without knowledge of the rest of the team. Because of this, Rick has decided to work on the dynamics he seems to set up in the team, and on ways to smooth feathers. He surmises that he could use some help in achieving more clarity about himself, especially his personal needs in the job and the way he deals with pressures exerted by daily events.

Self Conduct

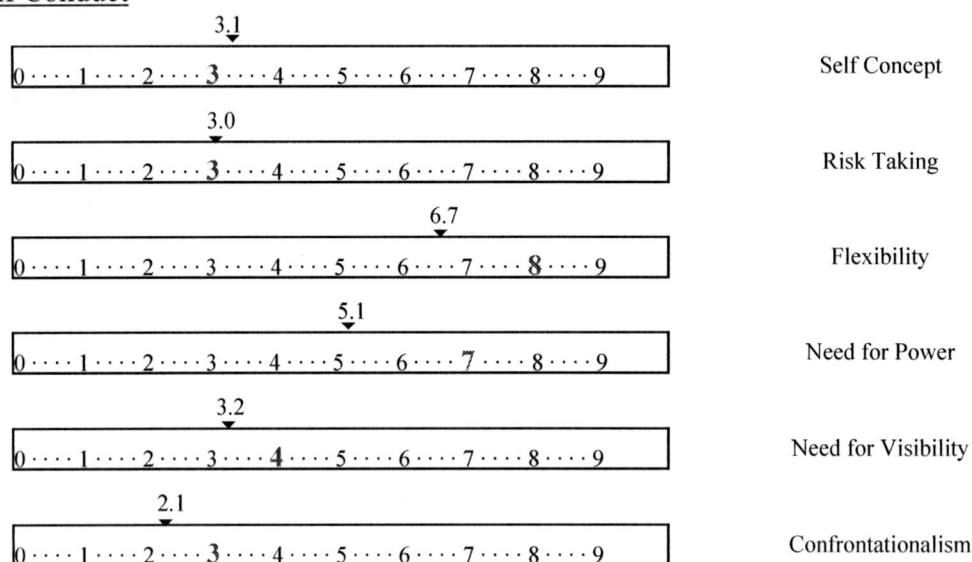

Fig. B.3 Rick's Self Conduct scores

It is interesting to compare the client's presenting problem with the behavioral description that is, essentially, below the client's level of consciousness. Below, Rick's self conduct variables have been translated from a numerical to a verbal form. Entries in **_italic bold_** in column 1 point to coaching issues (here, conduct flexibility and need for power).

NeedPress Profile		Behavioral Description of Client
Self Conduct		**Need: Client's relationship to self; nature of ego needs**
Self concept: _Strength of personal confidence_	3	Effective self concept, comfortable resilience and openness to others.
Risk taking: _Fear of failure, perceiving a narrow band of acceptability_	3	Workable combination of risk taking with sense of timing; sound judgment; views incomplete outcomes as learning experience.

Flexibility: *Ability to engage with novelty, diversity, and generate alternatives, experiment*	8	High need for creative independence; stays away from routinized procedures; easily bored with repetitive activities; seeks out diversity, looks for alternatives.
Need for power: *Relationship to power, need to control and direct others*	7	Blurring of leadership skills with ego needs; misplaced appraisals; manipulative posturing likely.
Need for visibility: *Desire to be visible, acknowledged, attract attention, need to be focused on personal achievements*	4	Outgoing, well-balanced, some desire for visibility, preferring to mingle.
Confrontationalism: *Need to berate or belittle others or self, need for verbal assault*	3	No felt need to berate self or others; seen as soft-hearted.

Table B.2 Rick's behavioral findings

Based on the above interpretation, a behavioral report written (or spoken) for purposes of feedback would emphasize the following aspects of Rick's behavior:

A. Client strengths
- Effective self concept, comfortable resilience with others.
- Sound judgment with good timing; open to learning.
- High need for creative independence.
- Reasonable need for being seen; not in hiding.
- No need to berate either self or others, and seen as soft-hearted.

B. Client challenges
- Blurring of leadership skills with ego needs; misplaced appraisals; manipulative posturing likely.
- Easily bored; seeks out variety for its own sake.

C. Summary of client's behavioral profile (coaching issues #1)
As seen, Rick's self conduct profile is, overall, very close to managerial norms. He has an effective self concept, makes sound judgments and is a creative individual who pursues his tasks independently of others, with no co-dependence and with a reasonable need for being acknowledged. He is also not vindictive and has no need to berate either himself or others. As his presenting problem conveys, Rick is sensitive enough, despite his long history with the company, to register that he is not always positively perceived by others who find him secretive, and easily tempted to bend team dynamics in the direction of his own personal and professional needs (mostly by making use of his close personal relationship with the CEO). As one can infer from Rick's self conduct findings, these perceptions by others can rather straightforwardly be derived from the challenges assessed by NPA (see B).

D. Developmentally focused summary (coaching issues #2)
4(5) {3:7:3}
To judge from his social-emotional score, Rick is at a point in his adult development where he has begun to detach himself somewhat from his own idiosyncratic value

system and integrity (cemented by his 'personality'). He is thoroughly embedded in a developmental position which makes him aware of the fact that his secure self concept, expertise, and fearless astuteness cannot entirely substitute for a lack of sensitivity when it comes to managing others or relating to peers. While his need for creative independence is a strength, it often entails a lack of engagement with (financial) detail and required mechanism (especially in an accounting firm), resulting in undue delegation of responsibilities to his team, and a neglect of supervisory duties. These issues are not helped by his difficulty with leadership, caused by a subjective need for power that often leads to the manipulation of others for reasons he mistakes as relating to his integrity. While Rick is certainly not any longer "a classical S-4," the distance he has journeyed in the direction of S-5 is diminished in relevance by his developmental risk of falling back on an orthodox self-authoring stance. The distance is also too small for him to be able to balance his need for power with a critical stance toward himself.

As the S-4 caricature puts it:

The changes they [S-4 individuals] author, however, will, more likely than not, be directed towards making the organization more responsive to themselves, authoring and moving it in directions approximating their own personal 'institution,' rather than one more universally self-sustaining. The climate they create will be one that follows the status quo, but taking on their own idiosyncratic values and operational principles as time passes. Since they are caught in their own frame of reference, they fail to appreciate the value of other frames of reference just as much, if not more, developed. This, by definition, limits the extent to which 'their' organization can learn-to-learn, grow, and further develop.

Although the above describes an orthodox S-4 individual, clearly the description rather directly speaks to Rick's own issues. His present developmental risk, to act from his present lower level (S-4), is equal to his potential to grow beyond S-4(5). For this reason, one might hypothesize that Rick is somehow *developmentally stuck* at his present Center of Gravity. The detailed reasons for this are not known (but can be ascertained). They are underscored by the fact that his developmental risk and potential are of equal strength, and his potential thus *frozen*. Should he indeed be 'stuck' developmentally, that would not bode well for successful coaching in terms of effective work of Rick's unconscious need, to blur the line between his obstinate focusing on 'integrity,' on one hand, and his leadership responsibilities, on the other.

E. Intake Feedback
In general, much of the effect of developmental coaching on coaching outcome (CROI) depends on the client's initial response to feedback. Clients who has an overly strong (arrogant) self concept and a high tendency to be confrontational, combined with low cognitive flexibility, may not enjoy any but highly positive (collusive) feedback. On the side of the coach, feedback that is given other than in line with the client's ascertained developmental level can easily misfire. It is essential in feedback, to be able to think systemically about links between developmental and behavioral scores, on one hand, and between outcomes for self conduct, task focus, and interpersonal perspective, on the other.

Rick received feedback after the coach had integrated the two developmental assessments with NPA findings. (The data set that feedback was given on actually was thus much larger than the variables here discussed.) By that time, the coach was reasonably familiar with the client's data and, through two in-depth interviews, with the client himself. Rick was astonished to hear many of the behavioral findings (deriving from the NPA), but more highly interested in the developmental ones. He confirmed based on his experience that the *internal tensions* he had been talking about seemed to relate directly to the relative proportion to which he was acting from one of the three levels within his developmental range.

Rick had the greatest difficulties with the behavioral *need for power* score, enough to become defensive. Initially, he flatly denied that he was interested in power. We discussed how power manifests in his domain of work, and how it might be perceived by others. Rick was adamant that some of the 'guys in the team' don't measure up to his own level of integrity. Astonishingly enough at S-4(5), he was unable to take responsibility for some of his own failings.

Regarding other findings, however, he was more open-minded. As to the need for power score, he gradually came around to seeing it more objectively as coaching continued. This shows that an objective score in and by itself, once 'put out there' as a challenge to the client, can induce helpful change processes. (For an S-3 coach, formulating such challenges would not be easy since it requires standing up to one's own values, here embodied by assessment outcomes.)

F. Coaching Strategy

In thinking over Rick's profile, I put in place the following (unfolding) strategy:

- Start from what is foremost on Rick's mind (e.g., the dynamics he seemed to create in the executive team).
- Minimize interpretations that Rick might want to 'shoot down' (given his defensiveness).
- Remain mainly an observer of what Rick is able to focus on, noting any defensiveness.
- (With his permission) talk to his reports, to see how they perceive Rick's blurring of ego needs with leadership responsibilities, and report the findings to him without identifying specific individuals.
- Role-play one or more upcoming team meetings, with him in the role of his most pronounced adversary, and with me playing Rick's role.
- Assign to Rick communication tasks that require him to try out more of an S-4/5 stance with a single partner; in this way, he may learn to detach from his habitual rigid separation of his own and other's integrity.
- Increasingly, engage Rick in becoming more reflective about his use of power – so far taken for granted by him.
- Overall, reduce the developmental Risk score and boost his Potential score in his RCP.

G. Expectable CROI

As the reader knows, coaching outcomes are not truly predictable. However, they can be measured, using the assessments taught in this book. In this particular case, no such post-test was done. What, then, could one reasonably expect would transpire during a one-year coaching process?

Here are some suggestions for calibrating CROI (which could be more ample if we were dealing with a complete data set):

- Presently stuck in a 'frozen' S-4(5) position, Rick's self assuredness is mainly based on his strong cognitive profile, mostly used defensively rather than for promoting a process of becoming unstuck.

- Cognitive coaching, focused on the thought forms he is presently <u>not</u> using, could contribute to giving his developmental potential more of a chance to take effect (see volume 2).

- Once Rick feels less strongly inclined to regress to S-4, he might actually make a developmental shift, but whether this would happen over a single year is not predictable.

- The best developmental outcome in his case would be a reduction of the developmental Risk score, linked to a boosting of the developmental Potential score; most likely, this would not result in a developmental shift (to S-4/5), but it could certainly prepare for such a shift.

- Regardless of such a shift, considerable behavioral changes, especially regarding work mechanics, due delegation, and misplaced appraisals (of people and projects) could be achieved. Such positive changes might contribute to Rick's feeling more secure in his developmental position, with less of a need to show that he is in charge (S-4).

- However, in the absence of a true developmental shift, behavioral changes generated in coaching may remain *cosmetic*, at least for a while.

CASE STUDY #2
Bob
4(3) {3:4:7}; alternatively = 4 {7:6:1}

<u>Profile and Presenting Problem:</u> Bob is a Director of HR and known as a successful developer of organizational training programs. He is presently part of a large software services firm, directing a project introducing new kinds of assessment products worldwide. While highly regarded by his colleagues and superiors, Bob reports to be 'wearing himself out,' in the sense of having to overcome what he calls 'numerous internal obstacles.' Bob has asked for a coach in order to better understand his fear of failure and tendency to circumvent potentially negative outcomes, and so as to feel more at ease in his creative endeavors. He doesn't think he will be able to continue coping with as much stress as he is presently experiencing.

<u>Task Focus</u>

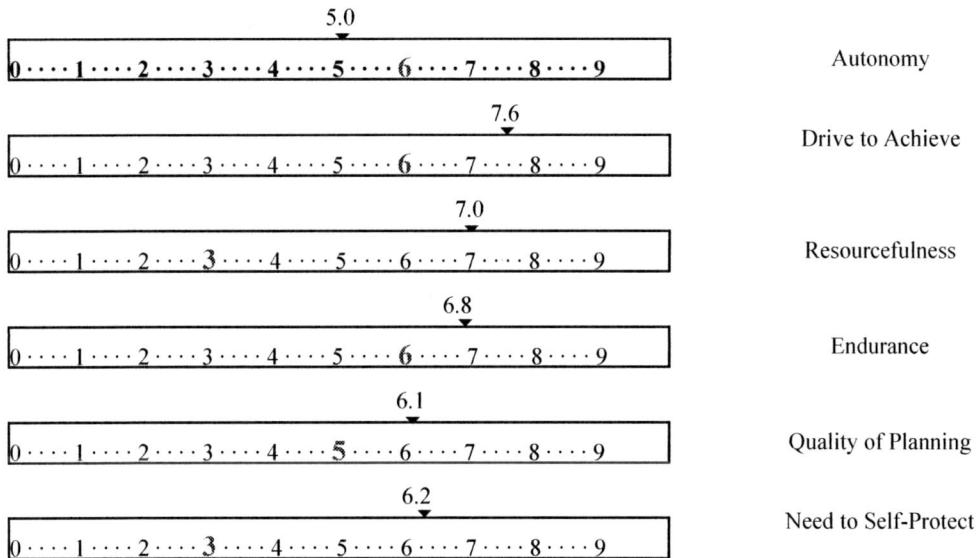

Fig. B.4 Bob's Task Focus scores

NeedPress Profile		Behavioral Description of Client
Task Focus		
Autonomy: *Degree of self reliance, resistance to influence, ability to defy authority and be unconventional*	6	Optimal combination of creative independence and accountability; no need to "crash" existing conventions; largely self-governing, self-reliant; willingness to experiment; openness to input from others.
Drive to achieve: *Ability to strive to do something difficult as well as quickly as possible; exercise authority*	6	Self-motivated approach; enjoys exploration, moving toward desirable outcomes; very goal oriented.
Resourcefulness: *Strength of motivation to overcome obstacles, ability to accept failure as a learning experience*	3	Weak performance under stress; does not marshal resources well; likely to circumvent negative outcomes; potentially overwhelmed by fear of failure.
Endurance:	6	Appropriate need for closure; good self-regulation; can be relied

Ability to invest continuous effort, complete a job under-taken despite obstacles		upon; able to set realistic goal; optimally motivated, sustained attention to tasks.
Quality of planning: *Degree of reliance on planning, scheduling, guidelines, need for "ground rules"*	5	Optimal utilization and even-handedness in carrying out activities; well organized; realistic; harnesses ideas well; precise.
Need to self protect: *Need to protect self by way of rationalization, taking a stand, make a case for oneself, offer excuses*	3	Limited, if not low, need to self-protect and defend own conduct; candid, open; "ego strength;" ability to maintain distance between self and work.

Table B.3 Bob's behavioral findings

We can summarize the above NPA data compactly as follows (variables in *italic bold* indicate coaching problems):

A. Client strengths
- Optimal combination of creative independence and accountability.
- No need to 'crash' existing conventions.
- Largely self-governing, self-reliant.
- Optimally motivated, with willingness to experiment.
- Openness to input from others.
- Self-motivated approach.
- Very goal oriented.
- Appropriate need for closure.
- Able to set realistic goals.
- Sustained attention to tasks.
- Optimal utilization and even-handedness in carrying out activities; well organized.
- Harnesses ideas well, is precise.
- Limited, if not low, needs to self-protect and defend own conduct (candidness).
- Ability to maintain distance between self and work.

B. Client challenges
- Weak performance under stress.
- Does not marshal resources well.
- Likely to circumvent negative outcomes.
- Potentially overwhelmed by fear of failure.

C. Summary of client's behavioral profile (coaching issues #1)
Reading the long list of this client's strengths, one might wonder why he would seek coaching. As an assessor, one might be tempted to play down any developmental risk or fragility. When one focuses on Bob's 'approach to tasks' alone — and thus disregards the other two sets of NPA variables here omitted, namely —— this first reaction is understandable. However, this evaluation holds water only from a strictly and narrowly

behavioral perspective which, as we know, is just what developmental coaching is meant to be a deepening and amplification of.

D. Developmentally focused summary (coaching issues #2)
4(3) {3:4:7}; alternatively = 4 {7: 6 :1}

Bob is presently at an *espousal* stage where the yearning to be self-authoring pervades all of his thoughts and actions. This holds true even more strongly since he manifestly possesses a strong potential for acting from an authentically self-authoring perspective. As a closer inspection of his re-written score shows, however, viewed from an S-4 perspective Bob's risk to resolve conflicts by espousal rather than actual self-authoring is exceedingly high (R=7). While his Center of Gravity is actually stronger at S-4 than S-4(3) [6>4], the higher center is clearly compromised by his high risk of regression to S-4(3). In short, Bob is presently in a stressful developmental position where he is not totally secure or 'himself' either in S-4(3) or S-4. While this position has nothing directly to do with his behavioral strengths and challenges, it certainly colors the way in which he demonstrates them to others. In particular, the developmental facts have a pervasive influence on his approach to tasks, where, as we have seen, his resourcefulness (in the broad sense outlined under 'challenges') leaves much to be desired.

For one thing, Bob's weak performance under stress and his tendency to circumvent negative outcomes – that is, disengage from projects feared by him to be unsuccessful — is clearly exacerbated by his developmental deficit in taking full responsibility for his actions (S-4(3)). Even where he is not actually overwhelmed by fears of failure, stressful situations easily lead to failures for him, due to a decisive lack of strong 'counter-action' on his part to avoid them. The stress in such situations is not primarily an external one. Rather, the stress that 'wears Bob out' is largely internally generated, and thus painful and counter-productive for him. It is not a 'character weakness,' but rather the outcome of his present developmental position.

E. Intake Feedback
In the feedback session, Bob was highly interested in how close he seemed to have come to a fully self-authoring position. He had felt for some time that he was nearing a peak of creativity in his life, and was confident of being on the brink of great achievements. He did not realize that the praises by others he was relying on actually only detracted from an S-4 stance since his reaction to them demonstrated his other-dependence (S-4(3) or lower).

Since the self conduct and interpersonal perspective scores emerging from the NPA were more problematic than the task approach scores here under discussion, Bob did not engage with the finding on lack of *resourcefulness* (counter-action) very deeply. He had other things to worry about. On the whole, he did not engage with many of the behavioral challenges brought up by feedback at all, but was more interested in the cognitive scores (here not discussed).
As a coach, this showed me that any emphasis on problematic behavioral scores would have to be postponed, until the client himself would express a need to engage with them more deeply. Consequently, the feedback session primarily centered on the topic of how Bob might best exercise his full creativity and autonomy without too high a

psychological cost to him (which he felt was presently exorbitant). I concluded the feedback session with much compassion regarding how uncomfortable it is to be under the influence of developmental scores such as stated above. The main goal that formed in my mind during feedback was to reduce the client's distress without myself falling into a facile espousal of his existing potential.

F. Coaching Strategy

In thinking over Bob's profile, I put in place the following (progressively unfolding) strategy:

- Focus client's attention on situations described as 'overwhelming' in terms of complexity or detail, to find out what precisely makes them over-whelming.
- Strengthen client's ability to delegate in order to strengthen self-authoring.
- Scrutinize company culture as a contributor to client's self doubt ("I can't possibly be that good!").
- Boost client's ability to declare 'breakdown' (of reports' motivation and resourcefulness) if situation and environment warrant that.
- Explore metaphors used by the client to describe 'complexity.'
- Explore thought forms used by the client to describe company culture and his relationship to it.
- Explore the high standards the client sets for himself regarding traces of espousal needed to keep internalized others at bay.
- Explore self-doubts linked to failures of harnessing own and others' resources effectively ("do I deliver the values I should provide?").
- Lead the client to articulate his notion of self-authoring more clearly, and role model situations in which he feels he is not measuring up.
- Assign to the client self observation tasks during meetings and presentations etc. as a potent source of self insight.
- Reinforce client's self confidence by appreciative inquiry, keeping developmental scores in mind.
- Strengthen client's attention to self-care as a way of reducing stress.
- Let client form new relationships as a manifestation of growth in self-authoring.

G. Expectable CROI

- Given the client's dilemma of being situated between stages S-4/3 and S-4(3) associated with major risk of regression, the realistically expectable outcome lies in diminishing the risk of regression to S-4/3 on one hand, and the boosting of the ability to act from S-4, on the other.
- Since major cognitive resources of the client are presently invested in being defensive about espousals vs. authentically upheld values, CROI will, in addition, depend on whether the coach can enhance the flexibility of the client's thinking about the context and the relationships he is embedded in.
- In terms of the client's approach to tasks, the self-generated internal stress is best reduced by demonstrating, and thereby reducing, the client's tendency to be blind to his own espousals (thoughts not matched by actions).

- Whether the highest client benefit will result in reducing developmental risk (S-4/3) or boosting developmental potential to act from S-4 [free of risks of regression] is hard to predict. However, at this juncture, focusing on potential seems premature.

CASE STUDY #3
Sarah
4 {9:7:4}; alternatively = 4(3) {3:6:11}

Profile and Presenting Problem: Sarah is a business coach with a thriving practice in which she focuses on higher-level executives of the banking industry. She has a strong background in Organizational Development as well as strong spiritual interests. Sarah asked to be mentored in order to become more effective with two particularly 'difficult' clients. One of them had conveyed to her that he felt she was, at times, 'pretty opinionated,' while Sarah perceived herself only as having strong personal convictions. The second client commented about her to peers that because of her idiosyncratic interpretations of what he brought to sessions he often did not feel 'understood' by her. Since Sarah had high opinions of her coaching expertise, and high standards of professional excellence, she was scandalized and shaken by her clients' reactions. She wondered whether there was something about herself that she did not entirely understand, some bottlenecks that it would be important for her to find out about.

Interpersonal Perspective

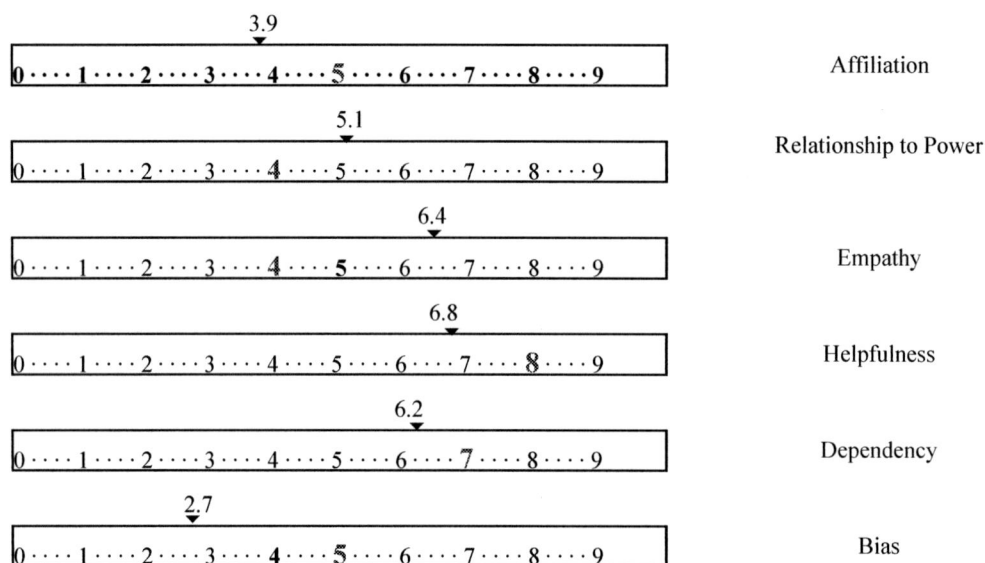

Fig. B.5 Sarah's Interpersonal Perspective scores

NeedPress Profile		Behavioral Description of Client
Interpersonal Perspective		
Affiliation: *Degree of cooperation and identification with others in the organization, ability to cooperate*	5	Generally cooperative; deals effectively with others; unlikely to alienate; realistic advocate of others.
Relation to power: *Ability to follow those in authority, accept others' suggestions, approach to conflict resolution*	4	Mature, respectful manner toward authority; unlikely to manifest hostile or subservient view; even-handed.
Empathy: *Ability to analyze one's own and others' motives and feelings; empathy, understanding of others' motivation and need*	4	Limited ability to empathize or distinguish own motivations from those of others; cloudy regarding impact on others.
Helpfulness: *Inclination and ability to extend oneself toward others, provide support, be generous and sharing*	8	Willingness to extend self; considerate; even-handed perception of others' problems; optimistic; generous.
Dependency: *Degree of reliance on others, also: willingness to identify with organization*	7	Relying on own resources; no undue leaning on others or need for help, reinforcement, or consolation; self-contained, inner-directed, self-governing.
Bias: *Degree of interpersonal aloofness and indifference; discriminatory stance toward others, and suspicion of their motives*	5	Somewhat distant and aloof; introvert; undemonstrative, reserved; likely to question others' motives.

Table B.4 Sarah's behavioral findings

A. Client strengths
- Generally cooperative, unlikely to alienate.
- Deals effectively with others.
- Realistic advocate of others.
- Neither hostile nor subservient toward others.
- Can respect authority.
- Willingness to extend self, considerate.
- Even-handed perception of others' problems, optimistic, generous.
- Optimistic regarding other's potential.
- Willing to extend self.
- Inner-directed and self-governing.
- No undue leaning on others.

B. Client challenges
- Limited ability to distinguish own motivations from those of others.
- Cloudy regarding own motivations and their impact on others.
- Limited ability to empathize with others.
- Somewhat distant and aloof, undemonstrative.
- Likely to question other's motive.

C. Summary of client's behavioral profile (coaching issues #1)

Looking at the parade of Sarah's behavioral strengths, above, her bewilderment about clients' critical reactions does not surprise a developmental expert. Any S-3 coach would swoon having such abilities confirmed, and rightfully so. Disregarding scores of self conduct and task approach (here omitted), Sarah does indeed seem to have a superb 'coaching personality.' However, her 'empathy' and 'bias' scores catch one's attention. They show that, in addition to adult-developmental issues (see below), there is also behavioral conflict.

In fact, the two deficient emotional intelligence scores pinpointed by NPA could easily reinforce each other. Where cloudiness regarding one's own motivation mixes with aloofness, bewilderment about oneself and others can easily build a home. The behavioral hypothesis is that this is what happens with and to Sarah. She therefore cannot 'fathom' some of her clients' reactions. How can one be optimistic about others' potential as well as nevertheless have limited ability to empathize with others, or at least be undemonstrative about it? No problem! Characters are not necessarily simple defense systems, and when they re-locate to a specific developmental position, many cherished assumptions about oneself and others may suddenly fall by the wayside!

D. Developmentally focused summary (coaching issues #2)

4 {9:7:4}; in terms of S-4 = 4(3) {3:6:11}

As often happens in developmental coaching, Sarah's developmental profile at the same time makes her situation more complex and her behavioral issues more understandable. Computing her RCP in two different ways, as shown above, here pays off. The sum of RCP elements [=20] gives one pause. The reason for 20 fragments to have been scored – incompetent scoring aside – must be that Sarah is developmentally 'highly distributed,' as shown below (which makes each of the scored positions more highly ambiguous):

	S ?	S ?	
4/3	4(3)	4	4(5)
3	6	7	4

Table B.5 Sarah's RCP

As we see right away, Sarah is presently almost equally 'at home' in S-4(3) and S-4, and consequently must be thoroughly confused by her own espousals. In addition to being 'jammed in' between two neighboring stages of almost equal strength, she has also not yet broken away from important internalized others that contribute to her cloudiness about herself, especially her motivations and impact on others (S-4/3=3). A third, easily misleading developmental fact is that she is not only quite embedded in S-4, but is also, it seems, beginning to distance herself from her own self-authoring (S-4(5)=4). (If a scoring error occurred regarding her profile at all, it must have been that the scorer mistook her espousals (of S-5) at S-4(5) — most likely 'spiritual claims' — for the real thing.).

In any case, Sarah is presently in a developmental pickle, which exacerbates her behavioral issues and conflicts. It is not really that Sarah is 'unpredictable.' That would almost be easier to deal with for others. Behavioral conflicts within a person's interpersonal perspective (as listed under strengths and challenges, above) do not so much make a person unpredictable than *predictably confused* about herself. If, in addition, the developmental profile contributes further causes of confusion, it can be really hard to be who one is at a particular developmental milestone. As is easily understandable, the mix of holding on to internalized others (S-4/3=3) with incipient steps beyond self-authoring (S-4(5)=4) can be totally confusing! Add to that the near-equal strength of two Centers of Gravity in Sarah's profile, and you have a pretty good snapshot of her present predicament.

E. Intake Feedback
Giving feedback to Sarah, especially since she was untutored developmentally, was not easy. A beginner in developmental coaching could easily have gone astray. To point out to her that her bewilderment has strictly behavioral causes (in her personality) could only make her defensive. Besides, it would be too much oriented to the past, 'character' and 'personality' being rooted in the pre-adult burdens a person carries into adult life. Particularly in this case, where Sarah came for mentoring, not coaching, a highly positive, forward-looking way to give feedback would have to be found. The second ingredient of such feedback would have to be *compassion* backed up by developmental explanation. One might say that coaching only from 'personality,' not 'Persona' (based on a conceptual framework yielding evidence) in this case could be ruinous. No S-3, and not even an S-4, mentor would be up to the task.

Under these circumstances, explanations of developmental dynamics, although necessarily somewhat abstract, can be very helpful. After all, conflict is the lifeblood of the developmental journey! Conflict is what propels one forward, given adequate cognitive resources. More generally, developmental language provides a somewhat 'objective' *vocabulary* that improves one's chances of giving effective feedback without lapsing into spiritual espousals.

For this reason, I began explaining to Sarah the equal potency of her two neighboring Centers of Gravity (S-4(3) and S-4), and then focused on the 'enormous' stretch between her attachment to internalized others (S-4/3), on one hand, and her attachment to spiritual goals and ideals (S-4(5)), on the other. I in no way questioned the authenticity of her spiritual experiences, but cautioned that she should not mistake them for existing developmental strengths, at least not presently. (I do indeed hold the view that spiritual leanings out of sync with developmental level can be pernicious for the self insight of the person concerned.)

Sarah's reaction was initially mixed. She found the developmental findings hard to fathom. Understandably, she wanted to know what to DO. (I told her that we were talking about BEING, not Doing, which she understood from a spiritual perspective.) She had no problem understanding the behavioral conflicts of her profile, having felt all along that her life seemed to be somewhat conflictual 'by nature.' What she felt was most difficult was how protracted her struggle to understand herself had been. She had my full compassion.

F. Mentoring Strategy
In thinking over Sarah's profile, I put in place the following (progressively unfolding) strategy:

- Take a step back from the behavioral 'foreground' of her issues with clients, in order to get at developmental causes and exacerbations
- Listen in depth to her spiritual interests and convictions, searching for espousals she might use to 'cover up' her unresolved issues by collusion with highly developed clients.
- Focus on her uneasy relationship between professional helping and being herself, the first predominantly defined according to S-4 (professionally underscored by aloofness), the second defined in terms of her spiritual interests (conveyed by an S-4(5) stance of self-transcendence).
- Demystify spiritual values as potential defenses against mental growth.
- Invent role plays that could make her see how she could work with her two 'difficult' clients in a, for them, less confusing way.
- Explore ways in which she might be 'overdoing,' or rushing to, helping, rather than first making sure she knew where her clients where coming from developmentally (they both sounded to me like solid S-4's) — in short, unburden her from too much interpretation and enactment, and strengthen the neutral focusing of attention in herself and (indirectly) her clients.
- In step with her own understanding of her adult-developmental issues, work toward her becoming open to recommending developmental assessments to both of her 'difficult' clients (this would facilitate her insight into how to compare herself developmentally to her clients).
- Re-assure her that I was open to giving developmental feedback to her clients together with herself (so that she wouldn't lose face).
- Assure her that I would continue to mentor her independently of her clients after feedback, — in short, use the interdevelopmental power of assessment-based coaching for alleviating her present inner conflicts as well as those with particular clients.

G. Expectable CROI

Although the case here discussed is one of *mentoring*, not coaching, some notions of CROI nevertheless make good sense:

- As an MCC, Sarah can expect from developmental mentoring a fuller understanding of her coaching dynamic with clients, to the extent that she is willing and able to understand the developmental causes of her often self-defeating impact on others.
- She can thus become 'a better coach' to the extent that she pauses to consider that her personality, skills, and expertises cannot guarantee making a positive impact, but that she needs to take her present developmental position into account when relating to clients.
- To the extent that she can embrace a consistent theoretical framework such as CDF, she can learn to act from a *Persona*, and leave her personality behind. This 'personality' — presently spread out between S-4/3 and S-4(5)) — has long held her back as it is.
- Once she can move out of her developmental predicament — between two equally powerful developmental stages and her spiritual overstretching that leads to developmental self-delusion — she will not only increase the benefits of her

work for clients, but will feel more ready to move on developmentally herself, experiencing less conflict than is presently the case.

Appendix C
Developmental Issues of Team Dynamics

So far in this book, I have focused on the developmental profile of individuals. The reader will have wondered whether any new information and insight emerges once we consider an entire team in terms of developmental stage scores and associated RCPs. This step implies an 'aggregation' of individual data, for the purpose of studying team and group dynamics.
In this chapter, I will briefly explore this important issue.

I first outline a TEAM TYPOLOGY based on members' Center of Gravity, and then use the information the typology yields to discuss developmental team dynamics. Going one step further, in section D, I proceed to applying the methods taught in this book to larger groups.

Throughout this book, we have actually assembled a team of individuals. When we introduced Rick in Appendix B, we heard of the executive team he was part of that often was unhappy about his impact on the team's behavior and its effectiveness overall. It might be of interest for the reader to see how the individuals we have discussed in this book would work together as a *team*.

Let's pretend, for argument's sake, that the individuals who figure in our demonstrations together make up Rick's executive team. I am thinking of the following individuals:
1. Rick: S-4(5) {3:7:3}
2. Bob: S-4(3) {3:4:7}; re-writable as 4 {7: 6:1}
3. Sarah: S-4 {9:7:4}; re-writable as 4(3) {3:6:11}
4. Katherine S-4/3 {3:5:5}
5. Sam (CEO) S-4/3 {2:5:6}

To the four individuals previously discussed, let's add a CEO called Sam, with a score of S-4/3 {2:5:6}. This addition will complete our executive team. Essentially, we are looking at a team partitioned into two individuals at S-4/3, two at S-4(3), and one at S-4(5). The question this section of the Appendix is focused on is: **What can we say about the dynamics of the above team in terms of social-emotional scores <u>alone</u>?**

Having read Appendix B, the reader will appreciate that answers to this question would be more ample if we included behavioral, if not also cognitive, data. However, a first attempt at answering the above question can be made without such data. This is so since strictly behavioral data describe only *symptoms*, and therefore do not speak for themselves. One and the same piece of data can have multiple developmental meanings, depending on the ED/CD relationship embedded in it! While cognitive data may be crucial, it determines how the social-emotional profile of a person shows up in the real world, rather than directly influencing the score itself.

The notion of a Developmental Team Typology is quite simple. Speaking with E. Schein (1999, 149), it basically has to do with the issue of how *interpersonal process* in a team relates to *task process*. As we have shown throughout the book, each developmental position gives rise to its own peculiar 'psychology,' complete with desires, needs, degrees of accountability, self concept, and so forth. Therefore, it clearly matters what is the total developmental range of the team we are dealing with.

As a generic prediction one can say that whenever we deal with a team whose Center of Gravity is below S-4, interpersonal process will dominate task processes, to the detriment of the latter. This is so since internalized others get in the way too strongly to permit the task process to remain in focus. In our case, the team is living largely below S-4, being stretched out between S-3/4 (Katherine, Sam) and S-4/5 (Rick), thus over six intermediate steps. Such a distribution is not at all unusual and tells its own story to anyone who thinks developmentally.

The typology about to be introduced distinguishes teams in terms of what I initially called *main stages,* such as S-2 or S-3. A second characteristic regards the issue where the majority of team members presently reside relative to main stages. This is shown in Fig. C.1, below:

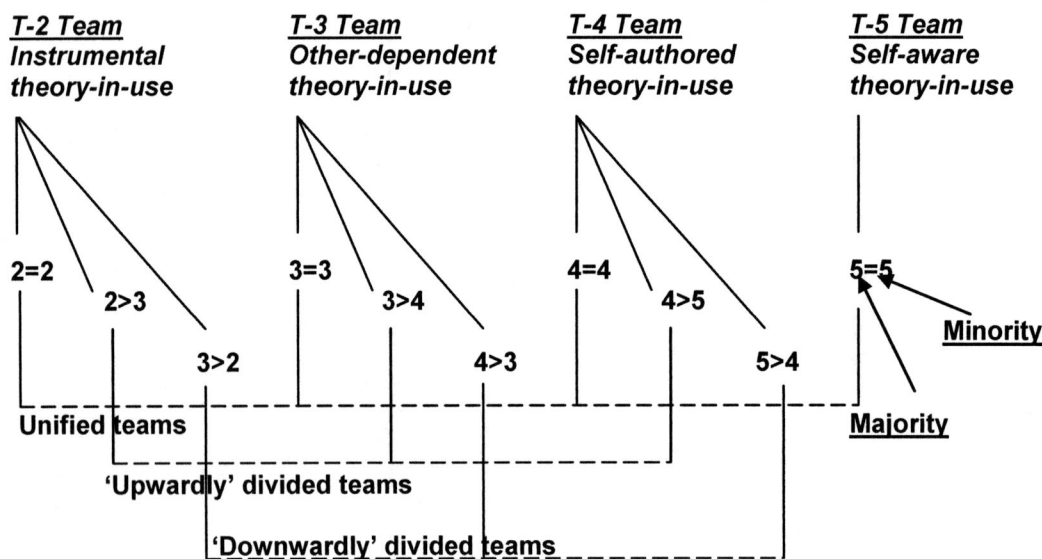

Fig. C.1 Developmental Team Typology

Overall, the Typology distinguishes three kinds of teams:

- **Unified teams** (T-2=2; T-3=3; T-4=4; T-5=5)
- **'Upwardly divided' teams'** (T-2>3; T-3>4; T-4>5)
- **'Downwardly divided' teams'** (T-3>2; T-4>3; T-5>4).

Here, the first integer refers to the **majority**, the second to the minority, of team members. I notate and label unified teams by '=', downwardly divided teams by indicating that the lower stage is dominating the higher one ('2 over 3,' or T-2>3), and upwardly divided teams accordingly (T-3>2).

Unified teams are those rare teams without either a majority or minority. In such teams, all members fall into a very close range, around a single stage. More frequent are divided teams comprising a clear majority and minority.

An *upwardly divided* team (e.g., T-2>3) comprises a majority of team members at <u>lower</u> levels, and a minority at higher levels. In such a case, the team is 'bottom' rather than 'top' heavy. For instance, if in a team of seven members a majority of five members reside at levels lower than the minority of two, the team is said to be 'upwardly divided,' toward the majority. In such a team, the majority of members reside closer to S-2 than S-3.

The opposite holds regarding *downwardly* divided teams (e.g., T-3>2), where the majority of a seven-member team resides closer to the <u>higher</u> level (S-3) than the lower one (S-2). Clearly, such a team is 'top heavy' in favor of S-3.

Let us investigate now how the team we formed above figures in the context of our Typology.

Team Member	Developmental Level	RCP	Spread
Sam (CEO)	4/3	{2:5:6}	3/4 to 4(3)
Katherine*	4/3	{3:5:5}	3/4 to 4(5)
Bob**	4(3)	{3:4:7}	4/3 to 4(5)
Sarah***	4	{9:7:4}	3/4 to 4(5)
Rick	4(5)	{3:7:3}	4 to 4/5
Mean	*4(3)*	*{3:5:5}*	*4 levels*

* distributed over 5 levels [S-3/4 to S-4(5), with very weak highest levels =1 @ S-4 and S-4(5)]
** distributed over 4 levels [S-4/3 to S-4(5) with a very weak highest level =1 @ S-4(5)]
*** distributed over 5 levels [S-3/4 to S-4(5) with very weak highest level =1 @ S-4(5)]

Table C.1 Developmental profile of an executive team

To judge from team members' developmental levels, this team is an **upwardly divided T-3 team,** with the majority of members in the range between S-3 and S-4. (We would have to call it a *downwardly divided T-4 team* if the majority of its members were 'living at' S-4 and beyond, which here is not the case.) **Various shades of closeness to level S-4 with some fragile extensions into the S-4 to S-5 range characterize the team.** The majority of team members reside between S-3/4 at the lower, and S-4(5) at the higher, end of the team's range. Only a single team member (Rick) reaches S-4/5, the *team ceiling*.

Before entering into the dynamics of our team, let's look a little more closely at the table below which briefly states *predictions* for each type of team the developmental typology distinguishes.

Type of Team	Description
T-2=2	<u>Unified T-2 team</u>: Group united by opportunistic strategy, but barely a group since members' instrumental objectives hinder consensual action. Fragility of group due to lack of truly common goal. No real task process. No leadership.
T-2>3	<u>Upwardly divided T-2 team</u>: Most team members reside at S-2, a minority closer to S-3. The majority's instrumental theory in use outweighs minority strivings toward consensual action. Common goals are espoused that are not truly shared. Argyris's Model-I self-sealing processes are the rule. Dominance of interpersonal over task process. Inconsistent and temporary leadership.
T-3>2	<u>Downwardly divided T-3 team</u>: Most team members reside at S-3, a minority closer

	to S-2. The majority's shared context and consensus is weakened or openly opposed by the minority's special interests. Majority consensus postures as 'leadership.' Task process is chaotic, overrun by interpersonal process.
T-3=3	Unified T-3 team: Strongly consensual group without leader, unable to transcend itself through principled action. Interpersonal process absorbs task process. Leadership, if existent, is limited to carrying out group consensus (with a largely managerial focus).
T-3>4	Upwardly divided T-3 team: Most team members reside at S-3, a minority closer to S-4 (or slightly beyond). Group with leadership potential groping toward a mission beyond itself. Leadership is fragile since exerted by minority member(s) potentially without power and support. Task process is largely determined by interpersonal process.
T-4>3	Downwardly divided T-4 team: Most team members reside at S-4, a minority closer to S-3. Group with hierarchical profile. Those defining guidelines beyond shared context are seen as authorities to follow. Task process is becoming nearly independent of interpersonal process.
T-4=4	Unified T-4 team: Status- and expertise-based group with respectful competition between different ideological systems. Group favoring hierarchical ('top down') solutions, unable to stand back from its own governing variables of action. Resistance to consensual team work, since members prefer to 'go it alone.' Divided or competing task processes.
T-4>5	Upwardly divided T-4 team: Most team members reside at S-4, a minority closer to S-5. Group minority is able to set transformational goals and exert leadership, but the majority is afraid of 'opening flood gates,' thus resists leadership as potentially self-threatening. Leader may use interpersonal process to advance task process, but his or her hold on the group is a fragile one. Need for support of leader, and for dealing with majority (Argyris' Model-I) defenses.
T-5>4	Downwardly divided T-5 team: Most team members reside at S-5, a minority closer to S-4. Group focused on self-transformation by empowering members. Focus on how to strengthen self-transformation without dismantling authority, by scrutinizing own governing variables of action. Interpersonal process absorbed into, and balanced with, task process.
T-5=5	Unified T-5 team: TOO GOOD TO BE TRUE (although ideal). Complete equilibrium of task and interpersonal process, where mutual self-transformation leads to consensual leadership, as in friendship. Performance risk: task process may get subordinated to transpersonal goals.

Table C.2 Developmental Typology of Teams interpreted

Two main contrasts are embedded in the above Typology, that between:
1. (political) power and level of self-awareness
2. task and interpersonal process.

The first contrast is that between actual power in a team, and the balance of that power with the level of members' self-awareness. Clearly, where power strivings or exertions outdo manifestations of self-awareness, important critical and reflective processes get cancelled in favor of brute force action and hyperactivity. The second contrast is that between what gets done (effectiveness) and how it gets done (Schein, 1999, 146 f.). As the reader will have noticed, in most teams listed above the two processes are not equilibrated. **Only once S-4(5) is transcended by the majority of a team is there a reasonable chance that they will be balanced.**

Focusing now on the team here composed for the sake of demonstrating the Typology, what can one say about it? The table above only provides a very general characterization of each team:

Upwardly divided T-3 team: Most team members reside at S-3, a minority closer to S-4 (or slightly beyond). *Group with leadership potential groping toward a mission beyond itself. Leadership is fragile since exerted by minority member(s) potentially without power and support. Task process is largely determined by interpersonal process.*

Another characterization of the team stems from Rick, the CFO we discussed in Appendix B, of whom I reported:

(Rick) has a strong and fruitful relationship with the CEO but is often at loggerheads with the rest of the executive team. He has been accused by his peers of being 'too close' to the CEO in terms of secret schemes the two are often pursuing without knowledge of the rest of the team. Because of this, Rick has decided to work on the dynamics he seems to set up in the team, and on ways to smooth feathers.

When we consider the dynamic of Rick's upwardly divided T-3 team, we begin to understand his issues, as well as his close association with Sam, the CEO. Here is what seems to be happening.

Behavioral issues aside, Rick is clearly the highest developed member of the team (S-4(5)). While Katherine, Bob, and Sarah also reach up to his level of self awareness, it is not their Center of Gravity, only the fragile ceiling of their present developmental profile. Therefore, while they may be able vaguely to 'intuit' him, it is impossible for them, spiritual leanings aside, to have a core understanding of his attempt to step outside his own ideological system (toward S-4/5).
In this situation, Rick may feel that support by a politically powerful team member, like the CEO, is helpful not only to him but the team as a whole. Although Sam is 'stretched down' all the way to S-3/4, in his best moments and supported by Rick, he reaches an espoused self-authoring stance (S-4(3)) which, combined with his power as CEO, can sway decisions in the direction Rick judges best to follow. Aside from their personal relationship, Sam and Rick therefore often form a club *for structural developmental reasons*, and are understandably suspected by the rest of the team to be secretive and to follow dubious schemes. (It is hard to say to what extent the secrecy observed by team members derives from their lack of grasp of higher developmental levels, and to what extent it is also rooted in Rick's and Sam's behavior.)

In light of this analysis, what are we to think of the general characterization of the team stated in the Table?

Upwardly divided T-3 team: Most team members reside at S-3, a minority closer to S-4 (or slightly beyond). Group with leadership potential groping toward a mission beyond itself. Leadership is fragile since exerted by minority member(s) potentially without power and support. Task process is largely determined by interpersonal process.

In the team, the absence of a clearly articulated S-4 position is glaring. What is a team to do in which four members (Rick, Sarah, Bob, Katherine) have leadership potential, and the official leader (Sam) cannot manifest independently as a leader? Since S-4 principled action is not the pervasive dynamic of the team, the interpersonal process between team members is always ready to absorb the task process where the real work gets done. In its groping toward a mission beyond itself, the team often gets bogged down in petty differences. Leadership is indeed fragile since carried by Rick who is not entirely trusted. A likeness of leadership only emerges when Sam, inspired and supported by Rick, takes action as CEO, putting his clout to use. In cases where Sam and Rick diverge, leadership is almost entirely suspended, except if consensus on the side of Bob, Katherine, and Sarah strengthens Rick (or Sam) in his pursuits. When Sam and Rick join hands, they are alienating the remainder of the team, and the heaviest blows come down on Rick (who therefore 'wears himself out.') **All of this is developmentally evident** without ever having looked at behavioral data as to 'personality' or 360 feedback!

Considering that Bob is 'wearing himself out' on the job, and that Katherine does not always 'find the courage' to be fully herself, Sarah could be tempted to posture as a substitute leader, self-assured and spiritually inspired as she is. Since she is often perceived as opinionated and has a limited understanding of herself and her impact on others, her leadership might, however, be less effective than Sam's who — while full of S-4 espousals — at least lacks her pretension.

The relationship between Rick and Sarah is another matter. Rick actually has the developmental foundations for spiritual understandings that Sarah lacks. However, given his role of CFO, he may not have sufficient experience with spiritual practice, to be acknowledged by her and others as spiritually motivated. Under these circumstances it is promising to hear from Rick (presenting problem) that he has decided to work on the dynamics he seems to set up in the team, and on ways to smooth feathers. Clearly, coaching Rick could have a fruitful influence on the team as a whole, although it would not close the power vacuum that now exists for him, nor would it bring the team closer to principled action. If Rick, Katherine, and Sarah were all coached, they might actually begin to understand each other more deeply, strengthening their S-4(5) position now so unevenly shared.

Team Coaching

How does one coach a developmentally diverse team such as the above, and how, in particular, an 'upwardly divided T-3 team'? From the vantage point of this book, it seems unthinkable to do so without developmental assessments based on which feedback can be given to team members regarding the developmental constellation the team is presently in. If such feedback is not forthcoming, the complexity of the team's dynamic is likely to get lost because will be entirely subsumed under the aspect of the different 'personalities' and their behaviors or 'preferences.' *However, behaviors and preferences ultimately explain nothing, since they are only symptoms, and themselves in need of explanation.* Also, personalities per se are not the issue. **These personalities are largely the manifestation of the developmental levels they presently embody!**

In the present case, where the least and most highly developed two team members (Sam and Rick) share a secret bond, that of power, it might be useful to split up the team into the dyad of Sam and Rick, on one hand, and the triad of Bob, Katherine, and Sarah, on the other. Occasionally, the full team could be coached together, once a better understanding of dyad and triad has been achieved. The reasoning behind this strategy would be that each of the two groupings comprises a highest level (Rick's S-4/5 and Sarah's S-4(5)) that could serve as the beacon toward which to draw the other members.

The disadvantage of the strategy would be that it may reinforce the lack of trust toward Rick that presently pervades the team.

On account of this, an alternative strategy would be to split the team up into two groups comprising Rick, Bob, and Katherine, on one hand, and Sam and Sarah, on the other. In this configuration, Sam and Sarah both share S-3/4 as their lowest level, with Sarah otherwise far ahead of Sam developmentally. Consequently, they both have an equally strong experience of powerful internalized others (S-3/4=2 and =3, respectively) from which coaching could attempt to pull them.

As to the second group (Rick, Bob, and Katherine), Katherine could be mentored by both Rick and Bob, although in different ways. In return, her spiritual ways, however tentatively expressed, might help the two men to strengthen their acceptance of each other, as well as the inkling of *something deeper that we could be connected to*. This, in turn, would give Katherine a doorway 'to test that (inkling),' and might provide a graceful way for her 'to bridge a gap that is not really a gap.'

Whichever coaching configuration is chosen, there are developmental risks and opportunities that arise. There is no recipe or best practice that can forestall or promote these, only the self-aware intervention of a coach with a cognitive profile commensurate with (minimally) S-4/5.

Appendix D
An Inkling of Capability Management

<u>Why Manage Capability?</u>
It is astounding that in a society in which most people define themselves by what they DO, or their work, there exists no comprehensive *theory of work*, even less a developmentally grounded one. As E. Jaques rightfully suggested (1994), if such a theory were to be formulated, one would have to distinguish what a person HAS — her competencies — from what a person IS — her capability. As Jaques saw it, this difference between what somebody 'has' and 'is' is of great relevance for the discipline of process consultation. I share his view. While one can suspend what one *has,* one can never suspend what one *is.* One is who one presently is.

As this volume has shown, much of what is considered 'behavior' in our culture is really a consequence of the developmental resources available to an individual at a particular time point. This also holds true for *work behavior,* or performance. In the Constructive Developmental Framework presented in this book, I address these resources summarily as **Capability**, to distinguish them from the various competencies a person might be credited with. Capability refers to what somebody IS, while Competence concerns what somebody HAS. The two are, of course, related, in the sense that the former is the *enabler* of the latter. **Capability grounds competencies. It concerns the use of competencies, and enables a person to use competencies in an optimal way.** As the reader now understands, one and the same competency is used differently at different levels of Capability.

The world of work including "human resources" would be a different world if the distinction between Capability and Competency had been understood. However, this is not the case. Neither industry (including adopters of the Scorecard) nor the military have so far grasped the difference between the enablers of competence (=capability) and competence itself. Nor can one say that the coaching community, whose work is largely behavioral, has grasped this distinction. Why is this an important societal issue?

If you remember Enron, you will probably agree that the people in that company were by no means any less competent than people in other big companies. In fact, executives and employees of Enron rightfully prided themselves on their intellectual smartness and social savvy. Considering what happened to them, the most likely hypothesis is that they were not scoundrels as much as *thoroughly immature developmentally.* This means that they acted from a developmental level at which they did not feel accountable in a way commensurate with their office and political power. Especially in the upper echelons of Enron, executives massively regressed to an S-2 vantage point, at least in decisions affecting corporate culture.

Since social-emotional and cognitive capabilities are so crucial to human achievement, it should astonish nobody that they directly determine what is going on in organizations, including corporate culture. Far beyond exerting their influence on teams, they shape every echelon of a company, and pervasively inform corporate climate.

It is an exciting idea that one might be able to assess the Capability of an entire company and express it in a form that indicates the developmentally rooted *business intelligence* a company embodies. As we have demonstrated in Appendix C, through **aggregation** of developmental data we arrive at valuable new insights into human resources at a level beyond the individual. In this last section of the Appendix, I further illuminate this gift of aggregation.

When we think about the Capability of entire companies, the question arises: can social-emotional and cognitive capabilities be *managed*, and if so, how? To answer this question, some clarifications are in order.

At the present time, both 'competencies' and 'talent' are the topic of management. What, then, could it mean to manage **Capability, a set of enablers of competence**? Such enablers are nothing else but the social-emotional and cognitive resources individuals bring to their work. Therefore, by *Capability Management* I mean the strategic harnessing of organizational human resources that are based on insight into the social-emotional and cognitive structure of the workforce. It is the purpose of Capability Management, to transcend the merely *transactional* activities of HR Departments and strengthen the *transformational* management capacity of organizations in the direction of learning organizations.

These are big words! Many schemes for bringing about learning organizations have been invented. They have all failed since the hidden dimensions of work capability, namely, social-emotional (ED) and cognitive (CD) resources, have been ignored or played down. At the very least, they have never been systematically assessed! As the 7-step model of learning to think developmentally in Chapter 9 implies, it take time to wake up to an understanding of Capability!

The Power of Aggregation
When, as in Appendix C, we reflected upon a particular team as an *upwardly divided T-3 team*, we took a step toward data aggregation. Leaving behind all individual detail, we characterized a number of individuals as a <u>unit</u> functioning at S-3, such that a minority of them stretched into S-4. We can easily enlarge the scope of aggregation to larger numbers of people.

As larger and larger numbers of people are taken into account, there is no need to assess every one. Rather, we can work with *sampling*, selecting a *sample* of the larger group (called a population). In order not to err when interpreting assessment outcomes, we need to begin by defining a **representative sample,** that is, a small group of people that statistically *represents* the larger group adequately. Putting together a representative sample of all line managers of a company, or all internal coaches by selecting the typical cases, would be an example of creating a *pure* sample. *Mixed* samples that comprise individuals having different functions and degrees of responsibility in a company require special deliberations.

What does aggregation tell us about a specific representative sample that investigating individual members of a population would not? It tells us what the group making up the sample has in common, and whether there are patterns showing deviations from a hypothetical Capability standard. For instance, if a representative sample of all internal coaches of a company were forming an upwardly divided T-3 team, considering that the standard for professional coaching is S-4, we would know that these coaches wouldn't be highly effective in coaching executives at levels such as S-4(5) and beyond. Although internal coaches don't typically form, and act as, teams, it might be crucial for the purpose of establishing excellence within an in-house coaching program, to know what the mean developmental level of the company's coaches is. A representative sample of such individuals will tell us whether the company's coaching program indeed has the quality the company thinks or professes that it does.

Competence versus Capability
When you think about the distinction between what people 'have' and 'are,' it is really no different from the one I have repeatedly made between the Horizontal and the Vertical, or between what is 'behavioral' and what is 'developmental.'

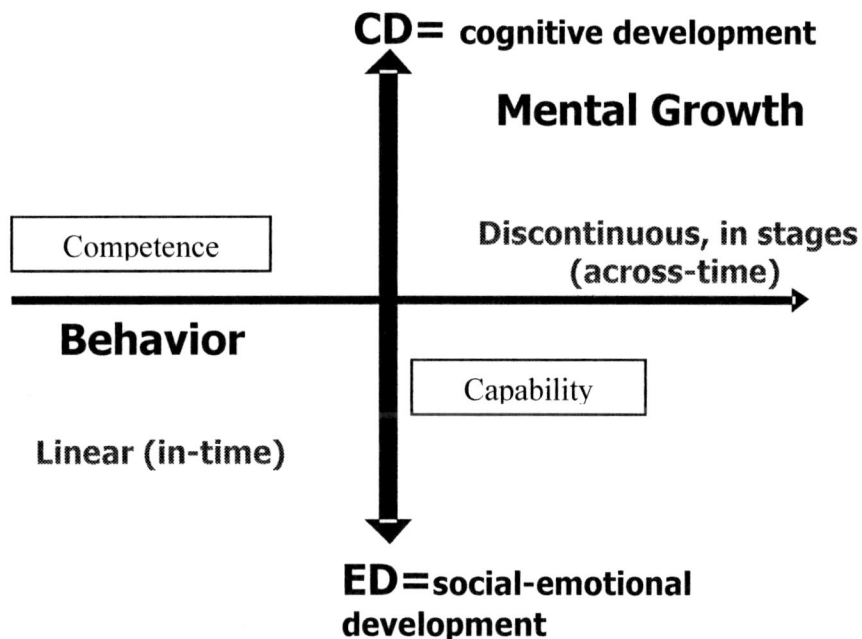

Fig. D.1 The Competence – Capability distinction

Competences are *behavioral* in the sense that they increase incrementally, in time, and thus can perhaps we improved through training. As you now know, Capabilities don't work that way. They are not based on performance skills but on *world views* (developmentally grounded personal attitudes), and they develop discontinuously, over stages. That means that if you have Competence X — such as the competence to coach or manage people — you will use that competence as a function of your Capability (e.g., developmental stage). That's why human capital management is crucially not about competences — they can be assumed — but about their actual USE in real time. And that use *can be predicted* since it has everything to do with Capability! For this reason, measuring

Capability would seem to make a great deal of sense. **Only what can be measured can also be managed.**

The Balance of Capability and Accountability

As E. Jaques was the first to point out in Requisite Organization (1998), the crucial issue for companies, and organizations generally, is the ability to balance people's capabilities — not their competences — with people's readiness to be held accountable for what they do. Of course, accountability varies with work complexity. We can therefore say that each company is defined by **two essential architectures.** As shown below, the first architecture is one of complexity levels of work (complexity architecture), while the second one is composed of different levels of capability (or developmental stages):

Work: Complexity Architecture   People: Capability Architecture

Stratum (Level of Work Complexity)*	Breadth of Time Span*	C D F	Formal Logic Type* [CD]	Fluidity Score [CD]**	Developmental Stage [ED]**
VIII	50 yrs		C4	>70	5(4)
VII	25 yrs		C3	>60	5/4
VI	10-20 yrs		C2	50-59	4/5
V	5-10 yrs		C1	40-49	4(5)
IV	2-5 yrs		B4	30-39	4
III	1-2 yrs		B3	20-29	4/3 to 4(3)
II	3 mo -1 yr		B2	10-19	3(4)-3/4
I	1 day - 3 mo		B1	<9	3(2) to 3

* Elliott Jaques (1998; 1994)
** Otto Laske (1999), elaborating work by R. Kegan (1982, 1994) and M. Basseches (1984 f.)

Table D.1 Two basic organizational architectures

On the left side of the table, you see a calibration of levels of work complexity, associated with time horizons varying between 1 day and 50 years (Jaques, 1998). The levels of work complexity are also called STRATA, and indicate different work demands and accountability levels, from janitor to CEO and Board Member. For work on each of these strata, a different *time horizon* is required. For instance, while a janitor typically does not have to think ahead more than at most a single day, a CEO at stratum VII ideally needs to look ahead 25 years or more to do her job well. Accordingly, different cognitive capabilities are required at different strata. (Coaches typically work within a time horizon of no more than 1-2 years which puts them at Stratum III, thus precisely where empirically speaking most of them developmentally are anyway, namely, between S-3 and S-4, and attempting to move into S-4). As said, this is not enough of a grounding for coaching individuals at stage S-4 and beyond.

On the right side of the table, you see a twofold calibration of CD and an associated ranking of ED. As you already know, ED scores are correlated with CD scores at about 0.6 (Laske & Stewart, 2005). This fact is implied by the table's right side, where different developmental stages are associated with different levels of cognitive grasp. (Cognitive grasp, dealt with in volume 2 of this book, is doubly calibrated, namely, by Type of logical reasoning, and by Fluidity score. These finer distinctions need not concern the reader of this volume.)

The purpose of the table is, of course, to convey that people at a particular social-emotional stage are ideally suited to work at a particular Stratum and not others. The hypothesis implied by Table D.1 says, that people presently making meaning in the range between S-4/3 and S-4(3) are best employed on Stratum III with which is associated a time horizon of 1-2 years. (Such people ought to have a cognitive fluidity scores lying between 20 and 29, and should be able to reason in terms of causality (B3)), as shown below:

SIZE OF ROLE			SIZE OF PERSON		
Stratum of Work Complexity	Time Horizon		Type of Reasoning	Fluidity Score	ED Range
III	1-2 yrs		B3	20-29	4/3 to 4(3)

Table D.2 Capability description of Stratum III

Let's consider some additional information on how complexity of work varies with Stratum, selecting for attention Stratum III. Jaques (1998, 67) describes Stratum III as follows:

In order to get on with work, including both overcoming obstacles and diagnostic accumulation, the person must first consider the situation and work out alternative pathways or routes by which the problems might be resolved. In particular, s(he) must find a path that stands a chance of coping with short-run requirements (say weeks or a few months), while at the same time providing the initial stages of a realistic path toward longer-term goals that could be a year or more ahead. The person must be able to change to alternative paths if the initial choice of path turns out to be unsatisfactory.

[To sum up], at Stratum-III, you must not only use direct judgment plus diagnostic accumulation, but you must also be able to encompass the whole process within a plan that has a pathway to goal completion that you have worked out in the first place — and have pre-planned alternative paths to change to if need be. ...

As you will realize this is a mixed cognitive and behavioral, not a social-emotional, characterization of organizational work at Stratum III. As we apply this description to external consultants such as most coaches, it's clear that any discrepancy between their social-emotional stage and their cognitive capacity points to potential bottlenecks in their work. (These issues will be dealt with in more detail in volume 2 of this book.)

Revisiting the Upwardly Divided 3-Team

The characterization of the two company architectures in the Table above is mainly focused on cognitive, not social-emotional, demands. The Table conveys a kind of *social engineering* point of view based mainly on cognitive levels, presently demonstrated by orthodox followers of E. Jaques. When we bring social-emotional issues into the discussion of Capability Management (as I do in this and the subsequent volume), the *relationship* between cognitive scores and social-emotional stages takes on central relevance. We know, after all, that even if an individual's cognitive profile satisfies the requirements of a particular work Stratum, that fact is no guarantee that the individual will deliver optimal work at that Stratum simply because his or her developmental stage could be incommensurate (too high or too low) with crucial Stratum responsibilities.

For instance, people working at Stratum III ought to have begun leaving behind internalized others at S-4/3 and be able to work from at least an 'espousal' perspective of S-4 (that is, S-4(3)). Where that requirement is not fulfilled, regardless of available cognitive resources and associated time horizons, the performance delivered by these individuals will be sub-optimal even if all competencies needed are available. This is the case since the way the existing competencies are *actually used* will be hampered by any social-emotional limitations that may exist.

Let's now return to the topic of a *representative sample* that stands in for a larger group of people whose capability we would like to learn about. To get a better idea of the issues posed by such a sample, lets us return to the upwardly divided T-3 team of Appendix C, and treat it as a very small sample standing in for a larger population. For this reason, let's forget the fact that in Appendix C this 5-person sample made up an executive team. For present purposes, let's rather assume that the sample is representative for an entire company echelon, that of **50 company managers** (thus forming a pure sample of people functioning at the same level of function and accountability). When we match the team's social-emotional scores to work Strata in the sense of the two company architectures outlined above, we find that the distribution of team members among different Strata is as follows:

1. Rick: S-4(5) {3:7:3} [V]
2. Bob: S-4(3) {3:4:7} [III]
3. Sarah: S-4 {9:7:4} [IV]
4. Katherine S-4/3 {3:5:5} [III]
5. Sam (CEO) S-4/3 {2:5:6} [III]

or, more compactly expressed:

Sample Member	Stratum (Level of Work Complexity and Accountability)
Bob, Katherine, Sam	III
Sarah	IV
Rick	V

Table D.3 Accountability distribution of representative mini-sample

As shown, Sam, Bob, and Katherine have the requisite ED scores to work at Stratum III. The trouble is that the people Sam represents ought to be at a much higher developmental level (and thus Stratum) than he actually is, — namely, minimally S-4(5), where we find Rick [Stratum V]. Sarah's ability to work at Stratum IV is precarious, due to her large developmental risk factor. Bob could conceivably work at Stratum IV, given his large developmental potential. However, only Rick is able to work at Stratum V. We can say, then, that the representative sample — here demonstrated by way of a mini-sample — lacks a sturdy Stratum IV — and S-4 — center.

When we look more deeply into the composition of our representative mini-sample and consider not only the level per se, but the developmental spread of the sample between the lowest and highest level of its range as well as the developmental potential of sample members, we arrive at a more differentiated view of the Capability of the company's line managers that the sample stands in for:

Team Member	Size of Role [Stratum]	Size of Person [ED Stage]	Spread	Potential [in RCP]
Rick	V	4(5)	4 - 4/5	4/5
Bob	III-IV	4(3)	4/3 - 4(5)	4(5)
Sarah	III-IV	4	3/4 - 4(5)	4(5)
Katherine	III	4/3	3/4 — 4(5)	4(3)
Sam	III	4/3	3/4 — 4(3)	4(3)

Table D.4 Distribution of Strata for mini-sample

Here, I have placed Bob and Sarah in between Strata III and IV, – Bob because of his high potential to move to Stratum IV, and Sarah because of her excessive risk to regress to Stratum III.

Assuming now that the appropriate level for a company's line managers is S-4, we can see from the above mini-sample that the actual presence of S-4 in the entire population of line managers is woefully lacking in strength. In short, the company's line managers are largely under-qualified in terms of their present Capability, *their competencies and so-called experience notwithstanding*. More specifically, the company's line managers are split into three groups, as follows:
1. those barely at S-4 (40%) – the requisite ED level
2. those under S-4 (40%)
3. those above S-4 (20%).

The first partition is close to the managerial standard for line managers, but barely so. The second partition lacks the requisite Capability for functioning in the line manager role, while the third partition's Capability exceeds the standard required for that function. In short, the company's Capability *at the line manager level* is presently woefully inadequate. This inadequacy is not removed by using excess capability (20% represented by Rick). Using workforce members at higher Capability levels in order to close a Capability gap is simply wasteful. It wears out the higher Capability levels with no apparent long-term benefit.

Under these circumstances, company management would do good to take note of the developmental potential available at the line manager echelon. As shown by the outer, 'Potential,' column in the above table, 40% of the line manager group has a potential to reach S-4(3), and another 40% can potentially perform at an ever higher Capability level.

Capability Metrics

The discussion above, about the distribution of Capability within a workforce (or a certain echelon thereof) has nudged us toward the notion of a *Capability Metric*. It is the purpose of such a metric to show, using representative samples, **what is the present overall capability distribution of a company's workforce or partition thereof**. This purpose is an extension of the team typology discussed in Appendix C, where we looked at the Capability level of an entire team. Here, we have broadened that view and are considering the issue of how Capability is distributed within a larger group of the workforce, that of a company's line managers.

When we work with Capability Metrics, our purpose is to arrive at a precise notion of what part of a workforce (or echelon thereof) has the *requisite Capability* for functioning at a specific Stratum (such as Str-IV), and what part of the workforce has a Capability below or above the requisite standard. Answering this question is important since it will contribute to decisions about what strategic tasks management can assume the workforce is presently able to handle. **Capability Metrics** are thus tools for long-term strategic thinking about human resources (and company mission), as well as their impact on overall organizational functioning.

At this point, an example of a Capability Metric is in order.

Let's return to Bob, whom we got to know in Appendix B. Bob is Director of HR who is known as a successful developer of organizational training programs. He is presently part of a large software services firm, directing a project that introduces new kinds of assessment products worldwide. Recently, Bob has been given the mandate to report to the company Board and CEO about the chances of success of a planned entry of the company into a large software Consortium. The Consortium in question has the mandate to build a large internet banking product, and Bob's company, still small, would stand to gain substantially if it were to enter the Consortium and successfully meet the milestones for a part of the planned project.

The question CEO and Board are asking themselves is whether the company has the wherewithal to deliver high quality internet software modules in a timely manner. **What tools could Bob best use to help him make an assessment of the company's present chances to participate successfully in the Consortium?** The answer is that Bob could use a CAPABILITY METRIC. Here is why.

What Bob really needs is a way to create a representative sample of all the people in the company who would engage with the Consortium project. These people would form a mixed, not a pure, representative sample, since they would most likely include the CFO, HR personnel, line managers, and the leaders of the software teams who are going to write and test the code for the software to be delivered through the Consortium. Let's say this would be 100 people in all. As I have said, you don't have to make an assessment of all 100 people. Rather, you define a REPRESENTATIVE SAMPLE of people, and for statistical reasons it would be good to work with a sample size of at least 20, better 25. This means you would assess 25% of the total Consortium team.

Bob now has to begin thinking about who should be included in the representative sample, and this is a discussion he needs to have with the CEO and the Board.

Let's say now this hurdle has been taken, and Bob has created his representative sample in collaborations with his management. Let's say also that the decision has been made to consider developmental stage S-4 as the *standard for members of the representative sample*. The people that are members of the Consortium team need to be at S-4 and thus cognitively function at Stratum IV. This is where the Capability Metric comes in. The metric is a summary of the Capabilities available to a company at a certain Stratum of work or echelon of accountability at a particular time. Before I present an example of such a metric, let us first go over the steps that Bob and his collaborators must take in order to get the Capability Metric off the ground.

Steps Required for Establishing a Capability Metric
The figure below shows the steps Bob and his collaborators need to take.

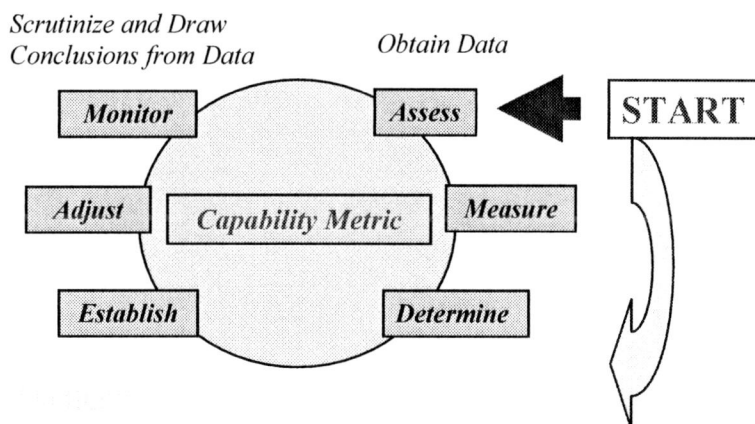

1. **Assess** *size of role* **= CD & ED Job Requirements**
2. **Measure** *size of person* **= Current CD & ED Capability of Consortium members**
3. **Determine** **gaps between (1) and (2)**
4. **Establish** *interventions to improve the capability profile (if possible)*
5. **Adjust** *(1) to (2) or vice versa – restructure & reassign roles, fire/hire*
6. **Monitor** *the balance of capability distribution over time.*

Fig. D.2 Steps in establishing and using a Capability Metric

As shown, the first step for Bob to take is to determine the cognitive requirements of those who are to work as a member of the Consortium team (both CD and ED). This will define the *size of role (level of work complexity)* in contrast to the "size of person" (Capability). To define "size of role," Bob would have to talk to the company's line managers and other supervisors of individuals who are to work on the Consortium team, since they know best what cognitive resources a particular contribution to the team requires. As we have seen in Table D.1, this means to decide the formal logic type and fluidity score needed by candidate Consortium members. Clearly, a certain minimal amount of systems thinking and critical thinking will be required. In addition, Bob needs to stipulate a standard cognitive fluidity score that further defines the level of work complexity. Flexibility of thinking is clearly a must for successfully working as part of the Consortium team.

Once the CD score has been stipulated, Bob can proceed to formulating a social-emotional standard. This will require familiarity with CDF, the *Constructive Developmental Framework* outlined in this book. It will also entail consulting the HR data base to consider records of past social behavior of candidate Consortium Team members. In the case below, I have assumed that Bob considers S-4 as the standard for participating in the Consortium. We are thus measuring Consortium Team members against a standard of S-4, associated with the appropriate CD scores for Stratum IV (see Table D.1, above).

Having now assessed *size of role*, or level of work complexity, Bob and his co-workers need to proceed to determining *size of person*, answering the question of **what is the Capability of individuals making up the representative sample, and how commensurate is their *size of person* with the *size of role* (level of work complexity) required by Consortium work?** Giving an answer to this question entails making actual developmental assessments as outlined in this book. This can be done either by Bob and co-workers internally (once they have been trained in developmental assessments), or by experts in developmental process consultation.

The steps that Bob needs to follow are now evident:
- Determine gaps between (1) size of role and (2) size of person.
- Establish HR interventions to improve capability profile — formulate a data based human capital strategy for work on the Consortium Team.
- Adjust size of role to size of person or vice versa, by restructuring & reassigning roles, firing and hiring (if there is time).
- Monitor the balance of capability distribution over time (for future engagements).

Since in this case managing existing capability has priority over fostering more capability — which could be done through hiring the right people — the main utility of the established Capability Metric in the present case is to suggest **how to select members for the Consortium Team.** Trainings might be considered at this point as well. Once both sizes (of role and person) have been determined, the soundness of the company's *balance* between level of accountability and of individual capability can easily be determined, by considering the Capability Metric (below). Before studying the metric itself, let's consider what such a metric actually accomplishes.

Essentially, a Capability Metric partitions a chosen representative sample along lines of capability 'at,' 'below,' and 'above' the level of work complexity required of sample members. When presented visually, the metric shows the proportions that exist between workers *at, below, or above* the Capability level requisite for their work.

We might want to think of the partition achieved by the metric in terms of colors (not shown in the book). All members of the sample below the standard that was set fall 'into the red.' They do not qualify for the work intended. Those members whose Capability surpasses the standard, fall 'into the green.' Using them in Consortium work would amount to a waste of Capability that is better used in more complex tasks. Members of the metric who actually embody the standard that was set for Consortium work fall 'into the gray.' Only sample members 'in the gray' are presently in the right spot in terms of balancing accountability and capability. (In the figure below, this gray area has been normalized to 1, in order to permit a visual comparison of the proportions of sample members falling either below or above the standard).

The partitioning of the representative sample described clearly introduces an objective, Capability based, standard for work on strategic tasks in the organization. As a consequence, to the extent that entries exist below and above the standard adopted for the metric, the company is put on notice that it lacks requisite organization regarding the Consortium team. The Capability Metric below indeed shows a lack of balance between accountability and capability in the representative sample, and this does not bode well for the company's success as a member of the Consortium.

Results Shown by the Capability Metric

Let us now inspect Fig. D.3, below, that shows the metric in full detail.

On the left, the reader sees a listing of aspects of Capability that have been assessed using CDF, while on the right, the results of the assessment are displayed in terms of a bar graph. Since the diagram above is in black and white, the reader has to imagine the left partition to be red, the middle to be gray, and the right side to be green in color. The standard against which the red and green areas are measured is normalized to '1' in the gray zone of the diagram. Consequently, those members of the representative sample who adhere to the CD and ED standards made requisite for the Consortium Team fall into the gray zone. As you can see, there is considerable imbalance, both in terms of lack (red, on left) and of excess Capability (green, on right). As shown, different aspects of Capability are shown by the metric to be out of synch with job accountability to a variable degree.

On the left side of the Figure above, a distinction is made between three aspects of Capability:
- Applied Capability (= performance)
- *Current* potential Capability (CD)
- *Future* potential Capability (ED)

Applied Capability is simply the capability that is presently applied by workers, and thus equals 'performance' (Jaques, 1994). It is here measured by the NP questionnaire that appears in Appendix B and again in volume 3 of this book. NP outcomes fall, as we say in CDF, 'into the horizontal.' This is so since performance is a behavioral issue, and performance improvements are a matter of incremental learning, not adult development (shift in terms of stages).

Profile of a Representative Sample

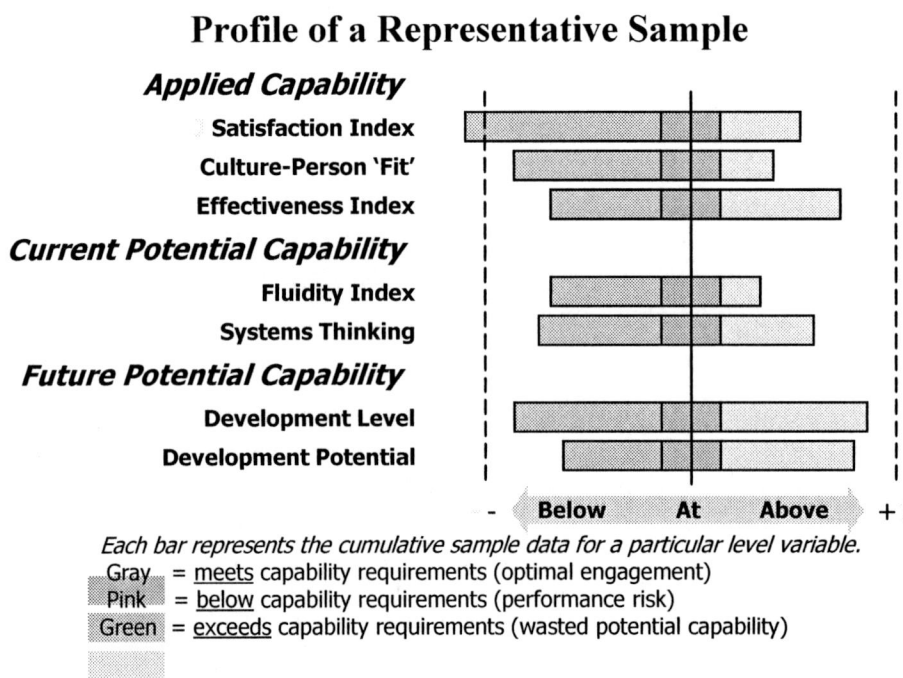

Fig. D.3 Capability Metric for a representative sample

Potential Capability — whether current (CD) or future (ED) — is a matter of adult development that underlies performance, and enables optimal performance in the first place. The difference between 'current' and 'future' potential Capability is not one of time, but of *degree of unfolding*. It is a developmental difference between what can currently be achieved by members of the representative sample when all of their cognitive resources are actually used, on one hand, and what is just emerging in terms of social-emotional Capability, on the other. (As we know, these two strands of adult development are correlated, strengthening or weakening each other as the case may be.)

As Fig. D.3 demonstrates, a Capability Metric may also include behavioral assessment outcomes, as it does here under "Applied Capability." This indicates that such a metric can become part of a larger Human Resources Management System. At IDM, we call such a system CAMDS, which stands for *Capability Assessment, Management, and Development System*. As we learned in the case studies (Appendix B), it is exactly the intersection between Horizontal and Vertical, Competence and Capability, that is of central importance in evaluating and strategizing the use of human resources in companies.

Let's return to our example.

As Bob studies the Capability Metric, above, what is he going to realize? Essentially, he is going to understand that he CANNOT advise CEO and Board to go ahead with the Consortium project at this time. The evidence against participation of the company in the Consortium is too strong to be ignored. In the order of capabilities indicated in Fig. D.3, here is what the Metric shows:

- 42% of sample members show lack of job satisfaction
- 30% of sample members are not attuned to the company's corporate culture
- 42% of sample members are not effective in their present role
- 32 % of sample members do not measure up to the CD standard set for flexibility of thinking and systemic grasp
- 30% of sample members make meaning either below or above S-4.

Bob might say that there are 'lots of people in the green,' meaning they have more Capability than is needed for Consortium work. But this would be counter-productive. Filling capability gaps by sacrificing excess Capability is depleting company resources, and wasting them as well. The amount of people falling into the gray zone of requisite capability IS SIMPLY TOO SMALL for the company to proceed with its Consortium plans!

Another way out that Bob might think of is to develop new resources immediately. But interventions and training programs that could be instituted — training, coaching, mentoring — will take time to take effect, and this time is not available to Bob's company since a decision about the Consortium needs to be made NOW. As shown, building a Capability Metric makes it possible for a company to make objective decisions about how to use its available human resources strategically, and what the pitfalls are the company needs to avoid. **Whether company management is up to making evidence based decisions in terms of its own developmental level is another issue.** (The executive team may prefer espousal over reality. This will occur by nature if the majority of its members live below S-4).

It is worth noting here that the case described above is decided, not on the basis of 'lack of competences,' but of 'lack of Capability.' These are two different things. What the Capability Metric above is telling Bob is **that even if all required competences were in place, the company would still fail as a member of the Consortium.** This kind of insight cannot be attained through either performance management or competency modeling measures, since what is being considered by a Capability Metric are not primarily the competences but their *enablers*. In short, the metric focuses on the issue of HOW WILL EXISTING COMPETENCIES ACTUALLY BE USED? (not what are they?), and that depends on the developmental resources of individuals (what they ARE), not their competences (what they HAVE). Assessing what people 'have' results in a snapshot of their past, while what they 'are' can only be revealed by developmental assessment, and is an integral part of their future. **Only when scrutinized in terms of Capability does a satisfactory level of competence have any real meaning for strategic management decisions!**

***

Concluding Reflections on Appendices C and D

In the last two sections of the Appendix (C & D), I have broadened the application of the methods taught in this book to teams and entire work groups in organizations. Exactly the same methods taught by the book for purposes of process consultation and the coaching of individuals have been employed. The only difference has been that these methods have been used with a larger number of people, and that assessment results have been aggregated to a higher level. Because of aggregation, the confidential details of individual assessments have dropped away. An anonymous data base has been created based on which one can judge entire teams and companies in developmental terms, of Capability, without having to trace findings to specific individuals. This involves a conceptual as well as managerial distinction between a <u>confidential</u> data base for purposes of workforce *development*, and an <u>anonymous</u> data base for purposes of formulating and *executing human resources strategies*, an issue I will consider more closely in volume 4 of this book.

Reflecting on Appendices B and C together, there is an eerie sameness between the Capability imbalance of the upwardly divided T-3 team discussed in Appendix C and the non-requisite representative sample of the planned Consortium team in the present section of the Appendix. In both cases, the professional S-4 standard for organizational work is not adhered to, neither in the five-person team nor the larger sample representing 100 line managers.

Since executive teams are rightfully held responsible for companies' corporate culture, one can well imagine how their Capability imbalance may pervade and determine entire companies. It could thus well be that, if we investigated the executive team of the software company at issue in Appendix D, we would find a similar *lack of requisite organization* as we did in our study of the executive team in Appendix C. If that were so, the illusions often generated by members of management teams could be revealed, and could be addressed in an evidence-based manner.

GLOSSARY

'=>' points to a cross reference

Behavioral profile	In CDF, data derived from the NP questionnaire on self conduct, task approach, and interpersonal perspective (emotional intelligence)
Capability	-- A person's cognitive and social-emotional maturity level that acts as an 'enabler' of the person's => *competence* and ability to perform.
Capability, applied	-- The capability presently applied in a person's work, measured in terms of the person's => *behavioral profile* (in CDF considered an objective indicator of the person's present => *performance*.)
Capability, current	-- Another term for <u>cognitive</u> capability; according to Jaques (1994, p. 25) "the highest level of work a person could currently carry, in work that s(he) valued and for which s(he) had the necessary skilled knowledge and experience." It is a function of complexity of mental processing.
Capability, future potential	-- For Jaques, "a constitutionally established maximum future potential capability maturing at a predictable rate from infancy to old age (1994, p. 59). In CDF, following Kegan, a <u>social-emotional</u> capability whose 'ceiling' is reached at different ages and cannot be predicted.
Capability Metric	-- Abstractly, a tool for strategic human capital management in the form of an assessment of a group's or entire company's capability level(s); concretely, a diagrammatic presentation of developmental findings for an entire group or company in the form of a bar graph.
Capability, potential	-- A person's developmental potential, measured in terms of cognitive development (systems thinking, higher than logical forms of thinking) and social emotional development *(=> developmental stage).*
Center of Gravity	-- => *(main) developmental stage.*
Clarity (Index)	-- In the => *Risk-Clarity-Potential Index* (RCP), the degree of embeddedness in one's present Center of Gravity.
Coaching level	-- A mode of functioning as a coach that depends on the professional's present developmental level and potential; there are three <u>main</u> coaching levels (other-dependent, self-authoring, self-aware).
Competence	-- What a person 'has' rather than 'is' (which equates with =>Capability).
Constructive Developmental Framework (CDF)	-- A conceptual framework based on research in adult development that is based on the notion that people's social and physical "world" is internally constructed by them, making them move in a world of their own (meaning) making.

Developmental compatibility
>-- Consultant-client compatibility based on both parties'
=>potential Capability (social-emotional stage [future] and
systems thinking [current]).

Developmental consultant (or coach)
>-- A consultant educated in developmental theory who is expert
in developmental interviewing, listening, analysis, and scoring of
interviews.

Developmental feedback
>-- Feedback on assessment results based on the consultant's
insight into the client's => developmental profile.

Developmental hypothesis
>-- A hypothesis regarding the client's present => *developmental stage*
required for, and used in, expert interviewing.

Developmental interviewing
>-- A 1-hr conversation based on a semi-structured protocol of
=> *developmental prompts* probed by the consultant during a =>
subject-object interview.

Developmental level -- => *developmental stage.*

Developmental listening
>-- Listening focused on how clients use language (their speech),
for the sake of discerning how they presently make meaning of
their internal and external experiences and, consequently, act in
the world.

Developmental potential
>-- A person's potential for making a single-step developmental
shift 'upward,' to the subsequent => *developmental stage.*

Developmental Process Consultation
>-- The developmental deepening of => *Process Consultation* in
which consulting to a client's mental process is based on an
understanding of the cognitive and social-emotional profile of the
client.

Developmental profile
>-- The set of developmental and behavioral data that defines a
client's professional and/or life situation, in CDF composed of
CD, ED, and NP findings.

Developmental prompts
>-- A noun, adjective, or short phrase that invites interviewees to
project themselves into the prompt for telling a story revealing
their => *developmental stage.*

Developmental range
>-- The range of levels within which a client presently makes
meaning; foremost all intermediate stages between two => *main
stages* such as S-2 to S-3, S-3 to S-4, and S-4 to S-5. In an
expanded meaning, we speak of any developmental zone – e.g. S-
3/4 to S-4(5) -- as a range, regardless of the presence of => *main
stages.*

Developmental shift -- The movement in consciousness by which the present =>
Center of Gravity is transcended as well as included, and a new
Center of Gravity established one step above the previous center
(Wilber).

Developmental strands
-- Dimensions of mental growth, such as cognition, self
awareness, faith, ethical stance, social-emotional maturity.

Developmental stage -- A way of, and frame of reference for, being in the real world,
based on what a person is 'subject to' (cannot take responsibility
for) and what the person can make into an object of reflection
(can take responsibility for).

Downwardly divided team
-- A team whose majority lives at, and acts from, a higher
developmental level than the team's minority.

Emotional intelligence
-- In CDF measured by the NP questionnaire under
'interpersonal perspective,' and never considered out of context
with => *developmental profile.*

Espousal
-- A mindset that typically takes hold of a person just before
reaching a new => *main stage* by which the person enters a new
=> *developmental range* (such as S-2 to S-3).

Horizontal (dimension)
-- In contrast to the vertical, developmental dimension the
behavioral, 'in time' dimension in which learning takes place.

Intermediate stage -- A stage between two stages that define the lower and higher
level (ceiling) of a => *developmental range*; e.g., S-3/4 is
intermediate between S-3(4) and S-4/3.

Level of work complexity
-- The degree of cognitive complexity of work, linked to the
accountability attached to doing the work, and associated with a
particular => *time horizon* (Jaques).

Loss of Self
-- The loss of one's present => *Center of Gravity* by which a new
Center of Gravity is established.

Main stage
S-2, S-3, S-4, or S-5, respectively.

Mental process
-- Emotional as well as intellectual processes by which persons
establish a social presence and individual identity in the world.
(Emotional processes are *always mediated* by cognitive functions,
rather than standing in contrast to intellectual functioning.)

Performance
-- The effectiveness of a person's work that is commensurate
with his or her =>*current potential capability* (which is cognitive) as
well as =>*future potential Capability* (which is social-emotional).

Potential
-- The developmental resources available to an individual for
making **developmental** a => *developmental shift* to a subsequent
level or stage (=>Center of Gravity).

Process Consultation -- A model of consultation in which the emphasis falls on
consulting to the client's => *mental process*, in contrast to
delivering solutions or diagnoses.

Risk, developmental -- The likelihood of regression to a lower => *Center of Gravity*, as indicated by the => RCP.

Risk-Clarity-Potential Index (RCP)
-- An index of social-emotional maturity that indicates a client's present degree of being embedded in a particular stage (clarity), the associated risk of regression to a lower stage (risk), as well as the client's potential for advancing to a subsequent => *developmental stage*.

Subject-Object Interview
-- A developmental interview invented by R. Kegan and his research group that is focused on what a client is presently 'subject to' (cannot take responsibility for) and can hold as object of reflection. The interview is 'semi-structured' by the re-occurrence of certain verbal => *developmental prompts*. The template provided by prompts makes interviews more easily comparable to each other, and also structures the interviewer's and client's tasks during the interview.

Subject-Object Relations
-- The relations each person has to his/her self and others, from the point of view of what the person is 'subject to' (is unaware of) and can hold as an 'object' of reflection (can be held responsible for).

Time horizon -- The span of days, months, or years of foresight required by different => *levels of work complexity* (Strata)

Upwardly divided team
-- A team whose majority lives at a lower developmental level than a minority of its members.

Vertical (dimension) -- The dimension of cognitive and social-emotional development, set apart from the horizontal dimension of learning, perception, and competence that is typically covered by behavioral assessments.

SELECTED BIBLIOGRAPHY

Aderman, M. See Hawkins, R. E. (1970).

Adorno, Th. W. (1999). Negative dialectics. New York: Continuum.

Ahrendt, H. (1971). The life of the mind. San Diego: Harcourt Brace Jovanovich.

Argyris, C. (1993). Knowledge for action. San Francisco: Jossey-Bass Publishers.

Argyris, C. (1999, 2nd ed.). On organizational learning. Malden, MA: Blackwell Business.

Basseches, M. (1980). Dialectical schemata: A framework for the empirical study of the development of dialectical thinking. Human Development, 23, 400-421.

Basseches, M. (1984). Dialectical thinking and adult development. Norwood, N.J.: Ablex.

Basseches, M. (1986). Dialectical thinking and young adult cognitive development. In R.A. Mines and K.S. Kitchener (Eds.), Adult Cognitive Development. New York: Praeger.

Basseches, M. (1989a). Toward a constructive-developmental understanding of the dialectics of individuality and irrationality. In D.N. Kramer & M. J. Bopp (Eds.) Transformation in clinical and developmental psychology. New York: Springer.

Basseches, M. (1989b). Intellectual development: The development of dialectical thinking. In E.P. Maimon, B.F. Nodine, & F. W. O'Connor (Eds.). Thinking, reasoning, and writing. White Plains: Longman.

Basseches, M. (2003). Adult development and the practice of psychotherapy. In J. Demick and C. Andreoletti (Eds.), Handbook of Adult Development (ch. 29, 533-563). New York: Kluwer Academic/Plenum Publishers.

Commons, M., Richards, F.A., Armon, C. (Eds.) (1984). Beyond formal operations: Late adolescent and adult cognitive development. New York: Praeger.

Cook-Greuter, S. (1990). Maps for living: Ego-developmental stages from symbiosis to conscious universal embeddedness. In M.L. Commons, C. Armon, L. Kohlberg, F. A. Richards, T.A. Grotzer & J.D. Sinnott (Eds.), Adult development vol. 2, Models and methods in the study of adolescent and adult thought (79-104). New York: Praeger.

Cook-Greuter, S. (1999). Postautonomous ego development: A study of its nature and measurement. Doctoral Thesis, Harvard Graduate School of Education. Ann Arbor, MI: Bell & Howell.

Demick, J. & C. Andreoletti (2003). Handbook of adult development. New York: Kluwer/Academic Plenum Publishers.

Flaherty, J. (1999). Coaching. Butterworth Heinemann.

Fuglsang, L. (2005). www.interdevelopmentals.org/Ezine/0605.html.

Grant, A. 2003. (Keynote). Keeping up with the cheese! Research as a foundation for professional coaching in the future. In Stein, I. (Ed.) Proceedings, First ICF Coaching Research Symposium. ICF, 2003.

Grant, A. (2004a). Toward a profession of coaching. International Journal of Evidence-based Coaching and Mentoring, vol. 2.1.

Grant, A. (2004b). What is evidence-based executive, workplace and life coaching? In Grant, A.M., Cavanash, M.J., & Kemp, T. (Eds.) Evidence-based coaching, 1, Australian Academic Press, Sydney.

Grant, A. (2005). Workplace and executive coaching: An annotated bibliography from the peer-reviewed business literature.

Graves, C. (1981). The Emergent, Cyclical, Double-Helix Model of the Adult Human Biopsychosocial System, Boston, May 20, 1981. (Quoted by Wilber, 2000, 40; 227).

Havens, L. (1993). Coming to life: Reflections on the art of psychotherapy. Cambridge, MA: Harvard.

Havens, L. (1986). Making contact: Uses of language in psychotherapy. Cambridge, MA: Harvard.

Hawkins, R.E. (1970). Need-Press Interaction as Related to Managerial Styles Among Executives. PhD thesis, Illinois Institute of Technology.

Hesse, H. (2002). Mit der Reife wird man immer juenger (In maturing one only gets younger), Munich, Germany: Insel Verlag [ISBN 3-458-34557-4].

Hudson, F. (2001). The adult years. San Francisco: Jossey Bass.

Jaques, E. (1998). Requisite organization. Falls Church, VA: Cason Hall & Co.

Jaques, E. (2002). The life and behavior of living organisms. Westport, CT: Praeger

Jaques, E. & K. Cason (1994). Human capability. Falls Church, VA: Cason Hall & Co.

Kegan, R. (1982). The evolving self. Cambridge, MA: Harvard.

Kegan, R. (1994). In over our heads. Cambridge, MA: Harvard.

Kegan, R. (2002). How the way we talk can change the way we work. San Francisco: Jossey-Bass.

Kornfield, J. (1993). A path with heart. New York: Bantam Books.

Lahey, L. Souvaine, E., Kegan, R., Goodman, R., Felix, S. (1988). A guide to the subject-object interview: Its administration and interpretation. Laboratory of Human Development, Harvard Graduate School of Education.

Laske, O. (1999a). Transformative effects of coaching on executives' professional agenda. PsyD. dissertation (2 volumes, order # 9930438). Ann Arbor, MI: Bell & Howell.

Laske, O. (1999b). An integrated model of developmental coaching. Consulting Psychology Journal, 51.3, 139-159.

Laske, O. (2000). Foundations of scholarly consulting: The Developmental Structure/Process Tool (DSPT™). Consulting Psychology Journal, 52.3, 178-200.

Laske, O. (2001). Linking two lines of adult development: The Developmental Structure/Process Tools (DSPT™). Adult Development: Bulletin of the Society for Research in Adult Development, 10.1.

Laske, O. (2003a). An integrated model of developmental coaching: Researching new ways of coaching and coach education. In Stein, I. F. (Ed), Proceedings, First ICF Coaching Research Symposium, 52-61.

Laske, O. (2003b). Executive development as adult development. Demick, J. & C. Andreoletti (Eds.), Handbook of adult development, ch. 29, 565-584. New York: Plenum/Kluwer.

Laske, O. (2004a). Can evidence based coaching increase ROI? Intern. J. Evidence Based Coaching and Mentoring, 2.2, 1-12. London, UK.

Laske, O. (2004b). Looking for patterns in clients' developmental-behavioral dance with coaches. In Stein, I. F., Campone, F. and L. J. Page (Eds.), Proceedings, Second ICF Coaching Research Symposium, 131-138.

Laske, O. (2006). From coach training to coach education: Teaching coaching within a comprehensively evidence based framework. Intern. J. Evidence Based Coaching and Mentoring, 4.1 London, U.K.

Laske, O. & B. Maynes (2002). Growing the top management team: Supporting mental growth as a vehicle for promoting organizational learning. J. of Management Development, 21.9, 702-727.

Laske, O., Stober, D., & J. Edwards (2004). What is, and why should we care about, evidence based coaching? In Stein, I. F., Campone, F., & L. J. Page (Eds.), <u>Proceedings, Second ICF Coaching Research Symposium</u>, 169-174.

Laske, O. & N. Moynihan (2004 f). <u>Hidden dimension insights.</u> IDM Newsletter series (see www.interdevelopmentals.org/e-zine.html).

Laske, O. & S. Stewart (2005a). <u>Developmental foundations of HR: Three webcasts.</u> (www.bettermanagement.com).

Laske, O. & A. Dawson (2005b). <u>There is more to what your client tells you than you think: How deeper answers to questions surface.</u> Presentation, 10th ICF International Conference, San Jose, CA.

Luborsky, L. (1988). <u>Who will benefit from psychotherapy?: Predicting therapeutic outcomes</u>. New York: Basic Books.

Murray, H. (2005). See http://<u>www.allpsych.com/personalitysynopsis/murray.html</u>, <u>http://murray.hmdc.harvard.edu/</u>. <u>http://www.wilderdom.com/personality/traits/PersonalityTraitsNeedsHenryMurray.html</u>.

Schein, E. (1999). <u>Process consultation revisited.</u> Reading, MA: Addison-Wesley.

Stein, I. (2003). <u>Proceedings, First ICF Coaching Research Symposium.</u> International Coach Federation.

Wilber, K. (2000). <u>Integral psychology.</u> Boston: Shambhala.

Wilber, K. (2005). <u>Integral spirituality.</u> Integral Institute.

Index

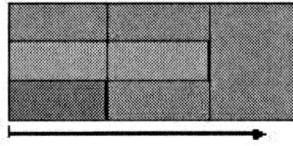

IDM PRESS

51 Mystic Street

Medford, MA 02155, USA

Where professionals go for deeper questions

and profound answers

QUICK ORDER FORM

Email order: orders@interdevelopmental.com

Fax orders: 781.391.2361. Announce your intention to send a fax by phone 781.391.2361 first, then send this form.

Postal orders: IDM Press, c/o Interdevelopmental Institute, Attn. Otto Laske, 51 Mystic St., Medford, MA 02155.

Inquiries: idmpress@interdevelopmentals.org.

Please send FREE information on non-certificate and certificate courses as well as developmental assessments and modalities of developmental mentoring to:

Name: _____

Address: _____

City: _____ State:_____ Zip: _____

Telephone: _____

Email address: _____

Sales tax: Please add 7.75% for orders shipped to California addresses.

Payment:
1. Check
2. Paypal
3. Money order
4. Credit card:
   Visa
   MasterCard
   AMEX
   Discover

Card number: _____
Name on card: _____**Expiration date:**_____

Printed in the United Kingdom
by Lightning Source UK Ltd.
117466UKS00001B/16